ENCYCLOPEDIA OF RACISM IN THE UNITED STATES

ENCYCLOPEDIA OF RACISM IN THE UNITED STATES

VOLUME ONE, A–H

Edited by Pyong Gap Min

GREENWOOD PRESS
Westport, Connecticut • London

Library of Congress Cataloging-in-Publication Data

Encyclopedia of racism in the United States / edited by Pyong Gap Min.
    p. cm.
    Includes bibliographical references and index.
    ISBN 0-313-32688-6 (set : alk. paper) — ISBN 0-313-33249-5 (vol. 1 : alk. paper)
— ISBN 0-313-33250-9 (vol. 2 : alk. paper) — ISBN 0-313-33555-9 (vol. 3 : alk.
paper) 1. Racism—United States—Encyclopedias. 2. United States—Race
relations—Encyclopedias. 3. United States—Ethnic relations—Encyclopedias.
4. Minorities—United States—Social conditions—Encyclopedias. I. Min, Pyong Gap,
1942-
    E184.A1E773 2005
    305.8'00973'03—dc22   2005008523

British Library Cataloguing in Publication Data is available.

Library of Congress Catalog Card Number: 2005008523
ISBN: 0-313-32688-6 (set)
        0-313-33249-5 (vol. I)
        0-313-33250-9 (vol. II)
        0-313-33555-9 (vol. III)

First published in 2005

Greenwood Press, 88 Post Road West, Westport, CT 06881
An imprint of Greenwood Publishing Group, Inc.
www.greenwood.com

Printed in the United States of America

The paper used in this book complies with the
Permanent Paper Standard issued by the National
Information Standards Organization (Z39.48–1984).

10 9 8 7 6 5 4 3 2 1

CONTENTS

PREFACE

The racial and ethnic diversity caused by the influx of new immigrants, the expansion of ethnic-studies programs in colleges and universities, and the gradual shift since the 1970s in the government's policy from Anglo-conformity to multiculturalism have contributed to the phenomenal increase in the number of high school and college courses relating to immigration, ethnicity, and racial- and ethnic-minority relations. These courses are offered in the disciplines of sociology, urban studies, anthropology, and history, as well as in various ethnic-studies programs. To meet the increasing demand, a number of encyclopedias covering new immigrant and minority groups and multicultural education have recently been published. Many high school and college students who study American history, immigration, ethnicity, and racial and ethnic relations need to understand concepts, theories, issues, and historical events related to racism. However, despite this need, no encyclopedia of racism in the United States existed.

Several recently published books focus on racism.[1] Some of them offer conceptual and theoretical clarifications relating to racism, and others concentrate attention on white racism against blacks, drawing on ethnographic research or public documents. But none of them is a reference work offering a comprehensive list of concepts, theories, and historical events relating to racism in the United States. Information about historical events that reflect prejudice, discrimination, and physical violence against minority racial groups can be found in books that cover the histories of particular minority groups. But none provides a comprehensive list of historical events pertaining to various racial and ethnic minority groups in the United States. Several handbooks and encyclopedias, such as the *Encyclopedia of the Civil Rights Movement* and the *Encyclopedia of Indian Holocaust*, specialize in racial issues relating to particular minority groups, but no comprehensive encyclopedia covering racial victimization for all racial and ethnic minority groups in the United

States had been published before this book, the *Encyclopedia of Racism in the United States.*

SCOPE OF COVERAGE AND CLASSIFICATION OF ENTRIES

To prepare the *Encyclopedia*, I reviewed most of the major books that specialize in race and ethnic relations or that focus on particular minority groups in the United States. In consultation with a five-member advisory board, a list of entries was devised for inclusion in the *Encyclopedia.* The selected entries, whether directly or indirectly related to racism in the United States, can be broadly classified into the following six categories:

1. Social-science terms, concepts, and theories related to racism
2. Historical and contemporary events, figures, and organizations reflecting or supporting racial discrimination and racial violence against minority groups
3. Racial prejudice and discrimination in employment, housing, and other areas
4. Reactions of minority groups to racial discrimination and of minority leaders who have fought against racism
5. Governmental measures, programs, and agencies, and court cases related to either discrimination or prevention of racial discrimination against minority groups
6. Major books either supporting or exposing racism

Most entries also refer to particular racial and ethnic minority groups. The groups are broadly divided into the following eight categories:

1. Native Americans/American Indians (terms used interchangeably)
2. African Americans
3. Hispanics/Latinos (terms used interchangeably)
4. Asian Americans and Pacific Islanders
5. Muslims, Arabs, and Middle Easterners
6. White ethnic groups (e.g., Jews, Italians, Irish)
7. Immigrants and their children
8. All ethnic groups

Many entries, such as Derogatory Terms and Hate Crimes, fall into category 8; that is, they relate to all racial and ethnic minority groups. These two ways of classifying entries, which are clearly reflected in the "Guide to Related Entries," will help users of the *Encyclopedia* trace broad themes and topics across the entries and will also assist readers who are searching for related groups of topics that interest them or that meet their study or research needs.

The *Encyclopedia of Racism in the United States* is heavily cross-referenced. For instance, readers searching for an organization by acronym, such as AIM, will encounter a cross-reference that sends them to the main entry under the full name of the organization—in this case, they will be instructed to *See* the American Indian Movement. A reader searching for the term *all-weather bigots* will be instructed to *See* Bigots, Types of, the entry in which "all-weather bigots" are described and discussed. The ends of most of the entries also feature *See also* cross-references that list other, related entries. Most entries also conclude with a "Further Reading" section that lists references the reader can turn to for more detailed information on the entry subject. A detailed person and subject index offers greater access to terms and concepts within entries. The *Encyclopedia* also includes an introduction that traces the history of American racism, a general bibliography of important and useful works on racism and minority and ethnic groups, a brief chronology of racism in the United States, and a selection of the full text or excerpts of important primary documents relating to U.S. racism.

Of the *Encyclopedia*'s 447 entries, 25 (e.g., Affirmative Action) are longer entries of 2,000–3,000 words covering complex topics or concepts, while about 180 are midsized entries of 500–1,000 words. The remainder are entries on issues, people, events, or organizations for which basic information and importance can be conveyed in fewer than 500 words. Each contributor to the *Encyclopedia* committed to write one long essay and several medium and short entries on topics within his or her particular field of expertise, and a continuity of thought and style across many related entries is the result.

PRACTICAL VALUE OF THE *ENCYCLOPEDIA* FOR MODERATION OF RACISM

Despite all the democratic ideals emphasized in the Declaration of Independence, the U.S. Constitution, and many other government documents, the United States has probably been the most racist country in the world, with the exception of South Africa under apartheid between 1948 and 1994, and Nazi Germany. Although federal and local governments have made significant changes since 1970 in support of multiculturalism, they have done little to achieve racial equality and to moderate institutional racism during the same period. White Americans are receptive to ethnic and racial diversity to a much grater extent than they were in 1970, but they do not always accept African Americans as friends, as members of their social clubs, or even as neighbors.

Given the seriousness of the problem of racism and racial inequality in contemporary American society, it is important for everyone to join the effort to moderate it. To moderate racism and racial inequality, education of the general public, especially high school and college students, about historical cases of racial injustices and contemporary forms of racism is needed. Students can learn as much about racism from researching a chosen topic as from listening to lectures.

I undertook the extremely difficult task of editing the *Encyclopedia* mainly because of its practical value for contributing to the moderation of racism. I hope the *Encyclopedia* will be helpful to high school and college students who are conducting research on race-related and minority issues and that it will serve as a valuable resource for graduate students and faculty members who teach and conduct research on race relations, racial inequality, and particular minority groups in social science, history, and ethnic studies programs.

NOTE

1. See Eduardo Bonilla-Silva, *Racism without Racists: Color-Blind Racism and the Persistence of Racial Inequality in the United States* (New York: Rowman & Littlefield, 2003); Benjamin P. Bowser and Raymond G. Hunt, *Impacts of Racism on White Americans*, 2nd ed. (Thousand Oaks, CA: Sage Publications, 1996); Martin Bulmer and John Solomon, *Racism* (New York: Oxford University Press, 1999); Christopher Bates Doob, *Racism: An American Caludron*, 3rd ed. (New York: Longman, 1999); Joe Feagin and Melvin P. Sikes, *Living with Racism: The Black Middle-Class Experience* (Boston: Beacon Press, 1994); Andrew Hacker, *Two Nations: Black and White, Separate, Hostile, Unequal*, 2nd ed. (New York: Random House, 1995); Paula S. Rotenberg, *White Privilege: Essential Readings on the Other Side of Racism* (New York: Worth Publishers, 2002); Neil J. Smelser, William J. Wilson, and Faith Mitchell, eds., *America Becoming: Racial Trends and Their Consequences*, vol. 2 (Washington, DC: National Research Council, 2001).

ACKNOWLEDGMENTS

I would like to acknowledge my gratitude to a number of people who helped me complete this encyclopedia project. First of all, I am grateful to the contributors, especially the main contributors, who wrote one or two sets of sixteen to eighteen entries, for their commitment to and personal sacrifice in completing their essays. In particular, I feel obligated to express my deep gratitude to Mikaila Arthur and Dong Ho-Cho, who each wrote essays for thirty-six entries, or approximately seventy manuscript pages. Their contribution to the encyclopedia has been enormous. I also appreciate the gracious cooperation of the encyclopedia's contributors during the revision process.

I would like to thank the five members of the advisory board for reviewing the original list of entries. Their suggestions and additions have made the list of entries more comprehensive and balanced. In particular, I am grateful to Charles Jaret for his invaluable assistance in shaping the final list of entries, finding two contributors for me, writing essays on a set of entries, and supporting my career activities, both as my dissertation advisor at Georgia State University and as one of my closest friends.

I received the Queens College Presidential In-Residence Release-Time Award in the 2003 fall semester for my book project comparing Indian Hindus and Korean Protestants. But I spent much of the released time in completing this encyclopedia project. I express my sincere gratitude to the president of Queens College and the award committee for granting me release-time that was indispensable to completing the project.

Four students at Queens College—Keiko Hirota, Tiffany Vélez, Kelly Corcorom, and Soyoung Lee—aided me in creating the original list of entries, editing entries by contributors, collecting original documents, reviewing copy-edited manuscripts, and/or communicating with contributors through e-mail. Their aid was essential because the project was completed with no institutional monetary support.

I started this encyclopedia project three years ago when Wendi Schnaufer, acquisitions editor at Greenwood Press, encouraged me to initiate it. I wish to acknowledge that she helped me create the list of entries and collect primary documents, and she edited the final version of the entire manuscript. I also owe my gratitude to John Wagner, development editor at Greenwood Press, who edited every essay, took care of format and references, and arranged all entries in alphabetical order.

Finally, I need to acknowledge my heartfelt thanks to my wife, Young Oak, for spending a great deal of time and energy editing many essays, classifying entries, and reading page proofs. Moreover, her loving support and encouragement were essential to completing probably the most difficult project in my career in sociology.

INTRODUCTION

THE PREVALENCE OF RACISM IN EARLY U.S. HISTORY

African Americans

In its classic form, racism refers to the belief that on the basis of their genetic difference some racial groups are innately superior to other racial groups in intelligence, temperament, and attitudes. Racist ideology began to develop during the fifteenth century, the Age of Discovery, when white Europeans began encountering large numbers of non-white peoples in the New World, Asia, and Africa. In North America, South America, the Caribbean Islands, and South Africa, European colonial rulers established slavery as an effective way to control and exploit African workers on plantations. White racial supremacy was institutionalized with the establishment of the racial slavery system. To justify this system, European Christian settlers emphasized their cultural and moral superiority to African blacks. To perpetuate the system, Europeans tightly supervised and controlled the behaviors and movements of African slaves.

By far, the most rigid form of racial slavery developed in the American South. It has been noted that the absence of a substantial intermediate group of free people of color set the stage for a sharp dichotomy between whites and blacks in the antebellum South.[1] Meanwhile, less restrictive manumission requirements enabled more sizable and socially significant free colored groups to develop in the slave societies of South America, the Caribbean, and South Africa. The racial caste system characterized the form of slavery in the American South, but it did not fit the other three slave societies, where many free blacks married white settlers and thereby gained higher status.

Black slaves in the American South were liberated from slavery after the Civil War, in 1865. But the white violence and physical intimidation—espe-

cially with the rise of the Ku Klux Klan during Reconstruction (1865–1877)—
effectively prevented black men from competing with white workers in the
labor market. Thus, African Americans endured worse economic conditions
during Reconstruction than they had under slavery. Moreover, the failure of
Reconstruction in 1877 led to the establishment by Southern states of Jim
Crow segregation laws to control the black threat to the economic and social advantages of white Americans. Jim Crow segregation laws and other
statutes that disenfranchised blacks helped maintain the de facto racial caste
system in the South until the early 1960s. In 1903, when black nationalist
W.E.B. Du Bois wrote that "the problem of the twentieth century is the problem of the color line," he was mainly concerned about racial separation and
inequality as it existed at the time in the United States. The United States pre-
served a very rigid racial caste system for more than three centuries, from
the time of the agrarian economy of the eighteenth and nineteenth centuries
into the industrial economy of the twentieth. Only the apartheid system established in South Africa in 1948 was more rigid than the racial caste system
in the United States.

As Michael Roberts points out in his entry Race Riots in this encyclopedia,
African Americans are mistakenly understood to be mainly responsible for race
riots in the United States because race is usually ascribed to minority groups
rather than to whites. However, race riots of the Jim Crow era were almost
always white-on-black riots, that is, the attempts of "white mobs . . . to maintain the status quo of Jim Crow." Most of these riots occurred when white
workers attacked black workers, who were often used by white business owners or managers as strikebreakers. Approximately 250 race riots occurred between 1898 (Wilmington, Delaware) and 1943 (Detroit), claiming the lives of
approximately 4,300 blacks. Also, numerous minorities, mostly blacks, were
victimized by lynching, another common form of white-on-minority violence.
More than 3,500 instances of lynching occurred in the United States between
1885 and 1914.[2]

Native Americans

Other racial minority groups in the United States, while spared slavery, were
subjected to other forms of racial prejudice and discrimination. Ethnocentrism, conquest, and racial domination-subordination strongly characterized
the relationship between European whites and Native Americans. From the
beginning of their encounters, European white Protestant settlers perceived
Native Americans as uncivilized and intellectually and morally inferior. Plantation owners in the South used some Indians as slaves but preferred blacks
to Indians because in the case of Indian servitude white physical security and
control could not be guaranteed: Indian slaves could obtain help and support
from their own, nearby peoples and territories.[3] White settlers initially tried
to solve the "Indian problem" by killing them all.[4] When this failed, the U.S.
government tried by force to remove Indian tribes from their native lands in
the East and relocate them to unfamiliar and barren lands west of the Mississippi. In the process, many Indians died and most Indian tribes lost all or a
portion of their lands. In the late nineteenth century, a change in government

Indian policy from separation to assimilation only ended up taking more lands from Indians, who were also left culturally uprooted.

Mexican Americans

Mexican Americans, who account for approximately 60 percent of the Latino population in the United States, also were initially absorbed into American society as a conquered group, a fact that set the stage for the colonial pattern of their race relations with American Anglos. Texas, which won its independence from Mexico in 1836, was annexed, over Mexican objections, by the United States in 1845. About half of the remaining Mexican territory, including California and New Mexico, came to the United States at the end of the Mexican-American War (1846–1848). Under the terms of the Treaty of Guadalupe Hidalgo, which ended the war, the U.S. government guaranteed the Mexican residents of these territories political and property rights and promised to safeguard their culture, especially by guaranteeing the right to use the Spanish language and to practice the Catholic religion. However, English gradually replaced Spanish as the standard language, and Anglos in the Mexican states began to develop and exhibit prejudice against Mexican Catholics. Moreover, Anglos gradually took the property of Mexicans through official and unofficial means and through fraud, thus transforming the Mexicans into a colonial work force.

By virtue of their in-between racial status, Mexican Americans and other Latinos have been treated better than African Americans in terms of selection of residential areas, public accommodation, and access to social-club membership. Yet, their physical and cultural differences and generally low economic status have also subjected them to prejudice, discrimination, police harassment, and racial violence. According to a study of a South Texas community, Anglos believed Mexicans to be unclean, prone to drunkenness and criminality, hostile, and unpredictable.[5] The lynching of Mexicans was common in the mining camps of Los Angeles in the nineteenth century.[6]

Asian Americans

The migration of Asians to the United States started after the California Gold Rush of 1848–1849, when Chinese farmers were recruited to California to work in mining and railroad construction. Initially, Californians praised Chinese immigrants as "hard-working" and "compliant." Yet, white workers came to believe that industrious Chinese immigrants were a threat to their employment; thus, prejudice against and stereotypes of Chinese immigrants quickly developed among whites. Lobbying by white workers, and the overall anti-Chinese sentiment on the West Coast, led to passage of the Chinese Exclusion Act in 1882, which prohibited the immigration of Chinese for more than sixty years.[7] The Chinese Exclusion Act is the only U.S. government measure to ban the immigration of a particular national-origin group.

Enforcement of the Chinese Exclusion Act led to the recruitment of Japanese and other Asian workers in Hawaii and California. But these groups also encountered a series of immigration restrictions by the U.S. government, which culminated in the National Origins Act of 1924.[8] Moreover, Asian immigrants were not allowed to be American citizens until 1952. In 1913, California passed the Alien Land Law to prohibit Japanese immigrants from owning farmland, and other West Coast states passed similar laws targeting Japanese and other immigrants. California and other states later used the law to prevent Asian immigrants from purchasing real estate. As noncitizen residents, Asian immigrants before World War II did not receive legal protection even if they were victimized by racial violence. Finally, all Japanese Americans living on the West Coast (excluding Hawaii), including native-born citizens, were incarcerated in internment camps during World War II for "security" reasons. Because of their incarceration, innocent Japanese Americans in relocation camps incurred not only monetary and property losses but also psychological damage.

White Immigrant Groups

Catholic, Jewish, and Eastern Orthodox Americans of heavily eastern and southern European ancestry have today been incorporated into mainstream white American society. But, when large numbers of these non-Protestant European immigrants arrived in the United States at the end of the nineteenth and beginning of the twentieth century, they were considered physically different from native-born Anglos and thus were subjected to prejudice, discrimination, and racial violence.[9] Southern Italians suffered not only antagonism directed against Catholics in general but also severe anti-Italian sentiments because of their peasant background. Italians suffered physical violence as well as negative images and stereotypes. Killings and lynchings of Italian immigrants occurred in the United States, especially in the South, between 1890 and 1910.[10] Nicola Sacco and Bartolomeo Vanzetti, two Italian immigrants, were charged with and found guilty of murder and armed robbery and executed in 1927, even though numerous witnesses testified that they were not involed in the crime.

For many centuries, Jews suffered negative stereotypes, prejudice, and discrimination, including legal discrimination, in European Christian countries. Although American Jews fared better than European Jews in terms of legal discrimination, they also encountered anti-Semitism in different forms.[11] Anti-Semitism in the United States increased in the 1880s with the influx of eastern European Jewish immigrants and reached its high point in the 1920s and the 1930s. The Ku Klux Klan and some white industrialists, such as Henry Ford, filled the media with anti-Semitic propaganda, spreading the idea of a "world Jewish conspiracy."[12] Jews were often denied accommodation at hotels and admission to social clubs. As the number of Jewish students in prestigious universities and professional schools increased, the latter took measures to restrict Jewish admissions. Jewish Americans were also subjected to discrimination in professional occupations, especially in law, medicine, and academia.

Nativist reactions to and prejudice against Jewish, Catholic, and Asian immigrants in the United States in the first decade of the twentieth century contributed to the development of "biological racism," a racist ideology that sees so-called Nordic races as genetically—and therefore also intellectually and morally—superior to other races, including eastern and southern Europeans, African Americans, Mexicans, and Asians.[13] Such well-known psychologists as Lewis Terman and C. W. Gould argued that based on scores of IQ tests, eastern and southern European immigrants and African Americans had lower levels of intellectual ability but tended to "outbreed" people of "Nordic" races. Their arguments supported the eugenics movement, which emerged after World War I. These ideas also contributed to the passage of discriminatory immigration laws in the early 1920s, which severely reduced immigration from eastern and southern European countries and entirely banned Asian immigration.

THE PERSISTENCE OF RACISM IN THE POST–CIVIL RIGHTS ERA

The passage of civil rights laws, including affirmative action programs, in the 1960s may lead many people to believe that racism is no longer an important factor for the adjustment of minorities in the twenty-first century. The ethnic and racial diversities created by the influx of Third World immigrants, the increasing emphasis on multiculturalism by government and schools, and the increase in intermarriages since the early 1970s may further enhance the belief about the insignificance of racism in contemporary American life. Jews, Italians, and other turn-of-the-century white immigrant groups have been incorporated into mainstream America.[14] However, the social-science literature accumulated since the 1980s reveals that African Americans still suffer high levels of racial prejudice and discrimination in all aspects of their lives, and other nonwhite minority groups also experience different forms of unequal treatment because of their nonwhite status.[15] Based on their findings, the authors of these studies have suggested that the color line continues to divide American society in the twenty-first century, just as it did in the twentieth.

Although legal discrimination against African Americans ended with the civil rights legislation of the early 1960s, enough evidence exists to support the view that African Americans still have to deal with racism—both individual and institutional—on a daily basis. Many people tend to believe that racial prejudice and discrimination are problems confronted only by poor blacks concentrated in inner-city neighborhoods and that well-educated, middle-class blacks do not have to deal with it. However, based on personal interviews with middle-class blacks, two social scientists, Joe Feagin and Melvin Sikes, have challenged this view. They conclude that "racism is the everyday experience" for middle-class blacks as well and that experiences with serious racial discrimination "have a cumulative impact on particular individuals, their families, and their communities."[16] Summing up his view of white-black separation in contemporary America, political scientist Andrew Hacker similarly commented that "America's version of apartheid, while lacking overt legal sanction, comes closest to the system even now being overturned in the land of its invention" (South Africa).[17]

Sociological studies show that the high level of segregation for African Americans has not been moderated since the 1970s.[18] Housing discrimination by real estate agents, commercial banks, and local white community leaders, and the racial gap in socioeconomic status are partly responsible for what has been called "American apartheid."[19] But racial prejudice against blacks on the part of white Americans is mainly responsible for racial segregation. Residential isolation, in turn, further enhances antiblack racial prejudice and creates further socioeconomic disadvantages for African Americans.[20] Segregated black neighborhoods are characterized by all kinds of social ills, such as high poverty and unemployment rates, high mortality and crime rates, and poor educational and health-care facilities.

Since the 1978 publication of his controversial book, *Declining Significance of Race*, William Wilson has paid keen attention to the class division within the African American community and focused on poverty among residents in inner-city black neighborhoods.[21] He has argued that the disappearance of blue-collar jobs from black neighborhoods, which is a result of deindustrialization rather than racism, is the main cause of poverty among inner-city black residents. However, various studies reveal that regardless of their class background, blacks experience racial discrimination in the labor market.

No doubt, deindustrialization, along with the poor school performance overall of black children, is an important contributing factor to the exceptionally high unemployment and poverty rates among young blacks. But the preference of employers for Latino legal and illegal workers over black workers is also responsible for the difficulty young blacks have finding employment. Studies by Roger Waldinger and Michael Richter have found that regardless of industry, employers and managers prefer Latino immigrants to blacks because they perceive the former to be more "subservient" and "docile."[22] Moreover, Feagin and Sikes have shown that black professionals also encounter discrimination in finding employment and in salaries, evaluations, and promotions.[23] According to an analysis of census data by Hacker, black men with a bachelor's degree earned $764 for every $1,000 earned by their white counterparts.[24] It can be argued that the racial gap in earnings is caused mainly by racial discrimination.

The influx of immigrants from the Caribbean Islands since the 1970s has contributed to a phenomenal increase in the black immigrant population.[25] Unlike African Americans whose ancestors were brought to the United States by force for economic exploitation, Caribbean immigrants are voluntary migrants who came here for better economic and educational opportunities. An interesting question is: will the adaptation of Caribbean black immigrants and their descendants follow the pattern taken by voluntary minority groups or by colonial minority groups?[26] Mary Waters' 1999 study of Caribbean immigrants in New York City reveals that the children of lower-class immigrants assimilate quickly, becoming African American children.[27] This finding indicates the importance of race as well as class for the racialization of Caribbean immigrants.

Although Latinos in the United States are currently better accepted than African Americans, they are also subjected to prejudice, stereotypes, and discrimination. Their in-between physical characteristics and their generally lower economic class and immigrant backgrounds enhance the negative image of Latinos. The influx of legal and illegal Mexicans immigrants during recent years has led to stereotypes of native-born Mexican Americans as undocumented residents and manual laborers.[28] Because of a long history of Anglo-Mexican racial stratification, Mexicans in Texas, in particular, still experience semi-involuntary segregation in using public facilities and racial harassment by the police similar to that experienced by African Americans.[29] Probably because of their darker skin, Puerto Ricans experience residential segregation from white Americans that is more similar to that of African Americans than to other Latino groups. Moreover, Puerto Ricans, regardless of generational status, exhibit low educational and occupational levels and a high poverty rate comparable to African Americans.

Most Asian-American groups currently have a higher socioeconomic status than whites.[30] Moreover, approximately 40 percent of U.S.-born Asian Americans engage in intermarriages, in most cases with white partners.[31] These facts have led some social scientists to predict that Asian Americans are likely to be incorporated into white society in the near future.[32] However, contemporary Asian immigrants are socio-economically polarized, with one group representing professional and business classes and the other group consisting of poor refugees from Indochina and working-class migrants.[33] Moreover, the social-science literature on Asian Americans indicates that not only Asian immigrants but also U.S.-born Asian Americans encounter racial violence, racial discrimination, and rejection because of their nonwhite racial characteristics. In the past two decades, dozens of incidents of racial violence against Asian Americans have occurred in many U.S. cities, killing a dozen people. Studies based on personal interviews with or personal narratives by second-generation Asian Americans reveal that most informants experienced rejection, with such taunts as "Go back to your country" or "What country are you from?"[34] Third- and fourth-generation white Americans have an option to choose their ethnic identity or not, because they are accepted as full American citizens.[35] However, one ethnographic study showed that society forces most third- or fourth-generation Japanese and Chinese Americans to accept their ethnic and racial identities, even though they, like multigeneration white Americans, are thoroughly acculturated to American society.[36]

The influx of large numbers of Latino, Caribbean, and Asian immigrants into a predominantly white society since the 1970s has increased anti-immigrant prejudice and actions, including a resurgence of white supremacist groups.[37] In particular, Mexican immigrants, accounting for about one-fifth of total immigrants, have been subjected to nativist attacks for serving the interest of their homeland, not being assimilable, and taking welfare monies.[38] In the late 1980s and early 1990s, California, Florida, and other states passed referenda making English the standard language, which partly reflects anti-immigrant attitudes toward Latino immigrants. In 1994, Californians also passed Proposition 187, which was intended to make the children of illegal residents ineligible for free medical treatment and education. Although the proposition was invalidated, it targeted mainly Mexican illegal residents.

Although the separation of church and state and the emphasis on religious pluralism have helped many ethnic groups preserve their ethnic traditions through the practice of religious faith and rituals, white racism and Protestantism, as the foundational elements of American culture, have served each other since the colonial era (see the entry Religion and Racism, by Khyati Josh). At the end of the nineteenth and beginning of the twentieth century, Jewish and Catholic immigrants from eastern and southern Europe suffered prejudice and racial discrimination by native Protestants. At the beginning of the twenty-first century, Muslim, Sikh, and Hindu immigrants from South Asia and the Middle East are experiencing prejudice and discrimination by white Christians, especially by white evangelical Protestants. As documented in detail by Bozorgmehr and Bakalian in this encyclopedia, many Middle Eastern and South Asian Muslims and Sikhs have been subjected to two types of discrimination and physical violence in the post–September 11 era. First, they have become targets of hate crimes and bias incidents, such as arson, assaults, and shootings perpetrated by ordinary American citizens. Second, they have been subjected to supervision, detentions, and other forms of civil rights violations carried out by the U.S. government at the federal and local levels. Although Jewish Americans have successfully assimilated into white society, they are not safe from hate crimes either. Several white supremacist organizations, such as the Ku Klux Klan, the Christian Identity Movement, and skinheads, target Jews as well as other racial minority groups.[39]

CONTEMPORARY FORMS OF RACISM

To better understand the contemporary forms of racism in the United States, we need to make a series of distinctions among different types of racism. Until the 1960s, social scientists focused on individual racism, the belief that some racial groups are morally, intellectually, or culturally superior to other races. However, following the path-breaking book *Black Power* (1967) by Stokely Carmichael and Charles Hamilton, two black-nationalist leaders, social scientists now usually distinguish between individual racism and institutional racism. Institutional racism means that social institutions are arranged in such a way that they are disadvantageous to minority racial groups.[40] According to one source, "Institutional racism, unlike individual racism, is not an immediate action but the legacy of a past racist behavioral pattern."[41] Specifically, institutional racism refers to "the discriminatory racial practices built into such prominent structures as the political, economic, and educational system."

Racial minority groups in the United States, especially African Americans in the post–civil rights era, suffer more from institutional racism than from individual racism. As shown by Francois Pierre-Louis in his essay on this topic (Institutional Racism) in this encyclopedia, there are many examples of institutional racism, such as cultural biases in intelligence tests and the low quality of schools in inner-city black neighborhoods that keep children of lower-income black families at a disadvantage. The 1973 Rockefeller Drug Laws in New York state are another salient example of institutional racism. The laws have imposed severe penalties on those who have sold or possessed narcotic drugs and crack cocaine, and as a result of these laws, the state's prison population has increased rapidly. Most of the prisoners are African American men because users of crack cocaine are heavily concentrated in this population.[42]

Social scientists also tend to divide individual racism into two types: biological racism and symbolic racism.[43] As previously noted, biological racism, which emphasizes the intellectual superiority of northwestern Europeans, was popular in the first decade of the twentieth century. By contrast, symbolic racism focuses on a racial minority group's purported behavioral deficiencies, such as being welfare dependent, lazy, and criminally oriented, which conflict with traditional American values such as hard work and self-reliance.[44] Individual racism against minority groups in the post–civil rights period usually takes the form of symbolic racism. That is, white Americans generally attribute the lower socioeconomic status and poverty of African Americans and other minority groups to the latter's lack of motivation and work ethic, and to their unstable families. Most white Americans seem to accept the culture-of-poverty thesis endorsed by conservative scholars and policymakers.

Given the contemporary knowledge of human development, few people could persuasively argue for the genetic basis of the intellectual superiority of particular racial groups. Nevertheless, biological racism has reemerged among academics in contemporary America. In his controversial 1969 article, Arthur Jensen, an educational psychologist, argued that Asians have the highest level of cognitive abilities, blacks have the lowest, and whites are in the middle, and that these differences were largely determined by biology. Based on his findings, Jensen suggested that the Head Start program that was created at that time to boost the IQ of minority children would have a limited impact. About twenty-five years later, Richard Herrnstein and Charles Murray made a similar argument for biologically determined differences in cognitive abilities among Asians, whites, and blacks.[45] They further claimed that the differences in the cognitive abilities account for some of the social stratification among the three groups.

Joel Kovel made a distinction between dominative racism and aversive racism.[46] This distinction is also of great use for understanding the nature of racial separation in contemporary America. While dominative racism involves unfair treatment of minority members, "aversive racism" refers to the tendency to try to avoid contact with blacks and other minority members. This form of racism is the main cause of the high level of residential segregation of African Americans from white Americans and the lack of white-black social interactions at the personal level. Since the unwillingness of white Americans to contact minority members at the personal and neighborhood levels does not involve civil rights violations, the government cannot use any short-term measures to facilitate interracial friendship and dating.

Finally, most contemporary Americans can be said to commit color-blind racism, which is a form of racism that serves to maintain the racial dominance of whites by ignoring the continuing effects of historical prejudice on the life chances of minority members.[47] Many whites believe that because minority members have enjoyed equal opportunity since the enforcement of the civil rights laws the racial category should no longer be considered as a factor in college admission or employment. They claim that the United States should be a color-blind society that gives reward only based on individual merits. Those who embrace color-blind racism argue that race-based affirmative action programs are not only unfair to white Americans, they are also demeaning to minority members of society because they imply that minorities are not equal to white Americans. The main problem with their argument is that they ignore how minorities' opportunities for socioeconomic attainment have been affected by past and current racial discrimination.

Color-blind racism can be said to be "unintentional racism" in that some white Americans do not pay attention to the current status of racial inequality and the special needs of American society's minority members mainly because they are ignorant of the lingering effects of past racial discrimination and of different forms of current racial discrimination. But many other white conservatives intentionally avoid discussion of racial issues and vaguely emphasize meritocracy to protect their racial privileges.

The "California Ballot Initiative to Ban Racial Data," or California Ballot Proposition 54, was the most exemplary public expression of color-blind racism. This proposition, made by University of California regent Ward Connerly in 2002, would have prohibited state and local governments in California from classifying students, contractors, or employees by race, ethnicity, or national origin. This initiative was an effort to block researchers' and policymakers' access to racial data in employment, public education, and governmental contracts. California voters defeated the proposition in October 2003. If it had been approved, researchers and policymakers would not have information about how underrepresented blacks or Latinos are, for example, in the Los Angeles Police Department or in the student body of the University of California system.

Opponents of racial data collection argue that any kind of racial classification is arbitrary because the human species is biologically and anatomically diverse, and that it "foments separatist racial identities and promotes practices of ingroup/outgroup inclusion and exclusion."[48] But the ulterior motivation of many of the opponents is to control information about the levels of direct and indirect racial discrimination taking place in employment, education, heath care, law enforcement, and other public settings. Racial classification in public documents, however arbitrary it may be, is necessary to understanding the level and nature of racial discrimination and racial inequality, because "race serves as a basis for the distribution of social privileges and resources."[49]

NOTES

1. George Frederickson, *White Supremacy: A Comparative Study of American and South African History* (New York: Oxford University Press, 1981).

2. Terry Ann Knopf, *Rumors, Race and Riots* (New Brunswick, NJ: Transaction Books, 1975).

3. Pierre van den Berghe, *The Ethnic Phenomenon* (New York: Elsevier, 1981).

4. Russell Thornton, *American Indian Holocaust Survival: A Population History since 1492* (Norman: University of Oklahoma Press, 1987).

5. Ozie G. Simmons, "The Mutual Image and Expectations of Anglo-Americans and Mexican-Americans," in *Chicanos: Social and Psychological Perspectives,* ed. Nathaniel N. Wagner and Marsha J. Haug (St. Louis, MO: Mosby, 1971).

6. Carey McWilliams, *North from Mexico: The Spanish-Speaking People of the United States* (New York: Greenwood Press, 1968).

7. Alexander Saxton, *The Indispensable Enemy: The Labor and the Anti-Chinese Movement in California* (Berkeley, CA: University of California Press, 1971); Ronald

Takaki, *Strangers from a Different Shore: A History of Asian Americans* (Boston: Little, Brown, 1989).

8. Bill Ong Hing, *Making and Remaking of Asian America through Immigration Policy* (Stanford, CA: Stanford University Press, 1993).

9. Noel Ignatiev, *How the Irish Became White* (New York: Routledge, 1995).

10. Richard Gambino, *Vendetta* (Garden City, NY: Doubleday, 1977).

11. Frederic Cople Jaher, *A Scapegoat in the New Wilderness: The Origins and Rise of Anti-Semitism in America* (Cambridge, MA: Harvard University Press, 1994); Louise A. Mayo, *The Ambivalent Image: Nineteenth-Century America's Perception of the Jew* (Rutherford, NJ: Fairleigh Dickenson University Press, 1988); Stephen L. Slavin and Mary A. Pratt, *The Einstein Syndrome: Corporate Anti-Semitism in America Today* (New York: World Publishers, 1982).

12. Martin Marger, *Race and Ethnic Relations: American and Global Perspectives*, 5th ed. (Belmont, CA: Wadsworth, 2000).

13. Madison Grant, *The Passing of the Great Race* (New York: Charles Scribner's Sons, 1916); John Higham, *Strangers in the Land* (New York: Atheneum, 1955).

14. Nancy Foner, *From Ellis Island to J.F.K. Airport: Immigrants to New York City* (New Haven, CT: Yale University Press, 2001); Ignatiev, *How the Irish Became White*.

15. Benjamin P. Bowser and Raymond G. Hunt, *Impacts of Racism on White Americans*, 2nd ed. (Thousand Oaks, CA: Sage Publications, 1996); Joe Feagin, "The Continuing Significance of Race: Anti-Black Discrimination in Public Places," *American Sociological Review* 56 (1991): 101–116; Joe R. Feagin and Karyn D. McKinney, *The Many Costs of Racism* (Lanham, MD: Rowman & Littlefield, 2003); Joe Feagin and Melvin P. Sikes, *Living with Racism: The Black Middle-Class Experience* (Boston: Beacon Press, 1994); Andrew Hacker, *Two Nations: Black and White, Separate, Hostile, Unequal,* 2nd ed. (New York: Random House, 1995); Douglas S. Massey and Nancy Denton, *American Apartheid: Segregation and the Making of the Underclass* (Cambridge, MA: Harvard University Press, 1993); Paula S. Rotenberg, *White Privilege: Essential Readings on the Other Side of Racism* (New York: Worth Publishers, 2002); Howard Schuman, Charlotte Steeh, Lawrence Bobo, and Maria Krysan, *Racial Attitudes in America: Trends and Interpretations*, rev. ed. (Cambridge, MA: Harvard University Press, 1997); Stephen Steinberg, *The Ethnic Myth: Race, Ethnicity, and Class in America*, 2nd ed. (Boston: Beacon Press, 1988); Roger Waldinger, *Still the Promised City? African Americans and New Immigrants in Postindustrial New York* (Cambridge, MA: Harvard University Press, 1996); Cornel West, *Race Matters* (New York: Vintage Books, 1994).

16. Feagin and Sikes, *Living with Racism*, 15–16.

17. Hacker, *Two Nations*, 4.

18. Reynolds Farley, Charlotte Steeh, Maria Krysan, Tara Jackson, and Keith Reeves, "Stereotypes and Segregation: Neighborhoods in the Detroit Area," *American Journal of Sociology* 100 (1994): 750–780; Massey and Denton, *American Apartheid*.

19. Massey and Denton, *American Apartheid*.

20. Ibid.

21. William Wilson, *The Declining Significance of Race* (Chicago: University of Chicago Press, 1978); Ibid., *The Truly Disadvantaged: The Inner City, the Underclass, and Public Policy* (Chicago: University of Chicago Press, 1987); Ibid., *When Work Disappears: The World of the New Urban Poor* (New York: Knopf, 1996).

22. Waldinger, *Still the Promised City*; Roger Waldinger and Michael I. Richter, *How the Other Half Works: Immigration and the Social Organization of Race* (Berkeley: University of California Press, 2003).

23. Feagin and Sikes, *Living with Racism*.

24. Hacker, *Two Nations*, 101.

25. Philip Kasinitz, *Caribbean New York: Black Immigrants and the Politics of Race* (Ithaca, NY: Cornell University Press, 1992); Mary Waters, *Black Identities: West Indian Immigrant Dreams and American Realities* (New York: Russell Sage Foundation, 1999).

26. Robert Blauner, *Racial Oppression in America* (New York: Harper and Row, 1972); John Ogbu, "Immigrant and Involuntary Minorities in Comparative Perspective," in *Minority Status and Schooling: A Comparative Study of Immigrant and Involuntary Minorities*, ed. Margaret Gibson and John Ogbu (New York: Garland Publishing, 1991).

27. Waters, *Black Identities*.

28. Min Zhou, "The Changing Face of America: Immigration, Race/Ethnicity, and Social Mobility," in *Mass Migration to the United States: Classical and Contemporary Periods*, ed. Pyong Gap Min (Walnut Creek, CA: AltaMira Press, 2002), 82.

29. Leo Grebler, Joan W. Moor, and Ralph C. Guzman, *The Mexican-American People: The Nation's Second Largest Minority* (New York: Free Press, 1970).

30. Arthur Sakamoto and Chomghwan Kim, "The Increasing Significance of Class, the Declining Significance of Race, and Wilson's Hypothesis," *Asian American Policy Issue* 12 (2003): 19–41; Arthur Sakamoto, Jeng Liu, and Jessie Tzeng, "The Declining Significance of Race among Chinese and Japanese American Men," *Research in Social Stratification and Mobility* 16 (1998):225–246.

31. Sharon Lee and Marilyn Fernandez, "Trends in Asian American Racial/Ethnic Inter-Marriage: A Comparison of 1980 and 1990 Census Data," *Sociological Perspectives* 41 (1998): 323–342.

32. Herbert Gans, "The Possibility of a New Racial Hierarchy in the Twentieth-First Century United States," in *The Cultural Territories of Race: Black and White Boundaries*, ed. Mechele Lamont (Chicago: University of Chicago Press, 1999).

33. Pyong Gap Min, "An Overview of Asian Americans" in *Asian American: Contemporary Trends and Issues* (Thousand Oaks, CA: Sage Publications, 1995).

34. Pyong Gap Min and Rose Kim, eds., *Struggle for Ethnic Identity: Narratives by Asian American Professionals* (Walnut Creek, CA: AltaMira Press, 1999); Pyong Gap Min, *The Second Generation: Ethnic Identity among Asian Americans* (Walnut Creek, CA: AltaMira Press, 2002).

35. Mary Waters, *Ethnic Options: Choosing Identities in America* (Berkeley: University of California Press, 1990).

36. Mia Tuan, *Forever Foreigners or Honorary Whites? The Asian Ethnic Experience Today* (New Brunswick, NJ: Rutgers University Press, 1999).

37. Charles Jaret, "Troubled by Newcomers: Anti-immigrant Attitudes and Action During Two Eras of Mass Immigration to the United States," *Journal of American Ethnic History* 18 (1999): 9–39.

38. Richard D. Lamm and Gary Imhoff, *The Immigration Time Bomb: The Fragmenting of America* (New York: Truman Talley, Dutton, 1985).

39. Amy Ferber, *White Man Falling: Race, Gender, and White Supremacy* (New York: Rowman & Littlefield, 1998); Slavin and Pratt, *The Einstein Syndrome*.

40. Christopher Bates Doob, *Racism: An American Cauldron*, 3rd ed. (New York: Longman), 8; Joe Feagin, *Discrimination, American Style* (Englewood, NJ: Prentice Hall, 1978); Feagin and Sikes, *Living with Racism*, 3; Thomas Pettigrew, ed., *Racial Discrimination in the United States* (New York: Harper and Row, 1975), x.

41. Doob, *Racism*, 8.

42. Aaron Wilson, "Rockefeller Drug Laws Information Sheet," Partnership for Responsible Drug Information, 2000.

43. Doob, *Racism*, 15; Hacker, *Two Nations*, 23–27; David Sears, "Symbolic Racism,"

in *Eliminating Racism: Profiles in Controversy*, ed. Phyllis Katz and Dalmas Taylor (New York: Plenum, 1988).

44. Sears, "Symbolic Racism."

45. Richard J. Herrnstein and Charles Murray, *The Bell Curve: Intelligence and Class Structure in American Life* (New York: Free Press, 1994).

46. Joel Kovel, *White Racism: A Psychohistory* (New York: Pantheon, 1970).

47. Eduardo Bonilla-Silva, *Racism without Racists: Color-Blind Racism and the Persistence of Racial Inequality in the United States* (New York: Rowman & Littlefield, 2003).

48. Yehudi Webster, "Racial Classification: A Wrong Turn," *Footnotes* 31 (January 2003): 8–9.

49. American Sociological Association, "The ASA Statement on the Importance of Collecting Data and Doing Social Science Research on Race," American Sociological Association, February 2002.

LIST OF EDITORS, ADVISORY BOARD MEMBERS, AND CONTRIBUTORS

EDITOR

Pyong Gap Min

Professor
Queens College and CUNY Graduate Center

ADVISORY BOARD MEMBERS

Steven Gold

Professor and the Acting Chair
Department of Sociology
Michigan State University

Ramon Gutierrez

Professor and Endowed Chair
Ethnic Studies Department
University of California at San Diego

Charles Jaret

Professor
Department of Sociology
Georgia State University

Ronald Taylor

Professor
Department of Sociology
Vice Provost, Multicultural and International Affairs
University of Connecticut

Min Zhou

Professor
Department of Sociology
Chair, Asian American Studies Interdepartmental Degree Program
University of California at Los Angeles

MAIN CONTRIBUTORS
   Each main contributor wrote a series of at least 14 entries of varying lengths, including one long essay on a broad topic of special significance. Each contributor's long essay topic is listed below.

Daisuke Akiba

Assistant Professor
Elementary and Early Childhood Education
Queens College
Japanese American Internment

Mikaila Mariel Lemonik Arthur

Doctoral Student
Department of Sociology
New York University
Anti-Semitism in the United States

Anny Bakalian

Associate Director
The Middle East and Middle Eastern American Studies Center
September 11th (2001) Terrorism, Discriminatory Reactions to

Sandra L. Barnes

Assistant Professor
Department of Sociology
Purdue University
Culture of Poverty Thesis

Mehdi Bozorgmehr

Associate Professor
Co-Director, The Middle East and Middle Eastern American Studies Center
Hunter College and the Graduate Center of City University of New York (CUNY)
September 11th (2001) Terrorism, Discriminatory Reactions to

Michael Roberts

Assistant Professor
Department of Sociology
San Diego State University
Race Riots

Robin Roger-Dillon

Assistant Professor
Department of Sociology
Queens College of CUNY
Biological Racism

Benjamin F. Shearer

Independent Scholar
Tallahassee, Florida
Financial Institutions and Racial Discrimination

Philip Yang

Associate Professor
Department of Sociology and Social Work
Texas Woman's University
Affirmative Action

OTHER CONTRIBUTORS

Nicholas Alexiou

Adjunct Professor
Department of Sociology
Queens College of CUNY

Jane Davis

Associate Professor
Department of English Literature
Iowa State University at Ames

On Kyung Joo

Library Media Specialist
Davison Avenue School
Long Island, New York

Rose Kim

Doctoral Student
Sociology Program
The Graduate Center of CUNY

Etsuko Maruoka-Ng

Doctoral Student
Department of Sociology
State University of New York (SUNY)—Stony Brook

Victoria Pitts

Associate Professor
Department of Sociology
Queens College of CUNY

Tiffany Vélez

Graduate Student
Department of Speech Pathology
Queens College

Barbara J. Webb

Associate Professor
Department of English Literature
Hunter College and the Graduate Center of CUNY

CHRONOLOGY OF RACE AND RACISM IN THE UNITED STATES

1790	Congress passes the Naturalization Act establishing the first rules and procedures to be used in granting citizens to immigrants
1800	Gabriel Prosser leads slave uprising in Virginia
1820	Congress enacts the Missouri Compromise by admitting Missouri as a slave state but prohibiting slavery in Louisiana Purchase territories north of Missouri's southern boundary
1822	Denmark Vesey leads a slave insurrection in Charleston, South Carolina
1824	Bureau of Indian Affairs (BIA) is created as part of the U.S. War Department to manage encounters and interactions with Native Americans
1831	In *Cherokee Nation v. Georgia*, the U.S. Supreme Court declares Georgia laws confiscating Cherokee lands unconstitutional
1831	Nat Turner leads a slavery uprising in Virginia
1833	American Anti-Slavery Society is formed in Philadelphia
1835	Publication of Alexis de Tocqueville's *Democracy in America*, an analysis of the nature of American democracy in the early nineteenth century
1836	New Philadelphia, the earliest known black town, is established in Pike County, Illinois
1838–1839	Trail of Tears: U.S. government forcibly removes the Cherokee from their lands in Georgia to Oklahoma
1845	Publication of the *Narrative of the Life of Frederick Douglass*, the autobiography of ex-slave abolitionist Frederick Douglass

1845	Term *Manifest Destiny* is coined by journalist John L. O'Sullivan in the July–August edition of the *United States Magazine and Democratic Review*
1845	United States annexes Texas
1848	Signing of the Treaty of Guadalupe Hidalgo, ending the Mexican-American War
1849	Bureau of Indian Affairs (BIA) is transferred to the U.S. Department of the Interior
1850	Congress passes a new Fugitive Slave Act as part of the Compromise of 1850
1850	Know-Nothing Party, a nativist, anti-immigrant political party, is founded
1852	Publication of Harriet Beecher Stowe's novel *Uncle Tom's Cabin*
1852	California enacts the Foreign Miners License Tax to protect white miners from foreign competition, especially from Chinese immigrants
1854	Kansas-Nebraska Act repeals the Missouri Compromise and opens all territories to the possibility of slavery
1857	In the Dred Scott Decision, the U.S. Supreme Court strikes down the Missouri Compromise (1820), declaring that Congress has no power to prohibit slavery
1859	Abolitionist John Brown raids the federal arsenal at Harper's Ferry, Virginia, in an effort to initiate a slave uprising
1862	President Abraham Lincoln issues the Emancipation Proclamation
1863	Believing they are being forced to fight and die for African Americans, with whom they are in competition for jobs, Irish immigrants riot against the Civil War draft in New York City
1865	Thirteenth Amendment is ratified, abolishing slavery in the United States
1865	Freedmen's Bureau is established by Congress to oversee all matters relating to war refugees and freed slaves
1865	Ku Klux Klan is founded in Tennessee
1866	Race riots erupt in Memphis, Tennessee, when white mobs attack African American soldiers and residents
1868	Fourteenth Amendment is ratified, requiring equal protection under the law for all citizens
1871	Anti-Chinese race riot erupts in Los Angeles after a white man is accidentally killed while trying to stop a dispute between two Chinese men
1877	To settle the disputed presidential election of 1876, the Democrats concede victory to Republican Rutherford B. Hayes, who

in turn withdraws federal troops from the South, thereby allowing white governments to overturn the political and social advances made by blacks during Reconstruction

1877–1950s   Southern states and municipalities pass and enforce a series of enactments known as Jim Crow Laws, which are designed to create and maintain racial segregation and to discriminate against blacks

1882   Congress passes the Chinese Exclusion Act, which prohibits Chinese laborers from entering the United States and denies naturalized citizenship to Chinese already in the country

1884   Publican of Mark Twain's novel *Adventures of Huckleberry Finn*

1887   Congress passes the Indian Allotment Act, known as the Dawes Act, to distribute parcels of tribal land to each tribal member or family on the reservation

1890   U.S. troops massacre Lakota Sioux Indians at Wounded Knee, South Dakota

1894   Immigration Restriction League is founded in Boston to protect the American way of life from and influx of "undesirable immigrants," mainly Jews and Catholics from southern and eastern Europe

1896   In *Plessy v. Fergusson*, the U.S. Supreme Court declares the separate but equal doctrine constitutional

1898   United States annexes Hawaii

1903   Publication of W.E.B. Du Bois's classic work, *The Souls of Black Folk*

1905   Asiatic Exclusion League, originally called the Japanese and Korean Exclusion League, is formed by white nativist labor unions

1905   Niagara Movement is founded by W.E.B. Du Bois to advocate full civil rights and full manhood suffrage for African Americans

1906   San Francisco School Board orders the segregation of Japanese and Korean children in the city's schools

1907   Bellingham Riots begin when a mob of white men, who fear the loss of their jobs to immigrants, attacks a Hindu community in Bellingham, Washington

1908   Japan accepts the so-called Gentlemen's Agreement, agreeing to issue no passports for immigration to the United States except to relatives of Japanese workers already in the country

1909   National Association for the Advancement of Colored People (NAACP) is founded by an interracial group of citizens in Springfield, Illinois

1911   Dillingham Report on immigration to the United States is issued by the U.S. Commission on Immigration, a congressional commission chaired by Senator William P. Dillingham

1913	Alien Land Law is passed in California to prevent immigrants from owning or leasing land for more than three years
1913	Anti-Defamation League of B'nai Brith is founded to combat prejudice, discrimination, and violence against Jews
1915	Release of D. W. Griffith's film, *Birth of a Nation*, a racist view of U.S. history that is instrumental in the revival of the Ku Klux Klan
1915	Leo Frank, a Jew convicted of murdering a girl in Georgia in 1913, is abducted from prison and lynched, despite the existence of evidence that casts doubt on his guilt
1915	Ku Klux Klan is refounded in Georgia by William J. Simmons
1916	New York chapter of the Universal Negro Improvement Association (UNIA) is established by organization founder Marcus Garvey
1916	Publication of Madison Grant's widely read *The Passing of the Great Race*, which argues that race is a primary factor in differences in intelligence, work ethic, and social and psychological characteristics
1917	Congress prohibits all immigration from the "Asiatic Barred Zone," which includes various parts of Asia and the Middle East
1917	Competition for jobs leads to a deadly white-on-black race riot in St. Louis, Missouri
1920	American Civil Liberties Union (ACLU) is established
1922	In *Ozawa v. United States*, the U.S. Supreme Court declares that a Japanese person is not eligible for citizenship in the United States
1923	In *United States v. Thind*, the U.S. Supreme Court denies citizenship to Asian Indian immigrants
1924	Congress passes the National Origins Act, severely restricting the flow of immigrants to the United States
1924	Congress passes the Indian Citizenship Act, granting U.S. citizenship to all Native Americans who are not already citizens under some other law or treaty
1927	Execution of Nicola Sacco and Bartolomeo Vanzetti, two Italian American anarchists convicted, on largely circumstantial evidence, of two murders committed during a robbery in 1920
1928	Meriam Report on Indian reservations is issued to the Secretary of the Interior
1929	League of United Latin American Citizens (LULAC) is founded to advocate for Hispanic civil rights
1930	Japanese American Citizens League (JACL) is founded to protect the civil rights of Japanese and other Asian Americans
1930	Nation of Islam (Black Muslims) is founded in Detroit by Wallace D. Fard

1932–1972 U.S. Public Health Service conducts and funds the Tuskegee Study of Untreated Syphilis in the Negro Male, which exploits and misleads hundreds of African American men in the name of science

1934 Federal Housing Administration (FHA) is created

1934 Congress passes the Indian Reorganization Act, also known as the Wheeler-Howard Act, to increase Native American self-governance and to foster tribal economic independence

1934 Congress passes the federal Anti-Lynching Law in response to the racially motivated murders of African Americans

1935 Congress passes the Wagner Act, also known as the National Labor Relations Act, giving workers the right to independent, union representation for purposes of collective bargaining with their employers

1942 Emergency Labor Program, popularly called the Bracero Program, is established to allow Mexican workers into the United States to meet the labor needs of southwestern agriculture growers during World War II

1942 Congress of Racial Equality (CORE) is founded as a pacifist group seeking to fight racism, integrate public facilities, and work for civil rights for African Americans

1942 President Franklin D. Roosevelt signs Executive Order 9066, clearing the way for internment of Japanese Americans

1942 War Relocation Authority (WRA) is established by executive order of President Roosevelt as the government agency responsible for removing persons believed to be threats to national security

1943 Detroit Race Riot comprises a series of violent encounters, sparked by competition for jobs and housing, between whites and African Americans in Detroit, Michigan

1943 Zoot Suit Riots, consisting of white attacks on Mexican American youths, erupt in Los Angeles

1944 In *Korematsu v. United States*, the U.S. Supreme Court case upholds the internment of Japanese Americans during World War II

1944 National Congress of American Indians (NCAI) is founded to lobby for Native American rights and causes

1946 Congress creates the Indian Claims Commission (ICC) to hear and determine claims against the U.S. government made by any Native American tribe or group

1947 Jackie Robinson joins the Brooklyn Dodgers, becoming the first African American player in major-league baseball

1948 President Harry S. Truman issues Executive Order 9981 racially integrating the U.S. military

1948	In *Shelley v. Kraemer*, the U.S. Supreme Court rules that the equal protection clause of the Fourteenth Amendment prevents racially restrictive housing covenants from being enforceable
1948	American GI Forum, an organization devoted to securing equal rights for Hispanic American veterans, is founded by Hector P. Garcia
1948	In *Oyama v. California*, the U.S. Supreme Court strikes down California's Alien Land Laws as unconstitutional
1952	Congress passes the McCarran-Walter Act, which eases certain restrictions on immigrants of particular national origins
1954	In *Brown v. Board of Education of Topeka*, the U.S. Supreme Court declares racial segregation in schools unconstitutional
1954	Publication of Gordon Allport's *The Nature of Prejudice*, an influential work examining and defining the nature of racial prejudice
1954	U.S. Immigration and Naturalization Service launches the controversial paramilitary repatriation program, "Operation Wetback," which targets Mexicans working "illegally" in the agricultural industry of the Southwest
1955	African American Rosa Parks refuses to give up her seat on a Montgomery, Alabama, bus to a white passenger, thereby initiating the Montgomery Bus Boycott
1955	Publication of John Higham's *Strangers in the Land*, a classic analysis of nativism in the United States
1956	Publication of Kenneth Stampp's *The Peculiar Institution*, which views slavery as a coercive and profit-seeking regime, a significant revision in the way historians have previously seen the institution
1957	Southern Christian Leadership Conference (SCLC) is created in New Orleans by a group of ministers, labor leaders, lawyers, and political activists concerned about the impact of segregation on their communities
1957	U.S. Commission on Civil Rights (USCCR) is created by the Civil Rights Act of 1957 as an independent, fact-finding arm of the federal government
1957	President Dwight D. Eisenhower sends federal troops to protect from angry whites nine black students attempting to integrate Central High School in Little Rock, Arkansas
1958	John Birch Society is founded by Robert Welch to advocate limited government, anticommunism, and American isolationism
1959	American Nazi Party is founded by George Lincoln Rockwell
1960	Student Nonviolent Coordinating Committee (SNCC) is founded at Shaw University in Raleigh, North Carolina, to coordinate nonviolent protest actions against racial segregation

1960	Publication of John Howard Griffin's *Black Like Me*, the story of the extensive loss of rights and privileges suffered by a white man who darkened his skin to pass for black
1961	President John F. Kennedy issues Executive Order 10925, which makes first use of the term *affirmative action* in calling on government contractors to treat employees "without regard to their race, creed, color, or national origin"
1961	Freedom Riders, blacks and whites who travel together across the South in buses, protest racial segregation
1961	Release of *West Side Story*, a groundbreaking film about white–Puerto Rican race relations
1962	National Farm Workers Association (NFWA), later the United Farm Workers (UFW), is founded by Cesar Chavez and Dolores Huerta
1963	March on Washington is organized to bring attention to the lack of job opportunities and civil rights for African Americans
1963	Martin Luther King Jr. delivers his "I Have a Dream" speech before the Lincoln Memorial in Washington, DC
1963	Martin Luther King Jr. writes his "Letter from a Birmingham Jail" while incarcerated for his role in antisegregation demonstrations in Birmingham, Alabama
1963	Reies Lopez Tijerina founds the Alianza Federal de Pueblos Libres (Federal Alliance of Land Grant) to reclaim Spanish and Mexican land grants held by Mexican and Native Americans before the Mexican-American War (1846–1848)
1964	Congress passes the Civil Rights Act to end the deeply entrenched practices of racial segregation and other forms of racial discrimination
1964	Bracero Program, which has allowed Mexican workers into the United States since 1942, is ended
1964	Organization of Afro-American Unity (OAAU) is founded by Malcolm X to coordinate political action and self-organization among blacks toward the goal of racial equality
1964	Harlem riot begins when a white police officer shoots and kills an African American youth in Yorkville, New York
1965	Congress creates the federal Department of Housing and Urban Development (HUD)
1965	Publication of Paul M. Siegel's groundbreaking article, "On the Cost of Being a Negro," which examines the true extent of the income gap between blacks and whites
1965	El Teatro Campensino, the Farmworkers Theater, is founded by Luis Valdez as part of the organizing effort of Cesar Chavez's United Farm Workers union

1965	Congress passes the Voting Rights Act, which requires certain state and local jurisdictions to get federal approval before altering their voting procedures
1965	Congress passes the Immigration Act, phasing out national-origin quotas and emphasizing the reunification of families
1965	Race riots erupt in the Watts neighborhood of Los Angeles
1965	Publication of Daniel Patrick Moynihan's *The Negro Family in America: The Case for National Action*, which blames the poverty and social problems afflicting African Americans on the breakdown of the family
1966	Black Panther Party for Self-Defense is formed by Huey Newton, Bobby Seale, and other radical black activists
1966	In *Miranda v. Arizona* (1966), the U.S. Supreme Court establishes suspects' right to an attorney and to be informed of their rights before questioning by police
1966	Maulana Karenga, professor of black studies at California State University, develops Kwanzaa as a cultural holiday to promote the African American experience
1967	Race riot erupts in Newark, New Jersey
1967	Publication of *Black Power: The Politics of Liberation in America* by Stokely Carmichael and Charles V. Hamilton
1967	Discrimination and poor housing for blacks spark violent race riots in Detroit, Michigan
1967	National Advisory Commission on Civil Disorders (the Kerner Commission) is formed by President Lyndon B. Johnson to investigate the causes and implications of the urban riots occurring in black sections of many major cities
1968	American Indian Movement (AIM) is founded
1968	Congress passes another Civil Rights Act to ensure fair housing practices (Title VIII, known as the Fair Housing Act) and confer various civil rights on Native Americans
1968	Bilingual Education Act is passed by Congress
1968	Kerner Commission (the National Advisory Commission on Civil Disorders) issues its report on the series of urban race riots that occurred in 1967
1968	Mexican American Legal Defense and Education Fund (MALDEF) is founded in San Antonio, Texas, to protect the civil rights of Latinos and promote their empowerment and full participation in society
1969	Arthur Jensen publishes a widely cited article in the *Harvard Education Review* attacking Head Start programs and claiming that African American children have a low average IQ that cannot be improved by social engineering

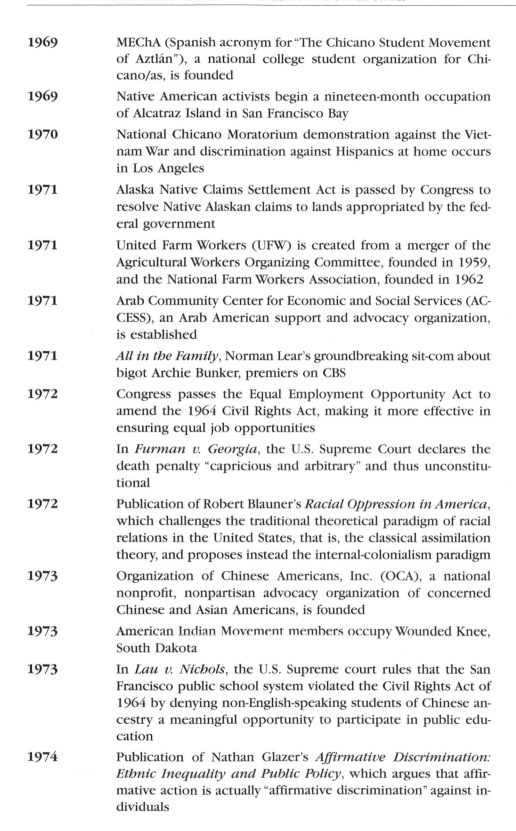

1969   MEChA (Spanish acronym for "The Chicano Student Movement of Aztlán"), a national college student organization for Chicano/as, is founded

1969   Native American activists begin a nineteen-month occupation of Alcatraz Island in San Francisco Bay

1970   National Chicano Moratorium demonstration against the Vietnam War and discrimination against Hispanics at home occurs in Los Angeles

1971   Alaska Native Claims Settlement Act is passed by Congress to resolve Native Alaskan claims to lands appropriated by the federal government

1971   United Farm Workers (UFW) is created from a merger of the Agricultural Workers Organizing Committee, founded in 1959, and the National Farm Workers Association, founded in 1962

1971   Arab Community Center for Economic and Social Services (ACCESS), an Arab American support and advocacy organization, is established

1971   *All in the Family*, Norman Lear's groundbreaking sit-com about bigot Archie Bunker, premiers on CBS

1972   Congress passes the Equal Employment Opportunity Act to amend the 1964 Civil Rights Act, making it more effective in ensuring equal job opportunities

1972   In *Furman v. Georgia*, the U.S. Supreme Court declares the death penalty "capricious and arbitrary" and thus unconstitutional

1972   Publication of Robert Blauner's *Racial Oppression in America*, which challenges the traditional theoretical paradigm of racial relations in the United States, that is, the classical assimilation theory, and proposes instead the internal-colonialism paradigm

1973   Organization of Chinese Americans, Inc. (OCA), a national nonprofit, nonpartisan advocacy organization of concerned Chinese and Asian Americans, is founded

1973   American Indian Movement members occupy Wounded Knee, South Dakota

1973   In *Lau v. Nichols*, the U.S. Supreme court rules that the San Francisco public school system violated the Civil Rights Act of 1964 by denying non-English-speaking students of Chinese ancestry a meaningful opportunity to participate in public education

1974   Publication of Nathan Glazer's *Affirmative Discrimination: Ethnic Inequality and Public Policy*, which argues that affirmative action is actually "affirmative discrimination" against individuals

1974	Asian American Legal Defense and Education Fund (AALDEF) is founded to protect the legal rights of Asian Americans
1975	Aryan Nations, a white-supremacist, anti-Semitic group, is founded by Richard G. Butler
1975	Congress amends the Voting Rights Act of 1965 to protect the voting rights of citizens of certain ethnic groups whose first language is not English
1975	Congress passes the Indian Self-Determination and Education Assistance Act to implement tribal self-determination in matters relating to delivery of educational, health, and other services to Native Americans
1976	In *Gregg v. Georgia*, the U.S. Supreme Court reinstates the death penalty
1976	Publication of Alex Haley's *Roots: The Saga of an American Family*, a semiautobiographical history of Haley's family and their experiences as slaves
1978	In *Regents of the University of California v. Bakke*, the U.S. Supreme Court upholds the concept of affirmative action
1978	Publication of William J. Wilson's influential *The Declining Significance of Race*, a polemic on the relative importance of race and class for life chances of African Americans
1978	Publication of Joe Feagin's *Discrimination, American Style*, which argues that racial discrimination is embedded in institutions and policies designed to address the concerns of white European males
1980	American-Arab Anti-Discrimination Committee is established
1981	U.S. Department of Education formulates a clear policy that Ebonics is a form of English, not a separate language, and thus not eligible for public funding
1982	Vincent Chin is murdered in Detroit, Michigan, by two white autoworkers who mistake him for Japanese and blame him for the loss of American jobs
1983	Publication of Thomas Sowell's *Economics and Politics of Race*, in which a conservative social scientist argues that culture makes a difference in the success of an ethnic group and that racial strife has affected human society throughout history
1984	Publication of Charles Murray's *Losing Ground: American Social Policy, 1950–1980*, a controversial examination of U.S. government social programs
1985	Arab American Institute is established to represent the interests of Americans of Arab descent in politics and to foster their civic and political empowerment
1985	Rainbow Coalition is founded by Reverend Jesse Jackson to unite people of diverse ethnic, religious, economic, and political backgrounds in a push for social, racial, and economic justice

1986	Howard Beach incident occurs, in which Michael Griffith, a black Trinidadian immigrant, is killed after he and two other men are attacked by a gang of white teenagers in the white Howard Beach neighborhood in Queens, New York
1986	Publication of Michael Omi and Howard Winant's *Racial Formation in the United States: From the 1960s to the 1980s*, a groundbreaking work on racial theory
1987	Dot-buster attacks occur, in which Latino gangs in Jersey City, New Jersey, threaten violence and vandalism against Asian Indian residents who do not leave the city
1988	Osama Bin Laden, the son of a Saudi billionaire, forms Al Qaeda, an organization that develops in the 1990s into a global terrorist network that promotes an extremist and militant form of Islam and attacks U.S. global interests
1988	Bensonhurst incident occurs, in which black teenager Yusef Hawkins is beaten to death by white youths in Bensonhurst neighborhood of Brooklyn, New York
1988	Congress passes the Fair Housing Amendments Act to strengthen provisions of the Fair Housing Act of 1968 by giving the Department of Housing and Urban Development (HUD) greater power to enforce the earlier legislation
1988	Congress approves the Civil Liberties Act, authorizing redress payments to Japanese Americans interned during World War II
1989	Publication of Stephen Steinberg's *Ethnic Myth: Race, Ethnicity and Class in America*, which challenges various prevailing ideas about race and ethnicity in the United States
1989	In *City of Richmond v. J.A. Croson Company*, the U.S. Supreme Court rules that a city affirmative action program violates the equal protection clause of the Fourteenth Amendment
1990	Congress passes the Hate Crimes Statistics Act, which requires the Department of Justice to compile annual national data on hate crimes and publish an annual summary of findings
1991	Yankel Rosenbaum, a Jewish yeshiva student, is murdered by a black mob in Crown Heights, New York
1991	Los Angeles police officers are taped beating Rodney King, an African American motorist, after King refuses to be pulled over
1991	Congress passes another Civil Rights Act to reverse recent court rulings that seem to weaken enforcement of earlier civil rights legislation
1992	Riots erupt in Los Angeles after the acquittal of the police officers accused in the Rodney King beating incident
1994	California voters pass Proposition 187, the Save Our State Initiative, which denies publicly funded nonemergency medical care, education, and social services to illegal immigrants and their foreign-born children

1994	Council on American Islamic Relations (CAIR) is to advocate for the civil rights of Muslim Americans
1994	Publication of scholar Cornel West's *Race Matters*, which examines the role of race in shaping the African American experience
1995	Minister Louis Farrakhan of the Nation of Islam sponsors the Million Man March on Washington to support African American families
1995	Publication of *Black Wealth/White Wealth: A New Perspective on Racial Inequality*, a book by Melvin L. Oliver and Thomas M. Shapiro detailing disparities in wealth between whites and blacks
1995	Right-wing extremists bomb the Alfred P. Murrah Federal Building in Oklahoma City
1995	O. J. Simpson, an African American football legend, is acquitted of murdering his wife, Nicole Brown Simpson, and Ron Goldman, who were both white
1995	Publication of John Yinger's *Closed Doors, Opportunities Lost: The Continuing Costs of Housing Discrimination*, examining various housing studies to determine how closely the housing industry is adhering to the Fair Housing Act of 1968
1996	Richard J. Herrnstein and Charles Murray publish *The Bell Curve: Intelligence and Class Structure in American Life*, in which they present statistical evidence that supposedly supports the notion of racial superiority based on IQ
1996	California voters pass Proposition 209, the California Civil Rights Initiative, which repeals affirmative action in public employment, education, or contracting
1996	In *Shaw v. Hunt*, the U.S. Supreme Court declares that race cannot be the sole factor in redrawing congressional districts
1997	California voters pass Proposition 227, the English Language Education for Children in Public Schools Initiative, which eliminates bilingual education in California public schools
1998	James Byrd Jr., a black man, is murdered in Jasper, Texas, by three white racists who slit his throat and drag his body behind a truck
1999	Publication of Mary Waters's *Black Identities: West Indian Immigrant Dreams and American Realities*, an award-winning book that explores the experiences of West Indian immigrants in New York
1999	Amadou Diallo, an immigrant working as a street vendor in New York, is shot by four undercover police officers, who mistake him for a rape suspect
1999	Wen Ho Lee, a Chinese American engineer working at the Los Alamos Research Laboratory, is accused of spying by the government and fired from his job in violation of his civil rights. He is later cleared of all charges

2001   Members of the militant Islamist organization Al Qaeda, acting on orders of the group's leader, Osama Bin Laden, launch terrorist attacks on New York City and Washington, DC, that kill almost 3,000 people

2001   Patriot Act is passed in the wake of the September 11, 2001, terrorist attacks to increase the effectiveness of U.S. law enforcement in detecting and preventing further acts of terrorism

2003   U.S. Supreme Court renders decisions in two University of Michigan affirmation action cases—*Grutter v. Bollinger* and *Gratz v. Bollinger*—declaring that race can be considered in university admissions decisions but cannot be a "deciding factor"

2003   California voters reject Proposition 54, the Racial Privacy Initiative (RPI), which would have banned the use and production of racially coded data by various state and municipal agencies

LIST OF ENTRIES

GUIDE TO RELATED ENTRIES

African Americans

"Acting White" Stage of Life

Affirmative Action

Afrocentrism

All-Black Resorts

Back-to-Africa Movement

Bensonhurst Incident

Black Anti-Semitism

Black Conservatives

"Black English" (Ebonics)

Black Family Instability Thesis

Black-Korean Conflicts

Black Nationalist Movement

Black Panther Party

Black Political Disenfranchisement

*Black Power: The Politics of Liber-
ation in America*

*Black Wealth/White Wealth: A New
Perspective on Racial Inequality*

Blacks, Wage Discrimination against

Block-busting

*Brown v. Board of Education of
Topeka*

Buffalo Soldiers

Busing

Byrd, James Jr.

Caribbean Immigrants, Attitudes
toward African Americans

Carmichael, Stokely

Civil Rights Movement

Color Line

"Cost of Being a Negro"

Culture of Poverty Thesis

Diallo, Amadou

Douglass, Frederick

Driving while Black, Stopping
People for

Du Bois, W.E.B.

Expatriation

Farrakhan, Louis

Freedmen's Bureau

Freedom Riders

Free Persons of Color in the Antebellum North

Garvey, Marcus

Harlem Renaissance

Concepts, Beliefs, and Theories

Immigration and Immigrants

Individuals

Powell, Colin

Randolph, A. Philip

Robinson, Jackie

Simpson, O. J.

Spencer, Herbert

Terman, Lewis

Thomas, Clarence

Thurmond, Strom

Tijerina, Reies Lopez

Wallace, George

Washington, Booker T.

Jews

Anti-Defamation League of B'nai Brith (ADL)

Anti-Semitism in the United States

Aryan Nations

Black Anti-Semitism

Frank, Leo

Jewish-Black Conflicts

Jewish Defense League (JDL)

Zionist Occupied Government (ZOG)

Laws, Treaties, Propositions, Constitutional Amendments, and Executive Orders

Alaska Native Claims Settlement Act of 1971

Alien Land Laws on the West Coast

Asiatic Barred Zone

California Ballot Proposition 54

California Ballot Proposition 187

California Ballot Proposition 209

California Ballot Proposition 227

Chinese Exclusion Act of 1882

Civil Rights Act of 1964

Civil Rights Act of 1968

Civil Rights Act of 1991

Equal Employment Opportunity Act of 1972

Executive Order 9066

Executive Order 9981

Fair Housing Act of 1968

Fair Housing Amendments Act of 1988

Fourteenth Amendment

Guadalupe Hidalgo, Treaty of

Hate Crimes Statistics Act of 1990

Immigrant Act of 1965

Indian Allotment Act of 1887

Indian Citizenship Act of 1924

Indian Reorganization Act of 1934 (IRA)

Indian Self-Determination and Educational Assistance Act of 1975 (ISDEAA)

Jim Crow Laws

McCarran-Walter Act of 1952

Missouri Compromise

National Origins Act of 1924

Naturalization Act of 1790

Voting Rights Act of 1965

Voting Rights Amendments of 1975

Wagner Act

Movements

Abolitionist Movement

Afrocentrism

Americanization Movement

Back-to-Africa Movement

Black Nationalist Movement

Chicano Movement

Civil Rights Movement

English-Only Movement

Eugenics Movement

Expatriation

Freedom Riders

Harlem Renaissance

Organizations, Groups, and Government Agencies

Al Qaeda

American-Arab Anti-Discrimination Committee (ADC)

American Civil Liberties Union (ACLU)

American GI Forum (AGIF)

American Indian Movement (AIM)

American Nazi Party (ANP)

Anti-Defamation League of B'nai Brith (ADL)

Arab American Institute (AAI)

Arab Community Center for Economic and Social Services (ACCESS)

Arab/Muslim American Advocacy Organizations, Responding to the Backlash

Aryan Nations

Asian American Legal Defense and Education Fund (AALDEF)

Asian Americans for Equality (AAFE)

Asiatic Exclusion League (AEL)

Black Panther Party

Bureau of Indian Affairs (BIA)

Congress of Racial Equality (CORE)

Council on American Islamic Relations (CAIR)

Federal Housing Administration (FHA)

Freedmen's Bureau

Freedom Riders

Immigration Restriction League of 1894

Indian Claims Commission (ICC)

Islamic Jihad

Japanese American Citizens League (JACL)

Jewish Defense League (JDL)

John Birch Society

Know-Nothing Party

Ku Klux Klan (KKK)

La Raza Unida

League of United Latin American Citizens (LULAC)

Mexican American Legal Defense and Education Fund (MALDEF)

Muslim Philanthropic Organizations, Closure of after September 11, 2001

Nation of Islam

National Advisory Commission on Civil Disorders

National Association for the Advancement of Colored People (NAACP)

National Congress of American Indians (NCAI)

Organization of Afro-American Unity (OAAU)

Organization of Chinese Americans (OCA)

Rainbow Coalition

Southern Christian Leadership Conference (SCLC)

Student Nonviolent Coordinating Committee (SNCC)

Texas Rangers

United Farm Workers (UFW)

U.S. Border Patrol

U.S. Commission on Civil Rights (USCCR)

U.S. Department of Housing and Urban Development (HUD)

War Relocation Authority (WRA)

Policies, Programs, and Government Acts

Affirmative Action

Affirmative Action, University of Michigan Ruling on

Anglo Conformity

Harlem Riot of 1964

Los Angeles Riot of 1871

Los Angeles Riot of 1992

Memphis Race Riot of 1866

Newark Riot of 1967

Race Riots

St. Louis Riot of 1917

Zoot Suit Riots

Slavery, Abolition, and Reconstruction

Abolitionist Movement

Civil War and the Abolition of Slavery

Douglass, Frederick

Dred Scott Decision

Emancipation Proclamation

Fourteenth Amendment

Freedmen's Bureau

Free Persons of Color in the Antebellum North

Guadalupe Hidalgo, Treaty of

Hayes-Tilden Compromise of 1877

Indentured Servants

Ku Klux Klan (KKK)

Lincoln, Abraham, and the Emancipation of Slaves

Literacy Test

Manifest Destiny

Missouri Compromise

Peculiar Institution: Slavery in the Ante-bellum South, The

Plantation System

Reconstruction Era

Roots

Sharecropping

Slave Auctions

Slaves Codes

Slave Families

Slave Revolts and White Attacks on Black Slaves

Slavery and American Indians

Slavery in the Antebellum South

Slave Trade

Underground Railroad

Sports, Entertainment, Culture, and Leisure

All-Black Resorts

El Teatro Campensino

Films and Racial Stereotypes

Fu Manchu

Godfather, The

Harlem Renaissance

Hollywood and Minority Actors

Minstrelsy

Morrison, Toni

Multiculturalism

Music Industry, Racism in

Robinson, Jackie

Simpson, O. J.

Sports and Racism

Sports Mascots

Television and Racial Stereotypes

Television Drama and Racism

West Side Story

Terrorism and 9/11

Al Qaeda

Arab/Muslim American Advocacy Organizations, Responding to the Backlash

Cultural Genocide

Government Initiatives after the September 11, 2001, Attack on the United States

"Green Menace"

Islamic Jihad

Middle Easterners, Historical Precedents of Backlash against

Muslim Philanthropic Organizations, Closure of after September 11, 2001

Muslims, Terrorist Image of

Oklahoma City Federal Building Bombing

September 11, 2001, Terrorism, Discriminatory Reactions to

Violent, Acts and Victims of

Asian Americans, Violence against

Bellingham Riots

Bensonhurst Incident

Byrd, James Jr.

Campus Ethnoviolence

Chin, Vincent

Cultural Genocide

Diallo, Amadou

Dot Buster Attacks

Frank, Leo

Hate Crimes

Howard Beach Incident

Italian Americans, Violence against

Ku Klux Klan (KKK)

Little Rock (Arkansas) Central High School, Integration of

Lynching

Mexican Americans, Violence against

Native Americans, Forced Relocation of

Non-Judeo-Christian Immigrant Groups, Violence against

Oklahoma City Federal Building Bombing

Rape and Racism

Rodney King Beating

Slave Revolts and White Attacks on Black Slaves

Wars and Military

American GI Forum (AGIF)

Buffalo Soldiers

Civil War and the Abolition of Slavery

Draft Riot of 1863

Executive Order 9066

Executive Order 9981

Guadalupe Hidalgo, Treaty of

Gulf War

Japanese American Internment

Mexican-American War

Native Americans, Conquest of

Philippine-American War

Sioux Outbreak of 1890

Spanish-American War

Texas Rebellion

War and Racial Inequality

War Relocation Authority (WRA)

White Supremacy

Aryan Nations

Duke, David

Ku Klux Klan (KKK)

Neo-Nazism

Nordic Supreriority

Oklahoma City Federal Building Bombing

Skinheads

White-Supremacist Movement in the United States

White-Supremacist Underground

Zionist Occupied Government (ZOG)

A

AAFE

See Asian Americans for Equality (AAFE).

AAI

See Arab American Institute (AAI).

AALDEF

See Asian American Legal Defense and Education Fund (AALDEF).

Abolitionist Movement

Instituted in the North in the early nineteenth century, the abolitionist movement was dedicated to the immediate abolition of slavery in the United States without compensation to the slave masters. The abolitionist movement is significant because it represented the first organized effort initiated largely by whites to combat the racial oppression of blacks.

Before the movement's inception in the 1830s, various Northern-based groups, such as the Quakers, opposed slavery for moral and ethical reasons, and antislavery efforts consisted of the Underground Railroad and individual action by those who opposed slavery. In 1833, three antislavery organizations, the New England Anti-Slavery Society, the New York Reformers, and the Philadelphia Quakers, met and formed the American Anti-Slavery Society (AASS) in Philadelphia. Under the leadership of William Lloyd Garrison (1805–1879), the organizer of the New England Society, the AASS called for the immediate emancipation of all slaves. By 1840, the AASS had spawned more than 2,000 local antislavery organizations and had a total national membership of more than 200,000.

Portrait of William Lloyd Garrison, organizer of the American Anti-Slavery Society.

Courtesy Thoemmes Continuum.

Garrison and other abolitionists believed that slaves should be afforded political and economic rights identical to those of whites. There were, however, varying public views regarding how the country should address the problem of slavery. Abolitionists initially attempted to sway Northerners and gain support from clergy and religious organizations, but these efforts met with only limited success. Some Northern whites supported abolition but feared economic and political competition should ex-slaves be given rights and opportunities equal to their own. Southern whites vehemently opposed the movement and attempted to thwart its influence. The AASS and the movement in general published numerous books and pamphlets, as well as such periodicals as the *North Star* and *The Liberator*. The AASS also bombarded Congress with petitions calling for the end of slavery. After the Civil War and the constitutional abolition of slavery, reform efforts focused on educating ex-slaves and aiding freed persons via the black churches. Besides Garrison, other noted leaders of the abolitionist movement included Frederick Douglass, John Brown, Henry David Thoreau, Arthur and Lewis Tappan, Theodore Weld, Charles G. Finney, and Harriet Beecher Stowe.

See also Civil War and the Abolition of Slavery; Douglass, Frederick; Dred Scott Decision; Emancipation Proclamation; Free Persons of Color in the Antebellum North; Lincoln, Abraham, and the Emancipation of the Slaves; Manifest Destiny; Mexican-American War; Missouri Compromise; *The Peculiar Institution: Slavery in the Ante-bellum South*; Plantation System; Reconstruction Era; Slave Auctions; Slave Codes; Slave Families; Slave Revolts and White Attacks on Black Slaves; Slave Trade; Slavery in the Antebellum South; Underground Railroad.

Further Reading

McKivigan, John R., ed. *History of the American Abolitionist Movement*. 5 vols. New York: Garland, 1999.

Sandra L. Barnes

Academic Racism

Academic racism refers to academic theories and scholarly research and writing that perpetuate the notion of racial superiority. Scientists and academicians in the United States have often used their work as the basis for advocating racist theories. Academic racism can emanate from a diversity of fields, including science, social science, history, and the humanities. As these theories of academic racism become dominant within academia, racism can be perpetuated through the higher-education curriculum, as well as through popular press and media. Because these theories are endowed with what is perceived to be the scientific and intellectual integrity of academia, they are often automatically conferred legitimacy and authority by students, popular media, and government decision makers.

Throughout the twentieth century, many eminent academicians in the United States used their work to advance theories of racial superiority. The most well known early example was the eugenics movement, which was forwarded in the United States by Charles Benedict Davenport, a biologist with a PhD from Harvard University. Embraced by public-health officials, activists, and intelligentsia, the eugenics movement resulted in as many as 20,000 forced sterilizations by the late 1930s and had a profound effect on public policy and in shaping the discourse on the emerging racial and ethnic diversity of the United States in the twentieth century.

Academic racism and its effects on public policy were most discernible during the period between the 1880s and the 1920s. Negative reaction to the changing immigrant stream in the United States led to one of the most evident applications of academic racism to national policymaking. The majority of immigrants during this period were unskilled workers or farmers from eastern and southern European countries who were radically different from the Protestant, English, German, and Scandinavian immigrants of the earlier immigrant flows. In the early 1900s, eugenicists such as scientist H. H. Goddard promoted the use of the new "intelligence quotient" test, the IQ test. When the United States entered World War I in 1917, eugenicists saw the potential for testing with a large sample and convinced the army to administer the IQ test on draftees, which resulted in a sample of almost two million draftees. Based on these results, Henry Laughlin from the Eugenics Record Office testified before Congress that more than 75 percent of the new immigrants were feebleminded and that their presence, along with their high fertility rate, was a threat to the biological makeup of the country. Based on this testimony, Congress passed the 1924 Immigration Act of 1924 (also known as the National Origins Act). This act placed stringent restrictions on immigration by setting quotas for incoming immigrants based on the 1910 census, rather than the 1920 census. This effectively stymied the flow of "undesirable" immigrants form southern and eastern Europe.

The field of psychology and the advent of the IQ test remains a racially contested arena. In the 1960s, William Shockley, a physicist at Stanford University and a Nobel Prize winner, advocated programs of voluntary sterilization of people with an IQ score lower than 100. In 1969, educational psychologist Arthur Jensen published an article in the *Harvard Education Review* attacking Head Start programs, claiming that African American children only have an average IQ of 85 and that no amount of social engineering would improve their performance. Within a few years Jensen's article had become one of the most widely cited studies in psychology. In the 1980s, J. Phillipe Rushton, a widely published Canadian psychology professor and an elected fellow of the American Association for the Advancement of Science, as well as of the American Psychological Association, argued that behavioral differences among African Americans, Whites, and Asians are the result of evolutionary variations in the reproductive strategies. African Americans are at one extreme, Rushton claimed, because they produce large numbers of offspring but offer them little care; at the other extreme are Asians, who have fewer children but indulge them; whites lie somewhere in between. Further, Rushton argued that African Americans have smaller brains and larger genitals than whites, making them less intelligent and more promiscuous. More recently, in their 1996 book *The Bell Curve: Intelligence and Class Structure in American Life*, Richard J. Herrnstein and Charles Murray presented an argument for racial superiority based on IQ, which, they claimed, was scientifically supported by large-scale statistical evidence.

Beyond introducing the racist ideology into public discourse, the consequences of academic racism can be observed in many areas of public policy. As evidenced by the Immigration Act of 1924, policymakers are liable to act on, and legislate based on, the racist theories that academics espouse. Present-day arguments against the welfare state often echo the theories of Social Darwinism. The eugenics movement has been reconstructed in recent decades in the form of cash incentives for the poor, who are disproportionately black, to undergo sterilization or other extreme forms of birth control. In the 1990s, legislators in Kansas backed a proposal to offer $500 to any welfare mother who agreed to have Norplant (a five-year contraceptive device) surgically implanted. Legislators in Connecticut and Florida also introduced bills that would offer cash bonuses to welfare recipients who would accept Norplant. In Florida, a bill was introduced to offer $400 to men living below the poverty line to have a vasectomy. In Colorado, legislators introduced a bill that would have offered early release to criminals who had a vasectomy. One scholar stated, that "the growth of scientific ideas within society is not normally haphazard. The ideas of scientists usually do not arise in some vacuum, but can be connected with underlying political or economic trends" (Billig 1998).

See also Biological Racism; Eugenics Movement; Jensen, Arthur.

Further Reading

Billig, Michael. "A Dead Idea That Will Not Lie Down." *Searchlight Magazine*, 1998.

Herrnstein, Richard J., and Charles Murray. *The Bell Curve: Intelligence and Class Structure in American Life*. New York: Free Press, 1994.

Mehler, Barry. "In Genes We Trust: When Science Bows to Racism." *The Public Eye: A Publication of Political Research Associates* 9, no. 1: 1995.

Tracy Chu

ACCESS

See Arab Community Center for Economic and Social Services (ACCESS).

ACLU

See American Civil Liberties Union (ACLU).

"Acting White" Stage of Life

The "acting white" stage of life refers to that phase of social identity develop-ment during which children of color have internalized social messages about the inferiority of their own race and act like white people. Studies show that even before they reach young adulthood, minority children in the United States usually accept consciously or unconsciously the messages about the inferiority of their physical characteristics and their cultures. They have developed an in-ternal ideology of racial subordination and ethnic inferiority and embraced it in a way that is manifested as a rejection of non-white characteristics. These negative ideations may be held simultaneously with and despite the existence of more positive ideas and feelings about their racial and ethnic groups. Among children and adolescents, feelings associated with acting white often involve embarrassment about the youth's ethnic/racial background.

There are both active and passive forms of acting white. Some people of color exhibiting passive, or "internal," forms are unaware of the degree to which their thoughts, feelings, and behaviors reflect the white mainstream ideology. They may demonstrate an unconscious identification with and ration-alization of the oppressor's logic system. Typical attitudes may include "people are people," "if I just work hard I will be judged by my merits," "the problem is that people of color who don't want to work hard enough mess things up for the rest of us," and "white people are generally smarter than people of color and they get ahead because they work hard." Among immigrants, a common ideation of acting white conflates the notion of becoming American—and thereby achieving social and financial success—with becoming more like white Americans. Indeed, among many immigrant groups the words *American* and *white* are effectively synonymous.

In the active form of acting white, a person of color may consciously iden-tify with the dominant group and its ideology. For example, some people of color are opposed to affirmative action because they believe people of color are less successful solely due to their own laziness and pathological culture. Behaviors include accepting and conforming to white social, cultural, and in-stitutional standards and seeking interaction with and validation from whites and white social groups. A person of color may also avoid organizations, com-mittees, and social groups that focus on race or racism because participation in such groups emphasizes the racial identity with which she is uncomfort-able. Likewise, she will often "go along with" or excuse the racist behaviors she observes.

Acting white can also be manifested as conflict with members of one's fam-ily or racial group. A person of color who is acting white will often refuse (or be unable) to recognize and acknowledge institutional racism. A person of color may also actively reject association with his or her ethnic group, such as by refusing to speak the home language with parents or peers, eschewing "ethnic" food and garb, or disassociating from ethnoreligious organizations. Alternatively, an individual may act white only in certain contexts, such as in the workplace or at school, but embrace her race and ethnic culture in other contexts.

When racism is perceived as existing only at the individual level, even negative race-based experiences can be rationalized as being external to the victim's own identity. People of color who retain this worldview successfully rationalize efforts on the part of others to change their consciousness. Even people of color who experience an urge to question their current status may find themselves seduced into remaining in place by the rewards offered from the dominant white society.

See also Internalized Racism.

Further Reading

Cross, William E., Jr. *Shades of Black: Diversity in African American Identity*. Philadelphia: Temple University Press, 1991.

Jackson, Bailey, and Rita Hardiman. "Conceptual Foundations for Social Justice Courses." In *Teaching for Diversity and Social Justice*, edited by Maurianne Adams, Lee Anne Bell, and Pat Griffin, 16–29. New York: Routledge, 1997.

Tatum, Beverly D. *"Why Are All the Black Kids Sitting Together in the Cafeteria?" and Other Conversations about Race*. New York: Basic Books, 1997.

Khyati Joshi

Active Bigots

See Bigots, Types of.

Adaptive Discrimination

Adaptive discrimination is a form of discrimination in which an individual acts in a discriminatory manner to conform to the prejudiced attitude of others, or the prejudiced attitude of the larger society. Although the person may not personally harbor any racial prejudice, he or she discriminates to "fit in" or adapt to society.

Adaptive discrimination is often seen as contrasting with overt discrimination, in which individuals discriminate based on their own prejudicial attitude. An example of adaptive discrimination would be a white landlord refusing to rent to an African American family because he or she feared that prejudiced white tenants might move out. On a macro level, adaptive discrimination can be caused by larger political mechanisms. For example, white British citizens who moved to South Africa during apartheid were compelled to accept a system of institutionalized racism that was completely alien to them. To adapt to white South African society, they had to accept and abide by discriminatory practices that were based in the racism of others. In his typology of people with a combination of prejudice and discrimination, Robert Merton referred to unprejudiced discriminators as "fair-weather liberals," and he called prejudiced nondiscriminators "timid bigots."

See also Bigots, Types of; Fair-Weather Liberals.

Further Reading

Merton, Robert. "Discrimination and the American Creed." In *Discrimination and National Welfare*, edited by R. M. MacIver, 99–126. New York: Institute for Religious and Social Studies, 1949.

Tracy Chu

ADC

See American-Arab Anti-Discrimination Committee (ADC).

ADL

See Anti-Defamation League of B'nai Brith (ADL).

AEL

See Asiatic Exclusion League (AEL).

Affirmative Action

Affirmative action is based on presidential directives, government guidelines and regulations, laws, and court decisions and can be defined as a government policy designed to combat discrimination and equalize opportunity for traditionally disadvantaged groups by giving preferential treatment to equally qualified minorities and women in employment, college admission, and government contracting. Literally, affirmative action means taking affirmative or positive steps to ensure equal opportunity for minorities and women. However, in the public mind, the meaning of affirmative action can be highly subjective and represent notions as varied as equal opportunity; proportional representation; special privilege given to minorities and women; reserved quotas of jobs, school spots, or government funding for minorities and women; or even government-mandated discrimination against white Americans.

No civil rights laws or executive orders on affirmative action authorize the use of reverse discrimination, quotas, or even preferential treatment. No laws or government regulations endorse the idea that unqualified or less qualified minorities or women can be hired, admitted, or given government contracts. In practice, however, some organizations did use quotas for minorities and women, lower standards to admit or hire less qualified minority and female applicants, or give contracts to less qualified firms owned by minorities and women. These practices violate the laws or regulations and are not what affirmative action intends to be. Court rulings, nevertheless, did sanction, either explicitly or implicitly, the use of preferential treatment of minorities and women.

For example, in the first significant case on affirmative action addressed by the U.S. Supreme Court, *Regents of the University of California v. Bakke* (1978), the Court held that while race could not be used as a quota to set aside specific positions for minority candidates, it could be considered as a factor in admission. As Supreme Court Justice Harry Blackmun put it, "In order to go beyond racism, we must first take account of race. There is no other way. And to treat some persons equally, we must treat them differently." Other rulings that allowed for a temporary use of preferential treatment for redressing past discrimination include *United Steelworkers of America v. Weber* (1979), which permitted the union to favor minorities in special training programs; *Sheet Metal Workers v. EEOC* (1986), which approved a specific quota of minority workers for the union; *International Association of Firefighters v. City of Cleveland* (1986), which gave the green light to the promotion of minorities over more senior whites; *United States v. Paradise* (1987), which endorsed favorable treatment of minority state troopers for purposes of promotion; *Johnson v. Transportation Agency, Santa Clara County* (1987), which approved preference in hiring of minorities and women over equally qualified men and whites; and *Metro Broadcasting v. FCC* (1990), which supported federal programs aimed at increasing minority ownership of broadcasting licenses.

Brief History of Affirmative Action

Before the 1960s, discrimination against minorities and women was widespread. Conscious efforts were made by the federal government in the 1940s and 1950s to reduce discrimination in employment. In the early 1940s, President Franklin Roosevelt issued executive orders to halt discrimination in the federal civil service and created the Fair Employment Practices Committee. During the 1950s, President Harry S. Truman issued two executive orders to establish fair employment procedures within the federal government structure, to nullify discrimination in the armed forces, and to formulate compliance procedures for government contractors. The basic approach then was voluntary nondiscrimination. However, the voluntary good-faith approach proved to be ineffective and insufficient in combating deeply rooted patterns of discrimination.

Affirmative action policy emerged in the 1960s as an alternative to the early voluntary approach. It originated from a series of executive orders issued by presidents John F. Kennedy and Lyndon B. Johnson and related legislation enacted during their presidencies in the 1960s. In March 1961, President Kennedy issued Executive Order 10925, in which the phrase "affirmative action" first surfaced. The order required government contractors and subcontractors to take "affirmative action to ensure that applicants are employed, and that employees are treated during employment, without regard to their race, creed, color, or national origin." That order did, for the first time, "place the full prestige of the presidency behind the moral imperative of non-discrimination."

In the mid-1960s, the civil rights movement entered its climax, as black protests escalated. The outcome was the passage of the landmark Civil Rights Act of 1964. Title VII of the act forbade discrimination "against any individual because of such individual's race, color, religion, sex or national origin." Seeking to appease the opposition to preferential treatment, Section 703(j) of Title VII stated that "nothing contained in this title shall be interpreted to require any employer, employment agency, labor organization, or joint labor-management committee subject to this title to grant preferential treatment to any individual or to any group . . . on account of an imbalance which may exist with respect to the total number and percentage of persons of any race, color, religion, sex, or national origin" (Bureau of National Affairs 1964).

However, simply making discrimination illegal by law was not enough. The government had to find an effective way to enforce the 1964 Civil Rights Act, to monitor the progress, and to ensure equal opportunity for every citizen. Under this context, President Johnson issued Executive Order 11246 on September 24, 1965, thereby laying an important ground for affirmative action policy. This order was a continuation of Executive Order 10925, but it proposed specific requirements. It mandated contracts with the government to include a nondiscrimination clause and federal contractors with 100 or more employees to take "affirmative action" to achieve the goal of nondiscrimination in "employment, upgrading, demotion and transfer; recruitment or recruitment advertising; layoff or termination; rates of pay or other forms of compensation; and selection for training, including apprenticeship." It required contractors and their subcontractors to submit compliance reports with information on the practices, policies, programs, and racial composition of their work force. It imposed penalties for noncompliance, in the form of cancellation, termination or suspension of federal funds, and ineligibility for further federal contracts. To implement the foregoing executive orders and the Civil Rights Act of 1964, the Equal Employment Opportunity Commission (EEOC) and the Office of Federal Contract Compliance (OFCC) located in the Department of Labor were founded.

In October 1967, President Johnson issued Executive Order 11375, which expanded affirmative action stipulations to include sex discrimination and required every federally funded organization with more than fifty employees and a contract in excess of $50,000 to submit a "written affirmative action compliance program" with goals and timetables. Goals consisted of expected percentages of new employees from various minority groups; specifically, the ethnic or racial makeup of an organization was expected to roughly match the makeup of the general population. The timetables were timelines for achieving the goals.

The enforcement of affirmative action policy continued even during the Nixon administration and Ford administration in the late 1960s and the 1970s. Executive Order 11478 of August 1969 issued by President Richard M. Nixon listed affirmative action steps. During the Carter administration, the Office of Federal Contract Compliance Programs (OFCCP, until 1975 was OFCC) published a *Construction Compliance Program Operations Manual* detailing the responsibilities of contractors, federal contract agencies, and the OFCCP. The regulations required contractors to include in affirmative action programs the utilization analysis of minority and women in the workforce and to increase their representation.

Although the executive orders and related regulations did not explicitly approve the use of preferential treatment, pressures to increase the representation of minorities and women resulted in the consideration of race, ethnicity, and gender in hiring, contracting, and college admissions. In various rulings, the Supreme Court ratified preferential treatment because the most important element of the 1964 act was to eliminate discrimination against minorities and women and to bring up equal opportunity. The Supreme Court called such an action of compensatory preferences for minorities and women benign race-conscious decision making.

In its most recent June 2003 rulings, the U.S. Supreme Court narrowly upheld the affirmative action policy of the University of Michigan Law School in considering race as a plus factor in the admission process. However, the Court also declared that universities cannot use rigid, quota-like point systems that use race as a decisive factor in undergraduate admissions and must adopt race-central policies "as soon as practical." These rulings do not draw an end to this controversy. Affirmative action will remain a highly controversial and divided issue in the years to come.

It should be noted that affirmative action was never intended to be permanent. It was considered a temporary measure for offsetting the effects of past and present discrimination. Once discrimination is no longer a major problem and everybody has an equal opportunity, affirmative action will not be needed. In his 1978 *Bakke* decision, Supreme Court Justice Blackmun speculated that race-conscious policy could be eliminated in ten years. In her latest opinion, Justice Sandra O'Connor wrote that the Court expects that twenty-five years from now racial preferences "will no longer be necessary."

Pros and Cons of Affirmative Action

Since its inception, affirmative action policy has been encircled by controversies and legal challenges. Over time three major arguments for affirmative action have been developed. The compensation argument contends that affirmative action is a remedy or a compensatory measure for correcting historical and contemporary discrimination against minorities and women. Since past and present discrimination put minorities and women in a disadvantageous position to compete with white males, *temporary* preferential treatment should be given to minorities and women until everybody is starting from the same point. This race/gender-conscious remedy is the prelude to color- and gender-blind competition.

Emphasized in recent debates, the diversity argument claims that affirmative action is necessary to diversify the student population and the workforce (e.g., Jackson 1995). This new argument departs from the compensation argument in moving affirmative action from a temporary measure to an open-ended task because of the necessity and desirability of diversity.

Finally, the effective argument maintains that affirmative action is effective and beneficial to the whole society. It has significantly increased the representation of minorities and women in educational institutions and the workforce; it has benefited not only minorities but also white women and their families as a result of now having two wage earners in their households; and it has helped corporations to diversify their labor force and to reach out to consumers of different ethnic groups.

At the opposite camp, opponents have made four major arguments against affirmative action. The reverse-discrimination argument argues that affirmative action is reverse discrimination against white males. Namely, white males have become victims of affirmative action. Some white men contest that since they personally have not discriminated against minorities or women, why should they be unfairly punished for past discrimination. Some argue that reverse discrimination has heightened racial division, resentment, and disharmony and that it pits one group against another.

The nonmeritocracy argument holds that affirmative action disregards individual merit and lowers the quality of the labor force or student body by giving positions or admissions to less qualified persons since set-aside quotas must be filled by less qualified candidates.

The ineffectiveness argument asserts that affirmative action is ineffective in advancing the positions of minorities and women (e.g., Smith and Welch 1984). Some contend that well-off minorities reap the benefits of affirmative action programs to the detriment of poor minorities, since they are more likely to be preferred over those truly disadvantaged who lack job skills, educational preparation, and resources (e.g., Wilson 1987). Furthermore, some whites who are rejected for college admissions or employment might be poor and disadvantaged ones who need help the most.

The counter-productivity argument contends that affirmative action hurts the very minorities and women it intends to help. On the one hand, qualified and competent minority members and women may be viewed as less qualified and as being favored by the government, and be stereotyped as people who cannot really make it on their own merit. On the other hand, it could create a feeling of inferiority or self-doubt among its beneficiaries and undermine their self-esteem. Along this line, some opponents (e.g., Sowell 1984) argue that affirmative action may discourage hard work and acquisition of skills since it encourages minorities to think that they can still get admitted or employed, even if they do not work at it.

Opposition to the existing affirmative action policy led to some collective actions at the state and national levels. Proposition 209 (the California Civil Rights Initiative), passed by California voters in November 1996 and effective in November 1997, was the first ballot measure in the nation that scrapped affirmative action policy. However, despite some countermaneuvers, affirmative action remains a national policy today.

Searching for a Solution

Both sides of the debate have their valid points. It is difficult to reconcile the conflicting interests involved. It is more fruitful to work out compromises or alternatives that could accomplish the same goals. Since affirmative action has never been intended to be permanent, the real question is, Is now the time to abolish this policy? There are currently two approaches to this question: "end it" represented by the conservative Republicans, and "mend it" represented by former president Bill Clinton. To determine whether to end it or mend it, some believe a comprehensive overhaul of affirmative action policy and programs is needed; specifically, we need to evaluate whether the goals of affirmative action policy have been accomplished and whether preferential treatment toward minorities and women (the means) is the best way to achieve the goals of affirmative action. An Associated Press poll conducted in February–March 2003 found that 59 percent of the respondents considered the country "not close" or "not too close" to eliminating discrimination against racial/ethnic minorities, while 38 percent responded with "very close" or "fairly close." Fifty-one percent of the respondents believed that affirmative action programs are needed to help minorities such as blacks and Hispanics, compared to 43 percent responding with "not needed." The Clinton administration completed a comprehensive review of all federal affirmative action programs in July 1996. Based on the review, Clinton declared that "when affirmative action is done right, it is flexible, it is fair, and it works." He set four criteria for all affirmative action programs to comply with: (1) no quotas, in theory or in practice; (2) no illegal discrimination of any kind, including reverse discrimination; (3) no preference for unqualified individuals for jobs or other opportunities; and (4) termination of programs once the goals have been achieved.

There are other alternatives to affirmative action beyond the yes/no framework. One alternative is affirmative action based on class or economic status, or giving preference to people who are at an economic disadvantage, regardless of their race or gender. This option is favored by most Americans of different races. Another alternative is to create diversity programs or use diversity approaches. Opinion polls found that most Americans favor diversity. But diversity can be achieved by programs other than affirmative action. The "top 10 percent rule" in college admissions in Texas is a telling example. Since 1997, the top 10 percent of students in each graduating class of the public high schools, including rich or poor ones and racially segregated or mixed ones, have received automatic admission to any of the public universities or colleges in Texas, including the flagship campus in Austin. This program appears to work well in maintaining the ethnic diversity in the University of Texas system. In California, ranking in the top 4 percent of the graduating class of any public high school makes students eligible for admission to at least one of the University of California campuses. Outreach programs that attempt to recruit or reach out to underrepresented minorities and women can help achieve the same goal of diversifying a student body or the workforce without using race or gender.

See also Affirmative Action, University of Michigan Ruling on; *Affirmative Discrimination: Ethnic Inequality and Public Policy*; Civil Rights Act of 1964; California Ballot Proposition 209; Legacy of Past Discrimination Argument for Affirmative Action; *Regents of the University of California v. Bakke*; Reverse Discrimination; Role-Model Argument for Affirmative Action.

Further Reading

Bureau of National Affairs. *The Civil Rights Act of 1964.* Washington, DC: Bureau of National Affairs, 1964.

Jackson, Jesse. "Affirming Affirmative Action." A press release to the National Press Club, March 1, 1995.

Murray, Charles. *Losing Ground: American Social Policy, 1950–1980.* New York: Basic Books, 1984.

Smith, James, and Finis Welch. "Affirmative Action and Labor Markets." *Journal of Labor Economics* (1984): 269–299.

Sowell, Thomas. "Black Progress Can't Be Legislated." *Washington Post Outlook,* August 12, 1984, sec. B, pp. 1–2.

Wilson, William Julius. *The Truly Disadvantaged: The Inner City, the Underclass, and Public Policy.* Chicago: University of Chicago Press, 1987.

Philip Yang

Affirmative Action, University of Michigan Ruling on

In the first ruling on affirmative action in university admission decisions in twenty-five years, the U.S. Supreme Court ruled on June 23, 2003, that race can be used in university admission procedures to achieve racial diversity in college classrooms. But the narrowly divided court also ruled that factoring race into admission decisions must be "narrowly tailored" to harm as few people as possible.

The University of Michigan faced two different but parallel lawsuits. One is *Grutter v. Bollinger*, involving the University's law school and Barbara Grutter. Grutter, a white woman who applied for the law school and was rejected, later found that there were African Americans and ethnic minorities who were admitted with admission scores lower than her own. She felt it to be an illegal discrimination and sued. She won the first round in U.S. District Court but lost in the Sixth Circuit Court of Appeals. The Supreme Court upheld the decision by a vote of 5–4. Justice Sandra Day O'Connor, who cast the deciding vote, acknowledged that the United States still needs affirmative action but hoped the days were numbered.

In the other case, *Gratz v. Bollinger*, the 6–3 majority ruled that the points system violated equal protection provisions of the Constitution. The University of Michigan had an affirmative action policy in undergraduate admissions that automatically awarded twenty points, one-fifth of the points needed to guarantee admission, to every single "underrepresented minority" applicant, based solely on race. The Court decided that the policy was "not narrowly tailored" to achieve the interest in educational diversity. Chief Justice William Rehnquist, representing the majority opinion, declared that while race can be used as a factor in admission decisions, it must not be a "deciding factor."

See also Affirmative Action; Legacy of Past Discrimination Argument for Affirmative Action; *Regents of the University of California v. Bakke*; Reverse Discrimination; Role-Model Argument for Affirmative Action.

Dong-Ho Cho

Affirmative Discrimination: Ethnic Inequality and Public Policy

Published in 1974 by Nathan Glazer, a distinguished Harvard sociologist, *Affirmative Discrimination: Ethnic Inequality and Public Policy* was the first systematic, vocal challenge to the government's affirmative action policy, which was designed to counter discrimination and equalize opportunity by giving preferential treatment to equally qualified women and members of minority groups historically discriminated against in employment, college admissions, and government contracting.

In this influential book, Glazer argues that as an effort to redress past discrimination against minority groups as well as women, the color- and group-conscious affirmative action policy implemented in the 1970s counters the traditional U.S. public policy that emphasizes the primacy of the individual and threatens to overturn the principle of fairness to the individual citizen. He concludes that despite its admirable intentions, affirmative action is indeed "affirmative discrimination" against individuals. He suggests a return to the simple and clear understanding of individual rights rather than group rights and an adoption of public policy that promotes fairness and equality regardless of race, color, or national origin. This book generated a huge controversy after its publication and set off an ongoing debate on affirmative action that continues today.

See also Affirmative Action; Affirmative Action, University of Michigan Ruling on; Legacy of Past Discrimination Argument for Affirmative Action; *Regents of the University of California v. Bakke*; Reverse Discrimination; Role-Model Argument for Affirmative Action.

Further Reading

Glazer, Nathan. *Affirmative Discrimination: Ethnic Inequality and Public Policy*. New York: Basic Books, 1974.

Philip Yang

Afrocentrism

Afrocentrism is a political and cultural movement that seeks to establish the primacy of African tradition over European culture in historiography and education. Conceived as a corrective to Eurocentrism, the chauvinistic claim to the superiority of European culture, Afrocentrism developed with a variety of black nationalist movements in the mid-1960s, such as the Moorish Science Temple, the Nation of Islam, and the Black Power movement. Afrocentrists strived to reexamine and reevaluate the history and culture of Africans and their descendents from their own perspective, creating an understanding of them not merely as passive objects but as active agents. But Afrocentrism has not been a unified movement at all. Some religionists created the myth of black supremacy, the exact reversion of the myth of white supremacy, in which blacks were the original creation of God and Whites the depredated race. Some historiographers argued that ancient civilization was indebted to the northeastern African civilizations, that is, Kemet (Egypt), Nubia, Axum, and Meroe. Martin Bernal, for example, proposed in his work *Black Athena: The Afroasiatic Roots of Classical Civilization* (1987) that ancient Greek civilization had its roots in Africa. Many schools, from elementary to college level, incorporated Afrocentrism into school curriculum. Research institutes were established in and outside universities, such as the Kemetic Institute in Chicago and the Association for the Study of Classical African Civilizations. Afrocentrism contributed to reclaiming the sense of dignity of African descendents and rediscovering the lost legacy of African civilization. But many criticized the movement as the retrospective projection of contemporary racial rhetoric onto ancient civilizations rather than truly illuminating historical scholarship.

See also Black Nationalist Movement; Black Panther Party; *Black Power: The Politics of Liberation in America*; Nation of Islam.

Further Reading

Bernal, Martin. Black Athena: The Afroasiatic Roots of Classical Civilization. New Jersey: Rutger University Press, 1987.

Dong-Ho Cho

AGIF

See American GI Forum (AGIF).

AIM

See American Indian Movement (AIM).

Alaska Native Claims Settlement Act of 1971

To understand the Alaska Native Claims Settlement Act, one must first know something about the history behind the territory of Alaska. It was the Russians who first showed interest in Alaska, because they perceived there was much profit to make in the fur seal and sea otter skin trade. Once this industry was depleted, the Russians proceeded to negotiate with the United States over the sale of the territory. The United States purchased Alaska from Russia for $7.2 million in 1867. In this transaction, the rights, status, and land ownership of Alaska natives were never considered. The United States declared that the "uncivilized tribes" in Alaska would be subject to U.S. laws and regulations.

The United States took more than 100 million acres of land for its own use from the territory's public domain, which caused a great controversy. The natives demanded that a freeze on federal land transfers be placed into effect on territorial land. This land freeze was imposed until Congress acted on the issue of how much land would be distributed to those who claimed it. There was a big debate over who exactly would receive the land. The natives claimed 40 million acres of land and also wanted part of the profits made by companies that mined resources from other parts of Alaskan land. The discovery of oil became a critical factor in determining the distribution of the territory.

Debate over land ownership came to a resolution in April 1971 when President Richard M. Nixon proposed to Congress that the Alaska natives would receive 44 million acres of land, $500 million in compensation from the federal treasury, and another $500 million in profits from the lands. Twelve regional corporations would be major recipients of the land. The Senate and the House passed separate bills in support of the president's original proposal to Congress. The Alaska Native Claims Settlement Act was passed as a compromise between the two bills.

See also Indian Claims Commission (ICC); Indian Reservations.

Tiffany Vélez

Alianza Federal de Pueblos Libres

See Tijerina, Reies Lopez.

Alien Land Laws on the West Coast

In the early twentieth century, Japanese immigrants on the West Coast enjoyed great success in farming and controlled a large proportion of the produce market. But their success posed a threat to white farmers, so in 1913, California passed the first Alien Land Law, which prevented immigrants from owning or leasing land for more than three years. In 1920, the law was extended so that aliens who were uneligible for citizenship could not hold land in guardianship for their American-born children. Although California was the first state to pass such a law, a number of other states—Arizona, Florida, Idaho, Kansas, Louisiana, Minnesota, Montana, Missouri, New Mexico, Oregon, Texas, Washington, and Wyoming—followed suit and enacted similar laws because they feared that Californian Japanese would invade their states.

The Alien Land Laws also had ramifications for Asian Indian immigrants. In a 1923 decision (*United States v. Thind*), the U.S. Supreme Court denied citizenship to Asian Indian immigrants, reversing two previous rulings that had conferred the right to citizenship upon Asian Indians. It declared that, although Asian Indians may be racially Caucasian, from a commonplace perspective only those from northern or western Europe could be considered white. The Alien Land Laws forced those Asian Indian farm owners either to become laborers again or to find some other way to register their land. In 1948, the Supreme Court struck down the Alien Land Laws as unconstitutional, in *Oyama v. California*.

See also Asian American Legal Defense and Education Fund (AALDEF); Asian Americans, Perceptions of as Foreigners; Asian Americans, Violence against; Asian Americans for Equality (AAFE); Asiatic Exclusion League (AEL); Japanese American Internment; Japanese Americans, Redress Movement for; *Thind v. U.S.*

Further Reading

McClain, Charles, ed. *Japanese Immigrants and American Law: The Alien Land Laws and Other Issues*. New York: Garland, 1994.

Tracy Chu

All-Black Resorts

In the twentieth century, all-black resorts grew out of the desire of a growing number of wealthy African American entrepreneurs to vacation in places that were free of segregation. Even before the Civil War, freed slaves established their own towns and created businesses to serve those communities.

The earliest known black town was New Philadelphia, which was established in Pike County, Illinois, in 1836. Princeville, North Carolina, established in 1885, was the first black town to be formed after the Civil War. Subsequently, numerous African American communities emerged, particularly in the industrial cities of the Midwest and Northeast. Many African American entrepreneurs and professionals accumulated considerable wealth, but the system of segregation denied them access to recreational facilities. All-black resorts thus were created by African Americans for African Americans who could afford them. The town of Oak Bluffs on Martha's Vineyard, an island off the southern coast of Cape Cod, started to be developed by African Americans at the end of the nineteenth century and has now grown into the prime resort serving well-to-do African Americans from the northeast. In 1930, Al Lewis, president of an African American insurance company, bought 200 acres along the coast of Amelia Island, Florida, and created the American Beach resort so that his employees could enjoy "relaxation without humiliation." The economic advancement of some African Americans led even a white businessmen to create an all-black recreational facility. Thus, in 1912, Idlewild, Michigan, better known as "the resort that segregation built," was established. Many of these resorts are now in decline, and redevelopment efforts are under way.

Dong-Ho Cho

All-Weather Bigots

See Bigots, Types of.

All-Weather Liberals

See Bigots, Types of; Fair-Weather Liberals.

Al Qaeda

In Arabic, *al Qaeda* means "the base" or "the foundation." Around 1988, Osama Bin Laden, the son of a Saudi billionaire, formed, with the aid of other Islamist groups, an organization named Al Qaeda, which in the 1990s became a global terrorist network with cells in a number of countries. Al Qaeda promotes an

Osama Bin Laden, second from left, founder of the global terrorist network Al Qaeda, with his top lieutenant Ayman al-Zawahri, second from right, and other Al Qaeda members, October 7, 2001.

AP/Wide World Photos.

extremist and militant form of Islam and seeks to attack U.S. interests around the world.

In the 1980s, Bin Laden financed and recruited Arab/Muslim men to fight on behalf of Afghanistan (not an Arab country, though a Muslim nation) against the Soviet invasion. These recruits came to be known euphemistically as Arab Afghans. When the effort against the Soviets proved surprisingly successful, Bin Laden was emboldened to redirect his *jihad*, or holy war, beyond Afghanistan, and Al Qaeda was formed. One of Al Qaeda's goals was to overthrow the U.S.-supported Saudi government. It believed that the Kingdom of Saudi Arabia, which houses Mecca and Medina, the two holiest sites in Islam, should not harbor the "infidel" U.S. armed forces that remained after the first Gulf War in 1990. Al Qaeda also wanted to challenge U.S. support for the Israeli government, which it held accountable for the oppression of the Palestinians.

Al Qaeda represents a fringe group in the Muslim world, and is based on an extremist and puritanical interpretation of the Qur'an, the holy book of Islam. Its followers distort religion to justify their global militant agenda, which includes attacking civilians and wreaking havoc on U.S. and Western interests.

Al Qaeda was responsible for the September 11, 2001, terrorist attacks, which killed 3,021 innocent people at the World Trade Center in New York City (2,843) and the Pentagon in Washington, DC, and, in an aborted attack, an airplane that crashed in Pennsylvania. This was by far the biggest terrorist incident on U.S. soil.

In response to 9/11, the United States launched the War on Terrorism, which included the invasion of Afghanistan to destroy Al Qaeda's bases and to overthrow the Taliban (literally, "religious students"), the country's strict fundamentalist rulers who harbored Al Qaeda. Domestically, Congress passed new legislation (the Patriot Act), and the U.S. Attorney General issued a series of initiatives meant to monitor and arrest potential terrorists. These policies were generally not effective in achieving their aim. Instead, they profiled persons of Middle Eastern and South Asian origin, leading to detentions and deportations of thousands of immigrants. They also reinforced commonly held stereotypes and suspicious beliefs about Arabs and Muslims. The United States in the post–9/11 period has been marked by a meteoric escalation of hate crimes and bias incidents. The FBI, which keeps statistics by the religious affiliation of the victim, not by ethnicity, reported "a very dramatic increase in the number of anti-Islamic crimes—28 in 2000 and 481 in 2001 (a 1,600% increase)." It is ironic that Al Qaeda's terrorism cost Middle Eastern American communities dearly, since these are the very people with whom it shared an ethnic and religious affiliation.

See also Arab/Muslim American Advocacy Organizations, Responding to the Backlash; Government Initiatives after the September 11, 2001, Attack on the United States; *Jihad*; Muslim Philanthropic Organizations, Closure of after September 11, 2001; Muslims, Prejudice and Discrimination against; Muslims, Terrorist Image of; September 11, 2001, Terrorism, Discriminatory Reactions to.

Further Reading

Gunaratna, Rohan. *Inside Al Qaeda: Global Network of Terror*. New York: Berkeley Publishing Group, 2003.

Mehdi Bozorgmehr and Anny Bakalian

American Anti-Slavery Society (AASS)

See Abolitionist Movement.

American-Arab Anti-Discrimination Committee (ADC)

James Abourezk, the first person of Arab descent to serve in the U.S. Senate, established the American-Arab Anti-Discrimination Committee (ADC) in 1980 as a membership-based civil rights advocacy organization. ADC's mission is to defend the rights of men and women of Arab descent and promote their cultural heritage. Through educational programs, media monitoring, and other efforts, ADC fights negative stereotypes of Arab Americans. It also provides legal services and counseling in cases of discrimination and defamation. Because many of ADC's members are concerned with establishing a more balanced U.S. Middle East policy, the organization's goals go well beyond the domestic issues implied by its name. Abourezk, a Democrat, who was a senator for South Dakota from 1973 to 1979, created the ADC in response to several trends, including the large influx of Arab immigrants brought about by changes in immigration policy in 1965, the increasing tensions and anti-American rhetoric in the Middle East, and the prevalence of anti-Arab bias in the American media and popular culture.

One of ADC's major contributions has been compiling and analyzing evidence of hate crimes and incidents of discrimination against Arab Americans in periodic reports (six since 1991). Its report "The Post–September 11 Backlash: September 11, 2001–October 11, 2002" revealed that in the nine weeks following the attacks, more than seven hundred violent incidents and eight hundred cases of employment discrimination were aimed at Arab or Muslim Americans, a marked escalation from previous years. Also of significance were the "new discriminatory immigration policies" that resulted in the detentions and selective deportation of immigrants from the Arab World and the monitoring of students and young men from that Middle East. The report concluded that "Arab Americans suffered a serious backlash following September 11, 2001." Undoubtedly, immigrants of Arab origin were the targets of ethnic and religious profiling by the U.S. government.

ADC has joined coalitions of civil rights organizations in Washington, DC, and others across the country to advocate for Arab immigrants. The backlash has galvanized many to join ADC and fight for their civil rights. The organization has grown to about forty chapters in more than twenty-four states, and there are ADC members in every state in the union. Second-generation Arab Americans have been particularly active in energizing the ranks of ADC, as well as other advocacy organizations, in the post–9/11 period. Their mobilization has not only aimed at improving the civil rights of people of Arab descent in the United States, they have vociferously called for changes in U.S. policy toward the Palestinian people, the war in Iraq, and other conflicts in the Middle East.

See also Arab American Institute (AAI); Arab Community Center for Economic and Social Services (ACCESS); Arab/Muslim American Advocacy Organizations, Responding to the Backlash; Government Initiatives after the September 11, 2001 Attack on the United States; *Jihad*; Middle Easterners, Historical Precedents of Backlash against; Middle Easterners, Stereotypes of; Muslim Philanthropic Organizations, Closure of after September 11, 2001; Muslims, Prejudice and Discrimination against; Muslims, Terrorist Image of; September 11, 2001, Terrorism, Discriminatory Reactions to.

Mehdi Bozorgmehr and Anny Bakalian

American Civil Liberties Union (ACLU)

The American Civil Liberties Union (ACLU) was established in 1920 by a group of people concerned about violations of the Bill of Rights (the first ten amendments to the U.S. Constitution). The civil liberties movement, which culminated in the creation of the ACLU, was a reaction to the censorship, draft, and espionage laws enacted during World War I. From its inception, the ACLU has had a reputation for being radical, mainly because it mostly has defended radicals. The cases the ACLU has championed have been in line with the organization's credo of free speech, press, and assembly. The mission of the ACLU is to work through the courts and the legislature to defend the rights and liberties of individuals as granted by the laws and the U.S. Constitution, regardless of the politics, race, or religion of the individual. To this end, the ACLU has appeared before the Supreme Court and other federal courts on numerous occasions, both as direct counsel and by filing amicus briefs. Roger Baldwin, one of the founders of the organization, served as executive director of the ACLU from 1920 to 1950.

The ACLU boasts almost half a million members and has offices in most states. The main sources of funding for this nonprofit organization are annual membership dues and contributions from private foundations, but not the government. The ACLU has, historically, defended the civil liberties of all people, even during times of national crisis. Since the events of September 11, 2001, the ACLU, under new leadership, has expanded its outreach to the Arab and Muslim American communities across the United States, and has even hired a staff member to advocate on their behalf. The ACLU has been in the forefront of the legal and public relations battles, defending the civil rights of Arab and Muslim men who have been most affected by the passage of the Patriot Act. The ACLU published a report on civil liberties after September 11 that provides a historical perspective in times of crisis.

Mehdi Bozorgmehr and Anny Bakalian

American Dream Ideology

The American dream ideology is the belief that any American, regardless of ethnic or racial background, can achieve economic success and social mobility through hard work and determination. The tenets of this conservative ideology stress rugged individualism, personal achievement, a strong work ethic, frugality, delayed gratification, and the accumulation of material possessions such as homes and automobiles. This ideology also stresses the importance of education in the achievement of upward mobility. The American dream ideology, often referred to as mainstream or middle-class values, is rooted in notions of a Protestant work ethic as described by Max Weber (1930) in *The Protestant Ethic and the Spirit of Capitalism*. People who hold with the American dream ideology seldom recognize the social barriers to success encountered by minority groups.

Large numbers of immigrants from southern and eastern European countries, predominantly non-Protestant (Catholic, Jewish, and Eastern Orthodox), arrived in the United States between 1880 and 1920. They came to the United States with the belief that through hard work they could achieve the American dream and economic success in a manner that was difficult or impossible in their native countries. In the United States, members of these "new immigrant" groups initially experienced economic difficulty, prejudice, and discrimination. But they gradually achieved socioeconomic mobility. By the 1970s third- and fourth-generation Italian, Polish, Jewish, and Irish Americans had caught up with or outperformed Protestant ethnic groups in socioeconomic status. They also achieved high levels of social assimilation, as reflected in their exceptionally high (60–75 percent) intermarriage rates.

Native white Americans who are familiar with stories of their ancestors' hardships in this new land believe that all Americans, including members of racial minority groups, can make it here through hard work and determination. Their logic is this: our immigrant ancestors started in this country from the bottom, but they made it through hard work and determination, and over generations we have achieved high social mobility. If blacks and other minority group are motivated and work hard as our ancestors did, they too can make it. Thus, they fail to understand that as whites they have privileges in the United States and that many members of racial minority groups experience disadvantages owing to racism. Not only white Americans, but also many Asian Americans and even members of other disadvantaged minority groups, accept the American dream ideology. Some conservative blacks, such as U.S. Supreme Court justice Clarence Thomas, believe that many blacks are poor mainly because they lack motivation and a strong work ethic.

See also Black Family Instability Thesis; Culture of Poverty Thesis; "Model Minority Thesis."

Further Reading

Baritz, Loren. *The Good Life*. New York: Knopf, 1989.

Lewis, Oscar. "The Culture of Poverty." *Scientific American* 115 (1966): 19–25.

Quarles, Benjamin. *The Negro in the Making of America*. New York: Simon & Schuster, 1987.

Weber, Max. *The Protestant Ethic and the Spirit of Capitalism*. Los Angeles: Roxbury Publishing Company, 1930.

Sandra L. Barnes

American GI Forum (AGIF)

The American GI Forum (AGIF) is a civil rights organization devoted to securing equal rights for Hispanic American veterans. AGIF was founded on March 26, 1948, by Hector P. Garcia, a young army veteran and a physician from Corpus Christi, Texas. He was also a member of the League of United Latin American Citizens. When World War II was over in 1945, millions of veterans returned home, looking to the GI Bill rights, which guaranteed educational, medical, housing, and other benefits. But a significant proportion of Mexican American and other Hispanic veterans throughout the United States were denied those benefits. Garcia called for an organized struggle with more than 700 other Hispanic veterans to address problems of discrimination and inequalities they have endured.

AGIF demanded that the GI Bill of Rights of 1944 apply equally to Hispanic veterans. It also fought to ensure adequate hospital care for the wounded. The organization successfully put Mexican American representation on draft boards. In 1949, AGIF launched a widespread protest movement against racial discrimination by the director of the Rice Funeral Home in Three Rivers, Texas, who refused the use of the chapel for the funeral of Private Felix Longoria. The protest stirred the nation and finally forced political leaders, including Lyndon B. Johnson, then a senator from Texas, to intervene and have him honored at Arlington National Cemetery with a full military funeral. In 1954, the AGIF was involved with other organizations in a landmark civil rights legal case, *Hernandez v. The State of Texas*. Today, AGIF focuses on employment training and counseling for veterans through its two programs, the Veteran Outreach Program, which provides employment training and counseling in the Southwest, and SER—Jobs for Progress, which operates employment training centers and provides residential and other services in the continental United States and Puerto Rico.

Dong-Ho Cho

American Indians

See American Indian Movement (AIM); Indian Allotment Act of 1887; Indian Citizenship Act of 1924; Indian Claims Commission (ICC); Indian Occupation of Alcatraz Island; Indian Reorganization Act of 1934 (IRA); Indian Reservations; Indian Self-Determination and Educational Assistance Act of 1975 (IS-DEAA); Native Americans, Conquest of; Native Americans, Forced Relocation of; Native Americans, Prejudice and Discrimination against; Slavery and American Indians.

American Indian Movement (AIM)

The American Indian Movement (AIM) was founded in 1968 to advance the rights of Native Americans in the United States. AIM originated in Minneapolis/St. Paul, Minnesota, to protest the discriminatory police treatment of Native Americans, to lobby for improved services, and to establish "survival schools" to introduce Native American youth to their culture. AIM quickly developed into a national organization with over forty chapters advocating for political self-determination, recognition of treaty rights, and cultural awareness.

In the late 1960s and early 1970s, AIM participated in a number of dramatic protest actions. In 1969, its members participated with the United Nations of All Tribes in a nineteen-month occupation of Alcatraz Island in a San Francisco harbor, the site of an abandoned federal prison, to draw attention to the poor conditions on reservations and across the United States. In 1972, as part of a national protest called the Trail of Broken Treaties, its members took over the main office of the Bureau of Indian Affairs (BIA) in Washington, DC, and demanded a reorganization of the Bureau and recognition of past treaties between the U.S. government and Native American groups. In 1973, 200 AIM members and Lakota elders occupied the village of Wounded Knee, an Oglala Sioux community on the Pine Ridge Reservation in South Dakota and the site of the infamous 1890 massacre of Native Americans by U.S. troops. They demanded the end of corruption involving the BIA and the local tribal council and a Senate investigation of Native American problems. The seventy-one-day occupation ended in a standoff. In 1975 a shoot-out occurred on the same reservation, leading to the indictment of AIM members in the deaths of two FBI agents. While other defendants were acquitted, Leonard Peltier was convicted of the murders and sentenced to two consecutive life sentences in a trial that continues to be seen as very controversial. Succeeding internal conflicts debilitated AIM, though it experienced a modest revival in the 1990s, leading protests in 1992 against the 500th anniversary of explorer Christopher Columbus' arrival in the Americas.

See also Columbus Day Controversy; Indian Allotment Act of 1887; Indian Citizenship Act of 1924; Indian Claims Commission (ICC); Indian Occupation of Alcatraz Island; Indian Reorganization Act of 1934 (IRA); Indian Reservations; Indian Self-Determination and Educational Assistance Act of 1975 (ISDEAA); Native Americans, Conquest of; Native Americans, Forced Relocation of; Native Americans, Prejudice and Discrimination against; Pan-ethnic Movements; Slavery and American Indians.

Further Reading

Banks, Dennis, and Richard Erdoes. *Ojibwa Warrior: Dennis Banks and the Rise of the American Indian Movement*. Norman: University of Oklahoma Press, 2004.

Kenneth J. Guest

American Literature and Racism

Racism has been both present in topic and a topic of American literature for centuries. Thomas Dixon's novel *The Clansman*, for example, inspired D. W. Griffith's film *Birth of a Nation* (1915), which contains vivid scenes of a white woman jumping off a cliff for fear of being raped by a black man, and black politicians eating chicken and sitting with their feet on the desks in the legislature. The book and film were instrumental in the revival of the Ku Klux Klan. More recently, William Styron's 1960s novel, *The Confessions of Nat Turner*, was attacked by many black critics because of the fictionalized motivation for Turner's rebellion: Styron's Turner feels that he must kill to conquer his lust for a white woman. Hence, in his reinterpretation of the slave rebellion that took place in 1831 in Virginia (during which Nat Turner led almost seventy blacks, and which resulted in the deaths of approximately seventy whites), Styron places emphasis on Turner's desire for sex with a white woman, for which there is no factual evidence, more than on his desire for freedom.

Many readers have perceived racism to be present in the works of other major American writers as Harriet Beecher Stowe, Mark Twain and William Faulkner.

Uncle Tom's Cabin by Harriet Beecher Stowe, published in 1852, is a central novel in the debate about racism in American literature. Though the book is clearly arguing against slavery, its argument for blacks' worth is embodied in Uncle Tom, whose name has become a derogatory phrase denoting blacks who are servile and submissive to whites. While Stowe stresses her belief in Uncle Tom's unrelenting nobility as a result of his unwavering Christianity, his almost superhuman humility has proved objectionable to many readers and critics.

President Abraham Lincoln attested to the book's power as an abolitionist text with his oft-quoted description of Stowe as the "lady who caused this great war." Nevertheless, despite Stowe's emancipatory beliefs, the sentimentality of the novel in general and the portrayal of Uncle Tom in particular are perhaps what have given rise to much of the criticism of the book. For instance, in "Everybody's Protest Novel," included in his collection *Notes of a Native Son* (1955), James Baldwin crystallized the objection to Stowe's sentimentality and rejected attempts to defend the book by critics who stated that the book's power could be found in this very quality, which was also a convention of much nineteenth-century literature. Baldwin stated that sentimentality is actually characterized by hatred, that is, the inability to perceive, and thus portray, blacks as fully human, complex beings. Baldwin also believed that the novel tainted whites' perceptions of blacks for generations by crystallizing the myth of the docile and servile black. Thus, the critique of the meaning of the novel's central figure has raised questions concerning what sort of black person whites find acceptable, even admirable—thus leading to a dangerous literary and societal stereotype.

Mark Twain's novel *The Adventures of Huckleberry Finn*, published in 1884, also makes slavery prominent topic, in this case in the depiction of the relationship between Huck and the runaway slave, Jim. Long the subject of debate has been whether aspects of the text are racist. The more obvious focus of the controversy is the use of the word *nigger*, which appears in the text well over 100 times, most obviously referring to "Nigger Jim." While some may believe that Twain, as a regional writer, wanted to capture the language that would have been used by people in real life, others have demanded that the book be removed from elementary and secondary school reading lists because of this epithet. What is also intriguing is that as with Stowe, Twain incorporates elements that seem at odds with his criticism of racism, which is especially noteworthy, as much of the book condemns the moral corruption of society in general.

In addition to the use of the word *nigger*, the final part of the book has been the subject of intense criticism regarding the level of Twain's racial consciousness. When Tom Sawyer enters the book, the novel becomes a boy's adventure story, and Tom and Huck make sport of Jim by exploiting his superstitious nature, having him do such things as write in blood as they make a game out of his desire for freedom. The ultimate irony comes when the reader learns that Jim already is free, without his knowing it. The final part of the book undermines readers' perceptions of the bond that has developed between Huck and Jim. As African American novelist Toni Morrison points out in *Playing in the Dark: Whiteness and the Literary Imagination* (1992), "The humiliation that Huck and Tom subject Jim to is baroque, endless, foolish, mind-softening—and it comes after we have experienced Jim as a caring father and a sensitive man" (57). Yet, Morrison believes that the book is valuable in getting readers to analyze the nature of black-white interdependence as represented in Huck and Jim's relationship. In short, *Huckleberry Finn*, a classic American text, still inspires debates about Twain's view of race and about its inclusion in educational curricula.

William Faulkner is a particularly complex figure in the exploration of racism and American literature. While Faulkner has been hailed as a stylistic genius whose complex narratives make for intricately woven literature, he has also been the subject of criticism. Race and the fragmentation of Southern society after the Civil War and well into the twentieth century are two of Faulkner's recurring themes, evident in such novels as *The Sound and the Fury* (1929), *Light in August* (1932) and *Absalom, Absalom!* (1936). Yet, he is certainly not simply a critic of Southern racism; instead, at times he is an example of it.

Faulkner made several disturbing statements during the civil rights movement, which make evident that however flawed he thought the Old South was, it was more comfortable to him than the idea of change in the racial hierarchy of the era. For example, in an interview in the March 1956 issue of *The Reporter*, Faulkner stated that if desegregation led to a race war in the South, he would support segregationists, "even if it meant going out into the streets and shooting negroes" (Leeming 1994, 117). In an article written for *Life* in March 1956, in the aftermath of the *Brown v. Board of Education* decision, Faulkner also declared: "I was against compulsory segregation. I am just as strongly opposed to compulsory integration" (51). He argued that the Supreme Court should not impose integration on the South, and that such court decisions could lead to violence by whites. Faulkner also made a statement that reflects his belief that Southern whites became the "underdog" in the face of court-ordered integration. Comments Faulkner made in 1957–1958 during talks at the University of Virginia, collected in *Faulkner in the University* (1959), are equally troubling. He compares the integration of blacks into Southern society as letting "unbridled horses loose in the streets, or say a community of five thousand cats with five hundred unassimilated dogs" (209). Faulkner also claims that only whites could teach blacks "self-restraint, honesty, dependability, purity. . . . If we don't, we will spend the rest of our lives dodging among the five hundred unbridled horses" (211).

These comments raise the question of exactly what Faulkner's stance was regarding racism and segregation as laid out in his books. His novels seem to stop at diagnosing the societal and psychological problems of the racially divided South—they do not pointing toward a future where the problem of race can be addressed positively. Hence James Baldwin's remarks are important to examine in a discussion of the ideology behind Faulkner's writings, both before and during the civil rights movement: "Faulkner . . . is so plaintive concerning this 'middle of the road' from which 'extremist' elements of both races are driving him that it does not seem unfair to ask just what he has been doing there until now. Where is the evidence of the struggle he has been carrying on there on behalf of the Negro?" (Leeming 1994, 117).

Perhaps Baldwin's question is the one that underlies the controversy about racism and American literature. Many authors have raised issues about race, and some of them—for example, Stowe and Twain—seem to think their works were well intentioned. But the conflicted nature of representations of race in American literature shows that to many writers, race presented a difficult challenge to their imagination and their artistry.

See also Morrison, Toni; "Nigger."

Further Reading

Faulkner, William. "A Letter to the North." *Life*, March 5, 1956, 51–52.

Gwynn, Frederick L., and Joseph L. Blotner, eds. *Faulkner in the University*. Charlottesville: University of Virginia Press, 1959.

Leeming, David. *James Baldwin: A Biography*. New York: Henry Holt, 1994.

Morrison, Toni. *Playing in the Dark: Whiteness and the Literary Imagination*. Cambridge, MA: Harvard University Press, 1992.

Jane Davis

American Nazi Party (ANP)

Founded by George Lincoln Rockwell (1918–1967) in the 1960s, the American Nazi Party was dedicated to the preservation of white power. Rockwell, claiming to be inspired by reading Adolph Hitler's *Mein Kampf*, vowed to exterminate homosexuals, Jews, blacks, and other groups. In the 1960s, the American Nazi Party had only a small membership but gained notoriety

George Lincoln Rockwell, center, leader of the American Nazi Party, and his "hate bus," 1961.

AP/Wide World Photos.

nonetheless, particularly as a result of Rockwell's famous 1966 interview with *Roots* author Alex Haley for *Playboy* magazine and his public call for "White Power" in response to the Black Power movement. In the 1960s, Rockwell organized the harassment of civil rights workers in the South. In the 1970s, the ANP organized confrontations against integrationists and eventually spawned another organization, the National Socialist White People's Party. The American Nazi Party, now based in Michigan and run by Rocky Suhayda, uses the Internet to attract membership. The official symbol of the American Nazi party is a red flag bearing a black swastika, a variation of Hitler's Third Reich flag.

See also White-Supremacist Movement in the United States; White-Supremacist Underground.

Victoria Pitts

American "Obsession with Race"

Civil Rights leader Martin Luther King Jr. envisioned a society where people would not be judged by the color of their skin. There are indicators, though, that race impacts every aspect of life for Americans. Racial and ethnic minorities continue to be less well integrated in American society. There is a great amount of social distance between white Americans and racial minorities, especially African Americans. Public spaces are no longer officially segregated by race, but beyond the workplace and a select few educational institutions, Americans live racially segregated lives.

This segregation can be attributed to lingering racial prejudices that are directed at minority groups in the United States, especially African Americans. Levels of residential segregation are quite high for African Americans. Despite survey data, which indicates considerable changes in neighborhood composition preferences among all racial groups, whites continue to prefer neighborhoods with much fewer African American households than African Americans prefer. Away from the workplace, friendships between people from different racial groups remain the exception rather than the rule and this is particularly true for African Americans and whites. Levels of intermarriage between whites and African Americans are much lower than rates of intermarriage between whites and other racial/ethnic minorities.

Racial minorities are treated like second-class citizens in a number of ways in the United States. Racial profiling practices by law enforcement officials and other authority figures subject racial minorities to frequent harassment. Racial minorities, especially African Americans, are routinely followed around in stores because they "look" suspicious or pulled over for "driving while (being) black." Since the terrorist attacks in the United States on September 11, 2001, Arab Americans are often treated as if they are foreigners who might be engaged in terrorist activities or have connections to a terrorist organization, at the very least.

The criminal justice system is supposed to mete out blind justice, but arrest and convictions rates vary considerably by race, as does sentencing. Racial minorities, especially African Americans, continue to be treated as outsiders in the United States, rather than the citizens that they are. In many subtle, and even some overt, ways, race continues to determine one's social status in America.

See also King, Martin Luther, Jr.; Racialism.

Romney S. Norwood

Americanization Movement

In the first two decades of the twentieth century, a few federal, state, and local government agencies and many private groups consisting of native-born Americans (especially those of Anglo-Saxon ancestry) tried to transform the recently arrived immigrants in the United States by encouraging or coercing them to change their foreign cultural orientations, political loyalties, and social behavior to become, very rapidly, "thoroughly American." These efforts soon became known as the Americanization Movement. Its sponsors were concerned and fearful that the massive wave of immigrants arriving since 1890 were not giving up their Old World ways and adopting an American mode of living quickly and completely. Proponents of Americanization believed that the heavy influx of newcomers who appeared so different (and in their eyes seemed degraded and inferior) would harm and destabilize American society unless strong remedial measures were taken to resocialize millions of immigrants and their children. The Americanization Movement has been characterized as an attempt to strip the immigrants of their native culture and make them over into Americans along Anglo-Saxon lines. As one of this movement's leaders put it: "Our task is to break up these [immigrants'] groups or settlements, to assimilate and amalgamate these people as a part of our American race, and to implant in their children, so far as can be done, the Anglo-Saxon conception of righteousness, law and order, and popular government, and to awaken in them a reverence for our democratic institutions and for those things in our national life which we as a people hold to be of abiding worth."

The Americanization Movement's most intense activity took place during World War I (1914–1918). Out of fear that immigrants might support their home countries—some of which were U.S. enemies—in the war, possibly with espionage or sabotage, the primary focus in these years was immigrants' political allegiance and loyalty. Americanization leaders went into immigrants' work sites, schools, and gathering places, making speeches and distributing pamphlets that urged recent immigrants and their children to give up any attachment they had to political leaders or factions in their homeland and become patriotic, proud, flag-waving U.S. citizens via the naturalization process. Many business owners, such as Henry Ford, who employed large numbers of immigrants, reinforced these efforts by having their workers take classes about U.S. history, politics, and citizen education. Of course, an equally important thrust of the Americanization Movement involved attempts to make immigrants learn and use the English language. Evening classes were held in many venues, and immigrants were urged to attend and then shift to English as quickly as possible, both as a sign of their willingness to "convert" from "foreign" to "American" and to ease their passage into the social and cultural "mainstream."

Beyond adopting English, U.S. citizenship, and patriotism, the Americanization Movement also sought to change immigrants' social behaviors and perspectives in matters like style of dress, diet and food preference, selection of first or last name, and habits of work or play. Immigrant workers and their children were indoctrinated on the importance of being punctual, dependable, obedient employees. Groups of native-born women sometimes participated in the Americanization Movement by visiting immigrants' homes and making recommendations on how a mother/wife should make it less foreign and more American, via changes in diet or cooking, household cleaning, personal hygiene, or child rearing.

While President Theodore Roosevelt, with speeches condemning the "hyphenated-American" and extolling the "100 percent American," may be the most prominent figure who supported the Americanization Movement, organizationally the most central person in it was Frances A. Kellor. She helped start or led the most active groups in the Americanization Movement, including the New York branch of the North American Civic League for Immigrants (1909), the Committee for Immigrants in America (1914), the National Americanization (Day) Committee (1915), and the Division of Immigrant Education within the federal Bureau of Education (1915). Both Roosevelt and Kellor had a genuine, but conditional, respect for and appreciation of the immigrants they felt they were assisting—they welcomed them and saw them as a positive addition *only if* they took the transforming steps offered by the Americanization Movement.

The Americanization Movement faded out in the 1920s as American leaders embraced harsher and more negative beliefs about immigrants and decided to allow immigration from northern and western Europe but restrict immigration from southern and eastern Europe and from Asia. Those unwanted immigrants were alleged to be so inherently different and inferior by nature that no resocialization through English classes, civics lessons, or changes in dress or surname could turn them into suitable Americans.

Looking back, it is understandable that social scientists favorably inclined toward cultural diversity and pluralism severely criticize the Americanization Movement. One called it a "fundamentally misguided" and "semi-hysterical attempt at pressure-cooking assimilation" based on "thinly veiled contempt" and a mistrust of immigrants that did not show an understanding of the utility of immigrants' cultural retentions and slower-paced adaptations to American life (Gordon 1964, 106). Another suggests that despite the energies expended and the ethnocentric rhetoric disseminated, the Americanization Movement had only a small effect on the immigrants—most were not directly involved in its programs and in many ways adjusted to American life at their own pace and in their own manner.

See also Anglo Conformity.

Further Reading

Gordon, Milton. *Assimilation in American Life*. New York: Oxford University Press, 1964.

Hartmann, Edward G. *The Movement to Americanize the Immigrant.* New York: Columbia University Press, 1948.

Higham, John. *Strangers in the Land: Patterns of American Nativism, 1860–1925.* 1955. Reprint, New York: Atheneum, 1975.

Charles Jaret

Anglo Conformity

From the beginning of its history, one of the most challenging tasks for the United States has been how to build and maintain a nation-state out of peoples from all over the world. To meet the challenge, many different approaches have been proposed and used. Anglo conformity is one of them. Anglo conformity is an ideology or a government policy that has emphasized that minority groups—immigrated, conquered, annexed, or enslaved—should conform to the dominant Anglo-American culture and its institutions in the United States. New immigrants should learn English, adopt the Protestant faith, practice the customs, behavior, and manners of Anglo-Americans, and accept economic and political systems. Anglo conformity both as an ideology and a government policy was dominant in the late nineteenth and early twentieth centuries and influential until the early 1960s.

Conforming to Anglo culture and institutional arrangements was expected because the majority of the people living in the United States during the eighteenth century were of English descent. After British, white Anglo-Protestants established themselves as the dominant group, subsequent groups and indigenous Native Americans were expected to conform to this cultural and social layout. It was argued that such assimilation to Anglo culture and society was necessary for the unity of the country.

The whole effort of Americanization of new immigrants in the nineteenth/twentieth centuries was based on this ideology. Around 1890, the national origins of immigrants had begun to change from northwest European countries to southern and eastern European countries. These "new" immigrants were less skilled and educated than the "old" immigrants. They tended to stick together as immigrant groups. Alarmed by these new and different immigrants, the federal government initiated a number of programs to help Americanize them. The Bureau of Naturalization helped establish a large network of citizenship programs run by nongovernmental voluntary organizations. Through such programs immigrants were expected to learn English, acquire the civic knowledge of the dominant Anglo-Saxon and ultimately to abandon their ethnic characteristics to culturally assimilate.

In many cases such an Americanization effort was coerced with more substantial pressure. Some employers made the attendance of citizenship classes obligatory for their immigrant employees. Hiring and promotions in workplaces often were linked to the acquisition of citizenship. Congress even mandated that the newly established income tax was twice as high for "nonresident aliens." Some states forbade instruction in foreign languages in public schools, and some even prohibited the study of foreign languages in elementary schools. Thus, Americanization became equivalent to Anglicization.

Until the 1960s, the public school system had been used as a main vehicle for enforcing the policy of Anglo conformity. On the whole, people who favor Anglo conformity tend to oppose bilingual education and other changes for a more inclusive curriculum. They tended to advocate English-only education and Christian values and institutions and attempted to maintain them in the United States. These Anglo conformists were strongly suspicious of ethnic identity, ethnic enclaves, and ethnic communities. They tended to believe that forming and maintaining diverse ethnic groups within a nation-state can be a threat to national unity and eventually can lead the nation to conflict and dissolution.

Since the early 1970s, the U.S. government and schools have changed their policies toward minority and new immigrant groups from Anglo Conformity to cultural pluralism, but this did not happen voluntarily. The civil rights movement, Black Nationalist movement, Third World Movement, and feminist movement in the 1960s forced them to support multiculturalism and diversity. The influx of new immigrants since 1965 has further contributed to ethnic and racial diversities.

See also Americanization Movement; Indian Allotment Act of 1887; Multiculturalism.

Further Reading

Gordon, Milton M. *Assimilation in American Life*. New York: Oxford University Press, 1964.

Schlesinger, Arthur M., Jr. *The Disuniting of America*. New York: Norton, 1992.

Vogel, V. J. *This Country Was Ours*. New York: Harper Torchbooks, 1974.

Heon Cheol Lee

ANP

See American Nazi Party (ANP).

Anti-Catholicism in the United States

Although the First Amendment to the U.S. Constitution declares that "Congress shall make no law respecting an establishment of religion, or prohibiting the free exercise thereof," the history of United States is filled with religious bigotry, persecution, and discrimination. At the start of the new nation, white Protestant Anglo-Americans established themselves as a dominant group, and their Protestant ethos shaped the country. The free exercise of other religions, such as Judaism and Catholicism, is constitutionally guaranteed, but their followers have frequently been the victims of discrimination in the United States.

Anti-Catholicism was deeply rooted in the Protestant past in other parts of the world, but it became a virulent force in the United States, especially during the middle of the nineteenth century, when a significant number of Catholics started immigrating. Most of the immigrants were Irish Catholics, and about half the Germans were also Catholics. Later, Catholics from southern and eastern Europe joined them. Such a great wave of new but different immigrants created fear in the minds of many "native" Americans, who were concerned that recent arrivals were so different from mainstream Americans that they could not fit into American society or, worse, could eventually dominate it.

Irish immigrants in particular were targeted. As the Irish population in America grew and many of its members were politically active, moving into various municipal jobs, there was an outburst of anti-Irish and anti-Catholic propaganda. Many Americans were led to believe that the authoritarian organization of the Catholic Church was incompatible with the democratic institutions and ideals of American society. In the minds of many Protestant nativists, "Catholic traditions continued to look dangerously un-American partly because they did not harmonize easily with the concept of individual freedom imbedded in the national culture" (Higham 1972, 6). Such an idea was constructed, propagated, and used for many different purposes.

In 1834, Samuel F. B. Morse, the famous inventor of the telegraph, wrote several widely publicized pamphlets, including *A Foreign Conspiracy against the Liberties of the United States*, claiming that the papal conquest was under way. He urged all Protestants to unite against Catholics and to change the lenient immigration laws that allowed Catholic immigrants to keep coming to the United States. The influential Protestant clergyman Lyman Beecher also contended in *A Plea for the West* that Catholics were plotting to take control of the western United States by encouraging huge numbers of Catholic immigrants to settle there. His inflammatory sermons delivered in Boston led to the burning of the Ursuline Convent outside of Boston in 1834. Perhaps the most infamous of the many propaganda pieces against Catholics was Maria Monk's *Awful Disclosure of the Hotel Dieu Nunnery of Montreal*, published in 1836. Though it was subsequently discredited, Monk's sensationalist claims stated that the nunnery was rife with illicit sex between priests and nuns and that the babies born from these encounters were murdered. Her work was widely distributed, read, and believed. Ironically, Catholicism in Europe was then an embattled force, but "anti-Catholics in America conveniently portrayed the church as a juggernaut poised to crush the United States" (Marty 1985, 273).

Growing fears of large numbers of immigrants in general and the fear of Catholic immigrants in particular created fertile soil for the emergence of an anti-immigrant nativist political movement, led especially by the American, or Know-Nothing Party. Exploiting such a fabricated fear, the party expanded their political influence. Its single political agenda was to oppose immigration and control the political influence of new immigrants. Part of the party's platform called for limiting political offices to the native born and extending the period required for naturalization to twenty-one years.

Anti-Catholic beliefs and actions continued against the southern and eastern European Catholic groups who began coming to America in the 1880s. Later, it was Italians who turned into the chief target of anti-Catholicism. Under the influence of such anti-immigrant and anti-Catholic political groups as the

Know-Nothing Party and the Immigration Restriction League, the National Origins Act was enacted in 1924 to curtail immigration from southern and eastern European countries, as well as from Asia and Latin America.

See also Irish Immigrants, Prejudice and Discrimination against; Know-Nothing Party; Nativism and the Anti-immigrant Movements.

Further Reading

Higham, John. *Strangers in the Land: Patterns of American Nativism, 1860–1925.* 1955. Reprint, New York: Atheneum, 1975.

Jones, Maldwyn Allen. *American Immigration.* Chicago: University of Chicago Press, 1960.

Marty, Martin E. *Pilgrims in Their Own Land.* New York: Penguin, 1984.

Heon Cheol Lee

Anti-Chinese Sentiments

See Chinese Immigrants and Anti-Chinese Sentiments.

Anti-Defamation League of B'nai Brith (ADL)

The Anti-Defamation League of B'nai Brith (ADL) was founded in 1913 in the midst of the anti-Semitic furor that surrounded the famous Leo Frank case, in which a northern Jew was convicted and later lynched for killing a girl in an Atlanta factory. Established by Chicago lawyer Sigmund Livingston with $200 and the sponsorship of a German Jewish fraternal organization called the Independent Order of B'nai B'rith, the ADL undertook to combat prejudice, discrimination, and violence against Jews throughout the United States. Among the organization's earliest campaigns were efforts to stop the news media from stereotyping Jews. Later, the ADL worked to combat quotas against Jews in higher education and employment, as well as anti-Semitic actions by the Ku Klux Klan. In the 1950s, as the civil rights movement emerged, the ADL began to work to end other kinds of hatred and discrimination. The organization launched educational campaigns about segregation, the Holocaust, and neofascist groups. With thirty regional offices, the ADL continues today to work through the media and the courts on behalf of Israel, Jews worldwide, people of color in the United States, and those who face discrimination in any nation. Its campaigns at the beginning of the twenty-first century include keeping religion out of public schools, combating terrorism without giving up civil liberties, supporting Israel, and helping children grow up without hate.

See also Anti-Semitism in the United States; Aryan Nations; Black Anti-Semitism; Frank, Leo; Jewish-Black Conflicts; Jewish Defense League (JDL); Ku Klux Klan (KKK).

Mikaila Mariel Lemonik Arthur

Anti-immigration Movements

See Nativism and the Anti-immigrant Movements.

Anti-Iranian Stereotypes

See Iran Hostage Crisis and Anti-Iranian Stereotypes.

Anti-Semitism in the United States

Anti-Semitism refers to hateful beliefs about or actions taken against the Jewish people, individual Jews, or non-Jews who are perceived as Jewish. This hate can be based on Jewish people as a race, a culture, or an ethnic group, and has existed for most of Judaism's more than four-thousand-year history. In the United Nations's 1950 *Statement on Race*, anti-Semitism was acknowledged as a form of racism.

The History of Anti-Semitism prior to the United States

Anti-Semitism began like any other kind of nativism or xenophobia (fear and/or hatred of foreigners): nations surrounding the Middle Eastern areas in which Jews lived conquered and subjugated or enslaved them. A normal part of this subjugation was the requirement that Jews stop practicing their religion, often enforced through laws that specified that Jews who did not convert or stop engaging in Jewish practice would be put to death, or at least forced to pay special high taxes. Many polytheistic religions were able to incorporate the old and new religions together; for instance, by finding equivalencies between their traditional gods and the gods of the new religion. The Jewish religion and people set themselves apart from other religions and people surrounding them, however, through their adoption of monotheism and their unique rules of ritual and dietary purity. Later, the Jews' use of a language different from that which the local people spoke was also a source of distinction. They were not ready to convert after being conquered, which resulted in many massacres and expulsions, as well as the development of a hatred against Jews on the part of many conquering states. Before the emergence of Christianity, Jews had already faced such subjugation from Egypt, Babylonia, Greece, and Rome.

Christianity, and later Islam, intensified religious anti-Semitism because they saw their own religions as improving on Judaism, while Jews did not agree. Throughout the history of Christianity, various denominations have blamed Jews for the crucifixion of Jesus (who was born a Jew). This blame has been closely tied to the fact that the Jewish holiday of Passover occurs near the time of Easter and involves special foods, which Christian anti-Semitics libelously believe to be made with the blood of Christian children. Throughout the history of Christian Europe, countries and towns have expelled their Jewish residents, launched programs of violence and theft against them, and forced conversion. In most areas, Jews were not allowed to own property and were confined to certain specific professions, such as traveling sales and banking. Their association with banking would come back to haunt them in accusations of usury and world domination made in literature ranging from Shakespeare's *The Merchant of Venice* to anti-Semitic tracts like *The Protocols of the Elders of Zion*.

Jewish Immigration

Jews came to the New World from the beginning of its colonization. Jews were among the early residents of the Dutch colonies in North America, having arrived by 1654. Other early areas of Jewish settlement were Philadelphia, Pennsylvania; Newport, Rhode Island; Charleston, South Carolina; and Savannah, Georgia. Early Jewish settlers were primarily assimilated Jews from European countries such as England, Holland, Germany, Spain, and Portugal, and they were able to be active participants in colonial life in those colonies that granted religious freedom. Among these immigrants were Spanish Jews fleeing the Inquisition, including some whose families had converted to Catholicism in the earlier waves of the Inquisition but were now under scrutiny again. Jews who attempted to settle in other colonies, particularly the Puritan New England ones, faced severe religious persecution. Many of these early immigrants were Sephardic Jews, or descendents of those Jews who had settled in Spain and other Mediterranean areas of the Jewish diaspora.

Steady numbers of Jews immigrated to the United States throughout its early history, but immigration was most intense during the period that has become known as the first mass migration, spanning the years 1881 to 1928. During this time, more than 2.3 million Jewish immigrants arrived and stayed in the United States. As compared with the earlier immigrants, these Jews were less assimilated, less educated, and poorer. They were Ashkenazi Jews, who came from eastern European countries such as Russia, the Ukraine, and Lithuania, had names that were more clearly Jewish in origin, and spoke Yiddish, a mix of German and Hebrew. The assimilated Jews already in the United States founded organizations such as the Hebrew Immigrant Aid Society to help the new immigrants assimilate to life in the new country, partially because they feared that these more recognizably Jewish immigrants would draw more attention to Jews in general and bring on more anti-Semitism and discrimination.

This wave of migration came to an end with the passing of restrictive immigration legislation, including entry taxes that were hard for impoverished refugees to pay; a literacy requirement that was difficult for many Jewish women who were never taught to read; tests of mental capability that were often culturally or linguistically biased; and, finally, the National Origins Acts of 1921 and 1924. These laws restricted immigration to no more than 2 percent of the number of individuals of each nationality living in the United States as of 1890. Because Jews were not counted as a separate nationality, they were forced to try to enter the country on the miniscule quotas allocated to the eastern European nations they were fleeing. No exception was made for refugees.

The result of these laws was that when Hitler and the Nazis came to power in Germany in the 1930s, few Jewish refugees were able to flee. Those who could, traveled to countries with bigger immigration quotas and tried to obtain papers there, but this was a risky and expensive effort. Legislators in the United States refused to allow Jews to enter during Nazi rule, even as evidence of concentration camps came to light. President Franklin Delano Roosevelt, who, because of his involvement in fighting against Nazi Germany in World War II, has come to be seen as a savior of the Jews, was also complicit in the decision to refuse Jewish refugees' entry. The most horrific result of this decision was the turning away in 1939 of the *USS St. Louis*, a ship filled with 900 Jewish refugees. The ship was refused entry in American waters in New York and was surrounded by Coast Guard ships to prevent the refugees from jumping to freedom. After the ship returned to Europe, the passengers sought refuge in other countries. Most of them, however, were later killed in Nazi concentration camps.

It was not only in terms of immigration that anti-Semitism affected Jews in the United States during this period, however. Many well-known public figures in politics, business, and religion espoused anti-Semitism, including Henry Ford (creator of the Ford automobile) and Father Charles Coughlin, a Royal Oak, Michigan, radio priest who advocated social justice for the poor and blamed the Jews for economic problems. Additionally, white supremacist hate groups such as the Ku Klux Klan emerged during these years. The Klan is strongly nativist and blamed both Jews and blacks for the economic woes of the Great Depression. Klan violence over the years has included severe beatings, lynchings, arson, and cross-burnings, each of which has been directed against Jews. Jews also experienced violence from other immigrant groups, Irish gangs for instance.

Revisions to immigration laws after the Nazi Holocaust in World War II did eventually allow for refugees to come to the United States, and Jews continue to make use of this method for immigration. Jewish refugees today come primarily from Muslim countries in the Middle East and from the countries making up the former Soviet Union. These new Jewish refugees tend to be less educated than their counterparts already in the United States. Refugees from the former Soviet republics face particular challenges, as the anti-Semitic regimes there prohibited most Jews from learning anything about their religion. These changes in refugee laws were accompanied by the end of legal discrimination against Jews. In the United States, no legal measures openly discriminate against Jews, which is not the case in many other countries. These changes reduced anti-Semitism, though they did not eliminate it.

Discrimination in Social Life

Nonviolent anti-Semitism was even more prevalent. Many social clubs were closed to Jewish members. Elite colleges and universities established quotas limiting the percentage of Jewish students who would be admitted. For instance, Harvard University's quota, adopted in the 1920s, limited Jews to 15 percent of the student body. In the twenty years from 1920 to 1940, the percentage of Jews in Columbia University's medical school fell from 50 percent to less than 7 percent, and in 1940 Jews had one-tenth the chance of admission to Cornell's medical school that non-Jews had. Discrimination was also common in employment, with as many as 20 percent of job openings in the 1950s requesting non-Jewish applicants. Jewish applicants were also disproportionately rejected for executive jobs at leading industrial corporations.

Organized Hate

Organized hate groups that espouse anti-Semitism still exist in the United States. One of these groups is Christian Identity, a conservative coalition of groups calling for a Christian nation and violence against Jews, blacks, and homosexuals. This group believes Jews are descended from Satan and are the enemies of all humanity. Other anti-Semitic groups include Nazis and Neo-Nazis, skinheads, white women's groups, and far-right conservative political groups. A number of these groups are Holocaust Revisionists, which means that they believe that the Nazi killings of 6 million Jews were invented by Allied governments or Zionist activists as propaganda, or else that Jews invented the Holocaust to get sympathy and enhance their ability to dominate world affairs. Some revisionists do accept the idea that the Nazis wanted to rid their lands of Jews but do not believe that concentration camps existed to kill their internees; others believe that the entire subject is a fiction. Some anti-Semitic groups have also blamed Jews for the terrorist attacks on September 11, 2001, even though those who committed the attacks were part of anti-Semitic groups. It is not only white supremacist groups that are anti-Semitic. There are organized anti-Semitic groups among African Americans, as well. The most well known of these is Louis Farrakhan's Nation of Islam. Claims made by black anti-Semitic groups have included the charge that Jewish doctors deliberately infect black children with HIV, that Jews themselves inspire genocide, and that Jews in Hollywood deliberately conspire to subjugate blacks.

Bias Crimes

Bias crimes and hateful acts committed against Jews by organized anti-Semitic and hate groups as well as by isolated individuals made up over 10 percent of all hate crimes reported to the FBI in the year 2001, and 57 percent of religion-related hate crimes. These crimes range from physical assaults to arson and vandalism (including spray painting swastikas and other symbols and messages of hate) of synagogues and private homes. In 2002, anti-Semitic bias crimes overall increased by 17 percent, but vandalism declined by 4 percent. Incidents on college campuses have also increased, and there is a large number of anti-Semitic Web sites and chat rooms on the Internet, some of which propagate anti-Semitic e-mail chains.

Public Opinion

According to a 1999 Gallup poll, 8 percent of American adults would not vote for a Jewish candidate for president if their party were to nominate one (as compared to 63 percent in 1937 and 18 percent in 1978), so there has been a decline in anti-Semitism with time. Jews are more electable than homosexuals (41 percent would not vote for the latter) or atheists (51 percent), and are on a par with women. However, Americans are more willing to vote

Removal of a spray-painted swastika at a Jewish cemetery in New Jersey, 1995.

AP/Wide World Photos.

for blacks, Baptists, Mormons, and Catholics. There are still private clubs, especially country clubs, that exclude Jews. And some colleges still try to limit the percentage of Jews in their student bodies, though the quotas they once used are now illegal. Instead, they look for geographic diversity and limit the number of students they admit from certain areas with high Jewish populations. However, there are instances where Jews must resort to court action to stop colleges or employers from discriminating against them. As a result of settlement agreements some colleges have been forced to establish special sensitivity training and learning centers to counter anti-Semitism on their campuses.

Anti-Semitism and Anti-Zionism

Some of the anti-Semitism in the United States today is related to the existence of Israel as the state of the Jewish people. The ongoing conflict in the region between Israel, its Muslim Arab neighbors, and the Palestinian people has led to events in the United States where Zionists (supporters of Israel as the homeland for the Jewish people) and Jews have been targeted by anti-Israel protesters. These events have been common at antiwar demonstrations, as well as on college campuses. In the United States, it is not only Muslims but a wide variety of people who are anti-Zionist. Zionism and Judaism, like anti-Semitism and anti-Zionism, are not synonymous, and it is possible for people to disapprove of Israel, Israeli policies, and the actions of the Israeli state without being anti-Semitic. Anti-Zionist feelings and actions, however, often turn into anti-Semitic feelings and actions because of the close connection between Jews and the state of Israel.

It is important to take note of the connections between anti-Semitism and other forms of racism and hatred. Many different forms of hatred spring from the same sources, as can be seen by the views espoused by the hate organizations discussed above. The continuing existence of anti-Semitism is not merely an annoyance in the life of Jewish Americans but also a legitimating of the practice of other forms of hate. Anti-Semitism is also tied to the anti-Americanism of international terrorist groups and to anti-Israel actions of many Palestinian and Muslim activists. While these different kinds of hate are separate entities, the links between them clarify the need to act against racism, prejudice, and discrimination as an interrelated set of beliefs and actions, rather than targeting individual groups or kinds of hate one at a time. Jews have long experienced the fact that when one source of hate is suppressed (for instance, Nazi Germany), another may spring up in its place (the anti-Jewish policies of Stalinist Russia).

The Jewish Reaction to Anti-Semitism

Jews in the United States have acted to combat anti-Semitism in many ways. They have organized groups such as the Anti-Defamation League, the American Jewish Committee, and the Simon Wiesenthal Center that work to combat anti-Semitic activity both in the United States and around the world. These organizations conduct research on the current state of anti-Semitism, educate individuals and governments about what can be done, and contact the news media to ensure fair reporting about anti-Semitic incidents. Jewish organizations, including those whose primary mission is combating anti-Semitism as well as others, also conduct political activism in favor of laws and policies that help reduce anti-Semitism. Some of these laws include those against hate crimes, prohibiting prayer in schools, and requiring education about tolerance. Many of these laws are helpful to other minority ethnic and religious groups in the United States. Jewish groups also support actions to ensure diversity in higher education, though some affirmative action policies are not supported because of their similarity to the discriminatory quota systems that once kept Jewish students out of elite institutions. Rarely, Jews have turned to terrorist activity to try prevent anti-Semitic activity or to retaliate for actions that have already been taken. The most notable group of this kind is the Jewish Defense League. However, most Jewish groups that work against anti-Semitism are nonviolent and are eager to work with other ethnic and religious groups to further civil rights and nondiscrimination for everyone.

See also American Nazi Party (ANP); Anti-Defamation League of B'nai Brith (ADL); Aryan Nations; Black Anti-Semitism; Ford, Henry; Frank, Leo; Jewish-

Black Conflicts; Jewish Defense League (JDL); Ku Klux Klan (KKK); Zionist Occupied Government.

Further Reading

Carr, Steven Alan. *Hollywood and Anti-Semitism: A Cultural History Up to World War II*. Cambridge: Cambridge University Press, 2001.

Chesler, Phyllis. *The New Anti-Semitism: The Current Crisis and What We Must Do About It*. San Francisco: Jossey-Bass Publishers, 2003.

Jaher, Frederic Cople. *A Scapegoat in the New Wilderness: The Origins and Rise of Anti-Semitism in America*. Cambridge, MA: Harvard University Press, 1994.

Lipstadt, Deborah E. *Denying the Holocaust: The Growing Assault on Truth and Memory*. New York: Free Press, 1993.

Mayo, Louise A. *The Ambivalent Image: Nineteenth-Century America's Perception of the Jew*. Rutherford, NJ: Fairleigh Dickenson University Press, 1988.

Slavin, Stephen L., and Mary A. Pratt. *The Einstein Syndrome: Corporate Anti-Semitism in America Today*. New York: World Publishers, 1982.

Sleznick, Gertrude Jaeger, and Stephan Steinberg. *The Tenacity of Prejudice: Anti-Semitism in Contemporary America*. New York: Harper & Row, 1969.

Mikaila Mariel Lemonik Arthur

Arab American Institute (AAI)

The Arab American Institute (AAI) was established in 1985 to represent the interests of Americans of Arab descent in politics, notably on Capitol Hill, and to foster their civic and political empowerment through policy, research, and public affairs services. AAI offers training and strategies for candidates who want to run for political office at the local, state, and national level; conducts constituency research; and monitors U.S. opinion and policy makers on issues that are of concern to Arab Americans, including the U.S. government's Middle East policy. Like most Middle Eastern advocacy organizations, AAI's agenda focuses on both domestic and foreign policy issues. Since its inception, AAI has been active in debunking stereotypes of Arabs and Arab Americans in the media and the general public. To this end, it has published a pamphlet entitled "Arab Americans: Making a Difference," which highlights the lives of prominent Arab Americans, such as former Senate Majority Leader George Mitchell, former secretary of health and human services Donna Shalala, and the Green Party presidential candidate in 2000 and 2004, Ralph Nader.

After the events of September 11, 2001, AAI was, like most Arab and Muslim American organizations, overwhelmed with the increased demand for its services in fighting the backlash. Its president, James Zogby, appeared regularly on the media, advocating for his constituents and educating the American public about Arab Americans and the Arab world. AAI collaborated with civil rights groups and other sympathizers in fighting the various government initiatives that targeted Arab Americans, especially immigrants. It also tried to increase its membership across the nation by energizing chapters and establishing new ones. These chapters were especially visible in organizing "know your rights" forums for those in the immigrant communities, encouraging them to register to vote and become more active politically.

Since 1996, AAI's nonprofit arm, the Arab American Institute Foundation, has been supporting public information and education programs and sponsoring outreach. The goal of the Foundation is to promote a fuller and deeper public understanding of this ethnic community, its present and future goals, and its role in the ever-expanding diversity of America. The annual Kahlil Gibran: Spirit of Humanity Awards Gala in Washington, DC, is symbolic of the Foundation's mission. Named after the author of *The Prophet*, individuals and institutions that have demonstrated a profound commitment to values of equality, responsibility, understanding, and generosity are honored. Honorees have included Queen Noor of Jordan, rock star Sting, and the Aga Khan Foundation.

See also Arab Community Center for Economic and Social Services (ACCESS); Arab/Muslim American Advocacy Organizations, Responding to the Backlash; Government Initiatives after the September 11, 2001, Attack on the United States; *Jihad*; Middle Easterners, Historical Precedents of Backlash against; Middle Easterners, Stereotypes of; Muslim Philanthropic Organizations, Closure of after September 11, 2001; Muslims, Prejudice and Discrimination against; Muslims, Terrorist Image of; September 11, 2001, Terrorism, Discriminatory Reactions to.

Mehdi Bozorgmehr and Anny Bakalian

Arab Community Center for Economic and Social Services (ACCESS)

Based in Dearborn, Michigan, the Arab Community Center for Economic and Social Services (ACCESS) is one of the oldest and largest Arab American support and advocacy organizations in the United States. ACCESS provides a range of social, legal, employment, health, and education services. In 1971, a group of community activists united around domestic issues, such as urban renewal, immigration discrimination, and the inclusion of Arab autoworkers in the union. They were also concerned about foreign policy in the Middle East, and the misrepresentation of Arabs in the media. They came together to establish ACCESS, electing George Khoury as the organization's first president. Today, ACCESS is an advocate for pan-Arab causes, promotes fairness in the Middle East, and works toward equity within the Arab American community. It tries to mainstream Arabic culture through its cultural-arts program, gives clients a chance to compete more equitably in the labor force through its youth and employment programs, and offers families greater prospects for healthy lives through its managed-care program.

ACCESS undeniably achieves its goal as the premier Arab American human services center. Its budget exceeds $10 million a year, its programs are comprehensive, it serves over 50,000 clients, and it comes into contact with about a quarter of a million people annually, and it has won recognition as a national leader among nonprofit organizations. Through national outreach programs, ACCESS is building a national network of Arab American organizations, trying to empower this ethnic community, especially the new immigrants. This goal has become particularly pressing in light of the backlash that followed the events of September 11, 2001.

See also Arab American Institute (AAI); Arab/Muslim American Advocacy Organizations, Responding to the Backlash; Government Initiatives after the September 11, 2001, Attack on the United States; *Jihad*; Middle Easterners, Historical Precedents of Backlash against; Middle Easterners, Stereotypes of; Muslim Philanthropic Organizations, Closure of after September 11, 2001; Muslims, Prejudice and Discrimination against; Muslims, Terrorist Image of; September 11, 2001, Terrorism, Discriminatory Reactions to.

Mehdi Bozorgmehr and Anny Bakalian

Arab/Muslim American Advocacy Organizations, Responding to the Backlash

Arab and Muslim immigrants have experienced discrimination throughout most of their history in the United States, but they did not mobilize politically or establish advocacy organizations until the 1970s. A number of factors influenced this timing. One is the change in immigration laws in 1965, which brought a new wave of highly educated Arab/Muslim immigrants who found U.S.–Middle East relations to be skewed. The oil boom in the 1970s increased further the large-scale influx of college students from oil-rich Arab countries and Iran. As educated immigrants, these newcomers were more responsive to events in the Middle East. Another factor is the emergence of ethnic identity politics in the post–civil rights era, which particularly benefited the native-born Arab Americans. Yet another factor that contributed to the creation of advocacy organizations is the series of violent attacks on American interests by various Middle Eastern groups after the 1970s, and the way these were played out by U.S. media and politicians, created stereotypes of Arab terrorists and by association of Arab/Muslim Americans. Finally, a new generation of civic-minded professionals of Arab descent has come of age.

Arab and Muslim American organizations were established to educate the American public about their ethnic origin and culture and to address the bias they saw in U.S. foreign policy. They mobilized their constituents to take a more active political and social role at the local and national levels. They started a variety of programs, published news reports, organized conferences, created internships, and encouraged their members to write to their congressional representatives on specific issues and support the campaigns of "friends" of the Middle East, at home and abroad.

Undoubtedly, the post–9/11 backlash was the biggest test for Arab/Muslim American advocacy organizations. The scale of hate crimes and government initiatives necessitated that most of these organizations, regardless of their original mission and goals, engage in some advocacy on behalf of their constituents. The ethnic/religious professional organizations responded to the backlash as experts in their specific field. For example, the Arab American Bar Association in Chicago issued a "white" or position paper about the backlash, members of the American Muslim Law Enforcement Officers Association made public appearances at community forums and town meetings to speak about relations with the police, and the American Arab Chamber of Commerce in Dearborn, Michigan, the largest Arab American enclave, educated its members to be proactive with their customers.

Many organizations grew in size, in the number of programs they offered and, in a few cases, even branched into social services. Much of this growth was the result of unprecedented grants they received from major American philanthropic organizations soon after the backlash started. Until September 11, Arab and Muslim American communities were generally not on the radar screen of the foundation world, and this is another reason for the foundations' reaction to the crisis. Several new organizations were established as a result of the gaps and needs observed after 9/11. Mostly young, U.S.-educated men and women who were able to galvanize their peers in the community established these organizations. For example, the Association of Patriotic Arab-Americans in the Military (APAAM) was created by a U.S. marine of Arab descent.

The goal of most Arab/Muslim American organizations was to mobilize their respective communities. They encouraged their members to be politically savvy, know their rights, and exercise them. They organized public forums and town hall meetings, offering "know your rights" presentations by public officials and experts. For example, in Brooklyn, New York, home to many immigrants of Arab descent, various groups hosted about a dozen such events in the eighteen months following 9/11. Voter-registration campaigns became more frequent in this population as well, and young, second-generation activists led the way as volunteers. The Network of Arab-American Professionals (NAAP), New York chapter, was exemplary in strategically canvassing New York City's five boroughs, as well as New Jersey, to register voters.

A major emphasis of almost all the Arab/Muslim American advocacy organizations, irrespective of their mission, was to educate the mainstream American public about Islam, Arabs, and the Middle East. Some undertook long-term, labor-intensive projects. For example, the Council on American Islamic Relations (CAIR) launched the "library project" and solicited sponsors to donate to local libraries a set of recommended books about Islam. A year after the launch of this project, about half of the libraries in the major states where Arabs and Muslims reside in large number had received books on Islam.

No matter how successful these organizations were, they could not possibly meet their mission without building coalitions with civil rights/liberties organizations, interfaith initiatives, and other advocacy organizations, both within the same ethnic/religious groups and with others. They also established ties with government officials and agencies at the local and national level. Organizations located in Washington, DC, that serve the national interests of Arab/Muslim Americans tended to focus on policy issues. Many had a government-affairs officer or staff person devoted to meeting with congressional leaders and staffers and other government officials, but almost all of them allocated a proportion of their budget and time to policy.

Overall, the Arab/Muslim American advocacy organizations scrambled to meet the challenge by relying on material and connections they had already established. Yet they were also transformed, branching into uncharted territory and forging new ties. Yet, no matter how well established and endowed some of these organizations were, they were overwhelmed and stretched by the exponential increase in demand for their services, participation in public events, interaction with the media, and their need to establish coalitions. It is noteworthy that most of the Arab/Muslim American advocacy organizations successfully managed to walk a fine line as they addressed two somewhat contradictory goals: expressing loyalty to the United States and proving their patriotism and, at the same, defending their constituents against government initiatives.

In the post–9/11 era, if there is a silver lining to this otherwise sad episode in American history, it is an attempt on the part of the American public to better understand Arab culture and the Muslim faith. Here, too, representatives of advocacy organizations played a role in disseminating knowledge. They distributed books and other publications, participated in interfaith events, and appeared in schools, libraries, churches, and temples. It is remarkable that many ordinary Americans were receptive and even went out of their way to show tolerance and understanding.

See also American-Arab Anti-Discrimination Committee (ADC); Arab American Institute (AAI); Arab Community Center for Economic and Social Services (ACCESS); Council on American Islamic Relations (CAIR); Government Initiatives after the September 11, 2001, Attack on the United States; *Jihad*; Middle Easterners, Historical Precedents of Backlash against; Middle Easterners, Stereotypes of; Muslim Philanthropic Organizations, Closure of after September 11, 2001; Muslims, Prejudice and Discrimination against; Muslims, Terrorist Image of; September 11, 2001, Terrorism, Discriminatory Reactions to.

Mehdi Bozorgmehr and Anny Bakalian

Archie Bunker Bigotry

Archic Bunker was a television sitcom character featured in the controversial, groundbreaking show *All in the Family*, which was created by writer-producer Norman Lear and inspired by the British television series *Til Death Do Us Part*. ABC originally commissioned the pilot but then rejected it. Lear took the show to CBS, and it premiered there on January 12, 1971; its final episode aired in 1979. The show sparked controversy with its handling of previously taboo subjects, such as breast cancer, impotence, and rape, and with its handling of hot political topics, including the Vietnam War, gun control, and racism. For many Americans, Bunker personified the image of an endearing bigot. In the show, Bunker, played by actor Carroll O'Connor, depicted an uneducated, prejudiced, conservative, white, working-class guy, who lived at 704 Houser Street in the Corona neighborhood of Queens, New York, with his sweet, bumbling wife, Edith (whom he called Dingbat), his daughter Gloria, and his ultra-liberal, Polish American son-in-law Mike Stivic, a graduate student (also known as Meathead). An unabashed bigot, Bunker loathed virtually every minority group and, in unrestrained diatribes, called blacks "jungle bunnies," "coons," and "spades," Puerto Ricans "spics," and Chinese people "chinks." Though he loathed minorities, they were often nearby, both at work and at home. His next-door neighbors, the Jeffersons, were a black family. Louise Jefferson was one of Edith's close friends, while her husband, George, the owner of a small dry-cleaning business, despised Archie; their son, Lionel, a good friend of Mike's, often visited the house and enjoyed teasing Archie about his racist beliefs. The Jeffersons later spun off into their own series, building on the premise that the family's dry-cleaning business had produced enough wealth for them to move into tony Manhattan. A 1972 episode, in which the black singer/dancer Sammy Davis Jr. kissed Archie, is often cited as a historic moment in American race relations.

When the show was launched, network executives, including CBS president William Paley, who was Jewish, were so concerned about its potentially offensive nature that the network took the unusual step of introducing it with the following disclaimer: "The program you are about to see . . . seeks to throw a humorous spotlight on our frailties, prejudices and concerns. By making them a source of laughter we hope to show—in a mature fashion—just how absurd they are." While some viewers complained about its "liberal bent," the show, which was written by Lear and Bud Yorkin, also Jewish, turned out to be extremely popular and was ranked number one in ratings for five consecutive years, becoming an anchor for the CBS network. Further expressions of the show's success were an "Archie for President" campaign launched in 1972 and the enshrinement of "Archie's chair," a prop in which he regularly sat in the show, at the Smithsonian Institute in Washington, DC.

Although the show received much critical and popular praise for its frank, humorous handling of emotionally and politically charged topics, some scholars criticized it for reinforcing prior prejudices and stereotypes. By presenting Bunker as a cultural archetype, the series can be seen as inadvertently validating such beliefs. Black psychologist Alvin Poussaint condemned the show, saying its "disarming" nature was its danger: "Blacks, for their own survival, should be in a posture of being very angry with bigots." Television executives commissioned a study on the show's impact, hoping to prove its claim that the show promoted positive race relations; but when the study's researchers concluded otherwise, saying that the show in fact reinforced bigoted beliefs, television executives ended up ditching the report's findings.

After the show ended in 1979, the creators reshaped the focus, centering a new show on a bar in Astoria, Queens, that Archie purchased after his retirement, and it renamed the show "Archie's Place," which aired until 1983. Other spinoff series from the show included *Maude*, whose title character, a liberally minded feminist played by actress Beatrice Arthur, was first introduced as Edith's cousin on *All in the Family*. *The Jeffersons* and *Gloria* were other spinoffs. When O'Connor died in June 2001, he was remembered as television's Archie Bunker, despite a varied career that spanned films and stage.

See also Television and Racial Stereotypes; Television Drama and Racism.

Rose Kim

Aryan Nations

Aryan Nations is one of the best-known white nationalist and anti-Semitic organizations in the U.S. Christian Identity movement. Founded in the 1970s by Richard G. Butler, Aryan Nations traces its roots to Wesley Swift, a Klan organizer and leader of a Los Angeles church, the Anglo-Saxon Christian Congregation. Upon Swift's death, Butler declared his Church of Jesus Christ Christian to be the Congregation's direct descendent and later formed the Aryan Nations for the protection of the white race from Jews and race-mixers. Aryan Nations headquarters was established in Hayden Lake, Idaho, on a twenty-acre wilderness site. From this base, Butler and his followers hoped to create an exclusively white "national racist state" in the Pacific Northwest. The group holds annual summer festivals, called the World Congress of Aryan Nations, designed to recruit members and build alliances with other white nationalist, neo-Nazi organizations.

The Christian Identity movement, of which Aryan Nations is a part, is a racist and anti-Semitic religious sect whose theology purports that the Lost Tribes of Israel settled in Britain. Whites are their true descendants. Others (today's Jews) are impostors, the offspring of the seed of Satan, who seek to rob white Christians of their birthright. Blacks and other people of color are considered to be less than human. The Christian Identity ideology has been adopted by many in other neo-Nazi and racist organizations. Aryan Nations has struggled in recent years, in large part as a result of losing a $6.3 million lawsuit in September

Richard Butler, center, founder of the Aryan Nations organization, at an Aryan Nations rally, 1999.

AP/Wide World Photos.

2000. Since then the group has splintered into smaller regional factions, with the Idaho group taking the name Aryan National Alliance.

See also Ku Klux Klan (KKK); White-Supremacist Movement in the United States; White-Supremacist Underground.

Kenneth J. Guest

Asian American Legal Defense and Education Fund (AALDEF)

Founded in 1974, the New York–based Asian American Legal Defense and Education Fund (AALDEF) was the first organization on the East Coast to address the legal rights of Asian Americans. Over the years, AALDEF established itself as a leader on issues of voting rights, anti-Asian violence, labor and tenant rights, immigrant concerns, and most recently, the effects of 9/11 on the Asian American community in New York.

In 1985 AALDEF negotiated the first ever agreement with the New York City Board of Elections to provide Chinese-speaking voters with bilingual materials and assistance. In 1995, under terms of the federal Civil Rights Act, AALDEF successfully campaigned for the full translation of ballots in New York City into Chinese and English. Defending the rights of low-income tenants in Chinatown, an AALDEF lawsuit in 1986 blocked construction of a twenty-one-story luxury condominium. In the decision, *Chinese Staff and Workers Association v. City of New York*, the New York Court of Appeals required an impact assessment of new development on small businesses and low-income tenants, establishing a legal foundation for preserving low-cost housing.

AALDEF's work for immigrant labor rights and against sweatshops has included workers' rights clinics and free legal assistance to garment and restaurant workers. In 1997, AALDEF successfully represented striking workers at Chinatown's Jing Fong Restaurant—one of the largest in New York—winning a $1.1 million settlement to recoup skimmed tips, unfair wages, and unpaid overtime. After 9/11, AALDEF has represented the New York Asian population, managing legal and social-service claims, representing detainees, and documenting and advocating for victims of hate crimes, particularly South Asians and Filipinos.

See also Asian Americans, Perceptions of as Foreigners; Asian Americans, Violence against; Asian Americans for Equality (AAFE); Pan-Asian Solidarity.

Kenneth J. Guest

Asian Americans, Discrimination against

Asian Americans were subjected to formal discrimination by the government until the mid-1960s. Anti-Asian laws introduced during the period considerably limited the civil liberties of Asian Americans in three major areas of their lives: immigration, naturalization, and land ownership. Civil rights legislation was passed in the 1960s, but discrimination against Asian Americans still persists in many areas of society.

First, Asians encountered a more rigid form of discrimination in terms of their immigration to the United States and naturalization. In 1882, Congress passed the notorious Chinese Exclusion Act to ban the immigration of Chinese laborers, making the Chinese the only national-origin group singled out for exclusion from the United States. Following that measure, the U.S. government took a number of others to ban or restrict Asian immigration. The restrictive measures include the Gentlemen's Agreement of 1908, the Immigration Act of 1917 (the Asiatic Barred Zone), and the National Origins Act of 1924. The National Origins Act was passed mainly to restrict immigration from southern and eastern European countries, but it also banned Asian immigration by providing for the permanent exclusion of any alien not eligible for citizenship. The McCarran-Walter Act of 1952 loosened the restriction of Asian immigration by setting an immigrant quota of 105 for each Asian and Pacific Triangle country.

The 1790 naturalization act limited citizenship to "free white persons." Based on this act, Asian immigrants in the late nineteenth century and half of the twentieth were not eligible for naturalization. In 1922, the opinion for the U.S. Supreme Court case *Ozawa v. United States* declared that Japanese people were not eligible for naturalized citizenship because, while the definition of *whiteness* was unclear in the 1790 naturalization law, they were not "Caucasian." However, in 1923 when an East Indian immigrant, Bhagat Singh Thind, claimed his American citizenship based on his standing as a "Caucasian," the Supreme Court stated that any persons of East Indian descent were "aliens ineligible to citizenship" because, while technically designated as Caucasian, they were not "white." In 1946, the Luce-Celler Act finally granted the right of naturalization to East Indians and Filipinos; yet many other Asian groups were still excluded from American citizenship until the passage of the McCarran-Walter Act of 1952.

Taking advantage of their noncitizen status, a number of states passed land laws in the first half of the twentieth century to prevent Asian immigrants from owning or leasing land. In 1913 California authorized the Alien Land Act, which was amended in 1920 and 1923 to completely exclude Asians from owning and leasing any forms of property in California. Washington and Louisiana passed similar laws in 1921, followed by other states; for example, Idaho, Montana, and Oregon in 1923 and Kansas in 1925. In 1952, in *Sei Fujii v. the State of California*, the California supreme court finally found the Alien Land Law unconstitutional.

During World War II, approximately 120,000 Japanese Americans, including U.S.-born Japanese citizens, who had settled in the West Coast states (other than Hawaii) were incarcerated in internment camps. The ostensible reason for their interment was that Japanese American could work as spies in the war against Japan, but the true reasons were racial prejudice against Japanese/Asian Americans and white farmers' jealousy of Japanese immigrants' success in farming in California. Although the United States was fighting against Germany and Italy, as well as Japan, during World War II, neither Italian nor German Americans were interned. The internees suffered enormous financial damages and humilations. The interment also signaled to Japanese and Asian Americans that they were not going to be accepted as full American citizens.

In 1964, Congress finally passed civil rights laws that prohibited racial dis-crimination against minorities in public facilities, government programs, and employment. Although these new policies made all types of racial discrimi-nation illegal, discrimination against Asian Americans has persisted in the post–civil rights era. For example, when the proportion of Asian American students increased significantly in the 1980s, the University of California sys-tem and other private universities used a number of measures to restrict the number of Asian American students. Many Asian Americans encounter the "glass ceiling" problem in achieving promotion to upper management or into a prominent position in a company. As a result, Asian Americans are severely underrepresented in positions involving authority and power, although they have a significantly higher overall educational level than white Americans.

See also Alien Land Laws on the West Coast; Chinese Exclusion Act of 1882; Gentlemen's Agreement of 1908; National Origins Act of 1924.

Further Reading

Okihiro, Gary Y. *Margins and Mainstreams: Asians in American History and Cul-ture*. Seattle: University of Washington Press, 1994.

Takaki, Ronald. *Strangers from a Different Shore: A History of Asian Americans*. New York: Little, Brown, 1989.

Wu, Frank H. *Yellow: Race in America Beyond Black and White*. New York: Basic Books, 2002.

Zia, Helen. *Asian American Dreams: The Emergence of an American People*. New York: Farrar, Straus and Giroux, 2000.

Etsuko Maruoka-Ng

Asian Americans for Equality (AAFE)

Although the civil rights movement, which emerged in the 1950s, was pri-marily fueled by African Americans and their supporters, it was responsible for prompting political awareness in other communities of color as well. One of the first organized efforts toward Asian American empowerment was initi-ated when the community members in New York City were angered by a con-struction firm publicly expressing its intention not to hire Asian American workers for a federally funded project in Chinatown in 1974. In response to the firm's argument that Asian Americans lacked physical strength for con-struction work, a group of Asian American community members founded a volunteer organization, which later became Asian Americans for Equality (AAFE), to protest against the construction firm's hiring policy. This prompted the firm to establish a policy not to discriminate against workers of color. In-spired by this success, AAFE has devoted much of its energy to protesting against housing discrimination faced by Asian Americans.

Today, AAFE has grown to serve as an advocate for the rights of Asian Amer-icans and other people of color and immigrants throughout the city of New York. On the one hand, AAFE has expanded its campaigns against injustice, and it now deals not only with housing and employment discrimination but also with discriminatory public policies and practices, such as racial biases in criminal justice and immigration procedures. On the other hand, the organization provides hands-on financial, legal, and educational support for households of color and businesses owned by people of color, to facilitate their efforts toward realizing their American Dreams.

See also Asian American Legal Defense and Education Fund (AALDEF); Asian American, Discrimination against; Asian Americans, Perceptions of as Foreigners; Asian Americans, Violence against; Pan-Asian Solidarity.

Daisuke Akiba

Asian Americans, Perceptions of as Foreigners

A common perception of Asian Americans is that they are foreigners or not real Americans. This perception is so prevalent that all Americans of Asian descent are virtually viewed and treated as "perpetual foreigners" because of their physical appearance. There are countless instances. Many U.S.-born Asians, including those who have been in the United States for several generations, are often asked by their new acquaintances such questions as, "Your English is excellent. Where did you learn it?" and "How long have you been in this country?" These questions seem neutral or even complimentary but in fact are offensive, because they imply that the questionees are foreign. In the 1998 Winter Olympic Games in Nagano, Japan, Tara Lipinski won the gold medal in the ladies' figure-skating competition, and Michelle Kwan took the silver medal. After the competition, MSNBC published the following headline on the Internet: "American Beats Out Kwan." This headline implies that Tara Lipinski is an American because she is white, but Michelle Kwan is not because she is of Asian descent. Except for appearance, Kwan, who was born and raised in Torrance, California, was no different than other seventeen-year-old American teenagers. This was not accidental. On February 2002, also after the Winter Olympics, the *Seattle Times* published the headline "Hughes Good as Gold, American outshines Kwan. . . ." In May 2001, Congressman David Wu and his Asian American staffer Ted Lieu were not allowed into the Department of Energy building even after presenting their congressional IDs. They were repeatedly asked their citizenship and country of origin. It took fifteen minutes for them to get a supervisor to let them in. An Italian American congressman went to the same building the next day, and no questions were asked. These examples show the deep consciousness or subconsciousness of some people that Asian Americans are not Americans.

The underlying cause of the perpetual foreigner perception is racism, and it has had an adverse impact on Asian Americans. It can reduce the trust of the public in Asian Americans, weaken their political empowerment, and increase the likelihood of discrimination and violence against members of this community.

See also Asian American Legal Defense and Education Fund (AALDEF); Asian Americans, Discrimination against; Asian Americans, Violence against; Asian Americans for Equality (AAFE); Fu Manchu; Pan-Asian Solidarity.

Philip Yang

Asian Americans, Violence against

Of all Asian ethnic groups, Chinese Americans have the longest history—150 years—of immigrating to the United States. After the Chinese were excluded from immigration in 1882, Japanese, Filipinos, Indians, and Koreans immigrated to Hawaii or California at different time periods, until Asian immigration was totally banned in 1924. These Asian immigrant groups experienced discrimination and violence under different social circumstances. To some degree, this sequential immigration of one Asian group at a time made Asian Americans more vulnerable to violence within American society. At the same time, all Asian Americans were treated as one homogenous group, and thus all groups suffered prejudice directed against a particular Asian group. Sources of violence against all immigrant Asian ethnic groups were identical: job competition and other forms of economic conflict, and Americans' prejudice against Asian Americans. Because of their physical differences, Asian Americans, including U.S.-born children, have been treated largely as perpetual foreigners. The combination of these factors under certain social circumstances often sparked violence, in various forms, against Asian Americans.

Throughout the second half of the nineteenth century and the early twentieth century, it was mainly Chinese and Japanese Americans who became the target of violence. Chinese immigrants initially were welcomed because of severe labor shortages in California in the 1850s and 1860s. When economic conditions in California turned bad in the 1870s and 1880s, however, white workers had to compete with Chinese workers for jobs. Chinese workers were then threatened, beaten, killed, or driven out of towns. For example, in Los Angeles in 1871, about twenty Chinese workers were hanged or burned to death. In 1887, thirty-one Chinese gold miners were robbed and murdered in Hells Canyon on the Idaho and Oregon border. In San Francisco, Chinese immigrants were forcefully driven to an obscure, small area of the city.

Beginning in the early part of the twentieth century, it was Japanese immigrants and their descendants who experienced serious forms of violence. Although they had no legal right to own the land, they became successful farmers, in terms of both their cultivation of farmlands and their management of trucking farms. White farmers felt that their own economic survival was threatened, and their anger took the form of physical violence against Japanese Americans and, it can be argued, was a major reason behind the large-scale internment of Japanese Americans in various war camps at the beginning of World War II.

The 1965 revision of the restrictive American immigration law, which had previously placed a quota on the number of immigrants allowed into the United States, opened up immigration opportunities for people from various parts of Asia. Indeed, the revised law led to the diversification of Asian ethnic groups immigrating to the United States, and the total number of Asians in the United States multiplied rapidly. The 2000 U.S. census indicated that Asian Americans accounted for 3.5 percent of the U.S. population. As numbers of these groups have increased, they have become visible in all aspects of American life. Their phenotypic and cultural differences from white Americans further increase their visibility, which, coupled with economic competition, has increased various forms of violence against Asian Americans.

Since the second half of the twentieth century, two additional factors have further aggravated violence against Asian Americans. First, the image of Asian Americans as a successful, or model, minority has generated white Americans' admiration, envy, jealousy, threat, and hatred toward Asian Americans. Such mixed emotions have resulted in subtle and complex forms of discrimination and violence against Asian Americans. In Texas, for example, Vietnamese Americans' shrimp ships were attacked by nearby white shrimp-ship owners and their collaborators. Also, the concentration of some Asian American groups, notably Koreans, in small businesses in minority areas made them vulnerable to physical violence by local customers. Some Korean American business owners and employees in black neighborhoods in New York, Los Angeles, and other cities encountered physical violence by local residents in the 1980s and 1990s. During the 1992 Los Angeles riots about 2,300 Korean American–owned stores in South Central Los Angeles and Koreatown were partially or entirely destroyed by black and Latino rioters.

Second, in the global age, the international economic situation has also stimulated violent actions against Asian Americans. The U.S.-Japan trade imbalance, caused largely by the importation of Japanese cars in large quantities, in particular, has angered many Americans and intensified anti-Japanese and anti-Asian sentiments and violence. For example, in 1982 Vincent Chin, a twenty-seven-year-old Chinese American, was beaten to death by two unemployed white auto workers, who mistook him for being Japanese.

While the past violence against Asian Americans was often an open, collective behavior in the form of mob violence, today's violent actions against Asian Americans are often observed as the behavior of one or two individuals. For example, in 1989, Jim Loo, a Vietnamese American, was shot outside of a pool hall in Raleigh, North Carolina, by two white brothers who were strangers to him. Loo and his friends left the pool hall after enjoying several hours of playing pool. In Houston, Texas, on August 9, 1990, Hung Truong, a fifteen-year-old Vietnamese American boy, was walking down the street with three non-Asian American friends. Suddenly, two eighteen-year-old white boys got out of a passing car, shouting about white power, and severely beat Truong, who died the next day.

Many non-Asian Americans still consider Asian Americans a homogeneous group, and so the problem of victimization because of mistaken ethnic identity goes on. Asian Americans continue to be subjected to violence, though the forms it erupts into has become more varied and complex.

See also Asian American Legal Defense and Education Fund (AALDEF); Asian Americans, Discrimination against; Asian Americans for Equality (AAFE); Asian Americans, Perceptions of as Foreigners; Chin, Vincent; Japan Bashing; Japanese American Internment; Japanese Americans, Redress Movement for; Pan-Asian Solidarity.

Further Reading

Chan, Sucheng. *Asian Americans: An Interpretive History*. Boston: Twayne, 1991. See esp. chap. 3.

Hall, Patricia Wong, and Victor M. Hwang. *Anti-Asian Violence in North America: Asian American and Asian Canadian Reflections on Hate, Healing and Resistance*. Walnut Creek, CA: AltaMira, 2001.

United States Commission on Civil Rights. *Civil Rights Issues Facing Asian Americans in the 1990s* (Washington, DC: U.S. Government Printing Office, 1992).

Shin Kim and Kwang Chung Kim

Asiatic Barred Zone

On February 5, 1917, Congress passed a statute prohibiting all immigration from an area designated as the "Asiatic Barred Zone," which included various Southeast Asian (e.g., India) and Middle Eastern countries. This bill was designed to restrict all immigration of laborers from Asia; earlier (the Chinese Exclusion Act of 1882, which was later extended to include the Japanese) had essentially banned immigration of laborers from China and Japan. President Woodrow Wilson vetoed this bill, but Congress overrode his veto, and this bill went into effect as the law of the land.

However, from the White policymakers' perspectives, this statute, even in combination with others restricting immigration from Asia, did not sufficiently control the presence of Asians in the United States. This allegedly led to the introduction of the Immigration Act of 1924, which prevented Asian laborers not only from becoming American citizens but also from entering the United States altogether.

See also Chinese Exclusion Act of 1882.

Daisuke Akiba

Asiatic Exclusion League (AEL)

In 1905, white nativist labor unions led the formation of the Japanese and Korean Exclusion League, later called the Asiatic Exclusion League (AEL). After the passage of the Chinese Exclusion Act of 1882, Japanese laborers began to replace Chinese in agriculture and urban trades. As a result, Japanese and Chinese came to be seen as a single "Asian" population whose willingness to work for low wages threatened the jobs and wages of white workers. Adding to the rising anti-Japanese and anti-Asian sentiment and the sense of competition in the early twentieth century was Japan's emergence as an Asian military and economic power. In this context, white workers spearheaded the anti-Japanese movement, conducting boycotts of Japanese businesses and denouncing Japanese workers at mass meetings and rallies. The AEL quickly became a leading voice in the anti-Asian movement. In the politic arena, the AEL lobbied for legislation to extend the Chinese Exclusion Act to Japanese and Koreans. Ideologically, the AEL promoted the idea that the Caucasian and Asiatic races could not assimilate and that to preserve Caucasian racial purity in America, Asian immigration must be stopped. The work of organizations such as the AEL contributed to the growing anti-immigrant sentiments that culminated in the restrictive National Origins Act of 1924, which prohibited most immigration to the United States from countries outside western and northern Europe.

See also Chinese Exclusion Act of 1882; Gentlemen's Agreement of 1908; National Origins Act of 1924.

Kenneth J. Guest

Assimilation Theory

Assimilation theory is a theory describing and explaining the process of assimilation—the blending together culturally, socially, psychologically, and biologically—that eventually occurs when diverse groups have contact with each other in a multiethnic society. This homogenization is a process of boundary reduction and a process of losing racial and ethnic distinctions. Theories of assimilation vary in their focus and in the explanations they provide. Two assimilation theories, Park's race-relations cycle and Gordon's theory of assimilation, have been influential in explaining intergroup relations.

Robert Park was one of the first theorists to suggest a cycle of race relations through which new immigrant groups would pass, a sequence of stages leading eventually to full assimilation. According to Park, the race relations cycle takes the form of "contacts, competition, accommodation and eventual assimilation." The cycle is progressive and irreversible. Customs regulations, immigration restrictions, and racial barriers may slacken the tempo of the movement or halt it altogether for a time, but the cycle cannot change its direction. He maintained that this four-stage cycle is a universal process; that is, it pertains to race relations everywhere, not just to those of the United States.

Critics of Park's theory of the race-relations cycle theory have pointed out that such a cycle may describe fairly well the experiences of most white European immigrant groups in the United States but that it does not represent the experiences of the groups with distinctive physical markers who came to America either voluntarily or involuntarily. The experiences of African Americans and Native Americans are clear cases of groups not following his race-relations cycle.

Milton Gordon also contributed to an understanding of the assimilation process. He argued that multiple processes of assimilation occur to different degrees in different dimensions, that assimilation is not a single, distinct linear process. He identified seven different areas of assimilation: cultural, structural, marital, psychological, attitudinal, behavioral, and civic. This process is neither inevitable nor sequential. Any particular group may remain indefinitely at any one of these stages. According to Gordon, the cultural and structural stages of assimilation are the most important. Cultural assimilation refers to the adoption of cultural patterns of the dominant, or host, group by the subordinate groups. Structural assimilation, according to Gordon, refers to the integration of the subordinate immigrant group into the social institutions of the dominant group, especially at the primary group level. In other words, when subordinate groups, such as new immigrant groups, are well blended into cliques, clubs, friendships, and other primary social institutions, we may say that structural assimilation has occurred. Gordon argued that structural assimilation at the primary level is the key to all subsequent assimilation. Once structural assimilation has occurred, either simultaneously with or subsequent to acculturation, Gordon claimed that the other types of assimilation would naturally follow. It is possible, according to Gordon, that a group assimilates culturally but remains separate structurally.

Gordon's theory of assimilation, too, has been criticized on several different points. One serious shortcoming of his theory lies in its understanding of structural assimilation as entailing interaction with the dominant group only at the primary level. Structural assimilation, however, should occur at the secondary institutional level as well as at the primary level in intergroup relations. In other words, the integration of new immigrant groups in the areas of education, employment, and the political sector is crucial to determining eventual assimilation in other dimensions.

Both theorists place less emphasis on the situational variables affecting the assimilation process. But one important fact related to assimilation in the United States is that different groups encounter a variety of experiences during the process of assimilation, and many factors can affect the degree and forms of assimilation. Some of these factors are how and when a group enters a society, its size and dispersion, its cultural similarity to the dominant group, and its physical distinctiveness. For instance, when a large number from an immigrant group enter a society during a short period of time, are concentrated in certain geographic areas, and practice cultural patterns, such as language and religion, that are different from those of the dominant group or groups, they are less likely to assimilate. One of the key determining factors of assimilation in American society has been physical differences from the dominant group. When dominant groups do not allow subordinate groups to assimilate, those groups remain separate.

Further Reading

Gordon, Milton M. *Assimilation in American Life*. New York: Oxford University Press, 1964.

Park, Robert E. *Race and Culture*. New York: The Free Press, 1964.

Heon Cheol Lee

Aversive Racism

See Racism, Aversive versus Dominative.

B

Back-to-Africa Movement

The Back-to-Africa movement is a mass global movement of people of African heritage to establish their own nation-state on the continent of Africa. The movement saw a nation-state of Africans as the only viable solution to racial oppression in the United States and colonialism elsewhere in the world. In the early nineteenth century, Paul Cuffe (1759–1817) organized a movement to send African Americans back to Africa in an effort to establish an African American colony in Africa. But it was not until the 1920s, under the leadership of Marcus Garvey (1887–1940) that the Back-to-Africa Movement drew significant mass support not only from African Americans but also from Africans in the West Indies and the Caribbean. Inspired by the pan-African nationalism of the time, Garvey called for global solidarity of all Africans everywhere in promoting their economic independence, black entrepreneurship, self-government, and racial pride. Widespread disillusionment among African Americans after World War I provided a fertile ground for the African Redemption movement led by Marcus Garvey, also known as "Black Moses." To pursue the vision, Garvey founded the Universal Negro Improvement Association (UNIA) in his home country, Jamaica, in 1914, and organized a chapter in New York City shortly after arriving in the United States in 1916. By 1920 the UNIA had hundreds of chapters globally. The UNIA established the Black Star Line shipping company in 1919, later replaced by Black Cross Navigation and Trading Co., to foster pan-African trade and African Americans' resettlement in Africa. Despite unprecedented mass support, the movement failed because of intraorganizational conflict, mismanagement, and assaults both from other black leaders and the U.S. government. But his vision of African nationalism survived the failure to reincarnate in the Black Nationalist movement in the 1960s.

See also Garvey, Marcus.

Dong-Ho Cho

Bakke v. Regents of the University of California

See Regents of the University of California v. Bakke.

Barrios

Latinos are the largest minority in the United States, and 58 percent of this group are Mexican American. Many Latinos in the United States live in barrios (neighborhoods). Latino neighborhoods or communities dot the country from St. Paul, Minnesota, to San Antonio, Texas, and from New York to Los Angeles. Most barrios by far are populated with Chicanos, people of Mexican heritage, but significant numbers of Puerto Ricans and Dominicans live in New York City, Guatemalans in Houston, and Cubans in Miami. Barrios are not necessarily small ethnic enclaves. The Los Angeles barrio has an area of 193 square miles and a population of almost 2 million people.

Most barrios, like black ghettos, were spawned by racism. As the United States took control of the former Mexican territory before and after the Mexican-American War—including Texas, New Mexico, Arizona, and California—mob violence against Mexicans was not unknown. In fact, between 1848 and 1928, lynch mobs killed nearly 600 Mexicans as Anglos went about the task of "Americanizing" the new lands. Mexicans, especially mestizos (of "mixed blood"), were displaced from their land and left politically impotent. Landless and impoverished, they sought the only kinds of jobs they could get. Mexican men, thought to be lazy, turned to manual labor for survival, and Mexican women were seen to be good only for keeping house. Barrios sprung up around cities.

Mexicans poured into the United States after 1910 and up until the Depression, to escape the messy Mexican Revolution. During World War II and after, immigration again picked up as the United States tried to recruit Mexican workers through the Bracero Program. These new immigrants often found housing in the old barrios, and jobs in the cities or in agriculture. New barrios developed too, as did services and businesses within them. Barrios were separate, segregated societies. There were segregated public schools for Chicanos and Anglos, segregated restaurants, and segregated theaters. The legacy of separation based on race has left many barrios as impoverished neighborhoods defined by a culture of drugs and gangs.

See also Bracero Program; Chicano Movement; Mexican American Legal Defense and Education Fund; Mexican-American War; Mexican Americans, Prejudice and Discrimination against; Mexican Americans, Violence against; Mexican Illegals, Labor Exploitation of.

Benjamin F. Shearer

Bellingham Riots

On September 4, 1907, a Hindu community in Bellingham, Washington, was attacked by an angry mob of 500 white men, most of whom were locals working in the lumber mills. The mob invaded the homes of the "ragheads"—the racial slur they used to describe the people from South Asia—and dragged people onto the streets, beat them, and drove them from town. The attacks became known as the Anti-Hindu riots, or more generally, the Bellingham riots, and the conditions that gave rise to the Bellingham riots were part of a larger pattern of race riots across the United States during the early part of the twentieth century: angry white workers, concerned about losing their jobs to "non-white" immigrants, resorted to violence to exclude certain groups from the local job market. Racial conflict among workers was oftentimes encouraged by their employers, who purposely used "non-white" workers as strike breakers and scabs in attempts to bust unions. Many white union rank-and-filers were members of the Asian Exclusion League, whose motto was, "The preservation of the Caucasian race upon American soil."

In the 1890s, many South Asians—most of whom were Hindu—fled the exploitation of British colonial rule in India for the United States. Between 1899 and 1913 more than 7,000 "Hindus" settled in the Pacific Northwest, seeking work in booming lumber and railroad industries. Once there, Hindu immigrants faced the same kind of hostility by white workers and their unions in the lumber mills as Chinese workers faced in California. At the time, many unions practiced racial exclusion as a way to monopolize the best jobs in the area for their white members. When threats and intimidation against immigrant workers failed to drive them out of the industry, white workers resorted to violence.

But racial tensions did not come to violence in all communities. For example, Astoria, Oregon, was similar to Bellingham, Washington, in that the economy there was also based on the timber and railroad industries, but immigrants from South Asia were welcome there. According to a *Daily Astorian* article, dated April 26, 1976 (9B), one man was quoted as saying, "We were afraid of them [South Asians] at first, but my dad said, 'They have to make a living the same as the rest of us. We are foreigners too.'"

See also Asian Americans, Violence against; Los Angeles Riot of 1871; Race Riots; St. Louis Riot of 1917.

Michael Roberts

Bensonhurst Incident

On August 23, 1988, Yusef Hawkins, a sixteen-year-old black teenager, was fatally attacked by more than a dozen white youths in the heavily Italian American Bensonhurst neighborhood of Brooklyn, New York. Yusef and three of his friends were in the neighborhood to check out a used car that had been advertised. A mob of whites, on the lookout for a black boy who had been invited to the birthday party of one of their girlfriends, mistook Hawkins for the person they sought and beat him and his friends with bats; one man, carrying a gun, shot Hawkins to death. Coming just three years after the Howard Beach case, in which a young black man was killed while fleeing a pack of murderous white teenagers, the death of Hawkins once again inflamed racial tensions in New York City and drew national attention to the troubled state of the city's race relations. Black activists, such as the Rev. Jesse Jackson, spoke

The Rev. Al Sharpton and others march in Bensonhurst, New York, to protest the parole of a white man involved in the murder of Yusef Hawkins, June 6, 1998.

AP/Wide World Photos.

publicly about the assault, and the Rev. Al Sharpton acted as spokesman for the Hawkins family. Eight days after the murder, several thousand protesters marched in Bensonhurst on a "Day of Outrage." The protest drew counter-demonstrators and elicited violent reactions from white onlookers. The Bensonhurst incident was referenced in Spike Lee's film, *Do the Right Thing* (1989) and also was considered by many political analysts to have been a crucial factor in the defeat of three-term New York City mayor Ed Koch and the election of the city's first African American mayor, David Dinkins. Koch had accused black leaders and politicians of deepening tension with their protests, but Dinkins had argued that their reactions were justified and appropriate.

See also Hate Crimes; Howard Beach Incident; Jackson, Jesse.

Rose Kim

BIA

See Bureau of Indian Affairs (BIA).

Bigotry

See Archie Bunker Bigotry; Bigots, Types of; Fair-Weather Liberals.

Bigots, Types of

According to sociologist Robert K. Merton, active bigots are those who are racially prejudiced and discriminate. People often do not act as they believe, but active bigots are consistent in their racial attitudes and discriminatory behaviors. They discriminate against others because they are prejudiced. Merton proposed that racial prejudice and discrimination do not necessarily go together because the situational conditions, such as normative expectations and rewards, as well as one's racial prejudice, determine one's action (discrimination). It is highly probable that those who are prejudiced may not discriminate because of the situational conditions. By combining the existence or absence of racial prejudice and discrimination, Merton suggested four categories of people: prejudiced discriminators as all-weather bigots, prejudiced nondiscriminators as timid bigots, unprejudiced discriminators as fair-weather liberals, and unprejudiced nondiscriminators as all-weather liberals. These are conceptual types. In reality, people demonstrate different degrees of prejudice and discrimination.

Members of organizations such as the Ku Klux Klan or neo-Nazi parties in the United States exemplify active bigots. In the contemporary United States, many people are racially prejudiced but do not overtly discriminate against others because of the situational conditions, such as economic interests, social pressure, and outright illegality. Merton labels these people "timid bigots." An important implication of his typology for the reduction of racial discrimination is that we should focus on people's behavior, instead of their attitudes, by enforcing the laws.

See also Fair-Weather Liberals.

Further Reading

Merton, Robert K. "Discrimination and American Creed." In *Discrimination and National Welfare*, edited by R. M. MacIver, 99–126. New York: Institute for Religious and Social Studies, 1949.

Heon Cheol Lee

Bilingual Education

Bilingual education in the United States can be traced back to the eighteenth and nineteenth centuries in communities where German, French, Spanish, and other minority language speakers were concentrated (e.g., New Mexico, California, Louisiana, northern New England, the Midwest, and the East). However, bilingual education as a national policy did not emerge until 1968, as a result of the Bilingual Education Act (BEA) of 1968 enacted by Congress. This act legitimized bilingual education programs at the national level and allocated funds for teaching limited-English-proficiency (LEP) children of low-income families in their native languages while they were learning English. Over time, bilingual education programs have been expanded by a series of amendments to or reauthorization of the 1968 BEA.

Bilingual education means education in two languages. In the United States, this term describes a number of educational approaches using students' native language and English in instruction. There are four basic types of bilingual education programs.

(1) *Transitional bilingual education*. In this model, children learn school subjects (e.g., math, literature, arts, science, and social studies) in their native language while studying English in programs designed for second-language learners. The goal is to prepare students to enter mainstream English classrooms. (2) *English immersion*. The goal of this model is to assist students in achieving proficiency in English. Students are "immersed" in English, which is the language of instruction. Teachers deliver lessons in simplified English so that students learn English and academic subjects. (3) *Two-way bilingual education*. Its purpose is to help all students achieve proficiency in both English and their native language. Instruction is given in both languages. (4) *English as a Second Language*. This program uses a combination of methods to teach English to non-English-speaking students of different language backgrounds.

Bilingual education has been an issue of ongoing controversy. Proponents argue that bilingual education helps LEP students ease the transition to the regular English program; gives bilingual children advantages over monolingual children in cognitive skills, especially in the ability to analyze the form and content of language and knowledge; helps children develop language and literacy skills that are transferable to learning a second language, such as organization of a paragraph and arguments; and helps non-English-speaking students maintain their native language and culture. Opponents contend that bilingual education is not needed because, historically, non-English–speaking European immigrants in the late nineteenth and early twentieth centuries succeeded without federally sponsored bilingual education programs; because it slows down the transition of LEP students to the regular English program by totally or almost totally separating LEP students from other English-speaking children and by reducing the amount of time spent on learning English; and because it encourages ethnic separation and ethnic tribalism in schools and in society by reinforcing the loyalty of LEP students to their native languages and by delaying their integration into the English-speaking society.

In recent years, public sentiment against transitional bilingual education program has been rising. In 1997, California voters endorsed Proposition 227, which largely eliminated bilingual education in California public schools. In 2000, Arizona voters passed Proposition 203, an initiative similar to Proposition 227. In both states, the proportion of LEP students in bilingual education classes declined from about one-third to 11 percent after the initiatives became law. As in the cases of California and Arizona, Ron Unz, a Silicon Valley millionaire, also financed and launched campaigns in Colorado and Massachusetts that placed anti-bilingual-education initiatives on their state ballots. While Massachusetts voters ratified the ballot measure, Colorado voters rejected the initiative in their state.

Overall, available empirical evidence seems to provide some support for bilingual education as a proper education *option* for LEP students. Well-designed bilingual educational programs seem to be as effective as other methods in some learning settings, but there is no clear evidence that they are more effective than other programs. The controversy over bilingual education has more to do with social and political concerns than with pedagogical concerns. Bilingual education is a political issue as much as it is an educational one, maybe even more so. Some believe that whether to participate in a bilingual education program should be the choice of parents and students. In this vein, to achieve the maximum from bilingual education, educators ought to move in the direction of enrichment programs to make all students truly "bilingual."

See also California Ballot Proposition 227; English-Only Movement; *Lau v. Nichols*; Multiculturalism.

Further Reading

August, D., and E. E. Garcia. *Language Minority Education in the United States: Research, Policy, and Practice.* Springfield, IL: Charles Thomas, 1988.

Crawford, James. *Bilingual Education: History, Politics, Theory, and Practice.* 2nd ed. Los Angeles: Bilingual Education Services, 1991.

Philip Yang

Bilingual Voting

See Voting Rights Amendments of 1975.

Biological Racism

Biological racism refers to the idea that the races are biologically different and that some races are superior to others in intelligence and moral characteristics. Biological racism was most popular in the United States in the 1920s, when IQ tests were first developed. It also took the form of anti-immigrant reactions to the influx of non-Protestant immigrants from southern, central, and eastern European countries, the influx that peaked in the first decade of the twentieth century. Biological racism thus provided the intellectual justification for the Immigration Act of 1924, which drastically restricted immigration from these regions of Europe, as well as for the eugenics movement and antimiscegenation laws.

Madison Grant was the champion of the idea of biological differences among racial groups. In his 1916 book, *The Passing of the Great Race*, he argued that the races were in fact subspecies of man and that the "Nordic" race—those with light hair and eyes—was superior to "Negroid" and "Mongoloid" races. Grant argued against the idea that all people are created equal. Instead, he maintained that there were clear and immutable differences among the races that were reflected in physical attributes such as height, skin and eye color, and skull shape. He further argued that these physical characteristics were associated with spiritual, intellectual, and temperamental traits. He argued that the "white race"—the so-called great race of the title of his book—

was in jeopardy of being dominated by what he considered to be the inferior races.

A foundation of biological racism is the idea of hereditarianism. Hereditarianism dates back to the late nineteenth and early twentieth centuries, when Charles Darwin's ideas of evolution dominated much of the intellectual world. Darwin's theory of evolution posited that beneficial traits evolved through natural selection and that only the fittest species survive. This idea was later applied to human beings and called Social Darwinism. Social Darwinism held that people who were successful were fundamentally more "fit" than people who were not successful; that is, nature rewarded those who were biologically superior. The rich, therefore, were argued to be biologically different, and superior, from the poor overall.

Social Darwinists further argued that biologically inferior people passed that inferiority to their children. Similarly, they thought that biological superiority was also inherited. Based on this idea, Hereditarians of the late nineteenth and early twentieth centuries supported both limiting the reproduction of those thought to be biologically inferior and antimiscegenation laws that would prevent the race mixing they feared would degrade the white race. The attempt to limit reproduction of people deemed unfit—and in extreme cases such as Nazi Germany, the mass murder of such people to promote biological "purity"—is known as eugenics.

Social Darwinism has little to do with Darwin's ideas. Social Darwinism, particularly as it was understood in the Progressive Era, has more in common with the theories of Jean-Baptiste Lamarck. Lamarck, a French naturalist who achieved prominence during the early 1800s, developed a theory of evolution based on transmutation and the ability of each generation to inherit the traits acquired by its ancestors. Lamarck's theories had largely been discredited by the 1900s. Nonetheless, Social Darwinists such as Herbert Spencer and Sir Francis Galton had popularized the idea that human character is inherited. This social theory provided so-called scientific facts used to define the political debates over race, poverty, and immigration. One of the unique features about biological racism is its appeal to science to answer questions that normally are viewed as political or moral. Political and moral judgments are always subjective. Science is supposed to be objective. Biologically based arguments about racial differences can be particularly powerful because they claim to be objective fact. If specific racial groups are inherently inferior, for example, as some scientists at the turn of the century argued, then politicians who wanted to limit immigration could claim that what they were advocating was common sense, based on science, not political ideology.

In the early twentieth century, Lewis Terman, a Stanford University psychologist, popularized widespread IQ testing in the United States. Following the eugenicist movement of the time, Terman worried that individuals with low IQ scores could lower the quality of American "stock"—the biological fitness of the American population. As a result, he was a strong supporter of immigration restrictions and of sterilizing men and women with low IQ scores or other "undesirable" traits, such as mental illness. Like many eugenicists of the time, Terman believed that intelligence, morality, and other human traits were linked and heritable; therefore, he viewed limiting or eliminating the reproduction of people with those characteristics as sound goal for social policy.

Persuaded by the hereditary argument of Terman and other psychologists, the U.S. Congress passed the National Origins Act in 1924. A decade after the immigration act, fascism dominated much of Europe. Jewish refugees—one of the restricted groups—were turned away from the United States even though the total quota of immigrants had not been met. It has been estimated that 6 million southern, central, and eastern Europeans were barred from admission to the United States in the 1930s on the basis of their nationality or "race."

Eugenics and the argument that there are significant biological differences among the "races" began to become socially and politically unacceptable after World War II. The Nazis in Germany justified the holocaust on alleged biological inferiorities of Jews and other groups. The Nazi quest to produce a "super race" of so-called Aryans left many people deeply wary of claims that some "races" are biologically superior to others. Biological racism, however, has occasionally reemerged, particularly around social policies such as the Head Start program in the 1960s, which aims to improve the academic performance of low income, often minority, children.

In 1969, educational psychologist Arthur Jensen published a controversial article titled "How Can We Boost IQ and Scholastic Achievement?" In it, Jensen argued that different racial groups have different average intelligence levels. Based on tests that he performed in the 1960s on school children, Jensen divided cognitive ability into two groups, level-1, simple functioning, and level-2, higher-level thinking. Jensen argued that level-1 abilities were distributed across racial groups but that level-2 abilities were not. He wrote that Asians as a group have the highest level-2 abilities, and blacks the lowest, with whites in the middle. Jensen argued that the differences that he found reflected fundamental biological difference only slightly affected by environmental factors. Therefore, programs aimed at improving the academic functioning of minority children would have a very limited impact.

Some contemporary scholars continue to argue that race is a biological category and that differences in ability observed among racial groups are inborn. These researchers are often called racists by their critics, a label that they strongly resist and view as detrimental to open academic debate. One of the most prominent and controversial contemporary books on race and IQ is *The Bell Curve* (1994) by Richard J. Herrnstein and Charles Murray. Herrnstein and Murray, like the Social Darwinists of the late nineteenth and early twentieth centuries, argue that social hierarchies reflect real differences in ability. In other words, smarter people are more likely to be rich and powerful. Moreover, they argue that this is not just true for individuals that some groups, on average, have lower IQs than others. We therefore should not be surprised that some groups, notably blacks, do not do as well economically as other groups. Herrnstein and Murray do not argue that *all* blacks are less intelligent than whites. However, they do argue that there are real differences between the *average* cognitive abilities of East Asians, whites, and blacks that account for some of the social stratification that we see in the United States.

Critics of Herrnstein, Murray, and Jensen, notably Stephen Jay Gould, argue that their perspective ignores the well-documented effects of culture, racism, and testing bias in accounting for differences in IQ scores and social position. In his essay "Curveball," Gould accuses Murray and Herrnstein of omitting important facts, distorting statistics, and denying the political implications of their work. To Gould, much of the research on racial differences is politics disguised as science. Practitioners of this research, such as Jensen, counter that what they are doing is pure science that should not be constrained by political concerns. Being able to identify the biological basis of "racial" differences, however, depends on identifying the existence of distinct racial groups, which to date no one has been able to do. Race remains an important social and cultural category, but the most advanced genetic research casts doubt on the idea that it is a biological category. Thus, at this time observed differences in the IQ test scores and social status among the "races" cannot be attributed to biological differences.

Although biological racism typically targets blacks as an inferior race, this is not always the case. For example, in 1991 Leonard Jeffries, a professor of black studies at City College of New York (CUNY), made a controversial speech entitled "Our Sacred Mission." He claimed that Africans were the only true race and that all other races were a genetic mutation. He also argued that blacks were "sun people"—peace loving and community oriented—whereas whites were "ice people"—individualistic and aggressive. This idea is also based on the assumption of a biologically based racial hierarchy.

Gould has argued that the science behind biological racism is deeply flawed and that it serves primarily to perpetuate social inequality. In Gould's well-known book, *The Mismeasure of Man* (1981), he uses the example of intelligence testing and immigration policy to illustrate this point. At the end of the nineteenth century, Gould notes, H. H. Goddard, an early popularizer of intelligence testing in the United States, went to the Ellis Island Immigration Station in the New York Harbor, to test the various races. Groups that today are considered different ethnic groups, such as Italians and the Irish, were at that time thought of as different races. The concept of race—with its undertone of fundamental difference—implies much greater difference than the more culturally dependent concept of ethnicity does. Goddard found that, according to his measures, 83 percent of Jews and 79 percent of Italians were feeble-minded. Several years later Robert Yerkes, a Harvard professor, tested people drafted into the army and found that they had an average mental age of thirteen. Yerkes attributed the decline in American intelligence to the infusion of inferior races through immigration. He was particularly concerned about Jews, Italians, and Greeks—identified by Goddard as inferior races—and advocated a restriction on immigration to prevent inferior races from diluting the intelligence of Americans.

Yet, as Gould notes, the low scores obtained by Goddard on Ellis Island could easily be attributed to the fact that many of those being tested had never seen the objects that the tests asked about. For example, the tests had questions about bowling, pocket knives, and other objects that may not have been familiar to the new immigrants being tested. The testing environment was also less than ideal. An illiterate peasant from Italy might have great difficulty understanding a test being administered in a new country the moment he or she stepped off the boat, regardless of his or her intelligence.

The idea that there are biologically based differences among "the races" has lost credibility among academic researchers. Some researchers have argued that there is little reason to see "the races" as distinct biological groups at all. Classifications such as male and female, for example, have a biological basis. It is possible to identify an individual's sex based on his or her chromosomal makeup, if not through visual inspection. There is no comparable test for race. If there is no biological marker—only a socially based visual classification—then how can we claim this category is primarily biological?

Legally, race has been defined in many ways. In the South, there was the infamous "one-drop rule." This rule held that a person could not be classified as white if he or she had one drop of "black blood," meaning an African American blood relative. In the Jewish tradition, Judaism passes through the maternal line. The Japanese consider only those with Japanese paternity to be Japanese. Today, on the U.S. census form, a person can choose his or her own race. Race, most researchers agree, is a subjective, cultural category and not a biological one.

Biological racism is currently rejected by mainstream scientists, many of whom question whether there is any biological basis to the classification of "race" at all. In the popular debate, however, a weaker notion of biological differences among the races has persisted, and many people are surprised to learn that there is little biological basis to the idea of race.

See also Eugenics Movement; Intelligence and Standardized Tests, Cultural Biases in; Intelligence Tests and Racism; Jensen, Arthur; National Origins Act of 1924; Nordic Superiority; One-Drop Rule; *The Passing of the Great Race*; Racial Purity; Terman, Lewis.

Further Reading

Gould, Stephen Jay. "Curveball." *The New Yorker*, November 28, 1994.

———. *The Mismeasure of Man*. New York: Norton, 1981.

Grant, Madison. *The Passing of the Great Race*. New York: Charles Scribner's Sons, 1916.

Herrnstein, Richard J., and Charles Murray. *The Bell Curve: Intelligence and Class Structure in American Life*. New York: Free Press, 1994.

Jensen, Arthur R. "The Debunking of Scientific Fossils and Straw Persons." *Contemporary Education Review* 1, no. 2 (1982): 121–135.

———. "How Can We Boost IQ and Scholastic Achievement?" *Harvard Educational Review* 39, no. 1 (1969): 1–123.

Leslie, Mitchell. "The Vexing Legacy of Lewis Terman." *Stanford Magazine*, July/August 2000.

Robin Roger-Dillon

Black Anti-Semitism

Among certain segments of the African American population in the United States, anti-Semitism and anti-Semitic groups can claim a large following. Claims made by black anti-Semitic groups have included the charge that Jewish doctors deliberately infect black children with HIV, that Jews themselves inspire genocide, and that Jews in Hollywood deliberately conspire to subjugate blacks. This black anti-Semitism probably arose out of the need for African Americans to hold the perpetrators of slavery responsible for their actions, and the leaders of various groups arrived at the Jews as a suitable culprit. However, only about 50,000 Jews lived in the United States before 1850, and most of these lived in the North, where slavery was already outlawed. If they did live in the South, many were urban merchants rather than slave owners. The number of Jewish families who owned slaves is estimated at a few hundred, at the most. Jews in the United States in the civil rights era were particularly involved in the civil rights movement's efforts to address some of these very problems, though the emergence of Black Nationalism was disruptive to this coalition.

Black anti-Semitism is also linked to general Christian anti-Semitic attitudes. Many American blacks are members of evangelical Christian denominations that hold that Jews, and all non-Protestants, are heathens who are straight on the road to hell unless they convert. Many of these denominations pick up on the anti-Semitism of the Middle Ages that blamed Jews for poisoning wells, spreading the plague, and murdering Christian children. Evangelical Christians are encouraged to proselytize Jews. Black anti-Semitic beliefs began to spread in earnest after Israel became the Jewish state. African Americans came to identify with the Palestinian people living in the region and saw Israeli attempts to solidify control over the region and protect themselves from Arab terrorism as domination over people of color in general. This attitude was intensified as greater numbers of African Americans began to convert to Black Nationalist Islam, thereby becoming coreligionists with the Palestinians. African American feelings about Israel, however, are not indicative of their feelings toward Jews in the United States.

A final source of black anti-Semitic sentiment is the fact that, historically, many of the merchants operating in predominantly African American neighborhoods have been Jews. This was particularly true before the mass immigration from Asia, as these merchants have increasingly been replaced by Korean immigrants, while the Jews have become wholesalers and landlords. The residents of these neighborhoods blame the Jewish merchants, and by extension all Jews, for the inflated prices, lack of selection, and disruptive shoplifting suspicions in operation in the stores. At times, the residents of these neighborhoods have responded to their dissatisfaction with riots. To some extent, the merchants in these neighborhoods are responsible for these policies. However, other conditions of doing business are also responsible.

One of the most well-known, and violent, incidences of black anti-Semitic behavior was the murder of Yankel Rosenbaum in the Crown Heights section of Brooklyn, New York, in the summer of 1991. Rosenbaum was an Australian student in yeshiva (an institute for the study of Jewish religion and texts) who was stabbed to death by Lemrick Nelson, an African American man, as a mob shouted "Get the Jew!" This event was part of race riots in the area between African American and Jewish residents that included destruction of property and muggings as well as this brutal murder. The riots began after an African American child, Gavin Cato, was killed in an automobile accident, but Rosenbaum had nothing to do with this accident and was just an innocent Jew who happened to be chosen by the mob as the person through whom they would vent their rage. Additionally, the mayor of New York, David Dinkins who was black, did nothing to stop the riots.

Black anti-Semitic groups have picked up on such classic anti-Semitic literature as *The Protocols of the Elders of Zion* as well as publishing their own works, such as *The Secret Relationship between Blacks and Jews.* They have tried to claim, however, that they are not anti-Semitic, by saying that they do not believe in genocide or concentration camps. In other words, many of these groups believe that only the most extreme forms of anti-Semitism count as anti-Semitism. These groups also try to ignore the many examples of Jews who have dedicated themselves to working for black civil rights.

One of the most well-known black anti-Semitic groups is the Nation of Islam, a Black Nationalist Islamic group founded by Wali Farad Muhammad (born Wallace Dodd Fard) in 1930 and now run by Louis Farrakhan. This organization was originally set up as a religious movement aiming to help African Americans develop a sense of pride and civil rights. However, under the leadership of Farrakhan, beginning in 1977, the organization added outspoken anti-Semitism to their prior motive of fighting white domination. During and before the Million Man March in Washington, DC, to strengthen the black community in 1995, Farrakhan made statements about Jews (as well as Asians) sucking the lifeblood out of the black community.

See also Anti-Defamation League of B'nai Brith (ADL); Anti-Semitism in the United States; Black Nationalist Movement; Farrakhan, Louis; Jeffries, Leonard; Jewish-Black Conflicts; Jewish Defense League (JDL); Million Man March on Washington; Nation of Islam; Zionist Occupied Government (ZOG).

Further Reading

Baldwin, James. *Black Anti-Semitism and Jewish Racism.* New York: R. W. Baron, 1969.

Brackerman, Harold. *The Truth behind the Nation of Islam's "The Secret Relationship Between Blacks and Jews."* New York: Four Walls Eight Windows, 1994.

Mikaila Mariel Lemonik Arthur

Black Conservatives

Emerging in the Reagan era, Black conservatives are those African Americans who oppose the liberal policies and philosophies traditionally espoused by the African American community and generally support Republican policies, including the termination of affirmative action, the lowering or abolition of the minimum wage, proposals for enterprise zones in inner cities, and cutbacks in welfare programs for the poor.

Before the civil rights era, there had been some black conservatives, such as George S. Schuyler, a columnist of the influential black newspaper *Pittsburgh Courier* and the author of *Black and Conservative*, and Zora Neale Hurston, a writer of stories, novels, and anthropological folklore. It was, however, the publication of Thomas Sowell's book *Race and Economics* in 1975 that marked the upsurge of a more aggressive and visible conservative politics of African American leadership. Besides Sowell, the senior fellow at the Hoover Institution on War, Revolution, and Peace at Stanford University, among the influential black conservatives are Glenn C. Loury, a professor at Harvard's Kennedy School of Government, Walter E. Williams, a professor of economics at George Mason University, I. A. Parker, president of the Lincoln Institute for Research and Education, Inc., Robert Woodson, president of the National Association of Neighborhood Enterprises, and Joseph Perkins, an editorial writer for the *Wall Street Journal*. Clarence Thomas, associate justice of the U.S. Supreme Court, tried to modify affirmative action during the Reagan and Bush administrations. Recently George W. Bush's first term secretary of state Colin Powell, and Condoleezza Rice, national security advisor (first term) and secretary of state (second term), have pursued hawkish foreign policies. Another Hoover research fellow, Shelby Steele, is adding a new voice to black conservative politics.

Liberal interventions such as affirmative action and policies promoting multiculturalism, diversity, and Afrocentrism have failed to promote true racial equality and dignity, Steele argues, because they rely on the culture of victimization and group preference instead of the culture of excellence and achievement. To be free, blacks must rebuke dependency on anyone or anything like the government. They need to prove they can do as well as whites to whites and themselves. It requires robust individualism and the spirit of fair competition. These principles are said to be the natural extension of Christianity. In this way, black conservatives resuscitate the traditional Protestant ethic of hard work, self-help, and sexual restraint to advocate the Republican agenda such as the opposition to homosexuality, abortion, and government dependency.

The rise of black conservatives was a response to the crisis of black liberalism. The global economic and political transformation—the oil embargo, the Vietnam War, and the economic revival of Japan and Germany—in the mid-1970s severely undermined the Keynesian model of American liberalism, that is, economic growth accompanied by state regulation and intervention on behalf of disadvantaged citizens. It soon became obvious that the enforcement of the civil rights laws could not solve the ongoing plight of the black working poor and underclass. Focusing on the crisis, Black conservatives discredited the black liberal leadership as being outdated and ineffective. But economic hardship among the poor seemed to weaken their persuasiveness. They, however, opened up an opportunity for black liberals to reexamine their assumptions. On the other hand, the belief among black conservatives in the magic of the unregulated market would be no less naïve than black liberals' belief in government intervention. Whether the critique of liberalism will lead to a new vision of freedom and dignity for all is unknown.

See also Losing Ground: American Social Policy, 1950–1980; Powell, Colin; Thomas, Clarence.

Further Reading

Schuyler, George S. *Black and Conservative.* New Rochelle, NY: Arlington House, 1966.

Sowell, Thomas. *Race and Economics.* New York: McKay, 1975.

Steele, Shelby. *A Dream Deferred*. New York: HarperCollins, 1998.

West, Cornel. "Unmasking the Black Conservatives." *Christian Century* (July 16–23, 1986): 644.

Dong-Ho Cho

"Black English" (Ebonics)

Black dialect, or Ebonics, as it is often called today, is a method of communication and a cultural marker in some black communities. The term *Ebonics* is a derivative of the word *ebony*, meaning "black," and *phonics*, meaning "sound." It is postulated that these speech sounds originated from West African Hamito-Bantu languages that have expanded and transformed over time. Some advocates consider Ebonics on par with mainstream English. The most disparaging critics characterize Ebonics as an inferior, slovenly, and deviant speech that reflects cultural deprivation and renders speakers unable to adequately interact in the larger society. Some have argued that the black language reflects the anatomic and genetic deficiencies of speakers. Other critics reject biologically based exemplars but also reject Ebonics use. It has also been suggested that the use of both mainstream English and Ebonics can foster bidialectalism or multilingualism. However, it has been argued that the use of Ebonics in schools merely reflects an inadequate, short-term attempt to address more pressing, systemic problems such as poverty, racism, and segregation. Ebonics was catapulted into the national spotlight during the Oakland School Board's 1996 resolution acknowledging it as a language and a viable teaching tool and the subsequent resolution revision in 1997 prompted by negative media exposure. Since 1981, the U.S. Department of Education has held a clear policy that Ebonics is a form of English and not a separate and distinct language, and thus not eligible for funding. And although it has already been taught in schools in places such as Ann Arbor, Michigan, Oakland appeared to be the first district to suggest a system-wide change and plans to seek funding. The American Speech, Language and Hearing Association classified black English as a social dialect.

See also Bilingual Education; Multiculturalism.

Sandra L. Barnes

Black Family Instability Thesis

The black family instability thesis is a theoretical framework rooted both in the culture of poverty thesis and a pathology model that suggests that black poverty is largely a result of the instability of black families. Daniel Patrick Moynihan's report *The Negro Family: The Case for National Action*, released in 1965, is largely associated with the black family instability thesis. In the report, Moynihan argued that the disintegration of black families was the main cause of black poverty. He presented the following data from the 1960 census to illustrate the instability of the black family: nearly one-quarter of urban black marriages were dissolved; nearly one-quarter of black births were out-of-wedlock; almost one-quarter of black families were headed by females; and increasing numbers of black families were welfare dependent. According to Moynihan, black family instability was the primary cause of their poor economic conditions. His study included comparative data for blacks and whites on factors, such as marital status, and birth rates, as well as statistics on non-white unemployment rates and Aid to Families with Dependent Children (AFDC) cases, to illustrate the growing number of female-headed families among blacks.

According to Moynihan, female-headed families are more welfare dependent and their children's educational chances are more limited, which contributes to their poverty. Because of the legacy of slavery, he argued, black families are far more unstable—that is, far more likely to be headed by females—than white families. As a result, family instability and poverty maintain a vicious cycle in the black community. Therefore, he recommended that the government should take action to strengthen black families so that they can escape from poverty. If poor black families were to experience stability similar to their white and black middle-class counterparts, national interventions were needed to alter the "tangle of pathology" that prevented them from maintaining nuclear families and experiencing economic stability.

Although the 1965 Moynihan report is mainly associated with the Black family instability thesis, similar findings were intimated much earlier by W. E. B. Du Bois in *The Philadelphia Negro* (1899) and by Gunnar Myrdal (1944) in *An American Dilemma: The Negro Problem and Modern Democracy*. E. Franklin Frazier's chapter, "Family Disorganization," in his 1957 *The Negro in the United States*, also recognized the socioeconomic success of middle-class blacks and correlated poverty among blacks to matrilineal black families, negative urban conditions, and aberrant lifestyles. Moynihan cited Frazier's findings in his 1965 study.

Moynihan's black family instability thesis has been widely known to social scientists mainly because it has been subjected to severe criticism. The major critiques can be summarized into the following three categories. First, they have indicated that Moynihan stereotyped black families. Although his 1960 census data showed only one-fourth of black families were female-headed, he emphasized the "pathological" nature of black families as if all black families were female-headed. Second, he used white middle-class families as a norm in evaluating black families. Since 1960, the proportion of female-headed families has significantly increased for both the black and the white communities. Thus, there is a far greater diversity in family systems, and a two-parent family should not be a norm for evaluating other types of families. Third and most importantly, Moynihan focused on the effects of family instability on poverty when the two variables mutually affect each other. As has been adequately pointed out, black men's joblessness is the main determinant of black family instability. As a result of racial discrimination, black men have difficulty finding jobs, which undermines black family stability. Therefore, Moynihan's critics have pointed out that by focusing on family instability as the main cause of black poverty, Moynihan provided the blaming-the-victim argument. Although Moynihan was well intentioned in his attempt to help eliminate poverty in the black community, his cultural argument has conservative implications.

See also Blaming-the-Victim Argument; Culture of Poverty Thesis; "Model Minority Thesis"; *The Negro Family: The Case for National Action*.

Further Reading

Du Bois, W.E.B. *The Philadelphia Negro*. Philadelphia: University of Pennsylvania Press, 1899.

Fine, Mark, Andrew I. Schwebel, and Linda James-Myers. "Family Stability in Black Families: Values Underlying Three Different Perspectives." *Journal of Comparative Family Studies* 18, no. 1 (1987): 1–23.

Frazier, E. Franklin. *The Negro in the United States*. New York: Macmillan, 1957.

Moynihan, Daniel Patrick. *The Negro Family: The Case for National Action*. Washington, DC: Office of Policy Planning and Research, U.S. Department of Labor, 1965.

Myrdal, Gunno. *An American Dilemma: The Negro Problem and Modern Democracy*. New York: Harper & Row, 1962.

Sandra L. Barnes

Black Identities: West Indian Immigrant Dreams and American Realities

Mary Waters's *Black Identities: West Indian Immigrant Dreams and American Realities* is a groundbreaking, award-winning book published in 1999. The book is an exploration of the experiences of immigrants to New York from the West Indies (predominately from English-speaking nations there). Waters conducted interviews with working- and middle-class West Indian immigrants and their children to explore their economic and social adjustment to life in New York as well as the ethnic and racial identities that they develop. Her research has had important consequences for the understanding of the assimilation of contemporary immigrants to the United States, particularly immigrants of color. The second-generation West Indians that Waters interviewed developed identities as either West Indians or American blacks, depending on their socioeconomic status and other experiences. These findings lend support to segmented assimilation theory, as they show how second-generation West Indians can often experience downward mobility as they become more assimilated as Americans. Waters also discusses the strategies that those who continue to identify as West Indian use to mark themselves as being West Indian rather than American black.

See also Caribbean Immigrants, Attitudes toward African Americans; Caribbean Immigrants, Class Differences in the Second Generation; Caribbean Immigrants, Experience of Racial Discrimination; Oppositional Identity.

Further Reading

Waters, Mary C. *Black Identities: West Indian Immigrant Dreams and American Realities*. Cambridge, MA: Harvard University Press, 1999.

Mikaila Mariel Lemonik Arthur

Black-Jewish Conflicts

See Black Anti-Semitism; Jewish-Black Conflicts.

Black-Korean Conflicts

Since the Immigration Act of 1965 abolished the national-origins quota system, a new wave of immigrants started coming to America from Asia countries, including Korea. By the early 1970s, some of these Korean immigrants had created commercial niches in predominantly black neighborhoods in central cities. Following the pattern of ethnic succession, they took over businesses from retiring Jewish and other white merchants who had low commercial rents.

As Korean merchants opened their businesses—fruit and vegetable stores, grocery and liquor stores, gift shops, and wig shops—in black neighborhoods, a number of disputes between Korean merchants and black customers and the boycotts of Korean stores broke out in New York, Chicago, Los Angeles, and other major cities. The interracial black-Korean conflict usually started with a dispute between a Korean merchant or employee and a black customer at a Korean-owned store, followed by an organized black boycott of Korean store(s), escalating into a large-scale intergroup racial conflict. During these conflicts both Koreans and blacks have taken a variety of direct, overt, collective actions to achieve their conflicting goals: to keep the stores open or closed in predominantly black neighborhoods of urban America. In addition to the boycotts of Korean stores, the conflict took different forms. Arson of Korean stores and physical violence against Korean storeowners and employees occurred in Los Angeles and New York. Most significantly, about 2,300 Korean stores in black neighborhoods in South Central Los Angeles and Koreatown were burned and/or rooted, mostly by black rioters, during three days of the 1992 Los Angeles Riots. Korean immigrants in Los Angeles sustained approximately 45 percent of all damage that occurred during the riots.

For the Korean immigrants' business-related conflicts with blacks, black leaders have blamed antiblack racism among Korean merchants as the underlying cause. However, Korean merchants and community leaders argued that their treatment of black customers only appeared to be rude and disrespectful because of cultural differences and misunderstandings between these two groups. They also argued that black customers acted disrespectfully toward them. After recognizing the minor role of racial prejudice and cultural differences in merchant-customer relations, one observer, Heon Lee (1999), concluded that it was the nature of Korean businesses in black neighborhoods that mainly contributed to merchant-customer disputes. The viability of Korean stores as small but profitable businesses in black neighborhoods has become the liability in merchant-customer relations.

Focusing on merchants' efforts of maintaining civility in merchant-customer interactions, one scholar, Jennifer Lee (2002), concluded that most merchant-customer interactions are civil and ordinary. She found that merchants, to establish and maintain such civil relations, made considerable investments: hiring black employees to act as "cultural brokers," placing female employees at the front end of the business to serve as "maternal brokers," and yielding to customers' requests and demands in order to avoid conflict.

During the conflicts, the American public, especially the white media, viewed Korean immigrants sympathetically as the innocent scapegoats of black frustration over the lack of their own economic success. In line with this argument, sociologist Pyong Gap Min (1996) provided an insightful analysis of black-Korean conflict by utilizing the middleman minority theory. Focusing on the structural conditions of the ethnic stratification system in the United States, Min argued that Korean immigrants as a group have become economically successful but politically powerless and vulnerable. Like Jews in medieval Europe and the Chinese in Southeast Asia, Koreans as a middleman minority have been "caught in the middle" between the dominant white corporations and African American customers. Under the structural conditions of poverty, joblessness, and inequality, Korean businesses in low-income black neighborhoods can be direct targets of residents' anger and economic frustrations.

The Korean-black conflict at the collective level, represented in the form of boycotts, can be viewed as the social movement of black empowerment. The leaders of the boycotts have often used the boycott as a method of empowering blacks politically and economically. The ideology of Black Nationalism and Black Power has been employed not only against Korean merchants but also against dominant white institutions, such as the police, the media, and the courts. To understand the process of conflict development, therefore, it is important to look at the black-Korean conflict in the political context of black-white relations in urban America.

Race relations in the United States in the pre–1965 era were a matter of black-white relations, but since then, the influx of immigrants from Third World countries has made race relations in the United States far more complicated than before. Today, conflicts between minority groups are as serious as minority-majority conflicts. Black-Korean conflicts represent a typical example of minority-minority conflicts in the post–1965 era: blacks and Koreans are racial minorities in America in terms of their relative group positions against the dominant whites in the racial stratification system, but their "degrees of minority status" differ in various dimensions; for instance, whereas Korean immigrants are more successful in business ownership and overall socioeconomic adjustment, blacks are numerically and politically more powerful.

See also Los Angeles Riots of 1992; Middleman Minorities; Rodney King Beating.

Further Reading

Lee, Heon C. "The Dynamics of Black-Korean Conflict: A Korean American Perspective." In *Koreans in the Hood: Conflict with African Americans*, edited by Kwang Chung Kim, 91–112. Baltimore, MD: Johns Hopkins University Press, 1999.

Lee, Jennifer. "From Civil Relations to Racial Conflict: Merchant-Customer Interactions in Urban America." *American Sociological Review* 67, no. 1 (2002): 77–98.

Min, Pyong Gap. *Caught in the Middle.* Berkeley: University of California Press. 1996.

Heon Cheol Lee

Black Muslims

See the Nation of Islam.

Black Nationalist Movement

Black Nationalism is premised on the view that "Black America is an oppressed nation, a semi-colony of the United States" (Allen 1990, 1). The central idea that American blacks composed an internal colony represented a radical break from the racial integration goals of the civil rights movement. Black Nationalists argued for the parallels in the experience of blacks in the United States with that of Third World peoples, including Africans and Asians, who had been subjected to U.S. imperialism as sources of cheap labor, land, and natural resources. The key tenets of Black Nationalism emphasize racial solidarity and pride, self-determination, and self-defense tactics.

The Black Nationalist movement is marked by different periods of mobilization led by various and distinct leaders and organizations. The goal of Black Nationalism is to unite and empower blacks to dismantle the institutionalized racism that has shaped their oppression and socioeconomic exploitation in the United States. Rejecting strategies of nonviolence employed by the civil rights movement, Black Nationalism promoted a militant stance and armed struggle. As Black Nationalists Stokely Carmichael and Charles V. Hamilton contend in *Black Power: The Politics of Liberation in America* (1967), "Those of us who advocate Black Power are quite clear in our own minds that a 'nonviolent' approach to civil rights is an approach Black people cannot afford and a luxury white people do not deserve" (53).

Key Leaders and Organizations

Marcus Garvey. Marcus Mosiah Garvey was born in Jamaica in 1887 of sharecropper parents. His observations of black workers harvesting plantations, loading ships, and building the Panama Canal during his travels to Central America made a powerful impression. Although black workers provided the necessary labor power to fuel Central America's economic growth, Garvey noted, they were powerless, isolated from each other and as a collective group. Upon his return to Jamaica, Garvey founded the Universal Negro Improvement and Conservation Association, later known as the Universal Negro Improvement Association (UNIA).

Originally conceived as a fraternal organization, the UNIA's motto was "One God, One Aim, One Destiny," reflecting Garvey's vision to unite all black people in the world. UNIA sought to uplift blacks and establish educational and industrial opportunities based on programs from Booker T. Washington's Tuskegee Institute. At Washington's invitation, thirty-five-year-old Garvey arrived in New York in 1916, approximately two years after the founding of UNIA, to expand his Black Nationalist program. Harlem, New York, became the headquarters of the Garveyism movement, which advocated for black racial pride, economic and political independence and self-reliance, although Garvey was mostly associated with promoting a Back-to-Africa movement. For a nominal fee of 35 cents and a pledge to support Garvey's nation-building program, persons of African descent could join the UNIA and gain a title and a uniform.

To foster economic development, the UNIA financed numerous commercial ventures, including laundries, restaurants, and newspapers, as well as a shipping line named the Black Star Line for the purpose of fostering international trade between blacks in the United States, the Caribbean, and Africa. By 1920, Garvey claimed nearly a thousand local divisions in the United States, the Caribbean, Central America, Canada, and Africa. A young J. Edgar Hoover, with the Federal Bureau of Investigation (FBI), was by then targeting Garvey as an "agitator." A year later, the Black Star Line was on the verge of bankruptcy and Garvey mailed promotional brochures with a photo of a ship that he did not own. Charged with mail fraud because the photo misrepresented the ownership of the ship, he was deported to Jamaica by the U.S. government in 1923.

Malcolm X. One of the most charismatic Black Nationalist leaders was Malcolm X (1925–1965), a protégé of Elijah Muhammad and the Nation of Islam until his break in 1963, when he formed his own organization, the Organization of Afro-American Unity. His infamous life story is richly documented in his autobiography as told to Alex Haley, and in Spike Lee's 1992 biographical film, *Malcolm X*. Born in Omaha, Nebraska, Malcolm Little was one of eight children of Rev. Earl Little, an organizer for Garvey's UNIA, and his West Indian wife, Louise Little, also a Garveyite. Malcolm's early life was marked by poverty and the ever-present threat of the Ku Klux Klan, who eventually murdered his father, which facilitated the mental demise and breakdown of his mother. His mother was committed to the state psychiatric hospital in Kalamazoo, Michigan, and Malcolm had little contact with her for the next twenty-six years.

Malcolm's exploits as a pimp, numbers runner, and drug hustler on the streets of Harlem in New York, and Roxbury, Massachusetts, eventually landed him in the Charlestown [Massachusetts] State Prison, convicted of a burglary charge. Later, he was transferred to the Massachusetts Norfolk Prison Colony, and it was while Malcolm served a seven-year prison sentence there that his brother, Reginald, introduced him to the Nation of Islam. Making great use of the prison library, Malcolm began an intensive process of self-education. As Malcolm describes, "Until I left that prison, in every free moment I had, if I was not reading in the library, I was reading on my bunk" (Haley and Malcolm X 1964, 173). His passion for reading and learning would continue to shape his intellectual prowess upon his release from prison.

In the spring of 1952, the Massachusetts State Parole Board approved Malcolm's release. He settled in Detroit and became active in Elijah Muhammad's Temple One. At this time, Malcolm ceased to use his surname and substituted an *X* for it. As he explained, "The Muslim's 'X' symbolized the true African family name that he never could know" (199). As a minister in the Nation of Islam, Malcolm X preached the teaching of Elijah Mohammad that "the white man is the devil" who brainwashed blacks to accept their subordination (200). Organizing new temples in cities with large black populations, including Los Angeles and New York, Malcolm X gained national attention. Malcolm X fought against white supremacy and internalized black racism by celebrating the rich history of Africans, honoring the beauty of black people, and advocating for their liberation and empowerment. He was a handsome, dynamic, and astute leader, and ultimately, his mentor Elijah Muhammad came to perceive his growing prominence as a threat.

Before his tragic and untimely death at thirty-nine years of age, Malcolm X traveled to Africa and the Middle East and embarked on a pilgrimage (*hajj*) to Mecca in Saudi Arabia, the most holy city in Islam. During his pilgrimage, he met Muslims of various racial identities and learned that not all whites are inherently racist. He reemerged as El-Hajj Malik El-Shabazz and promoted a more complex view of race in the United States. In contrast to the Nation of Islam's teachings that all whites were innately evil, Malcolm X's experiences and observations deepened his understanding of the mechanisms of institutionalized black oppression and whites' domination and benefit from racial privilege.

Malcolm X was to deliver a major speech on behalf of his organization, the Organization of Afro-American Unity, when he was assassinated in Harlem's Audubon Ball Room on February 21, 1965. His wife, Betty Shabazz, and five daughters witnessed his death. As documented in his autobiography, even months before his death Malcolm X had predicted that assassins would try to stop him from spreading his views. Three Muslim men were tried and convicted. However, many continue to suspect the involvement of Elijah Muhammad and the Nation of Islam in his assassination. Although he did not live long enough to develop the mission of his organization, Malcolm X is considered the "ideological father of the black power movement" (Allen 1990, 30), and his image and teachings continue to resonate worldwide today, especially among urban youth.

Black Panther Party

In the aftermath of the assassination of Malcolm X and the massive urban uprising in the Watts, sections of Los Angeles, California, in 1965, Oakland, California, black radical activist Huey Newton and several longtime friends, including Bobby Seale and David Hilliard, developed in 1966 the framework for an organization originally named the Black Panther Party for Self-Defense. As a revolutionary organization, the Black Panthers endorsed black empowerment and community control and provided basic social services referred to as "survival programs," such as the Free Breakfast for Children Program, health clinics, school and education programs, senior transport and service programs, and transportation to prisons, as well as prisoner support and legal-aid programs. The Black Panther Party included a clandestine military branch that engaged in armed struggle and battled the police in Chicago and Oakland.

The Black Panthers inspired the formation of similar radical nationalist groups among other racialized minorities, including the Brown Berets among Southern California's Chicano and Mexican Americans, the San Francisco Bay Area's Chinese organization, the Red Guard, and the Young Lords among Puerto Ricans in the Northeast. These organizations flourished during the late 1960s and early 1970s. Like the Black Panther Party, they provided much needed social services while undertaking militant actions, including armed struggle to demand social justice for their impoverished and marginalized communities. Similarly, senior citizens organized the Gray Panthers to address the human and civil rights abuses of the elderly. At its height, the Black Panther Party grew from a small Oakland-based organization to a national organization with chapters in forty-eight states. In addition, Black Panther coalition and support groups were formed in numerous countries, including Japan, China, France, England, Germany, Sweden, Mozambique, South Africa, Zimbabwe, and Uruguay.

In 1969, Federal Bureau of Investigation (FBI) director J. Edgar Hoover stated that "the Black Panther Party, without question, represents the greatest threat to the internal security of the country." Hoover used a counterintelligence program, known as COINTELPRO, established in 1956, to neutralize and police "political radicals" in the United States. Under Hoover's direction, the FBI actively employed informants and organized covert activities involving mayhem and murder in order to undermine and destroy the Black Panther Party. Several key leaders were assassinated, and by the late 1970s, the Black Panther Party was in disarray. However, former members of the Black Panther Party continue the struggle for Black liberation, including New York City councilor and 2005 mayoral candidate Charles Barron.

Central Ideas of Black Nationalism

A key tenet of Black Nationalism is that the subjugation of blacks in the United States is comparable to the colonization of African nations. As Malcolm X noted, "How is the black man going to get 'civil rights' before first he wins his *human* rights? If the American black man will start thinking about his *human* rights, and then start thinking of himself as one of the world's great peoples, he will see he has a case for the United Nations," (179). Stokely Carmichael coauthored the radical tome *Black Power*, which laid out the ideological rationale and action plan for Black Nationalism. Carmichael was an activist with the Student Nonviolent Coordinating Committee (SNCC) and organized sit-in demonstrations, marches, and voter registration drives in the South. Becoming frustrated with SNCC's integrationist goals and nonviolent strategies, Carmichael took over the SNCC chairmanship from John Lewis (in 2005, Congressman of Georgia's Fifth Congressional District). In 1966, under Carmichael's leadership, a radical faction of SNCC advocated black separatism and coined the term Black Power.

Black Nationalism viewed the condition of black Americans as a colonized people within the United States. As an internal colony, their economic, political, and social conditions paralleled those of Africans and Asians subjected to U.S. imperialism. Their political colonialization was achieved through indirect rule. While black elected officials seemingly allowed for self-governance, they acted and sustained the interests of the colonial power by "playing by the rules." Moreover, political redistricting and racial gerrymandering were tools to minimize black representation. Blacks were economically colonialized through economic dependency and exploitation of ghetto resources. Landlords and business owners frequently lived outside the neighborhood and took their profits elsewhere. Poor blacks often bought with credit and were vulnerable to loan sharks, predatory lending, discriminatory banking practices, and higher prices, which resulted in acute disinvestment in black communities. The economic subordination of blacks was also maintained by their labor-market incorporation as a seemingly endless supply of cheap or reserve labor. The social colonialization was evident in society's dehumanization of blacks in popular culture and social attitudes resulting in internalized self-hatred. The role of the police in forcefully maintaining the colonial status of blacks continues to be a key issue.

The Black Nationalist struggle against oppression was not a struggle for integration. Black Nationalism rejects integration because it leaves intact racist structures by accepting those blacks who are most like whites and, as result, siphons off critical human capital and resources from the black community. Integrationist policy strategies are premised on the idea that to obtain decent housing and education, blacks need to move into white neighborhoods. These policies reinforce the perception of whites as superior and blacks as inferior, which ultimately serves to maintain white supremacy. As Carmichael and Hamilton contended, "Black people have not suffered as individuals but as members of a group; therefore, their liberation lies in group action" (1967, 54). The goal is not to integrate blacks into mainstream society but to build, strengthen, and exercise self-help and self-rule in the black community, to gain and exert control over the neighborhood economy, housing market, and political institutions.

Black Nationalism is based on the fundamental principle of black unity. Before his untimely death, Malcolm X called himself a Black Nationalist freedom fighter and realized that for blacks to effectively battle racism, they must be united. Black racial solidarity was seen as necessary to bargain from a position of strength in a pluralistic society. As Carmichael and Hamilton argued, "Before a group can enter the open society, it must first close ranks," (44). Although Black self-determination was criticized as reverse racism or advocating black supremacy, Carmichael and Hamilton countered that "racism is not merely exclusion on the basis of race but exclusion for the purpose of subjugating or maintaining subjugation" (47).

See also Black Panther Party; *Black Power: The Politics of Liberation in America*; Garvey, Marcus; Internal Colonialism; Malcolm X.

Further Reading

Allen, Robert L. *Black Awakening in Capitalist America: An Analytic History*. Trenton, NJ: Africa World Press, 1990.

Brown, Elaine. *A Taste of Power: A Black Woman's Story*. New York: Doubleday, 1992.

Carmichael, Stokely, and Charles V. Hamilton. *Black Power: The Politics of Liberation in America*. New York: Vintage Books, 1967.

Cruse, Harold. *Rebellion or Revolution*. New York: William Morrow, 1968.

Haley, Alex, and Malcolm X. *The Autobiography of Malcolm X*. New York: Ballantine Books, 1964.

Martin, Tony. *Race First: The Ideological and Organizational Struggles of Marcus Garvey and the Universal Negro Improvement Association*. The New Marcus Garvey Library, no. 8, 1986.

Melendez, Mickey, and Jose Torres. *We Took the Streets: Fighting for Latino Rights with the Young Lords*. New York: St. Martin's Press, 2003.

Tabb, William K. *The Political Economy of the Black Ghetto*. New York: Norton, 1971.

West, Cornel. *Race Matters*. Boston: Beacon Press, 1993.

Tarry Hum

Black Panther Party

Originally called the Black Panther Party for Self-Defense, the Black Panther Party was organized in 1966 in Oakland, California, by Huey P. Newton and Bobby Seale. Inspired by Malcolm X, Franz Fanon, Marxism, and Socialism, the Party promoted racial pride and an alternative economic system. In contrast to civil rights leader Martin Luther King Jr.'s nonviolent tactics and integrationist goals, the Panthers advocated violent means and separatist goals. In the early years, the Party focused on a neighborhood patrol in Oakland to prevent police abuse in the African American community. The Panthers brought guns, insisting on their right to self-defense. They became well known for their penchant for calling the police "pigs" and for their free food program for children in Oakland. Later the Panthers grew into a national movement, adding chapters throughout the country and introducing prominent leaders such as Eldridge Cleaver, the Party's Minister of Information. A secret FBI report to President Richard Nixon in 1970 found that approximately 25 percent of African Americans had a great respect for the Black Panther Party, including 43 percent of African Americans under the age of twenty-one years. But the Black Panther Party went into decline largely because of harassment and infiltration by the police and the FBI. Many of its leaders, including Fred Hampton and Mark Clark, were shot to death in police raids or imprisoned. Throughout the years of the civil rights movement, the government simultaneously made concessions through Congress and acted through the FBI to harass and break up militant African American organizations.

See also Black Nationalist Movement; Internal Colonialism; *Racial Oppression in America*.

Dong-Ho Cho

Eldridge Cleaver, minister of information for the Black Panther Party, speaks at American University, 1968.

Courtesy Library of Congress.

Black Political Disenfranchisement

Black political disenfranchisement refers to the denial of civil and political rights to African Americans by U.S. state and local governments. Before the Civil War, blacks in the United States were considered to be three-fifths of a person and had no civil rights. But with the Emancipation Proclamation by President Abraham Lincoln in 1863 and the passage of the Fourteenth and the Fifteenth Amendments in 1866 and 1869, blacks were given their full civil, legal, and political rights. This entailed the right to vote, to run for office, and to elect one's representative.

From 1865 to the 1880s, blacks throughout the United States, primarily in the South, exercised their franchise by electing a number of African Americans to political offices. However, when Congress decided to remove federal troops from the South in 1877, blacks began to lose their civil and political rights. By the 1890s, Southern states passed a series of Jim Crow laws to segregate blacks in all aspects of public life. They also passed laws to prevent blacks from voting, including the poll tax, which required voters to pay a fee before they could vote; the literacy test, for which voters had to show their ability to read and write or answer certain questions; and the grandfather clause, which exempted those who had voted before the 1860s from either paying the taxes or taking the literacy test. The Civil Rights Act of 1964 eliminated these discriminatory laws, guaranteeing the right to vote to African Americans and other people of color.

See also Civil Rights Act of 1964; Fourteenth Amendment; Jim Crow Laws; Literacy Test; Poll Tax.

Francois Pierre-Louis

Black Power Movement

See Black Nationalist Movement.

Black Power: The Politics of Liberation in America

Published in 1967, *Black Power: The Politics of Liberation in America* by Stokely Carmichael and Charles V. Hamilton articulated a new direction of black freedom struggle beyond the traditional nonviolent civil rights movement. The book was written in a heightened sense of urgency amid the state violence against civil rights activists, the increasing disillusionment about the civil rights movement, and the explosion of ghetto riots. "Black Power" had already become a powerful rallying slogan and a controversial issue in the mass media before the book was published in 1967. The authors offered their book as the only viable hope for avoiding the destructive guerilla warfare. Although the media portrayed "Black Power" as reverse racism and a Black supremacy movement, Black Power meant nothing other than black people's self-determination, self-definition, and control over the most important issues affecting their lives. To achieve this goal, Black Power asked for all blacks to unite, recognize their heritage, and create a community. It sounded like a separatist movement, but only superficially so. Only the restriction of membership to blacks would give substantial bargaining power to blacks as a group. A true coalition would be possible only on the basis of blacks' autonomous power. This would be, then, the prerequisite for the full participation of blacks in the democratic decision-making process of an open, pluralistic society. Black Power did not refute or oppose the ideas of democracy and open society, but it did see the current form of representative democracy and the idea of assimilation falling short regarding the self-determination of racial minorities. The book also underlined the deep connection between the struggle for the liberation of blacks in America and that of the Third World for national liberation in Africa and Asia.

See also Black Nationalist Movement; Internal Colonialism.

Further Reading

Carmichael, Stokely, and Charles V. Hamilton. *Black Power: The Politics of Liberation in America*. New York: Vintage Books, 1967.

Dong-Ho Cho

Black Wealth/White Wealth: A New Perspective on Racial Inequality

Melvin L. Oliver and Thomas M. Shapiro, in their 1995 book *Black Wealth/White Wealth: A New Perspective on Racial Inequality*, systematically detailed the distribution of wealth for black and white Americans, paying particular attention to the inequities between the two groups. They argued that it is necessary to examine wealth as well as income to determine how well black families fared in comparison to white families, because wealth disparities between blacks and whites are much greater than income disparities. Three measures of wealth—income, net financial assets, and net worth—were examined to determine how total wealth for blacks compared with that for whites. Net worth consists of the value of all assets minus debts; net financial assets exclude home and vehicle equity.

Oliver and Shapiro found considerable differences in wealth between whites and blacks of all income levels. But they focused on the disparities between middle-class blacks and whites, as there was the perception that a strong and stable black middle class had emerged in the United States. Middle-class status was measured in multiple ways, but in each instance whites fared better than blacks in terms of income and wealth distribution.

The authors also demonstrated how precarious the black middle class was by illustrating that the typical white middle class family could survive without income at its present standard of living for slightly more than four months, whereas the typical black middle-class family would be unable to survive for even a month. One very notable finding was that net financial assets held by poverty-level whites were almost equal to those held by the highest-earning blacks. Oliver and Shapiro contended that past inequities, such as laws, that prevented blacks from accumulating wealth or participating in mainstream business endeavors had a cumulative effect that continues to be felt in the present.

See also Black Family Instability Thesis; Blacks, Wage Discrimination against; Racial Differences in Property Holdings; Racial Earnings Gap.

Further Reading

Oliver, Melvin L., and Thomas M. Shapiro. *Black Wealth/White Wealth: A New Perspective on Racial Inequality.* New York: Routledge, 1995.

Romney S. Norwood

Blacks, Wage Discrimination against

According to the U.S. Bureau of Labor Statistics' 2003 Current Population Survey, black workers make eighty cents for every one dollar that white workers make. These are significant differences in earnings that have consequences for the lives of black men and women: the wages one earns affect where one can live, how much leisure time one has, the amount and quality of education one can provide for one's children, the credit one can get from financial institutions, and access to health care, among many other factors. It is clear that the gap is not due entirely to discrimination in wages. For instance, black workers in the United States tend to have received somewhat less education overall than white workers. Individuals with less education often earn lower wages. Other factors that can explain part of the wage gap include the regional concentration of black workers and occupational clustering (when blacks are concentrated in certain types of jobs). But even when factors such as these are taken into account, the wage gap still persists.

Title VII of the Civil Rights Act of 1964 prohibits employment discrimination (including wage discrimination) based on race. The Civil Rights Act of 1991 provides for monetary damages in the case of intentional employment discrimination. So how is it possible for a wage discrimination gap to occur? Some companies refuse to hire black employees in well-paid positions, or they pay black employees less than white employees with the same job title. These laws, however, are difficult to enforce. Federal agents do not conduct audits of the payrolls of individual businesses to check compliance—an investigation must wait until an individual complains of discrimination. Though protection does exist for individuals who choose to complain, many do not for fear of losing their jobs and their livelihoods.

Companies also try to get around these laws by prescreening résumés in an attempt to avoid even interviewing black applicants (by looking at the neighborhood the applicant is from, for instance, or preferring applicants with memberships in exclusive country clubs). They may also create parallel job titles with substantially similar job requirements and segregate employees into separate pay categories this way (compare maid and janitor, chef and cook, gardener and laborer, or secretary and administrative assistant). Some states have enacted laws to prohibit this practice by requiring that employees with substantially similar work requirements be paid equally (termed "comparable worth"), but this sort of protection is far from universal and is, again, hard to enforce.

Additionally, small businesses employing fewer than fifteen workers are not covered by Title VII. Many of the lowest-paid jobs in the United States are with such small businesses, including small restaurants, stores, and individual homes. Households are particularly prone to paying low wages, as some employers choose not to report the income they pay their employees to the government, for the purposes of avoiding taxation and employee benefits. These jobs include housecleaning, health care, laundry, childcare, and garden work. The justification for excluding small businesses from Title VII and other employment discrimination laws is that compliance would place an undue hardship on them. The government, however, could choose to close this loophole.

It is important to note that the racial wage gap differs by gender—black men make seventy-five cents for each dollar earned by white men, and black women make eighty-six cents for every dollar earned by white women. There are a number of reasons why this might be true. For instance, black women are very heavily represented in the labor market compared to white women, who are more likely to have the means to choose to stay home with their children. In contrast, black men are less represented than white men in the labor market because of difficulties in securing well-paying jobs and because of the high incarceration rate black men face. Additionally, white men are distributed well across wage categories, from high-paying fields like medicine and law to low-paying ones like manual labor (though they most heavily dominate in managerial and professional occupations). Black men are concentrated in low-paying fields like janitorial work and unskilled manufacturing. While white women and black women tend to have different types of jobs (white women predominate in sales, teaching, and in clerical jobs, while black women largely have household, service, health care, and clerical jobs), these jobs differ more significantly in terms of prestige than wages. Black women also do better because they have higher levels of education than black men and because the strongest labor-market discrimination is directed against black men.

In 1965, only three-fifths of the wage gap between whites and blacks was accounted for by such factors as education, occupation, and regional concentration. That means that two-fifths of the gap was the cost of being black. The size of the gap varied with the amount of education but was highest for the most educated sectors of the population. There has been some progress in narrowing the wage gap since the 1960s, but not much. The most significant progress has been for those in the lowest income groups, and this progress has been because of increased access to education and more federal and state minimum-wage protections. Some of these gains have been counteracted by the loss of manufacturing jobs, employers' flight from the inner cities, and decreased union membership. However, as the gap narrows with increased education and better occupational distribution, more and more of it is caused by discrimination. Current estimates suggest that discrimination accounts for about fifteen cents of the twenty-five-cent wage gap between black and white men.

See also Black Wealth/White Wealth: A New Perspective on Racial Inequality; Civil Rights Act of 1964; Civil Rights Act of 1991; "Cost of Being a Negro"; Racial Earnings Gap.

Further Reading

Albelda, Randy, Robert W. Drago, and Steven Shulman. *Unlevel Playing Fields: Understanding Wage Inequality and Discrimination*. New York: McGraw Hill, 2001.

Darity, William A. *Persistent Disparity: Race and Economic Inequality in the United States since 1945*. Cheltenham, UK: Elgar Publishers, 1998.

Masters, Stanley H. *Black-White Income Differentials: Empirical Studies and Policy Implications*. New York: Academic Press, 1975.

Siegal, Paul. "The Cost of Being a Negro." *Sociological Inquiry* 35, no. 1 (1965).

Mikaila Mariel Lemonik Arthur

Blaming-the-Victim Argument

Explanations of socioeconomic problems among blacks and other disadvantaged minority groups have focused either on minority members' cultural deficiencies, such as lack of motivation and work ethic or family instability, or on racial discrimination and other social barriers encountered by minority members. In the 1950s and early 1960s, cultural explanations focusing on minority members' cultural deficiencies were popular. But since the late 1960s, structural explanations emphasizing racial discrimination and industrial structure have gradually replaced cultural explanations.

Whether they are scholars or policymakers, conservatives have often provided cultural explanations to blame minority groups for their socioeconomic problems. For example, Charles Murray (1984) argued that a ghetto family that depended on welfare programs was more likely to bear children who lacked motivation and a work ethic and that therefore ending welfare programs was the solution to the problem of ghetto poverty. This argument intended to blame the victims—poor families in the inner city—for their economic problems. But some liberals who did not intend to blame the victims have sometimes provided cultural explanations for minority groups' economic problems. For example, in his 1965 report on black families, *The Negro Family: The Case for National Action*, cabinet member Daniel Patrick Moynihan argued that the instability of African American families was the main cause of their poverty and that, therefore, the government should take action to help stabilize black families. Moynihan was a staunch liberal and wanted to eliminate poverty in the black community. However, because he focused on blacks' family instability rather than their social barriers as the main cause of poverty, his cultural argument had the effect of blaming the victims: inner-city African American residents.

Because of their conservative implications, cultural explanations are not popular in social-science discourses. Since culture and structure mutually influence each other, motivations and a work ethic do influence the attitudes and behavior of minority members. But even those social scientists who consider cultural mechanisms important for minority members' socioeconomic adjustments are careful not to emphasize cultural variables in their reports, because they often lose their argument when their facts are correct but they are "politically incorrect."

See also Black Family Instability Thesis; Culture of Poverty Thesis; *Losing Ground: American Social Policy, 1950–1980*; "Model Minority" Thesis; *The Negro Family: The Case for National Action*.

Further Reading

Mead, Lawrence. *The New Politics of Poverty: The Nonworking Poor in America*. New York: Basic Books, 1992.

Moynihan, Daniel Patrick. *The Negro Family: The Case for National Action*. Washington, DC: Office of Policy Planning and Research, U.S. Department of Labor, 1965.

Murray, Charles. *Losing Ground: American Social Policy, 1950–1980*. New York: Basic Books, 1984.

Sandra L. Barnes

Block-busting

Block-busting (or "panic-peddling") is a tactic used by unethical real estate agents to create high and rapid residential turnover, usually from white to black, in a neighborhood. Initially block-busting appears to be a step toward the racial integration of a neighborhood, but rather than seeking a stable or moderate interracial mix of residents in the area, real estate agents who engage in block-busting create fears about black neighbors or play upon existing prejudices of white residents to manipulate and encourage the whites to sell and move away. Then the agent finds black purchasers, who are steered into the area, for the houses in the neighborhood undergoing block-busting. Thus the cycle of racial turnover from white to black moves quickly. Several factors underlie block-busting: most often, concern over the social prestige of a neighborhood, an interest in maintaining property values and having them appreciate rather than depreciate, and fears about crime and the quality of local public schools. When dominant racial-ethnic group residents believe that their neighborhoods lose social status, decline in property value, and have more crime and worse schools when members of the racial-ethnic minority move in, then real estate agents can be successful in block-busting. When residents do not panic at the arrival of racial-minority neighbors and realize that this does not inevitably mean neighborhood decline, then they are more likely to resist real estate agents' offers to assist them sell their homes "while they can still get a good price for them," and block-busting is unsuccessful.

Charles Jaret

Border Patrol

See U.S. Border Patrol.

Boycotts

Boycotts are a tactic that social movements and other groups use to put pressure on their opponents so that they will change laws, policies, or behaviors.

This tactic involves refusing to support an organization or corporation financially by not purchasing its products, going to its stores, or spending money that it will benefit from. One reason for the popularity of boycotts is that the risk of physical or economic harm to those who participate is slight. As a result, groups engaged in boycotts can often induce individuals who are not part of their group but are sympathetic to their cause to participate, thus increasing the incentive for the target to change its ways. Martin Luther King Jr. and his followers, who were greatly influenced by Mahatma Ghandi, used boycotts and other forms of nonviolent action in the civil rights movement; the Montgomery Bus Boycott is one of the most famous examples. Other well-known instances of groups sponsoring boycotts are the boycott of grapes in sympathy with migrant agricultural workers in California in 1965 and boycotts of Korean grocery stores in New York and Los Angeles by African American and Latino groups who perceived the grocery store owners as racist.

See also Chavez, Cesar; King, Martin Luther, Jr.; United Farm Workers (UFW).

Mikaila Mariel Lemonik Arthur

Bracero Program

The Emergency Labor Program, popularly called the Bracero Program, was established by the U.S. government as a response to the labor needs of southwestern agriculture growers during World War II. Through a treaty with the Mexican government, manual laborers (braceros, from the Spanish *brazo*, or "arm") entered the United States to replace American workers under a contract-labor arrangement. By the time this guest-worker program ended in 1964, nearly five million braceros were employed in the United States, in both agriculture and industry.

Mexican braceros had been recruited directly by U.S. growers between 1942 and 1964 to meet labor shortages. The 1942 treaty between the U.S. and Mexican governments sought to address deficiencies and abuses in the previous arrangement. Mexican workers could not be recruited for U.S. military service; they were to be protected from discrimination; their transportation, living expenses, and repatriation were to be paid by the employer; and they were not to replace domestic workers. Even with the treaty provisions, poor treatment of braceros was prevalent, including low wages, inadequate housing, high food prices, salary deductions for food and health care, and a general lack of legal rights. Despite this effort to orchestrate and control the entrance of Mexican workers into the United States, historians note the parallel flows of undocumented Mexican immigrants during this time period and suggest they were stimulated by the bracero program.

During the Depression, as a means to reduce the welfare rolls, the U.S. government forcibly returned a large number of Mexican Americans, including many U.S.-born Mexicans, to Mexico. But when the United States suffered from the shortage of workers during World War II, the U.S. government arranged to bring Mexican workers back. This demonstrates that the United States's need for cheap labor is a more important factor for determining the U.S. government's immigration policies than the U.S. government's humanitarian consideration of providing opportunities for aliens.

See also Mexican Illegals, Labor Exploitation of.

Kenneth J. Guest

Brown v. Board of Education of Topeka

Segregation of white Americans and African Americans in public schools was not only lawful but also mandated in many states until this U.S. Supreme Court decision on May 17, 1954, which marked the end of legalized school segregation. Although there had been numerous legal attempts to end racially segregated schools as early as the 1840s (e.g., *Roberts v. City of Boston* in 1849), the case of *Brown v. Board of Education of Topeka* was the first to successfully lead to the decision that racial segregation in school was unconstitutional. Before school desegregation, legalized forms of racial discrimination, which were usually justified through the separate but equal doctrine, long affected every aspect of the lives of African Americans. Specifically, African Americans were denied access to schools that white Americans attended, under laws permitting or mandating race-based segregation.

African American children were forced to attend public schools with outdated facilities and limited educational resources in economically depressed areas. By contrast, their white American counterparts generally attended public schools with better facilities and better trained teachers in less distressed neighborhoods. Although some court decisions had previously acknowledged such discrepancies in the separate but equal doctrine (e.g., *Gebhart v. Belton* in Delaware in 1952), courts had been reluctant to rule segregation unconstitutional. In fact, in the case of *Plessy v. Fergusson* in 1896, the U.S. Supreme Court declared the separate but equal doctrine constitutional. These conditions served to maintain and widen the gaps in social positions between African Americans and whites that already existed largely because of slavery.

During the civil rights movement of the 1950s and 1960s, the members of African American communities and their supporters (e.g., NAACP) challenged the laws designed to permit and promote racial discrimination. They employed legal challenges, protests, boycotts and other strategies to accomplish their goals, and *Brown v. Board of Education of Topeka* was their first major victory. In this groundbreaking ruling, Chief Justice Warren questioned the separate but equal doctrine and contended that segregated schooling was inherently unequal, and it was hence unconstitutional. He made several socially profound observations in his ruling.

For example, Chief Justice Warren stated that providing African Americans with truly equal educational opportunity through desegregation will benefit not only African Americans but also the rest of the American society. He reasoned that a solid education was necessary for an individual to be a constructive citizen of the society, as education represented the means through which children are exposed to cultural values, opportunities to normative psychosocial adjustment, and pro-

Left to right: George E. C. Hayes, Thurgood Marshall, and James M. Nabrit exchange congratulations following the *Brown v. Board of Education* decision, May 17, 1954.

Courtesy Library of Congress.

fessional training. He further stated that racial segregation of schools deprives African American children of equal educational opportunities. In addition, Warren noted the psychological impact of segregation, particularly when it is legally sanctioned. He affirmed that the policy of racial separation unavoidably leads to the interpretation that African Americans are inferior, which, in turn, adversely affects African American children's motivation to learn and thereby impedes their educational and psychological development.

Following this ruling, segregation began to fade ever-so-slowly. Several states resisted the ruling and continued their sanction of school segregation. For example, two of the governors of Arkansas during desegregation, Orval Faubus and George Wallace, are notorious for disobeying the Supreme Court ruling and maintaining school segregation until 1963. In a similar attempt, a county in Virginia closed many of its public schools to resist desegregation; this prevented African American students from attending those schools, while their white counterparts received aid to attend private high schools. Although such blatant cases no longer exist, de facto school segregation continues today in various areas of the United States.

If the successful implementation of school desegregation seems to have occurred slowly, the supposed improvement in social and economic conditions for African Americans lagged even more, and African Americans still face adverse economic and social conditions. Nevertheless, *Brown v. Board of Education* signaled a victory for racial equality in that it provided a solid foundation upon which to base further civil rights efforts, not only for African Americans but also for other people of color and for women.

See also National Association for the Advancement of Colored People (NAACP); School Segregation; Separate but Equal Doctrine.

Further Reading

Bell, Derrick A. *And We Are Not Saved: The Elusive Quest for Racial Justice*. New York: Basic Books, 1989.

Marsh, Charles. *The Last Days: A Son's Story of Sin and Segregation at the Dawn of a New South*. New York: Basic Books, 2002.

Daisuke Akiba

Buffalo Soldiers

So named later by the Native Americans who fought them in the West, the Buffalo Soldiers were created by an act of Congress in 1866. What was unique about these troops of the 9th and 10th Cavalries was that their ranks were composed entirely of African Americans, most of whom were veterans of the Civil War. Although their officers were whites who often considered leading black soldiers a second-class assignment, the men of the 9th and 10th Cavalries proved themselves good soldiers with a desertion rate one-third that of white regiments.

General Philip Sheridan recruited the 9th Cavalry through offices in New Orleans and Louisville. Thus, most of the recruits came from Louisiana and Kentucky. Once established in 1867, the 9th was sent to Texas, not a hospitable territory for black soldiers. In Texas, the troops guarded travel and mail routes and attempted to keep the peace. As 1876 dawned, they were sent to New Mexico and then, five years later, to Arizona to fight the Apaches. In 1881 they were sent to Kansas and Indian Territory, then to Wyoming in 1891, their last western campaign.

The 10th Cavalry was put together by Benjamin Grierson at Fort Leavenworth, Kansas, with recruits from Missouri, Arkansas, and the Platte departments. Grierson soon moved headquarters to Fort Riley, Kansas, because of the overt racism of the Fort Leavenworth commander. From 1867 until 1875, when the 10th Cavalry was moved to West Texas, it was headquartered

Buffalo soldiers of the 25th Infantry, some wearing buffalo robes, Ft. Keogh, Montana.

Courtesy Library of Congress.

throughout Kansas and Indian Territory, and the troops' responsibilities were containing and fighting Native Americans, building forts, stringing telegraph wires, and exploring and mapping thousands of miles of uncharted territory. In 1885, the 10th was moved to Arizona to fight the Apaches, to Montana in 1891, and to the Dakotas until 1898.

These two black cavalries made significant contributions to the history and development of the West and distinguished themselves as excellent fighting forces under the most severe circumstances. In addition to the normal hardships experienced by all soldiers fighting on the frontier, these men were also subjected to the virulent racism that ran through frontier towns.

See also War and Racial Inequality.

Further Reading

Leckie, William H. *The Buffalo Soldiers: A Narrative of the Negro Cavalry in the West.* Norman: University of Oklahoma Press, 1999.

Benjamin F. Shearer

Bureau of Indian Affairs (BIA)

The Bureau of Indian Affairs (BIA) was created in 1824 as part of the U.S. War Department to manage encounters and interactions with Native Americans, including trade relations and, ultimately, the removal of Native Americans to reservations. Widespread dissatisfaction with the army administration of Native American affairs precipitated the BIA's relocation in 1849 to the U.S. Department of the Interior. However, the reorganized BIA was no more successful than its earlier incarnation in preventing conflict or protecting the rights of Native Americans.

Several key legislative acts, such as the 1887 Dawes Act (Indian General Allotment Act), the 1906 Burke Act, and the 1934 Wheeler-Howard Act (Indian Reorganization Act), facilitated the evolution of the BIA to become primarily a land-administration agency, acting as the trustee for over 55.7 million acres of land held in trust by the U.S. government for American Indians, Indian tribes, and Alaskan Natives. In addition to considering applications for federal recognition as a tribe, BIA manages federal programs that affect the 562 federally recognized American Indian and Alaska Native tribal governments. BIA's responsibilities include developing and maintaining forestlands and infrastructure, leasing land to ranchers, miners, and loggers, protecting water and land rights, providing health and human services, economic development, and managing Native American reservations and schools. Although a main objective of the BIA is to promote the self-determination of 1.4 million Native Americans, beginning in the early 1970s, Native American civil rights groups, such as the American Indian Movement (AIM), protested BIA's discriminatory and unfair practices. These complaints include mismanagement of funds owned by Native American tribes and individuals.

Native American groups are currently involved in the largest class-action lawsuit against the Bush Administration, claiming that the BIA engaged in unfair land-appraisal practices that have deprived Native Americans of the "fair market value" of property leases, and mishandled more than 300,000 Individual Indian Money trust accounts. In the 1996 *Cobell v. Norton* lawsuit (Gale Norton was then secretary of the interior), Elouise Cobell, treasurer of the Montana Blackfeet Indians, alleged that the U.S. government lost, misused, and usurped as much as $176 billion in Indian assets. This case is ongoing, and the BIA Web site is unavailable as a result of the lawsuit.

See also American Indian Movement (AIM); Indian Reservations; Native Americans, Prejudice and Discrimination against.

Tarry Hum

Bureau of Refugees, Freedmen and Abandoned Lands

See Freedmen's Bureau.

Busing

Since the late 1960s, the term *busing* has implied the forced assignment of students to schools outside of their community for the purpose of racial integration in education. In the 1954 *Brown v. Board of Education*, the U.S. Supreme Court ruled that separate schools for black and white students were unequal and unconstitutional. This landmark decision forced politicians and educators to integrate their school system. But it was not until 1971, after civil rights leaders and educators won other lawsuits that forced school districts to integrate their schools, that local districts began to implement busing programs. The theory behind busing was that black children would be exposed to white culture and also benefit from the same educational resources that whites enjoyed. By bringing together white and black children, society would ultimately benefit, because the races would be exposed to each other's culture and they would also become more tolerant of their differences. In its 1967 report, entitled *Racial Isolation in the Public Schools*, the U.S. Commission on Civil Rights argued that black children could not obtain a proper education if they were exposed only to substandard education in predominantly minority schools.

As a result of the Court order to integrate urban school systems whose minority population was over 50 percent, Cleveland, Boston, Yonkers, Buffalo, and other cities began to bus their children to schools that were predominantly white, or made arrangements with their local school boards to implement some form of desegregation. Many civil rights organizations, such as the Urban League, National Association for the Advancement of Colored People and American Civil Liberties Union supported busing, while many white parents who were forced to adopt busing vehemently protested the policy. In 1974, when the courts ordered the Boston school system to implement busing, white parents organized marches, protests, and boycotts to prevent the busing of their children to predominantly black schools.

Busing, which civil rights leaders advocated as the ideal solution to achieve racial equality in education, was a failure in many communities because of

Police escort school buses in South Boston during court-ordered integration.

AP/Wide World Photos.

white flight from the urban areas and inadequate government funding of school districts. Whites who did not agree with busing decided to remove their children from the public school system, or they moved to neighborhoods that had few black residents and thus the issue of busing was not even addressed. Moreover, politicians and civic leaders who were against busing initiated court actions to prevent it from taking place in their communities. The lawsuits delayed school integration in several communities because by the time a decision was reached, there was no longer a diverse student body to allow it to take place.

Four decades after the Court decision to desegregate public schools through busing, school districts in the major cities of the United States are more segregated than ever. In 1976, when the Cleveland school district was ordered to bus its black school children to predominantly white schools, there were 128,000 students attending the public school system, and 57 percent of them were African Americans. Today, the public school system has fewer than 77,000 children, and 70 percent of them are African Americans (Ravitch 2000).

Those opposed to busing have argued that the forced mixing of children through court-ordered busing has been a failure and that it is now time for the U.S. government and local school boards to do away with it. They have argued that the inability of black school children to learn has little to do with segregation but is related instead to their low socioeconomic conditions, the small amount of resources that are given to the schools they attend, and the unwillingness of parents to support the education of their children. School districts that were originally forced to bus their students are now asking the courts to release them from the busing program and to allow them to experiment with new programs to improve the educational performance of their districts. So far, courts seem willing to allow many districts to experiment with new programs.

See also Brown v. Board of Education of Topeka; School Segregation; Separate but Equal Doctrine.

Further Reading

Dentler, Robert A., and Marvin B. Scott. *Schools on Trial: An Inside Account of the Boston Desegregation Case*. Cambridge, MA: Abt Books, 1981.

Ravitch, Diane. "School Reform: Past, Present, And Future." *Case Western Reserve Law Review* 51, no. 2 (Winter 2000).

Francois Pierre-Louis

John William King and Lawrence Russell Brewer are escorted from the Jasper County Jail, June 9, 1998.

AP/Wide World Photos.

Byrd, James Jr.

James Byrd Jr. (1949–1998) was murdered in Jasper, Texas, on June 7, 1998, in a racially motivated attack by three local white racists. The assailants picked up Byrd, a 49-year-old African American, along a rural road as he was walking home. They slit his throat and then chained him to the back of a pickup truck, dragging his body for three miles. The brutality of the killing and its racist motivations received national media attention.

Three white men, John William King, 23; Shawn Berry, 23; and Lawrence Brewer Jr., 31, were arrested, tried, and convicted of the crime. King and Brewer received the death penalty, and Berry received a life sentence. As a result of the murder, the James Byrd Foundation for Racial Healing was created by the Byrd family to advocate for state and federal hate crimes legislation. In 2001, Texas governor Rick Perry signed the James Byrd Jr. Hate Crimes Act, which modified existing state law on hate crimes to specifically mention acts based on race, color, disability, religion, national origin or ancestry, age, and gender or sexual orientation. The act also strengthened penalties for bias-motivated violent crimes and property crimes.

See also Bensonhurst Incident; Hate Crimes; Howard Beach Incident.

Victoria Pitts

C

CAIR

See Council on American Islamic Relations (CAIR).

California Ballot Proposition 54

California Proposition 54, also called the Racial Privacy Initiative (RPI), or the "California Ballot Initiative to Ban Racial Data" was created in 2002 by Ward Connerly, the black University of California regent who had supported Proposition 209, a successful 1996 measure that abolished affirmative action in state-run agencies and educational institutions. Proposition 54 called for a ban on the use and production of racially coded data across a spectrum of state and municipal agencies. Both supporters and critics agreed that, if passed, the initiative would have a tremendous impact on how race relations were recorded, viewed, and interpreted in the future. Although controversial, the proposition was overshadowed by California's gubernatorial recall election, which resulted in the ouster of Governor Gray Davis and his replacement by actor Arnold Schwarzenegger. Appearing on the same ballot as the recall, Proposition 54 was defeated on October 7, 2003, receiving only 36 percent of the vote.

Connerly viewed Proposition 54 as an important step toward a truly color-blind society. He claimed that since 1996 state and local institutions had continued to collect and use racial data, which were used to side-step the anti-affirmative-action mandates of Proposition 209. Connerly envisioned Proposition 54 as a way of responding to these "violations" of the earlier measure. The RPI would have prevented state and municipal agencies from classifying people according to race, ethnicity, or national origin. It would have effectively barred the use and collection of racially coded data in public education, municipal social services, public contracting, and employment. Certain exceptions were allowed under the RPI's provisions, including data for medical research or data needed to meet federally mandated requirements. Some institutions would have been affected by both the ban and its exemptions. For example, the state Department of Education would have been required by federal conditions to continue tracking the performance of students from certain racial groups in some subjects (such as mathematics and language arts) but would have been banned under the RPI from doing so in other subjects (such as science or history). Approval of any exemptions from the RPI would have required a two-thirds majority in the state legislature.

Supporters of Proposition 54 argued that the multiracial character of California, where whites make up less than 50 percent of the population, made race-based classification increasingly anachronistic. A growing number of interracial marriages further muddied the clear racial divisions upon which data had hitherto been based. Continuing to collect racially coded data, according to supporters of the measure, would be time-consuming, costly, and ultimately misleading. A reliance on racial statistics could also mask the presence of other crucial factors that determine hiring practices, admissions practices, and the rewarding of government contracts. Proponents argued that the principles behind Proposition 54 thus reflected the shift in society toward an increasingly multiracial and color-blind outlook. They believed it was the duty of the government and its attendant institutions to reflect and legitimize this trend.

Critics argued that the "information ban" on racial data would have a pernicious effect on race relations and negatively impact the lives of countless people. In areas such as education, employment, and public health in particular, the absence of racial statistics would prevent the development of programs and policies specifically targeted toward vulnerable minority populations. Without racially coded data, litigation to combat racial discrimination would be impossible. Also, researchers and policymakers would be unable to track the changing economic and social conditions of various minority groups over time.

The heart of the opposition's argument was the principle that race is the fundamental marker and determinant of inequality in society. Opponents believed that race continues to affect the quality of education, the likelihood of exposure to environmental hazards or of contracting certain medical conditions, and an individual's ability to access fair housing and employment. Opponents argued that by "hiding" the role of race, Proposition 54 only provided the framework for further racial and ethnic discrimination. Although many people believed that passage of the proposition would cause other states to follow California's lead, defeat of the measure has at least temporarily cooled the issue.

See also California Ballot Proposition 187; California Ballot Proposition 209; California Ballot Proposition 227; Statistical Discrimination.

Further Reading

Coalition for an Informed California. http://www.defeat54.org.

El Nasser, Haya. "California Candidates Seize Prop 54 Issue." *USA Today*. September 8, 2003. http://www.usatoday.com/news/politicselections/state2003-09-07-prop54 -usat_x.htm.

Rossomondo, John. "California Initiative Seeks to End Racial Classifications." *Cybercast New Service.* December 31, 2001. http://www.conservativenews.org/politics/archive/200112/POL20011231a.html.

Sanders, Jim. "Racial Battle Line Drawn." *The Sacramento Bee.* August 10, 2003.

Rebekah Lee

California Ballot Proposition 187

The formal name of California Proposition 187 is the Save Our State Initiative. This 1994 proposition seemingly sought to address the problem of illegal immigration in California. But in essence, it reflects a high point in anti-immigrant sentiment and the nativism movement in the 1990s. Proposition 187 denies publicly funded nonemergency medical care and other health care to illegal immigrants and their foreign-born children; public elementary and secondary education to foreign-born children of illegal immigrants; public postsecondary education to illegal immigrants; and public social services to illegal immigrants. It requires law enforcement agencies to verify the legal status of every arrestee and notify the attorney general for deportation of illegal immigrants. It requires the state attorney general to maintain records of all reports on illegal immigrants received from state agencies and send them to the Immigration and Naturalization Service. It punishes any person who manufactures, distributes, or sells false documents by imprisonment or a fine and any person who uses false documents by imprisonment for five years or by a fine of up to $25,000.

Proposition 187 caused a huge controversy. Opponents attack the proposition's ineffectiveness in controlling illegal immigration, severe unintended consequences, and racist and scapegoating nature, while proponents defend its necessity, its benefits for cost savings and the economy, and its nonracist essence. California voters passed Proposition 187 with a margin of 59–41 percent on November 8, 1994. Except for a few measures on violation

Students rally against Proposition 187 during a protest in Los Angeles.

Photo by Rod Rolle/Liaison/Getty Images.

penalties, the major portions of Proposition 187 have been invalidated by federal district judge Mariana Pfaelzer.

See also California Ballot Proposition 54; California Ballot Proposition 209; California Ballot Proposition 227; Mexican Illegals, Labor Exploitation of.

Philip Yang

California Ballot Proposition 209

Initiated by two California State University professors, Glynn Custred and Thomas Wood, both of whom are self-described "angry white men," the 1996 Proposition 209 (the California Civil Rights Initiative) was the first ballot measure in the nation that sought to repeal affirmative action in public employment, public education, or public contracting. However, its real intent was disguised in neutral language, as shown in the following key paragraph: "The state shall not discriminate against, or grant preferential treatment to, any individual or group on the basis of race, sex, color, ethnicity, or national origin in the operation of public employment, public education, or public contracting."

Proposition 209 was passed by California voters on November 5, 1996, with 54 percent of the vote. Upon its passage, some anti-Proposition 209 groups immediately filed law suits. They contended that Proposition 209 contradicts federal civil rights laws, and that it violates the U.S. Constitution's equal-protection clause because it singles out women and minorities, making it more difficult for them to win passage of laws and policies that benefit them. After almost one year of legal battles, on November 3, 1997, the U.S. Supreme Court rejected, without comments, the appeal of the American Civil Liberties Union, clearing the way for the full enforcement of the nation's first across-the-board abolition of affirmative action in state and local government.

Proposition 209 has generated ripple effects across the nation. Other states and cities have initiated similar measures. Efforts were also made to push through Congress a bill to end affirmative action in public hiring and contracts. The latest Supreme Court rulings on lawsuits against the University of Michigan and its law school in admission policies virtually invalidate part of Proposition 209.

See also Affirmative Action; Affirmative Action, University of Michigan Ruling on; American Civil Liberties Union (ACLU); California Ballot Proposition 54; California Ballot Proposition 187; California Ballot Proposition 227; Statistical Discrimination.

Philip Yang

California Ballot Proposition 227

In November 1997, California voters passed Proposition 227 (The English Language Education for Children in Public Schools Initiative) with a large margin (61 percent yeas vs. 39 percent nays). The proposition was aimed at eliminating bilingual education in California public schools. It proposed the following key provisions:"All children in California public schools shall be taught English by being taught in English"; all children with limited English proficiency shall be placed in a sheltered English immersion program for a temporary period of no more than one year; under parental-waiver conditions (e.g., already with English proficiency, the child is age ten or older, or there are special physical, emotional, psychological, or educational needs), parents could request that their children be transferred to classes where children are taught through bilingual-education techniques permitted by law; and $50 million a year for ten years shall be allocated to fund programs of adult English-language instruction.

Cosponsored by Silicon Valley millionaire Ron Unz and Latino teacher Gloria Tuchman, Proposition 227 was an attempt to fix the problems of existing bilingual education in California, such as lengthy stays in bilingual-education programs, a lack of qualified bilingual teachers, and a deficiency in students' English proficiency, which is needed to compete in college and the labor market. However, there is no indication that the proposition's prescription has worked. Many parents have chosen to keep their children in bilingual-education programs. According to the California Department of Education, in the 1998–1999 school year, nearly 170,000 children remained in bilingual classrooms, down from 410,000 in the previous school year. Another 472,000 English learners received at least some "support" in their native language, compared to 306,000 in 1997–1998, despite threats of lawsuits by English-only advocates. Furthermore, Proposition 227 is seen to be shortsighted because it will turn potential bilinguals and multilinguals into monolinguals in an increasingly global economy. Some believe a legislative mandate for instructional programs is not needed and the choice should be left to parents and children.

See also Bilingual Education; California Ballot Proposition 54; California Ballot Proposition 187; California Ballot Proposition 209; English-Only Movement.

Philip Yang

Caló

Caló is a language of Chicano and Chicana youths that had its origin in the Segundo Barrio in downtown El Paso, Texas, in the 1920s and 1930s. Gang members there made up a language they called tirili, or hoodlum talk, which they used so that neither Mexicans nor Anglos could understand them. It was a source of pride that served to unite Spanish-speaking young people segregated from mainstream American life. Early in the 1940s, the gangs were run out of El Paso, and most of them moved to Los Angeles, taking with them an enthusiasm for wide brimmed hats, gold chains, trousers, and long coats, commonly referred to as zoot suits, and their secret language.

Caló is based on Spanish syntax and a Spanish lexicon, but with changed meanings. Although its roots are Spanish, Caló is not classic Spanish. Rather, it is a mix of Spanish Gypsy Caló, modern and archaic Spanish, Nahuatl, which is tied to Aztec culture, English, and invented words. English words, often swear words and those relating to drugs, are taken as is. Sometimes English words are the source of new words—*beer* becomes *birra*, *song* is *songa*, and *gang* is *ganga*—but *vatos* are *dudes*, *camarada* are *homeboys and home-girls*, *chingasos* is a *beating*.

Caló is used today by teens whether or not they are members of gangs. It has become the language of a teen subculture and has a vocabulary borrowed liberally not just from gang culture, but also from drug, prison, and urban street cultures. It is replete with expletives and other taboo language. Yet the interplay of language among generations and various groups naturally allows the Caló language to creep into otherwise normal speech. By its very nature, however, Caló is a dynamic language in a continual state of creation. At first a language used only by males, Caló remains today a source of Hispanic pride and unity for male and female youth.

See also Bilingual Education; "Black English" (Ebonics); Chicano Movement; Hispanics, Prejudice and Discrimination against; Zoot Suit Riots.

Benjamin F. Shearer

Campus Ethnoviolence

The term *ethnoviolence* refers to violent acts intended to do harm to individuals because of their actual or perceived membership in a particular group. Despite the word's linguistic roots, ethnoviolence does not refer only to acts committed because of ethnic or racial characteristics: gender, religion, national origin, sexual orientation, disability, and other such identifiers can also be involved. These acts can take many forms, from bias murders to racially offensive phone calls. They need not fulfill the popular definition of violence as requiring physical force: psychological and emotional harm falls fully under the definition of ethnoviolence.

When these incidents happen on college campuses, they are referred to as campus ethnoviolence. Acts that are considered ethnoviolence usually include one or more of the following: the use of epithets or slurs commonly directed against a particular group, the involvement of individuals or literature associated with hate organizations, the use of hate symbols, defacing or destroying property or events associated with a particular group, and acts fitting a pattern of prior attacks all targeted at a particular group. Perpetrators tend to be young adult males who are not affiliated with any organized hate groups. The Prejudice Institute has estimated that one out of every four or five Americans has been the target of ethnoviolence, most of whom have been targeted because of their racial or ethnic background. The Institute also believes that while the overall level of ethnoviolence has leveled off in recent years, more individual attacks are physically violent.

Ethnoviolence is different from the more widely known terms *hate crimes* and *bias crimes*, because actions that are considered ethnoviolence may not fit into the definition of a crime at all. Additionally, they may not involve an emotion as strong as hate, instead being perpetrated because of a desire for conformity, as part of some initiation ritual, or impulsively. However, the consequences of campus ethnoviolence affect both the individual victims of the acts and the entire community. After experiencing acts of ethnoviolence, many victims become subject to anxiety, fear, difficulty concentrating on work, and impaired social relations, and some may withdraw from school or move off-campus in response to an attack. It is estimated that only about one-fifth of victims of ethnoviolence report the attacks to campus officials, perhaps because of fear of reprisals, the belief that the officials will not care or believe them, or shame. The entire campus community can become racially or ethnically polarized after one or more attacks, resulting in difficult social interactions, uncomfortable classroom environments, and a bad reputation that can discourage the interest of prospective students. Because of the possibility of gaining a bad reputation, many college and university officials fail to report incidences of ethnoviolence to the federal government, despite laws requiring them to do so. Some college and university administrations have even gone so far as to seize copies of the campus newspaper that report on incidences of ethnoviolence so prospective students would not see the reports.

Many colleges and universities have, however, made a significant effort to prevent acts of ethnoviolence on their campuses and/or punish those responsible. Punishments can range from expulsion to compulsory community service, letters of apology, or sensitivity training. However, efforts to combat ethnoviolence are sometimes made difficult by the free-speech concerns of faculty and students. Regulations prohibiting racially motivated threats are seen by many individuals as limits on their free speech, which is guaranteed by the U.S. Constitution, in turn making free academic inquiry impossible. These individuals are particularly opposed to lumping speech in with physical action. However, institutional self-study committees have discovered ways to understand the kind of ethnoviolence occurring on campus, the sorts of individuals who perpetrate it, and potential solutions to the problem. One common approach is to create opportunities for intergroup dialogue and understanding so that potential perpetrators can learn how their actions might affect others. Additionally, self-studies that gather data on ethnoviolence can be used to combat the isolation of individual victims and help them speak out about their experiences to educate the wider campus community.

Further Reading

Hippensteele, Susan, and Meda Chesney-Lind. "Race and Sex Discrimination in the Academy: Rethinking Campus Ethnoviolence." *Thought and Action* 11, no. 2 (1995): 43–66.

Pincus, Fred L., and Howard Ehrlich. *Race and Ethnic Conflict: Contending Views on Prejudice, Discrimination, and Ethnoviolence.* Boulder, CO: Westview Press, 1999.

Mikaila Mariel Lemonik Arthur

Capitalism and Racial Inequality

Capitalism is an economic system that advocates the individual ownership of all the means of production that exist in society. These means of production include land, labor, capital, and machines. Capitalism is also based on the notion of free enterprise, minimum government regulations, and the exchange of goods based on supply and demand. Although Karl Marx introduced this term in the mid-nineteenth century to explain the economic system that existed in Western Europe, it was not fully adopted as a general definition of Western economies until the mid-twentieth century. Other important characteristics of capitalism are its emphasis on individual liberty and the promotion of entrepreneurship. Although capitalism has become the dominant economic system in the world today, it has been challenged for more than seventy years by communism, which is an economic system based on state ownership of the means of production and the private ownership of small businesses.

Capitalism began to emerge in Western Europe in the thirteenth century, but it was not until the eighteenth and late nineteenth centuries that it became the dominant economic system there. Since its beginnings, there has always been a correlation between capitalism and racial inequality. From the fifteenth to the nineteenth centuries, capitalist countries such as Holland, England, France, the United States, Spain, and Portugal used their power to colonize people of color around the world by extracting as much free labor and as many commodities as possible from the slave trade and their colonies.

As part of the capitalist system, these countries also created a racial hierarchy in which people of African origin and other people of color found themselves at the bottom of the ladder. Today, most of the wealthy countries are found in the Northern Hemisphere or in the white world, and the poor countries are located in the Southern Hemisphere. This racial hierarchy has had a great impact on the welfare of colored people in all societies, but primarily in countries that have a legacy of slavery, such as the United States and South Africa.

The United States is the most powerful capitalist country in the world today. It dominates the world's market in technology, agriculture, science, and entertainment and the arts. Although the United States is the richest country in the world, its minority population, composed primarily of African Americans, Latinos, and Native Americans, has not shared equally in the country's wealth. African Americans, for example, who suffered the most rigid form of slavery, still lag far behind whites in every economic and social indicator. Poverty remains a major obstacle to black Americans' advancement, and it is due primarily to the legacy of slavery, institutional discrimination, and subtle forms of individual discrimination.

Despite the great progress of capitalism in the twentieth century in economics, science, the arts, and technology, many capitalist countries have been unable to eliminate poverty in their society. The United States, for example, which is the most advanced capitalist country in the word, still has a large minority population that is poor and uneducated.

See also Economics and Politics of Race; Economics of Discrimination.

Further Reading

Manning, Marable. *How Capitalism Underdeveloped Black America*. Boston: South End Press, 1983.

Wilson, Julius. *The Truly Disadvantaged*. Chicago: University of Chicago Press, 1989.

Francois Pierre-Louis

Capital Punishment and Racial Inequality

Social-science research overwhelmingly indicates that race influences the decision to sentence a person to death. This research can be divided into two key categories. First, many studies show a disparity among those who are sentenced to the death penalty. Blacks are disproportionately receiving the punishment. In 2001, the Bureau of Justice Statistics reports that 55 percent of prisoners under a sentence of death are white and 43 percent are black (Snell and Maruschak 2002, 8). By way of comparison, the 2000 census indicates that 70 percent of the population in the United States is non-Hispanic and 12 percent is black. Some might argue that such a comparison is misleading, since it does not look at those people who are committing murder. Examining only those individuals arrested for murder and nonnegligent manslaughter in 2000—those most likely to be sentenced to death—48 percent are white and 48 percent are black, which still indicates a disparity, though not as glaring. Nevertheless, this trend does not seem to be decreasing, at least with respect to those receiving the ultimate sentence. Based on numbers supplied by the Bureau of Justice Statistics there was a 56 percent increase between 1991 and 2001 in the number of blacks under a sentence of death. For the same years, there was only a 35 percent increase in the number of whites being sentenced to death (Snell and Maruschak 2002, 1).

Second, in cases for which there is a black crime victim, an outcome of the death penalty is much less likely. One recent study by Amnesty International, for example, states, "While blacks and whites are murdered in roughly equal numbers in the USA, the killers of white people are six times as likely to be put to death. . . ." That same article further pointed out that studies in Illinois, Maryland, New Jersey, North Carolina, Pennsylvania, Texas, and Virginia and by the U.S. General Accounting Office all indicate similar findings (*USA Today* 2003, 14A).

One study indicating that race influences the likelihood of receiving the death penalty is cited by U.S. Supreme Court Justice Harry Blackmun: "A renowned example of racism infecting a capital-sentencing scheme is documented in *McCleskey v. Kemp*, 481 U.S. 279 (1987)[,] . . . a highly reliable statistical study (the Baldus Study) which indicated that, 'after taking into account some 230 nonracial factors . . . the jury *more likely than not* would have spared McCleskey's life had his victim been black.' 481 U.S. at 325 [emphasis in original] (Brennan, J., dissenting). The Baldus study further demonstrated that blacks who kill whites are sentenced to death 'at nearly *22 times* the rate of blacks who kill blacks, and more than 7 *times* the rate of whites who kill blacks.' *Id.*, at 327 [emphasis in original]" (*Callins v. Collins* 510 U.S. 1153–1154).

Currently, thirty-eight states, the U.S. government, and the U.S. military have capital punishment statutes. Alaska, the District of Columbia, Hawaii, Iowa, Maine, Massachusetts, Michigan, Minnesota, North Dakota, Rhode Island, Vermont, West Virginia, and Wisconsin do not have a death penalty statute. In the past, the death penalty has been found unconstitutional by the Supreme Court. In the case *Furman v. Georgia* (408 U.S. 238 [1972]), the high court held that the death penalty was unconstitutional due to it being capricious and arbitrary as to who is eligible for execution. Most states changed their laws to make the death penalty mandatory for certain offenses. This supposedly removed the problems with capital punishment statutes. Based on the revised statutes, the Supreme Court in *Gregg v. Georgia* (428 U.S. 153 [1976]) once again found the death penalty constitutional. Since then there have been 842 executions (Fins 2003, 9). The high court continues to grapple with this issue. Most recently, it held that the execution of the mentally retarded is unconstitutional (*Atkins v. Virginia*, 122 S. Ct. 2242 [2002]).

Although there are many powerful arguments against capital punishment, including its racial inequality, most people in the United States still favor it, which has been the trend since the early 1970s. A recent poll confirmed this trend, with 67 percent of respondents indicating that they favor capital punishment. However, when analyzing the responses to this poll by ethnicity, a different picture emerges. Whites overwhelmingly favor the death penalty (73 percent) as do Hispanics (63 percent). Blacks are least likely to favor the death penalty and are almost evenly split on the issue, with (46 percent favoring and 43 percent opposing) (*Sourcebook of Criminal Justice Statistics* 2001, 141). It is clear that this issue is divided along racial lines.

One of the most outspoken supporters of the death penalty is legal scholar Ernest van den Haag. With respect to racial disparity, van den Haag argues, "Even if poor or black convicts guilty of capital offenses suffer capital punishment, and other convicts equally guilty of the same crimes do not, a more equal distribution, however desirable, would merely be more equal. . . . The only relevant question is: does the person to be executed deserve the punishment? Whether or not others who deserved the same punishment, whatever their economic or racial group, have avoided execution is irrelevant. . . . [Additionally,] because most black murderers kill blacks, black murderers are spared the death penalty more often than white murderers. . . . The motivation behind unequal distribution of the death penalty may well have been to discriminate against blacks, but the result has favored them" (van den Haag, 2001, 267). Although the arguments against the death penalty seem to far outweigh those for it, the American public, for whatever reason, seems to favor the arguments of scholars such as van den Haag.

See also Criminal Justice System and Racial Discrimination.

Further Reading

Amnesty International USA. "Death Penalty Discriminates against Black Crime Victims." *USA Today*, April 29, 2003.

———. "United States of America—Death by Discrimination—The Continuing Role of Race in Capital Cases." *USA Today*, April 24, 2003.

Fins, Deborah. "Death Row U.S.A. Spring 2003." A quarterly report by the Criminal Justice project of the NAACP Legal Defense and Educational Fund, Inc. Found at http://www.deathpenaltyinfo.org/DEATHROWUSArecent.pdf.

Snell, Tracy, and Laura M. Masuschak. "Capital Punishment 2001." *Bureau of Justice Statistics Bulletin*. U.S. Department of Justice. Washington, DC, December 2002.

Sourcebook of Criminal Justice Statistics, 2001. Washington, DC: U.S. Government Printing Office, 2002.

van den Haag, Ernest. "The Ultimate Punishment: A Defense." In *Taking Sides: Clashing Views on Controversial Issues in Crime and Criminology*. 6th ed., edited by Richard C. Monk. New York: McGraw Hill, 2001. Originally published in the *Harvard Law Review* in 1986.

John Eterno

Caribbean Immigrants, Attitudes toward African Americans

Caribbean or West Indian immigrants from Jamaica, Guyana, Trinidad, Barbados, Haiti, and Grenada arrived in the United States in large numbers after 1965. The majority of them have settled in New York City where African Americans comprise a significant proportion of the population. In those countries, divisions purely along racial lines are not salient because blacks comprise the vast majority of their populations and possess a great deal of economic and political power there. Race is conceived as a continuum of color rather than a bipolar category, and class and race are intertwined in a fluid manner. Thus, Caribbeans come to the United States with identities based on nationality, social class, or political parties, as shaped by the individual history of their countries. Once in the United States, Caribbeans in the new context have, then, the option of adopting the identity handed down to them and to "become" black, continuing to identify themselves along individual nationalities, or else to retain their identities as become West Indians or Caribbeans. Their attitudes toward black Americans are influenced by how they identify themselves.

To date, there are no studies of Caribbean attitudes toward blacks based on representative samples. But Mary C. Waters, who conducted in-depth interviews with West Indian immigrants, found that once in the United States, they are ambivalent about identifying themselves in a manner that blurs all distinctions from American blacks (1999, 53–58). When asked about how they would answer a hypothetical census question about race, the interviewed Caribbean immigrants, particularly those who were of middle-class origin, light skinned, or of mixed-ancestry, expressed reluctance about saying they were black, even if they did so for lack of any other option. Others develop a "raceless" persona, saying that they never had thought themselves as black, or that being black made any difference in their lives. And a few volunteered that the census question about race was asked in order to discriminate against them.

Waters has found that "most immigrants distanced themselves from black Americans and wanted other people to know that they were not the same." Although some adopted the term *American* as part of their identity "they did not want to be seen as simply 'black American' because for most of them assimilation to black America was downward mobility." They pointed to the differences in cultures, attitudes toward work, and emphasis on family life as important characteristics that in their eyes separated them from African Americans.

A 1992 study of Caribbeans in New York also showed that often they preferred an ethnic to a racial identity. For example, the activities of voluntary associations, such as dinners, dances, beauty contests, and so forth, emphasized culture as a central factor in public identity. The author, Philip Kasinitz, points out that "intentionally or not, such activities tend to differentiate West Indians from African Americans." Yet, emphasis on ethnic differences does not imply that, as a whole, Caribbeans are apart from blacks. Early cohorts of Caribbeans, in addition to maintaining their own social networks and organizations, became part of the broader black community, often as their economic and political leaders. During the 1970s and 1980s West Indians and their descendents have been overrepresented in the political and economic leadership of the New York's black community. In this sense, many West Indians saw no contradiction between representing or working for the black community and maintaining an ethnic identity.

Caribbean immigrants' attitudes toward African Americans are context dependent, subject to economic and political forces, and above all they do not escape the larger societal race divisions. When they perceive discrimination against black Americans, or they find themselves in the minority, they side with blacks, assuming a racial identity; they tend to assume a West Indian identity when it is important to emphasize achievement in school or politics (Waters 1999, 63). As a minority in the U.S. context, Caribbeans rapidly come to terms with a white majority that holds positions of authority and has the power to discriminate. To this extent, foreign-born blacks have clear perceptions of racism in the workplace, and in public schools. The ethnic status adopted by Caribbeans appears to be no guarantee against experiences of racism.

See also Black Identities: West Indian Immigrant Dreams and American Realities; Caribbean Immigrants, Class Differences in the Second Generation; Caribbean Immigrants, Experience of Racial Discrimination; Proximal Host; Racialization.

Further Reading

Kasinitz, Philip. *Caribbean New York: Black Immigrants and the Politics of Race*. Ithaca, NY: Cornell University Press, 1992.

Waters, Mary C. *Black Identities: West Indian Immigrant Dreams and American Realities*. Cambridge, MA: Harvard University Press, 1999.

Carmenza Gallo

Caribbean Immigrants, Class Differences in the Second Generation

Regardless of country of origin, immigrants tend to adopt an identity based on their immigrant status in the United States. Thus, although to various degrees and by different means, the first generation's identities emphasize cultural aspects that differentiate them from nonimmigrants' identities. This seems to be true even when most identify as first generation immigrants along nonethnic characteristics, such as race, as is the case to some extent with Caribbean or West Indian immigrants. Yet, second-generation Caribbeans may adopt one among several identities, including at least an ethnic identity that preserves the characteristics emphasized by the first generation, or an American identity that emphasizes cultural commonalties with nonimmigrant groups.

In in-depth interviews with second-generation West Indian adolescents researcher Mary C. Waters found three dominant types of identities, largely depending on the adolescents' social class: ethnic, immigrant, and American identity (1999). Ethnic identity stressed distinctiveness from black Americans, particularly with respect to attitudes toward education, work ethic, and family. Youth with this type of identity believed that being a black American involved more than merely having black skin. But because they were conscious that the larger society could identify them by their skin color, they consciously tried to accentuate their ethnic traits, making sure others knew that they were not "merely" black (Waters 1999, 293–96). Immigrant identity, in turn, stressed nationality as a defining characteristic. Youth who adopted this identity were largely foreign born. It was different from an ethnic identity in that these youth "did not feel as much pressure to 'choose' between identifying with or distancing from black Americans as did either the American or ethnic respondents." They do not conceive of themselves as having a choice or of being perceived by others as black Americans (302–303). Last, American identity emphasized race as a defining characteristic, simultaneously embracing aspects of black American culture, including black English and music. According to Waters, for these youth, assimilation to America means assimilation to black America. Characteristically, this group perceived racism in the larger society and was aware of the generalized negative view of blacks held by whites. The author argues that this type of identity is similar to the "oppositional identity" adopted by stigmatized groups, which defines as good and worthy those very traits that the larger culture stigmatize.

The social-class background of the respondents in Waters' study influenced youth's identities. Middle-class youth in integrated neighborhoods, tended to adopt an ethnic identity, while those in poor neighborhoods tended to be immigrant- or American-identified. It appeared that middle-class children used ethnicity as a resource, given that in the neighborhoods they lived in and the schools they attended they had more contact with whites. It was thus important to draw differences between themselves and black Americans to strengthen assimilation to a middle-class status. This was not so with poorer second-generation immigrants who were generally in more segregated schools and neighborhoods and who consequently had less contact with whites.

The paths of identity formation among second-generation Caribbean immigrants suggest that the linear model of assimilation based on immigrants' experience at the beginning of the twentieth century is not applicable to the descendents of the 1960s immigrant wave. This model predicted that the second generation would be more culturally assimilated and less distinguishable than their parents. Now, as some studies with second-generation Cubans also suggest, economically mobile children tend to keep their ethnic identities, while less successful second-generation immigrants show greater assimilation with the American world they know and live in.

See also Black Identities: West Indian Immigrant Dreams and American Realities; Caribbean Immigrants, Attitudes toward African Americans; Caribbean Immigrants, Experience of Racial Discrimination; Oppositional Identity; Proximal Host; Racialization.

Further Reading

Portes, Alejandro, and Min Zhou. "The New Second Generation: Segmented Assimilation and Its Variants." *Annals of the American Academy of Political and Social Sciences* 530 (November 1993): 74–96.

Waters, Mary C. *Black Identities: West Indian Immigrant Dreams and American Realities.* Cambridge, MA: Harvard University Press, 1999.

Carmenza Gallo

Caribbean Immigrants, Experience of Racial Discrimination

Caribbean immigrants' experience of racial discrimination is shaped by two dominant factors: skin color and immigration experience. Insofar as direct and indirect institutional racism condenses the sources of social and economic inequalities based on race, Caribbean immigrants' experience of discrimination (particularly when they are poor), is no different from that of black Americans. As many Caribbeans are perceived as black in the United States, they mostly have access to housing in predominantly segregated black neighborhoods, where it is difficult to escape the effects of the discriminatory practices embedded in the economic, political, and educational institutions. Poverty and segregation have been shown to reinforce each other: living in a black-segregated neighborhood increases the likelihood of dropping out of high school and the risk of teenage and single parenthood, and it decreases the likelihood of going to college and of being employed. It also reduces income earned as an adult. This is so because segregation concentrates poverty and poverty's cultural and structural effects.

Substantial numbers of West Indian immigrants, however, are middle-class professionals. Indeed, Caribbean immigrants are often considered a model minority because of their economic success. They have been overrepresented among black professionals, businessmen, and political leaders. They also own their homes in large numbers and have a median household income higher than other minorities, notably, black Americans. In fact, on the basis of this economic success some scholars have questioned theories that argue that white racism handicaps blacks (Sowell 1981). Other scholars disagree, pointing out that color has confined West Indian professionals and businessmen to positions within the black community, and that even middle-class blacks are geographically segregated.

Furthermore, Caribbean immigrants' experience of discrimination is substantially mediated by whether they identify themselves as black, as Caribbean, or according to their individual nationalities. For one thing, West Indians emigrate from countries where blacks are the majority, and where discrimination is identified more with social class than with race. In addition, in these countries skin color is a continuum, not a bipolar classification. Once in the United States, Caribbean immigrants are surprised and skeptical about the importance of race in the social and economic realms of their lives. In addition, because immigrants come to the United States in search of economic opportunity, they believe that success depends on individual and family effort, not on immutable characteristics like skin color. Thus, although West Indians talk about racial discrimination at work or in the real estate market, for example, they, "like other voluntary immigrants, . . . are likely to see prejudice and discrimination as more isolated occurrences, and as temporary barriers to overcome. . . ." (Waters 1999, 147). This belief, according to researcher Mary C. Waters, may shield them against failure, helps explain their social and economic mobility, and separates them subjectively and politically from black Americans.

Economic success that provides the means to promote ethnicity and to celebrate Caribbean cultures as well as the continued arrival of new immigrants will, in all likelihood, help maintain or even enhance the importance of West Indians' ethnic identities and mediate their perceptions of race in the United States. Yet, economic success, at the same time, exposes Caribbean immigrants to greater contact with whites and thus the increased likelihood of experiencing interpersonal racism. These two trends will thus continue to play out in the near future with uncertain results in the contact between Caribbean immigrants and the larger society.

See also Black Identities: West Indian Immigrant Dreams and American Realities; Caribbean Immigrants, Attitudes toward African Americans; Caribbean Immigrants, Class Differences in the Second Generation; Proximal Host; Racialization.

Further Reading

Kasinitz, Philip. *Caribbean New York: Black Immigrants and the Politics of Race.* Ithaca, NY: Cornell University Press, 1992.

Massey, Douglas, and Nancy Denton. *American Apartheid: Segregation and the Making of the Underclass.* Cambridge, MA: Harvard University Press, 1993.

Sowell, Thomas. *Ethnic America.* New York: Basic Books, 1981.

Waters, Mary C. *Black Identities: West Indian Immigrant Dreams and American Realities.* Cambridge, MA: Harvard University Press, 1999.

Carmenza Gallo

Carmichael, Stokely (1941–1998)

A charismatic speaker and social activist, Stokely Carmichael is credited with helping to usher in the Black Power movement in the United States in the 1960s. Carmichael was born in Port-of-Spain, Trinidad, but grew up in a predominately white neighborhood in the Bronx, New York. At Howard University in Washington, DC, where he earned a bachelor's degree in philosophy in 1964, Carmichael became active in the civil rights movement and took part in sit-ins, marches, and other demonstrations. In 1966, he became the chairman of the Student Nonviolent Coordinating Committee (SNCC). During a speech, he challenged listeners toward "Black Power," and this theme became a hallmark symbol of black protest that was adopted by other groups such as the Black Nationalists and the Black Panthers, the latter of which Carmichael would later serve as prime minister. Although organizations such as the Congress of Racial Equality (CORE) and the National Association for the Advancement of Colored People (NAACP) were central to civil rights efforts, they

Stokely Carmichael addressing an audience, 1966.

Courtesy Library of Congress.

were often perceived as more conservative in their approach for racial redress. SNCC's younger membership galvanized efforts to fight racial discrimination and segregation. Carmichael emphasized the need for Black solidarity, cultural awareness, and political and economic empowerment.

In the late 1960s, Carmichael's activism took on a more global perspective, and he focused attention on the empowerment of Africa. He moved to Ghana to take part in the All-African People's Revolutionary Party and, in 1978, changed his name to Kwame Ture. He continued to tour as a lecturer and public intellectual until his death in 1998. Although various civil rights figures have been associated with the symbol of "Black Power," based on his selfless attempts to promote the empowerment of people of African descent, Carmichael is often considered the embodiment of the statement.

See also Black Nationalist Movement; Congress of Racial Equality (CORE); Internal Colonialism; Student Nonviolent Coordinating Committee (SNCC).

Sandra L. Barnes

Chavez, Cesar (1927–1993)

Chavez was a charismatic Mexican American labor activist who organized migrant farm workers in the western United States. In his lifetime, he became an icon of the American social-justice movement. Chavez was born near Yuma, Arizona, and when he was about ten, his family lost their farm and were forced to become migrant farm workers in California. Often on the move, Chavez attended thirty-seven schools. After his father suffered an accident when he was in the eighth grade, Chavez quit school to work as a migrant worker. At 17, he joined the navy and served two years in the western Pacific during World War II. Afterward, he returned to California, married Helen Fabela, and eventually had eight children. In 1952, he became a community organizer in the Latino community, working on issues such as voter registration and police brutality. Beginning in 1962, he focused on the plight of migrant farm workers, cofounding the National Farm Workers Association (NFWA) with Dolores Huerta.

In 1971, the union joined the AFL-CIO and became the United Farm Workers (UFW). Under his leadership, the union grew greatly in power and influence, especially during the 1960s and 1970s. An avid reader, Chavez was inspired by St. Francis of Assisi and Mahatma Gandhi and their ideas about public service and nonviolence. He organized dynamic, peaceful protests, such as boycotts, pickets, and marches, which won widespread public support, and he also endured many hunger strikes to draw attention to the workers' travails. In the 1980s and 1990s, the union's power began waning. Chavez died in his sleep on April 23, 1993, and at his request, he was buried at UFW headquarters in La Paz, California, in a simple pine coffin made by his brother, Richard.

See also Boycotts; El Teatro Campensino; United Farm Workers (UFW).

Rose Kim

Cherokee Nation v. Georgia

In December 1828, the Georgia legislature passed a law stipulating that the land in Georgia occupied by the Cherokee be divided into parcels and opened up for white settlement. The next year, it passed law declaring that all laws made by the Cherokee nation were null and void and that no Cherokee could testify in court against a white man. With the two new laws, the state of Georgia tried to evict the Cherokees out of the state. But the Cherokees responded with a lawsuit, claiming that the two Georgia laws were contrary to the U.S. Constitution, congressional legislation, and a treaty between the federal government and the Indians (the Treaty of Hopewell, 1785). The U.S. Supreme Court rejected the claim, arguing that the court did not have the legal juris-

Cesar Chavez, head of the United Farm Workers, championed farm labor and the working class.

Courtesy Library of Congress.

diction to hear the Cherokees' complaint because Indians were "domestic dependent nations" rather than foreign nations and that only the latter had the right to use the Supreme Court in a dispute with a state.

In 1831, Samuel Worcester and other white missionaries were arrested for living with Cherokees in violation of a law designed to prevent whites from encouraging the Cherokees to oppose the new state laws. Challenging his conviction, Worcester took the case to the court, claiming that this and other anti-Indian laws passed by Georgia were invalid. The case went to the Supreme Court, which this time gave a decision favorable to Worcester and the Cherokees. The chief justice, John Marshall, declared that the Cherokee nation was "a distinct community, occupying its own territory, with boundaries accurately described, in which the law of Georgia can have no force. . . ." (Jaret 1995,

543). He further declared that only the federal government had control over relations between Native Americans and U.S. citizens.

See also Native Americans, Conquest of; Native Americans, Forced Relocation of; Native Americans, Prejudice and Discrimination against.

Further Reading

Jaret, Charles. *Contemporary Racial and Ethnic Relations*. New York: HarperCollins, 1995.

Pyong Gap Min

Chicano Movement

The Chicano movement (also known as El Movimiento, La Causa, and La Raza) had its earliest roots in the federal government's attempts to avoid fulfilling the terms of the Treaty of Guadalupe Hidalgo, which ended the war between the United States and Mexico over the territory that now makes up Texas. This treaty, created in 1848, guaranteed citizenship and land rights to former citizens of Mexico who elected to remain in the areas annexed by the United States, but when these rights conflicted with the economic interests of new settlers (such as during the Gold Rush years), the treaty provisions often were ignored. However, the movement did not emerge as an organized entity until the mid-1960s, with the founding of the Crusade for Justice by Corky Gonzales and the effort to unionize farm workers in California spearheaded by farm-labor activist Cesar Chavez. These efforts resulted in the formation of the United Farm Workers (UFW) in 1970, the first union of farm workers in the country. It remains difficult to unionize the migrant laborers who make up the labor pool for American farms, particularly as many may not speak English and some are in the United States illegally, but the UFW has been able to unionize many workers and farms and win important benefits, such as pension plans for its members.

Before this time, the label "Chicano" was a derogatory term used to describe recent arrivals from Mexico, but the movement reclaimed the term as a way to demonstrate pride in their Mexican origins—particularly in light of the fact that many individuals of Mexican descent in the United States never immigrated to this country but instead became Americans because of the movement of national boundaries. Additionally, it is important to note that Chicanos, like many South Americans, are predominantly of mixed European-indigenous (mestizo) backgrounds, so the movement drew heavily on both the Spanish-Catholic tradition and Aztec mythology. The Chicano movement sees its homeland as Aztlán, a place grounded in Aztec myths and bounded by the United States-Mexico border to the south, the Pacific Ocean to the west, and the boundaries set by the Treaty of Guadalupe Hidalgo on the north and east.

One of the best-known instances of *el movimiento* (movement) activism was the Chicano Moratorium on August 29, 1970, in Los Angeles. This protest was against the Vietnam War, prompted in part by Chicano soldiers being killed in disproportionately large numbers. The organizers believed that the high casualties of Chicanos were caused by more of them being assigned to the frontline out of prejudice. The hundreds of demonstrators were predominantly non-violent, but the police used tear gas against them anyway, resulting in three deaths. One of those killed was Ruben Salazar, a journalist who was in a restaurant at the time of his death, not out demonstrating.

Around this time, the movement also created a political party called La Raza Unida. This party had a national convention in 1972 and ran candidates for office on a platform of equality, justice, and the provision of social services. It was a strong force in local politics in Texas and Southern California until its demise in 1981, which was variously attributed to new political opportunities (such as a Mexican organization within the Democratic Party), the criminal conviction of one of its leaders, and increasing immigration from other parts of Latin America that made the development of a more expansive Latino identity a necessity for national political success.

Another important organization formed in the early days of the Chicano movement was MEChA (the Spanish acronym for The Chicano Student Movement of Aztlán), founded in 1969. This was and remains a national college student organization for Chicano/as. MEChA has worked to increase options for Chicano studies on campuses where it is active, function as a support group for Chicano students, and resist political proposals unfavorable to Chicanos. The student component of the Chicano movement has been particularly strong in Los Angeles high schools and on University of California campuses. These students pushed for an end to admissions policies that discriminated against poor, underprivileged, and immigrant students; the provision of services like bilingual education and financial aid to help Chicano/a students get ahead; and the development of Chicano/a studies programs to provide a "relevant" education. It has remained at the forefront of the Chicano movement in more contemporary struggles, including those against California propositions 187 (cutting off many social services to illegal immigrants), 209 (ending affirmative action in public institutions of higher education), and 227 (abolishing bilingual education in California). Despite the efforts of MEChA and other organizations in el movimiento, all of these propositions passed, which demonstrates how much further the movement still has to go.

See also California Ballot Proposition 187; California Ballot Proposition 209; California Ballot Proposition 227; Chavez, Cesar; El Teatro Campensino; Hispanics, Prejudice and Discrimination against; La Raza Unida; Mexican American Legal Defense and Education Fund (MALDEF); Mexican Americans, Prejudice and Discrimination against; Mexican Americans, Violence against; Mexican Illegals, Labor Exploitation of; United Farm Workers (UFW).

Further Reading

Munoz, Carlos. *The Chicano Movement: Youth, Identity, and Power*. New York: Verso Books, 2003.

Navarro, Armando. *La Raza Unida Party: A Chicano Challenge to the U.S. Two-Party Dictatorship*. Philadelphia: Temple University Press, 2000.

Rosales, Franciso A. *Chicano! The History of the Mexican American Civil Rights Movement*. Houston: Arte Publico Press, 1997.

Mikaila Mariel Lemonik Arthur

Chin, Vincent (1955–1982)

In June 1982, Chinese American Vincent Chin, age twenty-seven, was murdered in Detroit, Michigan, by two white automobile-factory workers, who mistook him for being Japanese and blamed him for the loss of American automotive jobs. The ensuing court cases and community activism became symbolic of the ongoing fight of Asian Amerians against anti-Asian violence as well as their quest for the protection of their civil rights and equal protection under the law. On June 19, Chin was out with friends at a Detroit bar, celebrating his upcoming wedding, when Ronald Ebens and his stepson, Michael Nitz, taunted them and a fight broke out. Both groups were kicked out of the bar, but Ebens and Nitz went to their car, retrieved a baseball bat, and again accosted Chin and his friends in the parking lot. Ebens and Nitz chased them for twenty minutes, finally catching Chin outside a McDonald's restaurant. While Nitz held Chin, Ebens brutally beat him with the baseball bat, shattering his skull. Chin died four days later from his injuries.

Both men were charged with second-degree murder, but in a plea bargain, Ebens agreed to a lesser charge of manslaughter. In a much-criticized decision, Judge Charles Kaufman sentenced each of the men to three years of probation and fines of $3,870. Asian Americans in Detroit and eventually across the United States were outraged by the decision to issue such a light sentence for such a brutal murder. Chinese Americans joined with Korean, Japanese, and Filipino Americans to form Citizens for Justice to work for a just response to Chin's case. Chin's mother, Lily, overcame her limited English to become a prominent spokesperson for the cause. Her great-grandfather had immigrated to the United States in the nineteenth century to work in railroad construction. Chin's father, Hing, had immigrated to the United States in 1922 and served in the U.S. Army in World War II. The parents had worked in a Chinese laundry until Hing's death, when Lily began working in an automobile factory. But following her son's murder and the disappointing trial results, Chin's mother, feeling deprived of hope for a decent life in the United States, returned to China.

In response to the intense criticism of his decision, Judge Kaufman explained that the sentences were predicated on both men being citizens of the community; they were either employed (Ebens was an auto-factory foreman) or in school (Nitz had been laid off and was a part-time student); they had no prior record; and, in the judge's opinion, they were unlikely to repeat their offense. Newspaper editorials in Michigan decried the implication that if one was employed or in school one essentially could get a license to kill for only $3,800. After an investigation, the U.S. Justice Department found evidence of a civil rights violation, and in 1983 a federal grand jury indicted both men on charges of violating Chin's right to enjoy a public space. In 1984, a federal jury in the U.S. District Court found Ebens guilty but acquitted Nitz. Ebens was sentenced to twenty-five years in prison but was let go after posting a $20,000 bond. His conviction was later overturned on a technicality in a 1986 retrial. Neither man served jail time for the murder of Chin.

A documentary film, *Who Killed Vincent Chin?*, produced by Christine Choy and Renee Tajima in 1988, explored the case and the ensuing community activism. The film included recollections of those who knew Chin, those who had witnessed the events, the heroic appeals of Chin's mother, and, perhaps most striking, footage of Ronald Ebens. The film has become a classic in the continuing struggle to stop anti-Asian violence and protect the civil rights of Asian Americans. Chin's case played a significant role in mobilizing a new generation of Asian Americans to resist the stereotyping, discrimination, and violence that had been directed against their community for more than a century.

See also Asian Americans, Violence against; Chinese Exclusion Act of 1882; Chinese Immigrants and Anti-Chinese Sentiments; Hate Crimes; Pan-Asian Solidarity.

Further Reading

Chan, Sucheng. *Asian Americans: An Interpretive History*. New York: Twayne Publishers, 1991.

Wu, Frank H. *Yellow: Race in America beyond Black and White*. New York: Basic Books, 2003.

Kenneth J. Guest

Chinese Exclusion Act of 1882

A culmination of years of efforts to exclude Chinese economically and legally, the Chinese Exclusion Act of 1882 made it illegal for Chinese laborers to enter the United States and denied naturalized citizenship to Chinese people already in the country. Initially in place for ten years, the act was extended in 1892 as the Geary Act and made permanent in 1902. The Chinese Exclusion Act marked the beginning of efforts to restrict all immigration to the United States, which was finally codified in the National Origins Act of 1924 and only repealed in 1943 in deference to China's role as a U.S. ally in World War II. It stands as the first and only federal law to attempt to limit immigration of a particular national-origin group.

Anti-Chinese Sentiment and Early Attempts at Exclusion

Chinese immigrants first arrived in California in 1949 to participate in the Gold Rush, and they soon entered the agricultural sector and, later, railroad construction. Initially welcomed as cheap and cooperative labor, Chinese immigrants quickly drew the ire of white immigrant laborers, who considered these "coolies" to be a threat to their jobs and wages. California's nineteenth-century economy fluctuated wildly from boom to bust, and Chinese workers became an easy scapegoat for white workers' economic woes. Anti-Chinese sentiments spread quickly, as did acts of anti-Chinese violence, including riots, beatings, and lynchings.

California's politicians exploited nativist sentiment to attract the votes of white workers and enacted a series of laws designed to exclude the Chinese from full participation in California society and preserve California for "Americans." The Foreign Miners License Tax (1852) targeted the expanding Chinese population by levying a monthly tax of $20 on every foreign miner who did not desire to become a citizen. Precluded from citizenship by a 1790 U.S. federal law, Chinese miners fell under the tax until its repeal by the federal Civil Rights Act of 1870. In *People v. Hall* (1854) the California Supreme Court ruled that both American-born and immigrant Chinese could not testify for or against whites in court. In 1855, California imposed a landing tax of $50 per person for transporting persons of Chinese origin or descent into the state. The 1862 California law entitled "To Protect Free White Labor against Competition with Chinese Coolie Labor, and to Discourage the Immigration of the Chinese into the State of California," established a monthly tax of $2.50 on Chinese residents of California unless they operated a business or were licensed to work in a mine or agriculture. The 1875 Page Law prohibited the entry of Chinese prostitutes. Its concomitant interrogations and examinations intimidated and discouraged many potential women immigrants, leading to a 68 percent decline in Chinese women arrivals between 1876 and 1882, compared with the previous seven-year period.

Anti-Chinese sentiment was not limited to the U.S. West Coast. East Coast missionaries, merchants, and diplomats often disparaged the Chinese as godless, dishonest, and uncouth. When, after the opening of the transcontinental railroad in 1867, Calvin T. Sampson recruited seventy-five Chinese workers from California to break the strike at his shoe factory in Adams, Massachusetts, other manufacturers soon followed suit, and anti-Chinese sentiment spread quickly among white East Coast workers. As a result, when California politicians sought to enact anti-Chinese legislation on a national level, their efforts found a receptive audience. In a nation evenly divided between Republicans and Democrats, the threat of Chinese workers became a useful rallying cry for getting out the vote.

An initial attempt to enact Chinese exclusion on a federal level in 1879 passed both houses of Congress. President Rutherford B. Hayes vetoed the act, however, charging that it was an abrogation of the 1869 Burlingame-Seward Treaty. That treaty, while primarily serving to allow U.S. industry to recruit Chinese laborers, had also recognized the right of migration between China and the United States, marking a sea change in China's restrictive policies on trade and migration. To overcome President Hayes' objections, a new treaty allowing the United States to regulate Chinese immigration was negotiated in 1880 and signed into law in 1881. In 1882 the U.S. Congress passed the Chinese Exclusion Act again, and this time President Chester Arthur signed it into law.

The Act and Its Extensions

The passage of the 1882 Chinese Exclusion Act initiated a series of increasingly narrow federal laws designed to exclude Chinese immigrants and institute national origins as the criteria for restricting immigration and controlling the ethnic and racial composition of the U.S. population, a trajectory that culminated in the passage of the National Origins Act of 1924. The Chinese Exclusion Act, initially enacted for ten years, denied entry to Chinese laborers while providing exceptions for Chinese merchants, diplomats, teachers, students, and tourists. Later laws placed additional limits on Chinese immigrants already settled in the United States. In an 1884 Supreme Court case, a Chinese laborer residing in the United States returned to China and married. Upon returning together to the United States, the wife was denied admission. In its decision, the court ruled that Chinese women who married laborers were assigned their husbands' status upon marriage and so were prohibited admission. The 1888 Scott Act expanded exclusion to all Chinese except merchants. In addition, the Scott Act prohibited Chinese laborers who left the United States to return and canceled the reentry permits of those who had left previously and not yet returned to the United States, leaving more than twenty thousand Chinese stranded outside the United States, often separated from families and property. The 1894 modifications to the Scott Act allowed laborers with wives, children, or $1,000 in assets in the United States to return. The Geary Act of 1892 extended the Chinese Exclusion Act for ten more years and required Chinese laborers in the United States to obtain a certificate of residence. Failure to register within one year could be punished by deportation. In 1902, Congress extended the Chinese Exclusion Act indefinitely.

Impact on the Chinese Community in the United States

The passage of the Chinese Exclusion Act and subsequent efforts to strengthen and extend its provisions had a profound impact on the Chinese community in America. In the succeeding years the Chinese population contracted dramatically as fewer immigrants were able to enter the United States and those who left were unable to return. The severe restrictions on the immigration of women, coupled with the pattern of young men migrating alone, led to the emergence of a largely bachelor society unable to reproduce itself. While the 1880 census recorded 105,465 Chinese and the 1890 census, 107,488, by 1900 the number had dropped to 89,863 and by 1920, to 61,639. The impact on communities in China as well should not be underestimated, as men who had gone abroad were unable to return for visits without losing their right to reentry, and their wives were left in China, effectively becoming widows.

Faced with rising anti-Chinese sentiment and the need to rely on Chinese compatriots for protection, social networks, and economic support, Chinatowns began to emerge in the urban centers of the West Coast. Forced to retreat into their own cultural and economic colonies, in the late 1800s and early decades of the twentieth century, Chinese immigrants and their children converged on urban areas and shifted their employment niches from gold mining, agriculture, and railroad construction to laundries, restaurants, and light manufacturing, including garment factories. Chinatowns also began to attract white tourists, drawn to their images as exotic and foreign places.

Resistance to Exclusion

Escalating efforts by the U.S. government to prohibit Chinese immigration were met by increasingly creative efforts to circumvent those laws. The smuggling of Chinese workers across the Canadian-U.S. and Mexican-U.S. borders became a lucrative business for Chinese Americans and whites. But Chinese immigration to the United States, including laborers, continued, with entrants falling under the categories of merchant, student, teacher, diplomat, and tourist. Noncitizen laundrymen, laborers, and restaurant owners sought to represent themselves as "paper merchants" by buying shares in a merchant's company or by bribing a merchant to list them as a partner. Once recognized as a "merchant," Chinese immigrants were permitted to bring families to the United States under provisions of the Chinese Exclusion Act.

Statutes allowing citizens to bring wives and children to the United States led to the development of a "paper son" strategy. Children of citizens were automatically citizens of the United States even if born abroad. Children fathered by a Chinese American during a visit to China, for example, automatically became U.S. citizens and could enter the country. Many wives and children entered the United States legitimately under these provisions. Others entered as paper sons: men returning to the United States from visits to China would claim to have fathered a child while there, and they could then sell this "slot" to a family in China that desired to send their son to America. Entry for these children, either legitimate or paper, was not automatic. As Ellis Island became symbolic of European immigrants' entry into the United States through New York Harbor, Angel Island became symbolic of Chinese immigrants' entry through San Francisco Harbor. At Angel Island, Chinese immigrants were detained and examined to prove their identity. If unsuccessful, they would be deported immediately. In preparation for these interrogations, families prepared extensive coaching books filled with minute details of their home life. The hopeful immigrant would memorize the information, sometimes two hundred pages long, and toss the book into the harbor before arriving in San Francisco. The use of paper-son slots expanded dramatically after April 18, 1906, when an earthquake struck San Francisco. The resulting fires destroyed all municipal records, including birth records. Afterward, many Chinese men claimed to have been born in San Francisco, a claim that could not be contradicted. As U.S.-born citizens, they then availed themselves of the right to bring wives and children to the United States. It is uncertain how many Chinese men falsely claimed U.S. citizenship, but with the extreme imbalance of men to women at the time, by some estimates every Chinese woman living in San Francisco would have had to bear eight hundred children to account for all the men who claimed after the earthquake that they had been born in San Francisco.

Repeal of the Chinese Exclusion Act, and Its Aftermath

The Chinese Exclusion Act was repealed in 1943, in deference to China's role as a U.S. ally against Japan in World War II. After its repeal, Chinese immigration fell under the guidelines of the 1924 National Origins Act until its replacement in 1965. Under the national-origins provisions, Chinese were awarded an annual immigration quota of 105. For the ten years that followed, however, only an average of fifty-nine Chinese immigrants entered the United States. The repeal of the Chinese Exclusion Act also extended to Chinese immigrants the right to become naturalized citizens, and many then sought to reunite with their families. Chinese immigration to the United States after World War II was also bolstered by the War Brides Act and by refugee provisions available for Chinese fleeing communist China, often through Hong Kong. But true parity in immigration matters and the end of Chinese exclusion did not occur until 1965, with the passage of the Immigrant and Nationalities Act, which awarded an equal immigrant quota of twenty thousand to each country outside the Western Hemisphere. Since 1965, Chinese immigration to the United States has grown steadily, and the Chinese American community has increased both in numbers and diversity in origin.

See also Chinese Immigrants, Adaptation of to Female Jobs; Chinese Immigrants and Anti-Chinese Sentiments; Foreign Miners License Tax; Immigration Act of 1965; National Origins Act of 1924.

Further Reading

Hsu, Madeline. *Dreaming of Gold, Dreaming of Home: Transnationalism and Migration between the United States and South China, 1882–1943*. Stanford, CA: Stanford University Press, 2000.

Salyer, Lucy E. *Laws Harsh as Tigers: Chinese Immigrants and the Shaping of Modern Immigration Law*. Chapel Hill: University of North Carolina Press, 1995.

Takaki, Ronald. *Strangers from a Different Shore: A History of Asian Americans*. Boston: Back Bay Books, 1998.

Kenneth J. Guest

Chinese Immigrants, Adaptation of to Female Jobs

Chinese immigrants first arrived in the 1850s to work as miners and later worked on the transcontinental railroad, but by the 1870s, anti-Chinese sentiment and violence had driven Chinese immigrants out of these jobs. White laborers had become resentful of the Chinese, whom they had to compete against for work. These laborers instigated widespread violence and attacks on the Chinese and their property. This anti-Chinese sentiment also resulted in laws designed to exclude or alienate Chinese immigrants and culminated in the 1882 passage of the Chinese Exclusion Act. The combination of legal exclusion and violence drove Chinese laborers out of their jobs and forced them to cluster together for self-protection in urban enclaves both on the West Coast and in more remote parts of the country.

Effectively locked out of their former means of employment, the Chinese immigrants could only safely make a living by doing what was considered women's work, where they posed no perceived threat to white laborers. In mining towns, where there were few women to cook or clean, many Chinese men worked as domestic servants or opened laundries or tailor shops or ran restaurants where they served both Chinese and white workers. Laundries in particular required minimal English and little money to open. By 1900, most large American towns had many Chinese laundries, which employed as much as 75 percent of all Chinese men.

In adopting these traditionally female jobs, Chinese immigrants also began a tradition of self-employment and entrepreneurship. It was at this time that the tradition of small-business ownership by Chinese immigrants began. The Chinese were relegated to undervalued types of enterprises that were outside the general economy (i.e., laundries, restaurants, and grocery stores). The proliferation of these Chinese-owned businesses was not under heavy scrutiny by whites. Moreover, because of a strong tradition of rotating credit association, or *hui*, the Chinese were able to obtain large sums of investment money on short notice without using American banks. Under this system, all members of an association contributed a small sum every month, with the monthly total going to whichever member won a lottery or, in the case of associations that sought to accrue interest, whichever member put in a bid to pay the highest interest for use of the money. These low-interest or interest-free lump sums were of great importance to the Chinese immigrant business economy because it allowed the immigrants to circumvent American banks, which would have denied them credit or charged them higher interest rates than the credit associations did. Thus, the combination of this access to capital and the undervaluing of the traditionally female work that they were engaging in created a viable economic niche for Chinese immigrants who had been forced out of the mainstream labor market.

However, there was backlash against the Chinese immigrants who were assuming these female roles, as well as psychosocial ramifications that contributed heavily to the image of Chinese men as feminized and perverse. Though they no longer posed a direct threat to white male laborers, working-class white women who were then being displaced from the workforce, became active in protesting the Chinese immigrants' newly claimed niche. The founding of the Workingmen's Party of California (WPC) in San Francisco in the late 1870s was bolstered, in large part, by these mainly Irish, working-class white women. These white women participated in the street protests, labor unions rallies, and political committees. They also formed associations of white women laundresses for the sole purpose of competing with Chinese laundries.

The propaganda generated by the movement against Chinese laborers characterized Chinese immigrants simultaneously as emasculated slaves to the white man and as disease-ridden sexual perverts who could not be trusted in the private homes of middle-class white women. The threat of the Chinese worker's sexual perversion became a consistent theme in the labor propaganda. Wealthy white women who employed Chinese men in their home were warned of potential rape and molestation. The Chinese were also depicted as posing such an economic threat that working-class white women were in danger of being driven to their own sexual perversion. The labor press widely distributed stories of white women workers who were unsuccessful at competing with Chinese workers, found themselves unemployed, and were eventually forced into prostitution. These propaganda campaigns, the gender bias in immigration law, which produced a Chinese bachelor society devoid of intact families, and the adoption of female roles in the labor force all served to stigmatize Chinese masculinity as deviant.

See also Asian Americans, Violence against; Chinese Exclusion Act of 1882; Chinese Immigrants and Anti-Chinese Sentiments.

Further Reading

Light, Ivan. "Ethnic Enterprise in America: Japanese, Chinese, and Blacks." In *From Different Shores: Perspectives on Race and Ethnicity in America*, edited by Ronald Takaki, 82–92. New York: Oxford University Press, 1994.

Min, Pyong Gap. "A Comparison of Pre- and Post–1965 Asian Immigrant Businesses."

In *Mass Migration to the United States: Classical and Contemporary Periods*, edited by Pyong Gap Min, 285–308. Walnut Creek, CA: AltaMira, 2002.

Zhou, Min. "Chinese: Divergent Destinies in Immigrant New York." In *New Immigrants in New York*, edited by Nancy Foner, 141–172. New York: Columbia University Press, 2001.

Tracy Chu

Chinese Immigrants and Anti-Chinese Sentiments

Chinese immigrants first arrived in California in 1849 to seek their fortunes as prospectors and miners on Gold Mountain. The China they left behind suffered from drought, overpopulation, local wars and national chaos from imperialist intrusions after the Opium Wars (1839–1842), and a devastating civil war during the Taiping Rebellion. The immigration of Chinese, mostly young men, to the United States was a continuation of a centuries-old pattern of out-migration from southern China in search of economic opportunity. Leaving their wives and families behind for what they considered a short-term employment opportunity, they bought tickets to America on credit and quickly settled into California's rapidly expanding mining industry and agricultural sector. Employers initially welcomed the Chinese immigrants, commonly referred to as "celestials," as flexible, cheap, and cooperative. In the volatile economic times of the new California, employers often turned to Chinese workers because of their willingness to work for lower wages than white immigrants. In the 1860s, Chinese laborers engaged in railroad construction projects, including the building of the western spur of the transcontinental railroad. They served not only as laborers but also as cooks and laundry men, playing the role of female domestics because there were so few women at the work sites. Chinese immigrants eventually made up 90 percent of the construction force, at enormous savings to the Central Pacific Railroad, which paid white workers $31 a month plus housing, but Chinese $31 without housing.

California's nineteenth-century economy fluctuated wildly from boom to bust, leaving workers anxious and uncertain. White laborers considered the Chinese to be a threat to jobs and wages, and cheap Chinese labor became a scapegoat for their economic woes. In this environment, anti-Chinese sentiments spread quickly and Chinese workers became frequent targets of violence, including riots, beatings, and lynchings. California's nativist politicians, scrambling for workers' votes in a state evenly balanced between Democrats and Republicans, played upon whites' fears of foreigners and nonwhites. Beginning with the Foreign Miners License Tax in 1852, the California government enacted a series of laws to protect "California for Americans," particularly against the Chinese. The numerous exclusionary laws that followed were designed to marginalize Chinese immigrants, exclude them from full participation in California society, and secure the political support of the white working class. In 1855, the state levied a landing tax of $50 a head on the owner or master of any ship carrying immigrants who could not become naturalized citizens. In 1862, the state passed a law "To Protect Free White Labor

An 1877 engraving of San Francisco customs officers inspecting the belongings of Chinese immigrants.

Courtesy Library of Congress.

against Competition with Chinese Coolie Labor, and to Discourage the Immigration of the Chinese into the State of California" that established a tax of $2.50 each month on all Chinese residents of the state, with the exception of those who were licensed to work in mines, operating businesses, or engaged in certain kinds of agriculture. The 1,875-page law prohibited the entry of Chinese prostitutes, but the accompanying rigorous interrogations and cross-examinations hampered the immigration of all Chinese women. Arrivals of Chinese women declined by 68 percent between 1876–1882 compared with the previous seven-year period. In the 1854 case *People v. Hall*, the California Supreme Court ruled that Chinese, like blacks, mulattos, and American Indians, could not testify for or against whites in court, leaving Chinese Americans extremely vulnerable to discrimination and violence.

The opening of the transcontinental railroad in 1867 facilitated Chinese migration to the East Coast, where Chinese workers were drawn into labor conflicts and they quickly discovered that anti-Chinese sentiment was not limited to the American West. East Coast traders, missionaries and diplomats who had encountered Chinese immigrants as early as 1785, before the Gold Rush, often portrayed them as immoral heathens, dishonest and barbaric. Scientific racial classification projects expressed concerns over race mixing. In 1870, Calvin T. Sampson hired seventy-five Chinese workers from California to break a strike at his shoe factory in Adams, Massachusetts. The practice quickly spread, and anti-Chinese sentiments among white East Coast workers quickly escalated. The rise in anti-Chinese sentiments was initially brought to national attention by California politicians, but it found a receptive audience and culminated in the Chinese Exclusion Act of 1882, which banned the immigration of Chinese laborers into the United States. The Chinese Exclusion Act, enforced until its repeal in 1943, marked the beginning of efforts to restrict all immigration to the United States, finally codified in the National Origins Act of 1924.

See also Asian Americans, Violence against; Chinese Exclusion Act of 1882; Chinese Immigrants, Adaptation of to Female Jobs; Foreign Miners License Tax; National Origins Act of 1924.

Further Reading

Salyer, Lucy E. *Laws Harsh as Tigers: Chinese Immigrants and the Shaping of Modern Immigration Law*. Chapel Hill: University of North Carolina Press, 1995.

Takaki, Ronald. *Strangers from a Different Shore: A History of Asian Americans*. Boston: Back Bay Books, 1998.

Kenneth J. Guest

Christian Identity Movement

See White-Supremacist Movement in the United States.

Civil Rights Act of 1964

After the Civil War, the U.S. Congress made efforts to restore civil and political rights to African Americans by passing the Fourteenth and Fifteenth amendments to the Constitution. However, the Congressional Reconstruction came to an end in 1878 when the federal government withdrew its troops from the South. Southern white supremacists were able to do what they wanted to do to put African Americans back into conditions that closely resembled slavery. Southern states quickly established various segregation laws, known as Jim Crow laws, to maintain two separate societies between blacks and whites. With an institutionalization of the Jim Crow system, whites were able to maintain racial segregation in all aspects of their lives. In the infamous 1896 *Plessy v. Ferguson* case, even the U.S. Supreme Court justified the constitutionality of the idea of separate but equal treatment of whites and blacks.

When the U.S. Supreme Court finally challenged school segregation in the *Brown v. Board of Education of Topeka, Kansas* in 1954, the struggle of African Americans to dismantle the Jim Crow system received a long-awaited and welcome relief. Then the civil rights movement started with Rosa Parks' refusal to give up her seat to a white passenger in a bus in Montgomery, Alabama, in December 1954. The Montgomery bus boycott in 1955, the Selma March in 1960, and the ensuing nonviolent civil right protests in the South, led by Martin Luther King Jr., put pressure on the U.S. government to abolish segregation laws.

As a result of the efforts of the civil rights movement, Congress finally passed the Civil Rights Act of 1964 to end the deeply entrenched practices of racial segregation and other forms of racial discrimination. Although President John F. Kennedy originally proposed it in 1963, President Lyndon B. Johnson signed the Civil Rights Act into a law on July 2, 1964. It was the most comprehensive legislation in American history that sought to end racial discrimination in the public arena. Its core objective was to end de jure—that is, formal—discrimination based on race, color, or national origin, in various areas, such as voting, public accommodation, education, and employment.

Title I of the act aimed to make the voting system equally accessible to minorities. Many municipalities across the South maintained certain registration requirements, such as literacy tests, poll taxes, and grandfather clauses to prevent minority members from voting. Title I made these requirements unconstitutional. Title II declared any segregation or discrimination illegal in public accommodation. It banned discrimination at restaurants, hotels, or other public places. Title III originally included broad language empowering the attorney general but was later deleted. Interestingly, the act does not have Title III.

Title IV addressed discrimination in educational institutions. It required the commissioner of education to undertake a survey and report to the president on the availability of equal educational opportunities for individuals, detailed according to race, color, religion, or national origin. It also provided strong disincentives for discrimination by authorizing withdrawal of federal funds from higher educational institutions that practiced discrimination. It also authorized the attorney general to pursue racial desegregation of schools by undertaking legal actions as well. Along with these strong punitive measures, this title proposed the creation of special training institutions to improve the sensibilities of educators and school personnel in regard to racial discrimination.

Title V concerns the establishments of the Civil Rights Commission. Title VI deals with the nondiscriminatory distribution of funds by prohibiting racial discrimination in any program funded by the federal government. It stipulates that federal agencies must go beyond not participating in discriminatory practices themselves. Federal agencies must assume affirmative duty to prevent such discrimination by state or local agencies by cutting off federal funds, if necessary. Title VII concerns the creation of the Equal Employment Opportunity Commission (EEOC). The EEOC was empowered to investigate charges of discrimination by trade unions, schools, or employers involved in interstate commerce or doing business with federal government.

With such sweeping measures to prevent discrimination, the constitutionality of the act was challenged immediately. Nonetheless, the U.S. Supreme Court upheld its constitutionality in the case of *Heart of Atlanta Motel v. United States* in 1964. In spite of persistent challenges, this law has allowed federal law enforcement agencies to use the enormous power at their disposal in fighting racial discrimination in education, employment, voting, and the use of public facilities. It almost single-handedly dealt a death blow to the Jim Crow system in the South and discriminatory practices in the North.

The impact of the Civil Rights Act was significant in eradicating de jure discrimination. As might be expected, the enforcement of the act varies according to the presidential administration in power, but even with inconsistent reinforcement from the executive branch, de jure discrimination has almost disappeared in the United States. Yet, certain types of institutional discrimination remain entrenched.

See also Brown v. Board of Education of Topeka; Civil Rights Act of 1968; Civil Rights Act of 1991; Fourteenth Amendment; Jim Crow Laws; King, Martin Luther, Jr.; Parks, Rosa; Separate but Equal Doctrine.

Further Reading

Graham, Hugh Davis. *The Civil Rights Era: Origins and Development of National Policy*. New York: Oxford University Press, 1990.

Loevy, Robert, ed. *The Civil Rights Act of 1964: The Passage of the Law That Ended Racial Segregation*. Albany: State University of New York Press, 1997.

Whalen, Charles, and Barbara Whalen. *The Longest Debate: A Legislative History of the 1964 Civil Rights Act*. Washington, DC: Seven Locks Press, 1985.

Shin Kim and Kwang Chung Kim

Civil Rights Act of 1968

The U.S. Congress passed the Civil Rights Act of 1968 on April 11, 1968. The main component of the Act was to confer numerous types of civil rights to Native Americans. Nevertheless, Title VIII, the most well known section of the act, declared that "it is the policy of the United States to provide, within constitutional limitations, for fair housing throughout the United States." In other words, this title made discrimination based on race, sex, national origin, color, religion, or disabled or familial status in the sale, rental, financing, and advertising of housing in federally assisted units and most of the private housing market unlawful. One exemption was dwellings of up to four separate living units in which the owner maintains a residence. Thus, the act is often dubbed a "fair housing" act.

It is a far-reaching legal provision as far as housing is concerned. It is estimated that 80 percent of all housing in the United States is covered by Title VIII. The Civil Rights Act of 1968 was also known as the last of the sweeping civil rights legislation. With the passage of this act, most civil rights leaders believed that what could be written into law had been exhausted. They maintained that what was remaining was the will of the government in interpreting and enforcing civil rights acts to build a nondiscriminatory society.

See also Civil Rights Act of 1964; Civil Rights Act of 1991; Housing Discrimination; U.S. Department of Housing and Urban Development (HUD).

Further Reading

Committee on the Judiciary, House of Representatives. *Civil Rights Acts of 1957, 1960, 1964, 1968 and Voting Rights Act of 1965*. Washington, DC: Government Printing Office, 1968.

Shin Kim and Kwang Chung Kim

Civil Rights Act of 1991

From 1989 to 1991, the U.S. Supreme Court handed down decisions that undermined the protection granted by federal civil rights legislations. A case in point is four 5–4 decisions delivered in June 1989: *Lorance v. AT & T Technologies*, *Martin v. Wilks*, *Patterson v. McLean Credit Union*, and *Wards Cove Packing Co. v. Antonio*. By interpreting affirmative action narrowly, the

Supreme Court restricted the rights of individuals to protect themselves from employment discrimination and shifted the burden of proof from employers to employees in these cases.

Civil rights advocates lobbied Congress to enact measures that would overturn the court rulings, arguing that the court had undermined the intent of federal civil rights and equal employment legislation. In October 1990, Congress approved a bill that was designed to reverse the court rulings and strengthen provisions of the 1964 Civil Rights Act. President George H. W. Bush vetoed the legislation, stating that it would encourage hiring quotas. In 1991, after months of negotiation, the U.S. Congress passed a bill that provided additional remedies to deter harassment and intentional discrimination. On November 21, 1991, President Bush signed the Civil Rights Act of 1991 into a law. Even though the act had mixed signals on the affirmative action and group rights, one of its widely anticipated consequences was an increase in employment discrimination litigation.

See also Affirmative Action; Civil Rights Act of 1964; Civil Rights Act of 1968.

Further Reading

Cathcart, David A., Leon Friedman, Merrick T. Rossein, Mark Snyderman, and Steven H. Steinglass. *The Civil Rights Act of 1991*. Philadelphia: American Law Institute–American Bar Association, Committee on Continuing Professional Education, 1993.

Shin Kim and Kwang Chung Kim

Civil Rights Movement

The civil rights movement conventionally refers to the struggle of African Americans in the 1950s and 1960s to end the system of racial segregation, discrimination, and inequality in the United States. It may be a way of immortalizing the significant achievements of the social movement that marked the threshold of postwar U.S. history. But the conventional use of the term is misleading in several ways. First, it tends to ignore the long history of civil rights movements that existed before the mid-1950s. Second, it also tends to neglect the fact that Latinos, Native Americans, Asians, women, homosexuals, and many other minority groups as well as African Americans have fought for their own civil rights at the same historical juncture. Third, the term tends to confine the scope of blacks' freedom struggle of the 1950s and 1960s to the narrow issues of civil rights legislation and effective law enforcement and, thus, to marginalize the efforts to address inner-city poverty, de facto racial segregation by economic inequality, the unjust war on Vietnam, and neocolonialism. The canonization of the freedom struggle of the turbulent years as the civil rights movement means, of course, the public recognition of the movement's cause, which is undoubtedly an achievement in itself. But as soon as it is officially acknowledged, it can easily be forgotten that the aspirations of those who participated in the movement have yet to be fully realized. This essay focuses on the black freedom struggle in the 1950s and 1960s.

Explosive Mixture

The freedom struggle on such a massive scale that radically transformed U.S. race relations did not erupt from a vacuum. Since the outbreak of World War II, a large number of African Americans had departed from the South, looking for a better life in the North. It is estimated that during the period 1940–1950 1,599,000 blacks migrated, mostly to the northern metropolises. This was three times the number of Afro-Americans who had headed for the North, leaving the Jim Crow system of the South behind, during the Great Migration of the 1920s. The massive migration to the North continued in the 1960s, with an additional 1,380,000 blacks leaving the South. The concentration of Afro-American population in some northern cities, such as Philadelphia, Detroit, Indianapolis, Chicago, and New York, gained considerable leverage in both local and federal electoral politics. In 1940, for example, the Democratic Party platform included for the first time equal protection under the law and due process rights for African Americans, in an effort to win the presidential election. Even in the South, the acceleration of black vote registration in the 1940s threatened the political domination of whites in Georgia and Alabama. The demographic shift also meant economic progress for African Americans. From 1947 to 1974, the median income of black households more than doubled, although it still remained at the level of 62 percent of white household income. During the late 1940s and early 1950s, the black unemployment rate was less than 2 percent. African American purchasing power substantially increased, and the Black college population tripled. Northern white universities saw a dramatic increase in the number of African American students. African American celebrities disproved the notion of black inferiority. The National Association for the Advancement of Colored People (NAACP) litigation strategy had already been harvesting important legal victories in the area of public education since the Supreme Court case *Missouri ex rel Gaines v. Canada*, the 1938 decision requiring the University of Missouri Law School either to admit a single qualified applicant or to build him a law school. However, the more the NAACP-style litigation strategy gained its victories in the courtroom, the clearer its limits became: not only that civil rights politics remained a middle-class affair—hence, the NAACP was dubbed the "National Association for the Advancement of *Certain* People"—but also that the court decisions were usually ignored in the real world where political power lay in the hands of opportunists and extreme racists.

The end of World War II, the last imperialist war, encouraged nations' self-determination. Global movement toward decolonization and national liberation of the once colonized peoples revealed the inherent connection of colonialism and racial oppression. Blacks and Latinos found themselves colonized within the colonizer society and shared the fate of the peoples abroad fighting for their national liberation. In addition, the barbarity of racial segregation still officially existing in the United States became a burden on the international leadership of the new superpower. It was particularly burdensome because the cold war pressed the United States into the role of being a superior social system to the Soviet alternative. Within the United States, the merger of the AFL and CIO in 1955 and the sway of McCarthyism turned class politics into identity politics, marginalizing blacks, women, and other minorities from the benefits of the social contract between business and labor unions. In short, demographic shifts, general economic prosperity, the transformed terrain of domestic and international politics, the gains of the previous civil rights movement up to the mid-1950s, and the stubborn white resistance created an explosive mixture of heightened hope and an acute sense of frustration about race relations among African Americans. Any slightest pressure would trigger an unexpected chain of events leading to a racial revolution.

Infrastructure of Social Movement

The novelty of the civil rights movement in the mid-1950s and the 1960s was that it could organize and mobilize rank-and-file African Americans for the first time and that the goals and tactics of the movement were continuously debated and redefined as ordinary folks found their way into political involvement. The aspiration of African Americans for human dignity and a decent life had long been there and manifested itself in a variety of forms, such as revolts, sabotages, escapes, songs, sermons, poems, stories, research, education, entrepreneurship, co-ops, and political organizations. However, translating the culture of black resistance into a mass-protest movement required a deliberate effort to organize and mobilize.

Black churches proved to be one of the most fertile breeding grounds among protest organizations. Decades of African American Christianity provided not only the religious justification for the black freedom struggle but also the practical skills for organizing and fund-raising. Black churches were training camps and operation headquarters at the same time. Urbanization of the black population, the traditional black allegiance to their churches, and informal and formal connections among clergymen in and out of the denominational boundaries turned the black church into a formidable movement organization. Another decisive base for the mass protest movement was black educational institutions, including elementary and high schools, colleges, seminaries, and universities. Students, relatively free from societal obligations, had not only free time and boundless energy to pursue causes but also leadership skills and organizational resources. The organizations that had no mass base also played an important role in the movement. The NAACP, the most prominent protest organization in the first half of the twentieth century, was instrumental in developing local leadership, organizing skills and networks, and seeking justice through the courts. But the lesser-known organizations, such as the American Friends Service Committee, the Fellowship of Reconciliation, the War Resisters League and the Highlander Folk School, were also indispensable in disseminating the tactic of nonviolent direct actions, developing mass educational programs, and publicizing local movements.

The celebrated Montgomery Bus Boycott in 1955–1956 was not the first mass, direct-action movement. In 1953, there had been a successful large-scale, church-based bus boycott movement in Baton Rouge, Louisiana. The movement was mobilized through the local black churches and the United Defense League (UDL) under the leadership of the Reverend T. J. Jemison of the Mt. Zion Baptist Church. The news of the mass bus boycott was disseminated through the network of black ministers across the country. The Baton Rouge Bus Boycott movement introduced a new form of protest, different from the traditional NAACP-style legal struggle.

The Montgomery boycott, however, earned its recognition as the watershed of the civil rights movement because it was mobilized on a greater scale, lasted more than a year, and thus gained national and international attention. Rosa Parks' famous refusal to give up her seat to a white man on December 1, 1955, was a deliberate act of defiance by a person who was deeply involved in the black protest organizations. She had served as secretary for the local NAACP since 1943 and also organized the local NAACP Youth Council. She also served as a stewardess at the St. Paul AME Church in Montgomery. It was not just Parks' conscience but also her involvement in the protest organizations that triggered the mass boycott.

Immediately after her arrest, E. D. Nixon of the NAACP and Jo Ann Robinson organized a grassroots bus boycott movement with the help of local ministers, including Martin Luther King Jr. The 1954 U.S. Supreme Court's ruling in *Brown v. Board of Education* in 1954, which rejected the "doctrine of separate but equal facilities," encouraged the fight against state segregation ordinances. The white city council's determined resistance to the rather moderate demand for the modification of the segregation ordinance turned the one-day boycott into a yearlong struggle for total desegregation. For more than a year, Montgomery blacks walked, car-pooled, or bicycled to work, refusing to use the segregated public transportation that depended heavily on black passengers. The unforeseeable confrontation between the determined whites and the equally resolute blacks in the South finally gained attention from the national media.

Although reluctantly involved at first, Martin Luther King Jr. inspired millions of Americans, black and white, both in the South and the North, with his articulate Christian teaching of nonviolent but uncompromising resistance against injustice. The mass mobilization of the black community, combined with the NACCP's tactic of seeking redress through the courts, reached a successful conclusion in the Supreme Court's final decision in *Browder v. Gayle* on November 13, 1956, that the bus segregation ordinance was unconstitutional. The Montgomery buses were desegregated on December 21, 1956.

The victory in Montgomery inspired many African Americans in other cities, such as Tallahassee and Birmingham. At the center of the mass boycotts were the "organizations of organizations," including the Montgomery Improvement Association (MIA), the Inter Civic Council of Tallahassee (ICC), and the Alabama Christian Movement for Human Rights (ACMHR). These organizations were no less decisive for the unfolding civil rights struggle than for the immediate local victories they gained. Minister activists, while leading local boycotts, formed the Southern Christian Leadership Conference (SCLC) in 1957, with Martin Luther King Jr. as its president, to coordinate a Southern struggle. The decentralized organization of organizations benefited from the variety of organizational skills and tactics used by its local affiliates and thus expanded its base for the wider confrontations in the years to come. Drawing upon the teachings of Christianity and the methods of pacifist Indian leader Mahatma Gandhi, King formulated the method of nonviolent resistance: active but peaceful disobedience to the clearly unjust laws would provoke the regime's violent reaction and lead to the suffering of the protesters. The suffering of the innocent has such a redemptive power that it would move the conscience of the world at large, eventually giving moral edge and substantial support to the protest movement. Participants in demonstrations, boycotts, and sit-ins were expected to be ready to accept suffering without retaliation.

The Power of Organized Civil Disobedience

A series of student sit-ins in 1960 opened a decade of political turmoil. Between February 1 and April 1, 1960, thousands of students participated in sit-in demonstrations in about seventy Southern cities in order to nullify racial segregation at public lunch counters through direct action. It was sparked by the four African American students from North Carolina Agricultural and Technical College who sat at the whites-only luncheon counter in the Woolworth's store in Greensboro. They had been members of the NAACP Youth Council. Thanks to the movement's network of leaders, organizations, churches, and schools, sit-in protests spread to other stores and provoked sympathy demonstrations. Although the national office of the NAACP refused to support the Greensboro sit-ins, Martin Luther King Jr. fully endorsed them as part of the worldwide struggle for freedom, and appreciated their novelty by saying: "What is fresh, what is new in your fight is the fact that it was initiated, led, sustained by students. What is new is that American students have come of age." On February 13, 1960, about five hundred students, mainly from four black colleges in Nashville, Tennessee, launched their own sit-in demonstration. Highly disciplined in nonviolent action strategy, many of them, when arrested, prefered to go to jail rather than pay the fines, in protest against unjust law enforcement practices. Lunch counters in the city were integrated by May 10. On April 17, 1960, in the midst of sit-in struggle, the Student Nonviolent (in 1965, changed to National) Coordinating Committee (SNCC) was founded. The student movement had much wider political agendas than the equal treatment at lunch counters: to engage in political activity on all levels—local, state, and federal—so that no one is forced to endure second-class citizenship. The SNCC inspired the white student movement organization, Students for a Democratic Society (SDS).

The Freedom Rides launched by the Congress of Racial Equality (CORE) in 1961 galvanized the civil rights struggle. Initially, a small group of black and white activists rode an interstate bus from Washington, DC, to New Orleans to test whether buses and terminal facilities were desegregated. The riders were badly beaten in Alabama. But the SNCC and SCLA decided to continue with new activists. In Montgomery, they met angry white mobs. The intervention of the U.S. marshals rescued them from the threat. Now even more students, ministers, and others volunteered for the Freedom Rides, turning it into a mass movement. Like sit-ins, the Freedom Rides educated and inspired the black community by generating the tales, songs, and culture of protest. In an effort to reach, educate, and mobilize the black mass, the SCLC took over the Citizen Schools. African Americans from farms, plantations, and Southern cities were taught to raise questions about the power structure affecting their lives. They would organize their own communities and participate in demonstrations. More than anything else, a series of local victories taught them that organized civil disobedience could effectively nullify the system of racial oppression.

The most dramatic confrontation came on April 3, 1963. The SCLC carefully planned to stage a massive protest movement in Birmingham, as the city was one of its best organized centers, yet it remained under the control of rampant white segregationist power, symbolized by the police chief "Bull" O'Connor. The demonstration was marked by its large number of participants, including schoolchildren. Marchers demanded fair employment opportunities, desegregation of public facilities, creation of a committee to plan desegregation, and the dropping of charges against King and other activists. A large number of arrests were made, but it could not stop day-to-day demonstrations. On May 3, the Birmingham police attacked student demonstrators with dogs, billy clubs, and high-pressure water hoses, to which students responded with rocks and bottles. The scene of cruelty shook the world, as well as the nation. Sympathy demonstrations followed across the nation. The assassination of Medger Evers, the leader of the Mississippi NAACP, added fuel to the fire. The North and West saw as many protests as the South. They demanded better job opportunities and an end to de facto segregation in housing and education in New York, Philadelphia, Boston, Chicago, Los Angeles, San Francisco, and Englewood, New Jersey.

Finally, President John F. Kennedy proposed a civil rights bill. On August 28, 1963, when Congress debated the proposed bill, more than 200,000 blacks and whites gathered for the March on Washington for Jobs and Freedom, organized by labor and civil rights leaders with the support of Jewish, Catholic, and Protestant religious groups. Here King gave the famous "I Have a Dream" speech.

Disillusionment and the Unfinished Project

The civil rights bill proposed by Kennedy was finally ratified in February 1964 under the Johnson administration. The Civil Rights Act of 1964 was the most comprehensive legislation ever, giving the attorney general authority to protect citizens against discrimination and segregation in voting, education, and the use of public facilities. But its enforcement met violent resistance from whites. During the so-called long, hot summer of 1964 some twenty-four black churches were destroyed by arson or bombing. Many civil rights activists were abducted and killed. Southern whites resisted obstinately the voter registration drives, particularly in areas with a large black population. In 1965, three civil rights workers were killed in Selma, Dallas County, Alabama, where the county sheriff was infamous for the use of tear gas, whips, and clubs against demonstrators. In protest, the Selma-Montgomery march was launched, featuring two Nobel Peace Prize winners, Martin Luther King Jr. and Ralph Bunche. It was then that President Johnson proposed a voting rights act, which Congress passed with unusual swiftness. The Voting Rights Act of 1965 made it possible for African Americans to win seats in the Georgia legislature and in city councils of several Southern cities.

However, the gains in legislation and law enforcement, although impressive by themselves, paradoxically underscored the abyssal discrepancy between African Americans' heightened expectations and the tenacious reality of racial inequality and de facto segregation. Rent strikes, school boycotts, and demonstrations against discrimination in the building trade unions failed in Northern cities. The spontaneous riots of slum dwellers in 1964 and 1965 brought the enormity of the task ahead to light. Militant leaders, particularly in the SNCC and CORE, lost faith in the nonviolent direct-action strategy and white partnership. The two-party domination and the capitalist system of economy, they thought, would not deliver true equality to the colonized under the regime of internal colonialism. Only the revolutionary restructuring of the social system would do, with armed rebellion, if necessary.

Thus, during the 1964–1966 period, the civil rights leadership became increasingly divided on strategy and on the Vietnam War. The civil right movement in general was in decline. The slogan "Black Power" emerged in the summer of 1966 and enjoyed enormous popularity in the African American community, especially among youth. To the main advocates of the Black Power movement, the SNCC and the CORE meant blacks' substantial autonomy in politics and economy. At this point, the civil rights movement turned into a total revolution, calling for economic development in the black community, black control of the black community, and a fresh appreciation of black history and culture. Black nationalism and separatism regained their strength. In 1967, the Black Power Conference in Newark, New Jersey, called for the partitioning of the United States into two independent nations, one for white and the other for black. The Black Panther Party emerged as a prominent revolutionary organization when its members demonstrated, carrying guns, in the California legislative building. The Black Panthers multiplied as its chapters spread to cities across the nation and called for black control of all major cities. In 1969, the Black Economic Development Conference, organized under the leadership of James Forman of the SNCC, demanded that white Christian churches, synagogues, and all other religious institutions in the United States pay $500 million in reparation and surrender 60 percent of their assets for the rehabilitation of the black community. Ironically, the revolutionary rhetoric expressed desperation as much as confidence. By the time the Black Power slogan was in fashion, the movement at large had already lost its momentum. It was declining in size, finances, and efficacy. Meeting the fate of Martin Luther King Jr. gunned down in 1968, the dream of full freedom and equality he articulated so dramatically remained an unfinished project.

See also Black Nationalist Movement; King, Martin Luther Jr.; Malcolm X; Montgomery Bus Boycott; National Association for the Advancement of Colored People (NAACP); Parks, Rosa; Sit-ins; Student Nonviolent Coordinating Committee (SNCC); Southern Christian Leadership Conference (SCLC).

Further Reading

Eagles, Charles W., ed. *The Civil Rights Movement in America*. Jackson: University Press of Mississippi, 1986.

Franklin, John Hope, and Alfred A. Moss Jr. *From Slavery to Freedom: A History of Negro Americans*. New York: McGraw-Hill, 1988.

Levy, Peter B., ed. *Let Freedom Ring: A Documentary History of the Modern Civil Rights Movement.* Westport, CT: Praeger, 1992.

Lowery, Charles D., and John F. Marszalek, eds. *The Greenwood Encyclopedia of African American Civil Rights: From Emancipation to the Twenty-First Century.* Westport, CT: Greenwood Press, 2003.

Meier, August, Elliott Rudwick, and Francis L. Broderick, eds. *Black Protest Thought in the Twentieth Century.* 2nd ed. Indianapolis: Bobbs-Merril, 1971.

Morris, Aldon D. *The Origins of the Civil Rights Movement: Black Community Organizing for Change.* New York: Free Press, 1984.

Riches, William T. M. *The Civil Rights Movement: Struggle and Resistance.* New York: St. Martin's Press, 1997.

Dong-Ho Cho

Civil War and the Abolition of Slavery

The U.S. Civil War was the bloodiest conflict that ever took place on American soil. More than half a million people lost their lives, and several hundred thousands were wounded. There have been different interpretations of the causes of this conflict. One interpretation says that the country wanted to move to a modern industrial economy and was hampered by the South, which had an inefficient slave economy. Another interpretation is that through its court decisions and domination of the federal government, the South was moving toward imposing slavery nationally. Therefore, it had to be stopped by those who opposed the slave system. However, whatever interpretation is considered, slavery was a major reason for the Civil War, mainly because in 1776, the founding fathers failed to address this issue properly.

From the colonial era to 1865, slavery was the main economic and social system that produced a vast amount of wealth for the United States. In addition to being an economic investment, it was also a unique form of social relations, separating the North from the South. Unlike the North, which developed a capitalist economy, slavery gave rise in the South to what has been described as "a hierarchical society based on paternalism, an ideology linking dominant and subordinate classes in a complex pattern of mutual responsibilities and obligations" (Foner 1997, 89–90). This system resembled feudalism more than the emerging modern economies of that period.

The division at the foundation of the American republic between those who favored a slave-free society and those who wanted to continue the institution made it impossible for the Founding Fathers to take a firm position on this issue. Instead, they allowed the importation of slaves from Africa into the United States until 1808 and let Southern states count a slave as three-fifths of a person for purposes of taxation and representation. In 1820, a compromise was reached that banned slavery in the territories west of the Mississippi and Ohio valleys.

The slave economy that existed in the United States was primarily regressive. It depended on vast tracks of land, the use of free labor, and the acquisition of virgin land periodically to maintain the production of crops such as tobacco, cotton, and sugar cane. This use of land depleted the soil of its nu-

Freed slaves, escorted by Union soldiers, migrate to North Carolina after the 1863 issuance of the Emancipation Proclamation.

Courtesy Library of Congress.

trients faster than other crops, thereby rendering the land less productive. As a result of these conditions, it was very difficult for the South to abide by the Missouri Compromise to keep slavery out of the new territories. Moreover, as more Northerners began to challenge the institution of slavery through the abolitionist movement, it became harder for the South to justify slavery.

As a consequence, many Southern politicians began to talk openly about seceding from the Union. The desire for slave-holding states in the South to secede from the Union was probably the major cause of the Civil War. The Supreme Court decision against Dred Scott in 1857 further exacerbated the tension between the North and the South, contributing to the South's decision to secede sooner. Dred Scott was born into slavery in the South and then moved to Missouri with his master, who sold him to another person in the state. Later, Scott sued his new master to claim his freedom on the basis of his residency in a slave-free territory for seven years. When the predominately pro-slavery Supreme Court heard Scott's case, it declared that he was still a slave and that the agreement that banned slavery in the new territories was unconstitutional. The North, which opposed slavery, feared that the South was going to impose slavery in all the territories west of the Mississippi River.

The election of Abraham Lincoln as president of the United States in 1860 further strained North-South relations, as slave owners in the South perceived Lincoln as an advocate of the North whose agenda was to end slavery. In reality, Lincoln did not intend to abolish slavery. His major interest was to preserve the Union at any cost. But as the war progressed, he realized that to maintain the North's support, he would have to advocate the emancipation of the slaves. In 1863, he proclaimed the emancipation of slaves in states that were rebelling against the Union.

See also Abolitionist Movement; Dred Scott Decision; Emancipation Proclamation; Missouri Compromise; Slave Auctions; Slave Codes; Slave Families; Slave Trade; Slavery in the Antebellum South.

Further Reading

Fehrenbacher, Don E. *Slavery, Law and Politics*. New York: Oxford University Press, 1981.

Foner, Eric. "Slavery, The Civil War, and Reconstruction." In *The New American History*, edited by Eric Foner. Philadelphia: Temple University Press, 1997.

Francois Pierre-Louis

Closed Doors, Opportunities Lost: The Continuing Costs of Housing Discrimination

In *Closed Doors, Opportunities Lost* (1995), John Yinger examined the 1989 Housing Discrimination Study (HDS) and a few other housing studies to determine how well the housing industry was adhering to the Fair Housing Act of 1968. The HDS used fair-housing audits, which entailed sending out two audit teammates who were equally qualified to purchase a home but who differ in racial/ethnic background. All other characteristics (sex, age, and general appearance) were matched. Each audit teammate was also assigned the same personal background, received the same training on how to respond to the sales agent and was sent out under similar housing-market conditions. The teammates' order of viewing a home was also randomized. This was all done to mitigate any outside factors that might influence an agent's behavior.

Major findings of the HDS included that 20 percent of blacks and 13 percent of Hispanics learned about fewer housing opportunities than did their white counterparts; minorities were shown fewer properties and waited longer for assistance from housing agents; minorities were less likely to be asked about any special requirements they might have for a home, but they were more likely to be asked by an agent about their income; minorities received fewer positive comments about potential homes and were less likely to receive follow-up calls or to be asked to call the agent if they had any questions. Yinger also reported that housing opportunities for minorities were constrained because agents tended to steer them toward neighborhoods with higher minority populations, lower-income residents, and lower property values. He concluded that these subtle violations of housing laws contributed to other inequities, such as racial residential segregation, racial disparities in home ownership, wealth, education, and labor market disparities.

See also Fair Housing Act of 1968; Fair Housing Amendments Act of 1988; Fair-Housing Audit; Housing Discrimination.

Further Reading

Yinger, John. *Closed Doors, Opportunities Lost: The Continuing Costs of Housing Discrimination*. New York: Russell Sage Foundation, 1995.

Romney S. Norwood

College Admission, Discrimination in

Higher education is now and has long been a gateway to opportunity in the United States. However, access to this gateway has been constrained by many waves of discriminatory action at colleges and universities throughout the centuries, on the basis of socioeconomic status, religion, and gender as well as race. The earliest colleges all required a test of Christian religious faith for admission. The first not to require such a test was Brown University, founded in 1766. For many years, significant income was required to pay tuition costs at most colleges and universities unless an individual student was sponsored by a philanthropist. Individual colleges did not institute financial-aid systems until just before the twentieth century, and mass financial aid was only made possible by the GI Bill in the 1940s. Women were denied formal education at the level of men's colleges until at least 1814, when Emma Willard opened the Middlebury Female Seminary in Connecticut.

The first integrated college to officially and knowingly admit African American students, Oberlin College, did so in the early 1850s, though undoubtedly African American students had graduated from colleges by passing as white. This method became the impetus for admission of African American students to other colleges and universities as the schools saw individual students achieve academic success and graduate, and decided to open their doors to a few, selected others. Cheyney University, in Pennsylvania, founded in 1837, was the first institution of higher education founded specifically for the education of blacks. It was not an easy path to integration. The early African American students admitted were held to extremely high standards and few were admitted. Universities also began admitting small numbers of Asian and Latino/a students, at first as international students. Later, students of these racial backgrounds who had grown up in the United States were admitted to college, but they were often still treated as foreigners.

Later, as increasing numbers of southern and eastern European immigrants, including large numbers of Jews and Catholics, entered the United States, many universities and colleges instituted quota systems to ensure that their student bodies would remain primarily "white" and Christian. Specific percentage limits, ranging from 20 percent at Columbia in the early 1940s to 6 percent at Dartmouth in 1934, capped the number of Jewish students who would be admitted, regardless of their qualifications. Even after these systems were abolished, quota systems on the basis of geography (often specifically limiting the number of students who could be admitted from the New York metropolitan area) continued to discriminate against the ethnic groups concentrated in that area, especially Jews. Methods for determining the Jewish origin of applicants included requiring the attachment of photographs to the application, specific questions concerning race and religion, interviews, and restricted scholarships.

The U.S. Congress passed Title VI of the 1964 Civil Rights Act, barring federal funding of universities and colleges that discriminate on the basis of race. As almost all colleges and universities receive some federal funding, including at a minimum student financial aid or faculty research grants, this sort of discrimination is illegal. Other, more subtle forms of racial discrimination can continue; for instance, making it easier for students who have relatives who attended the college before it was racially integrated to be admitted or preferentially admitting students who have been involved in specific extracurricular activities that are primarily engaged in by white students (such as the game of squash), as well as the geographical quota systems already discussed. Additionally, many universities and colleges rely significantly on the SAT and similar tests in their admission processes. ETS statistics show that there is a clear racial gap in scores on the SATs, which put African Americans at a disadvantage.

A new debate over discrimination in admissions has arisen more recently. In the wake of the civil rights legislation and movement of the 1950s and 1960s, many universities and colleges instituted policies that have come to be known as affirmative action. These policies vary: explicit quota systems ensuring that a certain percentage of students of color will be admitted; processes whereby students of color receive some additional points in the scoring of their application; lowering test-score thresholds; and considering past racial disadvantage are a few examples. They are described as a way to make up for the legacy of past discrimination and resulted in significant increases in African American and Latino/a students at many colleges and universities. They have, however, been the source of significant controversy for decades. For instance, some white students have claimed that affirmative action policies constitute reverse racism against white students, who are being supplanted by underqualified students of color, though most affirmative action policies only admit students who meet some minimum qualifications to which all students are held. Some public universities have recently been forced to abandon their affirmative action policies, which has led to precipitous declines in the number of students of color, especially African Americans.

Asian American students have been left in a marginal position with respect to affirmative action: in some colleges and universities they are considered to be in the same group as African Americans and Latino/as as beneficiaries of programs aimed at all students of color, while other colleges and universities see the growing numbers of Asian American students as a reason to remove them from affirmative action programs. However, Asian Americans do not benefit from the removal of affirmative action programs in the way whites do. Preferences for legacy students (students whose parents or grandparents have attended the school) and certain types of extracurricular activities are a hardship for Asian American applicants. Additionally, emphasis on outstanding English skills can be a challenge for immigrant students and the children of immigrants. All of these factors resulted in several high-profile cases in the 1980s of Asian American students accusing universities of having anti-Asian American quota systems similar to those experienced by Jews in the early part of the twentieth century.

See also Affirmative Action; California Ballot Proposition 209; Civil Rights Act of 1964; Intelligence Tests and Racism.

Further Reading

Takagi, Dana Y. *The Retreat from Race: Asian-American Admissions and Racial Politics*. New Brunswick, NJ: Rutgers University Press, 1992.

Synott, Marcia Graham. *The Half-Opened Door: Discrimination and College Admissions at Harvard, Yale, and Princeton*. Westport, CT: Greenwood Press, 1979.

Wechsler, Harold S. *The Qualified Student: A History of Selective College Admission in America*. New York: John Wiley, 1977.

Mikaila Mariel Lemonik Arthur

Colonization Complex

The colonization complex, proposed by sociologist Robert Blauner, explains the processes of colonialism, and it includes four processes: (1) invasion of the territory and its population; (2) destruction and/or alteration of the social organizations and other systems inherent to the indigenous culture; (3) domination by the invaders of the indigenous population; and (4) oppression being justified through racist beliefs and ideologies.

Interestingly, Blauner suggested that the dynamics of the colonization complex may explain both external colonialism, whereby one nation gains control over another nation's political and socioeconomic systems, and internal colonialism, in which a particular segment of the population within a society assumes control over another group or other groups within the same society. He considers African Americans a typical example of an internally colonized minority because this group continues to suffer from institutional racism, through which their economic, political, educational, and other opportunities are limited.

See also Colonized versus Immigrant Minorities; Internal Colonialism.

Further Reading

Blauner, Robert. *Still the Big News: Racial Oppression in America*. Philadelphia: Temple University Press, 2001.

Daisuke Akiba

Colonized versus Immigrant Minorities

Involuntary minorities are people who have historically become members of a country through enslavement, colonization, or conquest. Involuntary minorities in the United States share at least two features: historically, they were forced against their will to become a part of the United States, and they interpret their presence in the United States as having been forced on them by others. Major examples of involuntary minorities in the United States include African Americans and American Indians. Other involuntary minorities include Mexican Americans in the Southwest, who were conquered and displaced from power, as well as native Hawaiians and native Alaskans. Because many early Chinese migrants were kidnapped or "tricked" into coming to the United

States in the nineteenth century to be exploited for labor, they can also be considered to be involuntary minorities.

Voluntary immigrants are those who migrate to a country by choice, most often with the expectation of improving their economic and social position. Their migration status is in direct contrast to that of involuntary migrants in that they have actively chosen to enter into American society and they do not perceive their presence as forced on them by the U.S. government or by white Americans. Voluntary minorities in the United States include Afro-Caribbean, Asian, and Latino immigrants.

In contemporary America, voluntary and involuntary minorities have had fundamentally different patterns of adjustment. Although involuntary minorities, such as African Americans, have the advantage of knowing the dominant language and are more familiar with American culture than newly arrived immigrants, they also have very different patterns of social adjustment and more negative outcomes. These differences, some theorists argue, are mitigated by their history of oppression and the culture that has arisen from those conditions of oppression. In comparing the situations and outcomes of voluntary and involuntary minorities, this essay looks at the work of three major theorists: Stanley Lieberson, Robert Blauner, and John Ogbu.

Stanley Lieberson's Theory of Migrant versus Indigenous Superordination

Stanley Lieberson's theory of voluntary and involuntary minorities is based on the way two groups, the migrant population and the indigenous population, make initial contact with each other. Lieberson's main argument is that the method by which a migrant group is initially introduced to a society has long-range effects on how the two groups will conflict with each other and exert power over each other. Rather than classifying migrant groups explicitly as "voluntary" and "involuntary," Lieberson constructs a typology of two categories based on the initial conditions of contact and dominance, migrant superordination and indigenous superordination. Although his theory does not specifically use the categories *involuntary* and *voluntary*, his work is an important precursor to later theorists who deal explicitly with the differences between voluntary and involuntary minorities.

Migrant superordination occurs when a migrant group dominates the indigenous, or established, population of the land to which it is migrating. Often, this domination occurs because the migrating population has superior technology and weaponry. Warfare and violent conflict is common in the early stages of contact, and it leads to a great decline in the numbers of the indigenous population. The migrant group then imposes its political, economic, and cultural institutions on the indigenous population. In the United States, the domination of American Indians and Mexicans by white settlers is an example of migrant superordination. Here, the white European settlers were the migrant groups who dominated the indigenous populations.

Indigenous superordination occurs when a migrating population assumes a subordinate position in the society that they are migrating to. The indigenous, or established, group dominates the migrants. Though there is definite, often violent, conflict between the subordinate migrant group and the established society, there is no outright warfare such as there was, for example, between American Indians and early white settlers. Voluntary immigrant groups, including eastern European and, more recently, Asian and Latino minorities, fall under the rubric of indigenous superordination. In this situation, the immigrants are the migrating groups that are dominated by the established social, cultural, and political institutions of the indigenous (i.e., the mainstream and largely white) American society. However, Lieberson's theory is not suitable for explaining African American race relations, because their history of forced migration does not fit into his typology.

Migrant superordination and indigenous superordination lead to different levels of racial and ethnic conflict and control. Lieberson argues that there is more ongoing racial and ethnic conflict in instances of migrant superordination than in instances of indigenous superordination. In situations of migrant superordination, warfare and nationalism frequently develop into a cycle of conflict between the subordinated indigenous group and the superordinate migrants. Oppression by a common enemy brings about a sense of racial and tribal unity among the subordinated indigenous population. This was the case, he argues, with the warfare between American Indians and early white settlers.

Lieberson argues that in contrast, when migrants come to a country and are dominated by the indigenous population, such as in the case of immigrants in the United States, there is less overtly violent racial conflict between the groups. There are only occasional periods of violence between immigrants and the dominant society, which are generally initiated by the dominant society as a reaction to what they consider to be threats to the social order, such as cheap-labor competition created by the presence of immigrant laborers.

Part of what makes the indigenous superordination a less conflict-ridden relationship is the fact that migrants often have the option of returning to their homeland if they are dissatisfied with how they are being subordinated. Also, Lieberson points out, there is less conflict in societies with indigenous superordination because the level of contact between the migrant and the dominant indigenous groups is controlled by the dominant group; the dominant group retains tight control over multiethnic contacts. Other racial and ethnic migrant groups are admitted in large numbers only in accordance with the economic needs of the dominant society. Examples of this in the United States included the influx of Chinese laborers in the mid-nineteenth century, as well as Japanese farm laborers, and, later, Latin American laborers. However, when a migrant group becomes too dominant or "indigenous" (i.e., large numbers and/or many generations of the minority group have settled permanently in the country), the dominant indigenous group can limit immigration and effectively "cut off" the source of conflict. Such was the case with early-twentieth-century anti-immigration laws in which Asian immigrants were stopped from immigrating to the United States and those who were already here were stripped of many rights because the dominant whites feared that they were becoming too powerful and too plentiful to remain subordinated.

Robert Blauner's Theory of Colonized and Immigrant Minorities

Marxist sociologist Robert Blauner emphasizes fundamental differences between involuntary or colonized minorities and immigrants. He argues that minority groups created by the colonization experience (such as American Indians, Mexicans, and to some extent early Chinese laborers) face more intense prejudice, racism, and discrimination than do minority groups created by immigration. Moreover, the disadvantaged status of colonized groups tends to persist longer and is more difficult to overcome than the disadvantaged status of voluntary migrants. Blauner argues that, because of this fundamental disadvantage, African Americans and American Indians have more difficulty in adjusting to society than immigrant groups do. According to his theory, there are three major conditions that differentiate voluntary and involuntary minorities: mode of entry, labor relationships with the dominant culture, and cultural policy of the dominant group toward the minority group.

The most basic difference between colonized minorities and immigrants is the condition of forced versus free entry into a country. Involuntary minorities are either forcibly brought to a country (e.g., African slavery), or they have had their native homeland colonized (e.g., Native Americans and Mexicans). Immigrant minority groups are voluntary participants in the host society and have at least some control over their destination and their position in the host society. Though immigrants may be restricted by rigid and preferential immigration regulations, they enjoy relative freedom of movement (both in terms of migration to the United States as well as internal migration once within the country) that minorities brought to the society by conquest or slavery do not enjoy.

The second difference that Blauner emphasizes is the forced labor that involuntary minorities often have to perform. Historically, involuntary minorities were forced into dependent labor relationships, either by being brought into the country as slaves (i.e., the African slave trade), or being conquered and subjugated economically and politically (i.e., American Indians). They did not have the power to choose where they would live and work, and they did not have full access to the labor market. In contrast, Blauner argues, voluntary migrants have more access to waged (free) labor markets and are able to concentrate in industrial centers.

The third differentiating condition is a cultural policy of the dominant group that restricts or destroys the values and way of life of the minority group. Involuntary minorities have historically been subjected to massive inequalities and attacks on their existing cultural and social organizations. They were also often placed in situations where any form of assimilation into the dominant culture was extremely difficult, and perhaps even forbidden. During slavery, Africans were unable to maintain their family systems or ethnic ties because the plantation owners would frequently break up families or communities that were developing group solidarity. In the case of American Indians, nineteenth-century policies outlawed their native religion, and any new religious movement in that population was forcibly put down.

Blauner argues that, despite the fact that early Asian immigrants were subject to forced migration, restricted movement and labor, and cultural persecution, they did not face the same level of oppression that other involuntary groups did. He argues that Asians were, on a whole, able to retain enough internal organizations and resources to pursue their own self-interests. Although in his later writing he acknowledges that immigrants of color, such as Asians and Latinos, are disadvantaged in American society because of their race and ethnicity, Blauner maintains that involuntary minorities such as American Indians and African Americans were subjected to a more or less total destruction of native culture and social formation.

John Ogbu's Cultural-Ecological Theory

Anthropologist John Ogbu argues that involuntary and voluntary minorities are guided by distinctly different cultural models. Their understanding of how society and its institutions work, as well as their understanding of their place in that working order, is intrinsically related to their history as involuntary or voluntary migrants. Ogbu considers outcomes such as low educational achievement in involuntary minorities as an adaptive response to the requirements of cultural imperatives within their particular ecological structure. He looks to the development of these cultural imperatives to help explain why African American students, even affluent African American students, do not perform as well in school as their counterparts who are not African American. Most notably, Ogbu's theory helps to explain why African Americans are often outperformed by ethnic immigrants (i.e., voluntary minorities), who face similar, sometimes harsher, structural barriers to success. He argues that the cultural imperatives of involuntary migrants are shaped by historical, structural, and cultural forces that are very different from those of voluntary minorities.

In Ogbu's theory, the difference between the success outcomes (e.g., education, employment, and income) of involuntary and voluntary minorities stem from a fundamental difference in cultural orientation. As involuntary minorities, African American students often adopt an oppositional social identity that holds an inherent distrust for mainstream (i.e., white) authority and rejects mainstream values such as educational achievement. To adopt the mainstream value system and excel in school would be a form of "acting white," which is interpreted as a betrayal of group solidarity and racial identity. Ogbu also asserts that African Americans often do poorly in school because, with this backdrop of historical disadvantage, folk theories of success develop, and these are very pessimistic, often legitimately so. For example, African Americans may believe that they have to work twice as hard or be twice as good as members of the dominant group to compete for the same job or social position. Moreover, they may develop other, nonmainstream, destructive survival strategies, such as drug dealing or violence, as a more viable path to success, an alternative to a mainstream system that lacks opportunities for them.

In contrast, although they often face the similar structural barriers, voluntary minorities tend to be more successful than involuntary minorities, regardless of race or class. For example, in the United States, Afro-Caribbean immigrants are often able to achieve greater success than even middle-class African American blacks who were born in the United States. Ogbu argues that this is because the lineage of historical and social forces that mediate their cultural orientation is so different from that of minorities who were forcibly brought to the country. Immigrants, such as Afro-Caribbeans, do not have a long history of degradation over many generations and instead experience American society as a new social environment. Voluntary minorities have a greater degree of trust or acquiescence toward members of the dominant group and the institutions that they control. They possess a social identity and collectivity that was formed before migration, rather than being developed in opposition to the social identity of the dominant group of the host society. As a result, they do not fear the stigma of "acting white" with the same intensity as involuntary minorities. Rather, they often see their cultural and linguistic differences from the dominant group as barriers that they have to overcome. They immigrate to the United States largely with the mentality of wanting to embrace American society, and its educational and economic system, as a means to further their success.

Voluntary migrants also possess a positive dual frame of reference that allows them to develop and maintain an optimistic view of their future possibilities. This frame of reference enables them to compare their present situation with their former situation, or with that of their family and friends "back home." Despite the menial labor or poor living conditions they face in the United States, often they find it to be more fruitful and to present greater opportunities than life in their home country. Involuntary minorities have no "back home" to compare their situation to. The only frame of reference they have is to compare their place in society with that of members of the dominant group. When they make such a comparison, involuntary minorities invariably conclude that they are worse off than they ought to be because of the way they have been treated by the dominant group.

See also Black Power: The Politics of Liberation in America; Internal Colonialism; Oppositional Identity.

Further Reading

Blauner, Robert. "Colonized and Immigrant Minorities." In *From Different Shores: Perspectives on Race and Ethnicity in America*, edited by Ronald Takaki, 149–160. New York: Oxford University Press, 1994.

———. "Some Self-Critical Reflections on Colonized and Immigrant Minorities." In *Still the Big News: Racial Oppression in America*, edited by Robert Blauner, 189–192. Philadelphia: Temple University Press, 2001.

Fordham, Signithia, and John U. Ogbu. "Black Students' School Success: Coping with the Burden of 'Acting White.'" *The Urban Review* 18, no. 3 (1986): 176–206.

Lieberson, Stanley. "A Societal Theory of Race and Ethnic Relations." *American Sociological Review* 66 (1961): 902–910.

Ogbu, John U. "Immigrant and Involuntary Minorities in Comparative Perspective." In *Minority Status and Schooling: A Comparative Study of Immigrant and Involuntary Minorities*, edited by Margaret Gibson and John Ogbu, 3–53. New York: Garland, 1991.

———. *Black American Students in an Affluent Suburb: A Study of Academic Disengagement*. (Mahwah, NJ: L. Erlbaum Associates, 2003.

Ogbu, John U., and Simons, Herbert D. "Voluntary and Involuntary Minorities: A Cultural-Ecological Theory of School Performance with Some Implications for Education." *Anthropology & Education Quarterly* 29, no. 2 (1998): 155–188.

Tracy Chu

Color-Blind Racism

Color-blind racism is a modern form of racism that functions to sustain the racial/societal dominance of whites by ignoring the continuing effects of historical prejudice. By its very logic, color-blind racism requires that individuals pretend a person of color is socially raceless. It is exemplified by the statement "I only see you, I don't see the color of your skin."

Color-blind racism can also be thought of as "unintentional racism," because it involves racial injustice but springs from ignorance, naïveté, or cultural and religious marginalization rather than from racial hatred. But it leads to undesirable outcomes: the marginalization and oppression of people of color by failing to acknowledge and respond to their distinctive needs, experiences, and identities. In contrast to both Jim Crow racism and multiculturalism, color-blind racism avoids direct racial discourse and thereby effectively safeguards existing structures of racial privilege. It is based on the principle that "all people are equal"; while this principle is valid, it ignores continuing racial inequality and disadvantage in contemporary society.

Today, one major manifestation of color-blind racism is efforts (such as California's Proposition 54, defeated by voters in 2003) to eliminate racial categories from census data and public documents. Laws eliminating racial categories would have the effect of preventing the targeting of important services, such as bilingual education and economic development assistance, toward the communities that need them.

See also Affirmative Action; California Ballot Proposition 54; Jim Crow Laws.

Khyati Joshi

Color Hierarchy

The term *color hierarchy* represents the correlation between skin color and society's continuum of success or dominance. The gradations from light to dark skin tone have economic, political, social, and cultural implications. While the color hierarchy is most obvious in the historical contrast between black slaves and white slave owners, it still exists in contemporary America as well. In the contemporary context, Whites may be understood as "on top," followed by Asian Americans, Latinos, and Native Americans, with African Americans occupying the least privileged position in the U.S. racial hierarchy. The color hierarchy can also be seen within individual ethnic communities, with lighter-skinned individuals tending to enjoy more or different opportunities and privileges—and less discrimination—than those with darker skin.

Of course, the color hierarchy interacts with other factors, such as English-language ability and legal status, so that lighter-skinned individuals and groups may nevertheless face more overall discrimination and disadvantage.

Khyati Joshi

Color Line

In the introduction to his 1903 classic book, *The Souls of Black Folk*, W.E.B. Dubois warned readers that his writings on the meaning and experiences of black American life should not only be of interest to African Americans but should interest all people, because "the problem of the Twentieth Century is the problem of the color line." This concept of a color line demarcating the separation of blacks and whites in American society has served as a powerful metaphor for the nature of racial inequality in the United States. In his 1881 essay entitled "The Color Line," published in *The North American Review*, ex-slave and famous orator Frederick Douglass described how "slavery is indeed gone, but its shadow still lingers over the country and poisons more or less the moral atmosphere of all sections of the republic." The legacy of slavery evolved into institutional practices and policies that maintained the segregation and dehumanization of African Americans. In Douglass' words, "Out of the depths of slavery has come this prejudice and this color line."

The color line refers to the de jure segregation enforced by Jim Crow laws and practices that shaped nearly every aspect of the social, economic, and political lives of African Americans for more than a century following the abolition of slavery. The 1896 *Plessy v. Ferguson* Supreme Court decision maintained that "separate" facilities for blacks and whites were not unconstitutional as long as the facilities were "equal." This doctrine of legalized segregation maintained a color line in public spaces, such as restaurants, theaters, residential patterns, and public schools, and was frequently sustained with threats and brutal acts of violence, including lynchings. A visible marker that demarcated the color line was the ubiquitous "colored" signs on water fountains, restrooms, and waiting rooms that designated the separation and subordination of African Americans.

See also De Jure and De Facto Segregation; Douglass, Frederick; Jim Crow Laws; Lynching; Residential Segregation; Separate but Equal Doctrine.

Tarry Hum

Columbus Day Controversy

October 12 has been recognized in the United States as Columbus Day to exalt the Italian voyager Christopher Columbus and to celebrate his "discovery" of the "New World" in 1492. Many Italian Americans observe Columbus Day as a celebration of their ethnic heritage. Historically, it is believed that the first Columbus Day celebration took place in New York in 1792. In 1937, President Franklin D. Roosevelt reserved October 12 as a national holiday, and since 1971 it has been observed as a federal holiday.

However, in recent decades, the commemoration has been a source of social controversy and political division among ethnic and racial groups. The controversy revolves around demands by many Native American and other non-European communities to remove Columbus Day as a federal holiday because it has its origins in conquest, colonialism, and slavery. This has caused a persistent conflict between Native Americans, and Italian and other white Americans.

Landing of Columbus in America, 1492. Critics argue against the federal celebration of the event because of its origins in conquest, colonialism, and slavery.

Courtesy Library of Congress.

In response to this controversy, Native American and other minority leaders argue that the federal government should establish a holiday that recognizes Native Americans. As a result, since 2000, more than twenty states in the United States do not recognize Columbus Day as a national holiday, and some states, such as South Dakota and Delaware, have taken the matter one step further and changed Columbus Day to Native American Day. Critics of commemoration and celebrations of Columbus do not necessarily deny the historical contribution of his legacy, but they argue that the existing celebrations of a specific understanding of the legacy of Columbus justify stereotypes of Native Americans or other minority groups and the racist ideology toward them and thus contribute to the maintenance of existing social inequalities against them.

Nicholas Alexiou

Competitive Race Relations

See Race Relations, Paternalistic vs. Competitive

Congress of Racial Equality (CORE)

The Congress of Racial Equality (CORE) was founded in 1942 as a pacifist group seeking to change racist attitudes in society, integrate public facilities, and fight for civil rights for African Americans. At its inception, it was an interracial group with a democratic, decentralized structure. As the group moved through the 1960s, sponsoring and cosponsoring events like the 1963 March on Washington and the Freedom Rides, the leadership became primarily African American so as to build the credibility of the group among more militant sectors of the civil rights movement. In the late 1960s and 1970s, CORE became more centralized and focused on issues of Black Nationalism, separatism, and capitalism. CORE has continued to be active to this day, returning to a more multiracial program of work on such issues as making Martin Luther King Day a national holiday and on welfare-to-work programs. It is concerned with ensuring equality for all sectors of society, but particularly with promoting political and economic empowerment of African Americans, through voter registration, support of African American candidates for public office, and economic issues facing inner-city populations.

See also Black Nationalist Movement; Freedom Riders; March on Washington Movement.

Mikaila Mariel Lemonik Arthur

Conservatives

See Liberal and Conservative Views of Racial Inequality.

Coolie

Coolie refers to a popular stereotype of Chinese working as cheap labor in mines, agriculture, and railroad construction in the nineteenth-century United States. Originally, the term referred to a system of indentured labor established by the British in the nineteenth century to recruit primarily Indian and Chinese workers for plantations in Asia, Africa, and Latin America. With the end of the African slave trade and the abolition of slavery at home, the British shipped tens of thousands of Chinese coolies—often war prisoners, kidnap victims, and debtors coerced into service—from southern China to Latin America, particularly Cuba and Peru, between 1845 and 1874, to work on plantations and in mines. Their transportation recalls the African slave ships, which were replete with death, disease, starvation, riots, murders, and mutinies. Recruiters delivered workers in this Chinese "pig trade" with signed contracts for terms of service that were then sold to the highest bidder upon arrival.

Most Chinese arriving in the United States in the nineteenth century, however, were not indentured laborers; they bought tickets on credit, repaying the fare with labor after arrival. The creditors' control of migrants after arrival, though, left many believing the credit-ticket arrangement varied from the coolie trade only in that the Chinese willingly participated in their subjugation. An American law prohibited coolies or indentured workers. But the image of slave-like living and working conditions, combined with the perceived threat to the jobs and wages of the American white working class, became a rallying cry for white American workers and formed the

Chinese laborers constructing the Central Pacific Railroad, 1860s.

Courtesy North Wind/North Wind Picture Archives.

base of the economic argument for Chinese exclusion later in the nineteenth century.

See also Chinese Exclusion Act of 1882; Chinese Immigrants, Adaptation of to Female Jobs; Chinese Immigrants and Anti-Chinese Sentiments; Foreign Miners License Tax; Indentured Servants.

Kenneth J. Guest

CORE

See Congress of Racial Equality (CORE).

"Cost of Being a Negro"

When John Howard Griffin's book *Black Like Me* was published in 1960, its readers learned how a white man who artificially and temporarily darkened his skin pigmentation and passed as a black man in the South paid a steep price in privileges lost as well as vanished opportunities, status, and trust. Newspaper accounts of that era told of even steeper penalties borne by blacks: real or imagined offenses that whites might commit and only be mildly chastised for could cost black men or women years in prison or even their lives.

In 1965, sociologist Paul M. Siegel initiated a new approach to this issue with the publication of his groundbreaking article, "On the Cost of Being a Negro." He drew on 1960 U.S. census data and, with statistical tables and graphs, provided the first quantitative analysis of whites' and non-whites' incomes that estimated how much of the interracial income gap still remained even after one took into account (controlled for) differences in whites' and non-whites' years of education, geographical locations, and occupational levels. Siegel found that in 1959, on average, black men with the same years of schooling, working in the same occupational category, and living in the same region as white men were paid $1,097 less than white men received. Siegel argued that this advantage to whites or deficit to blacks (about $1,000) was a rough indicator of the "cost" of being black due to racial discrimination: an undeclared and illegitimate tax for being nonwhite or bonus for being white. Further analysis by Siegel showed that this "cost" was not equal in size across all educational categories; in fact, the "cost" or "tax" for being black was largest for blacks with the highest educational levels. The conclusion he and civil rights activists drew from this research was that making blacks and whites more similar in terms of educational level, occupation, and region of residence would not be enough to bring about interracial economic equality—something had to be done to eliminate disparities in pay between blacks and whites who were equivalent on those other traits.

In the ensuing years, other social scientists have extended and revised Siegel's approach and findings. Researchers have published dozens of articles in which they add more control variables to the analysis, use more sophisticated statistical techniques and more current data, and decompose income or earnings inequalities among groups other than blacks and whites. For example, researchers now routinely include in the analysis variables such as the amount of work experience or job seniority a worker has, whether they are in urban or rural areas, the industry they are employed in, and whether or not they are labor-union members. In applying this approach to other groups, specialists in gender inequality examine how much of the average male-female earnings gap is left unexplained even after controlling for many variables known to affect workers' earnings, and upon finding that a substantial portion of the gap cannot be attributed to those variables, they argue that this may indicate gender discrimination in wages or salaries. Other researchers have studied the "cost" of being a Mexican American worker and compared it with the "cost" of being black or from several other racial/ethnic categories. One such study of male workers found that the cost of being Mexican American was higher than the cost of being black and that it had not declined over time as much as had the cost of being black. Of course, research on the "cost of being black" is quite relevant to the thesis advanced by William J. Wilson in *The Declining Significance of Race* (1978), and Wilson's critics often cited this work to show that "being black" (i.e., racial discrimination against blacks) still has substantial negative effects on socioeconomic and health status.

Scholars also have clarified and critiqued the statistical decomposition analysis (which is typically based on multiple regression) used in "the cost of . . ."

literature, showing some inherent interpretive ambiguities that make it difficult to say precisely how much of the income gap is due to discrimination. Nevertheless, research by Siegel and others in this tradition occupies an important place in the research on racial/ethnic and gender economic inequality and has at times (and with varying degrees of success) been useful in lawsuits against, or other challenges to, wage and salary discrimination. With the release of income data from the 2000 census more research and debate on the "cost of being black" and related topics is likely.

See also Blacks, Wage Discrimination against; Economics of Discrimination; Racial Earnings Gap.

Further Reading

Cotton, Jeremiah. "More on the 'Cost' of Being a Black or Mexican American Male Worker." *Social Science Quarterly* 66 (1985): 867–885.

———. "Discrimination and Favoritism in the U.S. Labor Market: The Cost to a Wage Earner of Being Female and Black and the Benefit of Being Male and White." *The American Journal of Economics and Sociology* 47 (1988): 15–28.

Siegel, Paul M. "On the Cost of Being a Negro." *Sociological Inquiry* 25 (Winter 1965): 41–57.

Charles Jaret

Council on American Islamic Relations (CAIR)

The Council on American Islamic Relations (CAIR) was established in 1994, but in the wake of the backlash against Muslims that followed the events of September 11, 2001, it has come to national prominence as the leading civil rights advocate for the growing number of Muslim Americans. This is probably because of its ability to fill an important void in addressing issues that are pressing for Muslim Americans in a period of crisis and to respond quickly to events through the use of electronic communication, and to the strength of its programs.

Through political and social activism, CAIR works to debunk negative stereotypes of Islam and empower its constituents. Its slogan, "Faith in Action," explains CAIR's programs, which include (1) media relations: monitoring the media for stereotypes and projecting a positive image of Islam, as in the "Islam in America" advertisement campaign in major newspapers; (2) publications: for example, the "Know Your Rights Pocket Guide," "An Employer's Guide to Islamic Religious Practices," and "Teaching About Islam and Muslims in the Public School Classroom;" and (3) action alerts: encouraging grassroots activism.

CAIR has been tallying cases of hate crimes and bias incidents that individuals report over the phone or via e-mail, as well as stories from the press. Periodically, a report is published summarizing this work, such as the May 2002 report entitled "The Status of Muslim Civil Rights in the United States: Stereotypes and Civil Liberties." Among CAIR's most popular programs is the daily electronic news it sends to its listserv group summarizing mentions of Islam, Muslims, and Arabs in the local, national, and international press. These daily e-mails also disseminate information on community events and fundraisers and encourage readers to write protest or encouragement letters to officials and the press. In its work, CAIR educates its membership on how to function effectively in the United States. CAIR's primary goals, however, remain the education of the larger American public about Islam.

See also Hate Crimes; Muslims, Prejudice and Discrimination against; Muslims, Terrorist Image of; September 11, 2001, Terrorism, Discriminatory Reactions to.

Mehdi Bozorgmehr and Anny Bakalian

Covert versus Overt Discrimination

Overt discrimination, sometimes called "old-fashioned" discrimination, refers to public or private conscious attitudes and behaviors intended to harm or damage a person or a group of people of color or to define people of color as inferior to whites and therefore less entitled to society's benefits. The discrimination typical of the Jim Crow era, such as lynchings, the use of racial epithets, the enforcement of laws designed to prevent minorities from voting, and terrorist acts by white supremacist organizations, represents discrimination as most individuals understand it. These acts, which constitute overt discrimination, have come to define what discrimination is.

By contrast, covert discrimination is hidden and much less public than overt discrimination. Examples of covert discrimination include cultural and religious marginalization, color-blind racism, and tokenism. Covert discrimination, a form of modern racism, is often not recognized by members of the majority group as being discriminatory. It is disguised with language that downplays the clearly racial aspects of the discrimination, and it is rationalized by invocation of or reliance on nonracial explanations more acceptable in the broader society. The existence of covert discrimination is therefore more difficult to prove than are acts of overt racism. In contemporary society, covert discrimination is more commonplace.

See also Jim Crow Laws; Lynching.

Khyati Joshi

Creation Generation

The term *creation generation* refers to the generation of Mexicans who became U.S. citizens as a result of the 1848 Treaty of Guadalupe Hidalgo, which ended the war between Mexico and the United States. The treaty is now considered to have unduly benefited the United States. Under this treaty, in an exchange for a payment of $15 million, Mexico surrendered 55 percent of its territories: areas that currently include New Mexico, Arizona, Texas, and parts of California, Colorado, Nevada, and Utah. In addition, Mexican citizens residing in these areas were granted U.S. citizenship.

The notion of involuntary immigrants (i.e., individuals who belong to social groups that were forced into becoming Americans) has primarily been applied to the experiences of African Americans, but other minority groups in the United States fit the same criterion. The creation generation of Mexicans is among them. Although the treaty provided an opportunity for these individuals to remain Mexican citizens, most did not opt to do so. Rather, they became Americans not through due democratic process, but simply by virtue of remaining at their own residences, which now fell on the American side of the new border. As an involuntary minority group, they encountered Anglo-centered ethnocentrism, economic exploitation, and political disfranchisement.

See also Guadalupe Hidalgo, Treaty of; Manifest Destiny; Mexican-American War.

Daisuke Akiba

Crime and Race

The relationship between crime and race in the United States is a subject of intense and very contentious inquiry. The controversy begins with large disparities in crime counts between blacks and whites. Differing explanations for these disparities keep the argument going. Complicating this issue is the fact that black Americans tend to have a less favorable view of the criminal justice system, especially the police.

Two of the most well-known measures of crime in the United States are the Federal Bureau of Investigation's (FBI) Uniform Crime Reports (UCR) and the Bureau of Justice Statistics' National Crime Victimization Survey (NCVS). Since 1930, the UCR has provided official statistics collected from police agencies throughout the United States. Police agencies voluntarily submit statistics on the crimes that are reported to them and the arrests they make to the FBI, which then collates the data. In 2001, nearly 17,000 agencies participated, covering 92 percent of the total population. The NCVS, on the other hand, collects data through the use of a telephone survey conducted by the Bureau of the Census. A nationally representative sample of about 45,000 households and 94,000 persons are asked whether they have been victims of crime and, if so, the characteristics of that crime.

Both the UCR and the NCVS show similar trends regarding the race of offenders. Generally, the number of minorities identified as offenders is disproportionately high compared with their overall numbers in the population. As Ronald J. Berger et al. advise the NCVS, "data are consistent with the UCR. The offenders in these types of crimes are disproportionately young, nonwhite, and male" (2001, 51). Even though both indicators show minorities as offenders in disproportionate numbers, there are well-known weaknesses with both measures, which means one must use extreme caution when interpreting these figures.

Arrest statistics for murder/nonnegligent manslaughter provide an example of how crime figures can be interpreted with respect to race. These

figures indicate that blacks generally have high rates of arrest disproportionate with their numbers in the population. In 2001, blacks were the subject of arrest in 48.7 percent of the murders/nonnegligent manslaughters,
and whites represented 48.4 percent of the arrests for those same crimes
(Federal Bureau of Investigation 2001, 252). Since whites make up approximately 75 percent of the population and blacks about 12 percent of the
population (based on 2000 census data for those reporting only one race),
this means that blacks are overrepresented in this arrest category. One way
to interpret this disparity is that it is because of overt discrimination by police in arresting more blacks. However, examining the characteristics of the
offenders (based on victims' descriptions) for murder/nonnegligent manslaughter, approximately 48 percent of offenders are identified as white and
49 percent of offenders are identified as black (*Sourcebook of Criminal Justice Statistics* 2001, 314). These offender percentages closely reflect the arrest percentages, suggesting that interpretation of these statistics must be
done cautiously, especially with respect to determining overt discrimination
in the system.

Regarding race as a correlate of crime, today researchers essentially accept
the paradigm that "although some of the racial differences observed in official
statistics can be attributed to differential responses by the criminal justice system, criminologists generally agree that there are real differences in behavior
as well. . . . However, . . . there has been a general reluctance 'to speak openly
about the race and crime connection' and thus the theoretical mechanisms
underlying the race-crime connection are not well understood" (South and
Messner 2000, 87–88).

Even though the connections between race and crime are not fully known,
explanations for this disparity are plentiful and have led to enormous debate.
Some of the more notable arguments to explain the disparity center on
poverty and disadvantage due to race; cultural phenomena, such as a subculture of violence; the neighborhood or area where minorities tend to live; family disruption; and similar causes. Multilevel analysis argues that there are many
causes and that explanations can be found by looking at the individuals, the
communities, and, some anecdotal work suggests, in discrimination rampant
in the criminal justice system.

Regardless of these arguments, it is clear that there is a racial divide in trust
of various aspects of the criminal justice system, especially the police. In a recent Gallup poll, 61 percent of whites expressed confidence in the police,
compared to only 34 percent of blacks. Additionally, high-profile incidents of
police brutality, such as in the Amadou Diallo, Abner Louima, Rodney King,
and Patrick Dorismond cases, certainly leave an impression of discrimination,
even though it may not be systemic.

Thus, the relationship between crime and race is not fully explored. Social
scientists generally agree that there is a disparity between whites and blacks
in crime statistics and in the response of the criminal justice system. The reasons for this disparity are the subject of continued scrutiny and debate.

See also Criminal Justice System and Racial Discrimination.

Further Reading

Berger, Ronald J., Marvin D. Free, Jr., and Patricia Searles. *Crime, Justice and Society: Criminology and the Sociological Imagination*. New York: McGraw-Hill, 2001.

Federal Bureau of Investigation. *Crime in the United States: Uniform Crime Reports*. Washington, DC: U.S. Government Printing Office, 2001.

Senna, Joseph J., and Larry J. Siegel. *Essentials of Criminal Justice*. 3rd ed. Belmont, CA: Wadsworth, 2001.

Sourcebook of Criminal Justice Statistics, 2001. Washington DC: U.S. Government Printing Office, 2002.

South, Scott J., and Steven F. Messner. "Crime and Demography: Multiple Linkages, Reciprocal Relations." *Annual Review of Sociology* 26, no. 1 (2000): 83–106.

John Eterno

Criminal Justice System and Racial Discrimination

The criminal justice system encompasses policing, criminal-court processes, sentencing, incarceration, and additional supervision. In each of these areas, research has shown race to be a significant factor in outcome. Frequently, race interacts with economic status, leading many prominent social scientists to conclude that justice policies targeting low-income and otherwise disadvantaged communities are likely to have a more severe impact on African Americans than on people of other races. Census data demonstrates that a disproportionately high percentage of black and Latino households fall below the poverty line, and Justice Department statistics demonstrate that blacks and Latinos make up a disproportionately high percentage of defendants, inmates, probationers, and parolees. Justice Department data also demonstrates that a higher percentage of black defendants than white or Latino defendants are indigent.

According to the Bureau of Justice Statistics, 9 percent of all African Americans were under correctional supervision of some sort (incarcerated, or supervised by probation or parole) in 1997, while only 2 percent of whites and 1 percent of all other races combined were under correctional supervision. In many U.S. cities, young black men are taken out of their communities through incarceration at very high rates. Although research has shown that there are race-based inconsistencies in the application of sentences, including capital punishment, the federal courts have been equivocal in response. In *Gideon v. Wainwright* (1963) and then in *Miranda v. Arizona* (1966) the Supreme Court established, respectively, the right to an attorney and the right of suspects to be informed of their rights prior to questioning in police custody. Both of these decisions had the effect of increasing protections that had previously been lacking for low-income suspects and defendants. However, these two decisions rested firmly on principles of equality before the law regardless of financial resources, thereby protecting against explicit discrimination. The Court has not, however, supported protections against implicit discrimination based on race.

The War on Drugs initiated by the Reagan administration mandates sentences based on type and weight of drug. Sentences for crack cocaine, a less expensive form of cocaine used primarily by African Americans, are one hundred times more severe than sentences for cocaine in its powder form, which is more expensive and more prevalent than crack among white drug users. This disparity alone is responsible for a significant portion of the increase in incarceration of African Americans since 1980. Many activists argue that American drug laws are disproportionately targeting minorities and are discriminatory. Whether or not there was any discriminatory intent in the law, it is clear that American drug laws are affecting minorities and minority communities to a greater degree than they are affecting white communities. There is also evidence that blacks and Hispanics are sentenced to longer prison terms than are their white counterparts.

Race is also a factor in who is questioned and arrested for crimes. There has been considerable controversy over racial profiling, which is the practice of questioning people, most often black men, who are statistically more likely to have been involved in

Waiting in a prison cell.

a crime. Critics of this practice argue that it constitutes racial harassment. The practice of police pulling over African American motorists has become so common that the "offense" has become informally known as a DWB—Driving while Black. After the terrorist attacks of September 11, 2001, racial profiling began to target men of Middle Eastern descent. Civil libertarian groups object to the practice of racial profiling because it violates the right to equal treatment under the law. Some law enforcement officials argue that it is an essential tool in combating crime and terrorism.

See also Crime and Race.

Further Reading

Beckett, Katherine, and Theodore Sasson. *The Politics of Injustice: Crime and Punishment in America*. Thousand Oaks, CA: Sage Publications, 2000.

Cole, David. *No Equal Justice: Race and Class in the American Criminal Justice System*. New York: New Press, 1999.

Kennedy, Randall. *Race, Crime and the Law*. New York: Pantheon, 1997.

Tonry, Michael. *Malign Neglect: Race, Crime, and Punishment in America*. New York: Oxford University Press, 1995.

                                                                Robin Roger-Dillon

Cultural Genocide

Cultural genocide refers to the deliberate and systematic destruction of the cultural heritage, religion, language, and way of life of a group of people. Initial drafts of the 1948 United Nations Convention on Genocide included an explicit statement forbidding cultural genocide, as well as biological genocide (e.g., restricting births, sterilization, compulsory abortions, and segregation of sexes), and physical genocide (killing—whether quickly as in mass murder, or slowly as in economic deprivation). Examples of cultural genocide include the forcible transfer of children to another group, the forced and systematic exile of individuals representing the culture of a group, prohibition of the use of the national language (even in private), the systematic destruction of religious works or books printed in the national language (as well as prohibition of new publications), systematic destruction of historical or religious monuments or their diversion to alien uses, and destruction or dispersion of documents and objects of historical, artistic, or religious value and of objects used in religious worship.

The United States immediately resisted the 1948 UN proposal (the Genocide Convention on the Prevention and Punishment of Genocide) to prohibit cultural genocide because U.S. politicians were concerned that U.S. treatment of minorities would be in violation of such injunctions. As a result, the subsequent version of the Convention has excluded any explicit mention of cultural genocide. In the United States, American Indians have historically suffered both physical and cultural genocide at the hands of the U.S. government. After the physical genocide of conquest, the remaining American Indians were subject to a cultural genocide in which their land was taken away, their icons were destroyed, their children were forcibly removed and taught to speak other languages and worship other gods, and their religious practices were forbidden.

See also Hate Crimes; Native Americans, Conquest of; Native Americans, Forced Relocation of.

                                                                Tracy Chu

Cultural Pluralism

See Multiculturalism.

Culture of Poverty Thesis

Definition and Origin of the Culture of Poverty Thesis

The culture of poverty thesis is a theoretical framework that has been used to explain the poverty of African Americans and other racial minority groups in the United States in terms of their cultural deficiencies. *Culture* can be broadly defined as the material and nonmaterial features of a group of people. Although few cultures exist in isolation, members of a cultural group have a similar ideology, behavior, norms, values, artifacts, and a shared set of experiences. The word *culture* is often used to distinguish groups based on characteristics such as race, ethnicity, religion, and national origin. The central feature of the culture of poverty thesis is that the poor share a common culture (i.e., attitudes, behavior, lifestyle, beliefs) that directly or indirectly perpetuates their impoverished conditions.

According to the thesis, because of dire economic conditions, the poor attempt to cope with feelings of hopelessness and despair that come with knowing that their chances for success in life are few. These adaptations include (1) a sense of resignation and passivity because of long-term poverty; (2) a present-time orientation because of pressures to survive day to day; (3) feelings of fatalism and powerlessness because of separation from the political process; (4) low aspirations from lack of opportunity; (5) feelings of inferiority because of society's contempt and aversion to the poor; and (6) an increased number of female heads of households due to lack of a male breadwinners and unstable families. Gaining popularity in the 1960s and early 1970s, the theoretical view was used to place the onus of escaping poverty on the poor.

Although various scholars and writers have espoused a culture of poverty thesis, anthropologist Oscar Lewis (1914–1970) is credited with having developed it. He performed research in impoverished Latin American barrios (neighborhoods), using participant observation and life-history analysis. According to Lewis, a culture of poverty had economic, psychological, and social features and was both an adaptation and reaction by the poor to their marginal position in a class-stratified society. Just as culture reflects a shared way of life, Lewis suggested, the poor he studied shared a common way of life that served as a coping mechanism but also perpetuated poverty. Thus, poverty created an environment that fostered more poverty. For persons who embraced a culture of poverty, it was difficult to exhibit attitudes and behavior that could help them escape poverty, and their condition became matter of fact. Lewis posited that the long-term self-perpetuating cycle of poverty also subsumed the children of the poor, who were socialized into this culture as well. Lewis suggested that economic changes in society as a whole would help the poor, as would involvement in trade-union movements and efforts to raise class-consciousness. Lewis's findings were published in *Five Families* (1959), *The Children of Sánchez* (1961), *La Vida* (1966), and *Anthropological Essays* (1970).

Moynihan's Report as a Typical Example of the Culture of Poverty Thesis

Daniel Patrick Moynihan's *The Negro Family: The Case for National Action* (1965) is quite possibly the most widely known example of the culture of poverty thesis applied to explain the poverty of a minority group in the United States. Moynihan suggested that poverty among blacks was primarily a result of black family instability evidenced by high divorce rates, female-headed households, out-of-wedlock births, and welfare dependency. Moynihan noted that the effects of slavery, racial discrimination, segregation, and poverty in urban cities made it difficult for many blacks to establish economically stable families, but that, for poor blacks to escape poverty, they must establish and maintain family stability. Moynihan concluded that social policy should be directed toward strengthening the black family.

Commissioned by President Lyndon B. Johnson, Moynihan's results were widely read and publicized and influenced how the academia and the wider public viewed black families. The Moynihan report resulted in numerous studies on poverty among blacks that emphasized a culture of poverty as the main cause of poverty in the black community. The theoretical basis of many of these studies was a pathology model that correlated chronic socioeconomic problems with inherent individual character flaws among the poor. The pathology model suggested that the long-term effects of poverty are linked to historic economic inequities but are largely a result of poor personal choices among the poor that create economic, social, and cultural conditions that are difficult to escape.

In contrast to the culture of poverty thesis applied to blacks and Hispanics, the model-minority thesis has been associated with Asian Americans. Some scholars and the mainstream media have applauded Asian Americans for possessing a strong work ethic and stable families, emphasizing education, exhibiting delayed gratification, and responding to racism and discrimination in less confrontational ways. They have attributed the socioeconomic success of Asian Americans to these positive cultural traits that poor blacks and Hispanics are encouraged to emulate.

The Culture of Poverty and the Structure versus Individual Agency Discourse

The culture of poverty thesis can be positioned within the broader "structure versus agency" academic discourse, where structure and agency represent two ends of a polemic to explain social issues such as poverty. By focusing on the effects of structural constraints on poverty, the structural approach considers macrolevel dynamics, most of which are outside the control of the poor, as the primary reasons most poor remain so and the ranks of the poor are growing. Structural constraints often associated with urban poverty are (1) deindustrialization that resulted in demand shifts from manufacturing to service occupations, (2) globalization, (3) the increase in demand for technical workers, (4) racism and discrimination, (5) residential isolation, and (6) out-migration of businesses and jobs from urban areas to the suburbs. From this perspective, poverty is not inevitable and economic improvements can occur for members of disadvantaged minority groups through social policy and government intervention.

In contrast, the agency discourse assumes that persons have free will or a choice in matters that directly affect them. In an open socioeconomic mobility system such as that in the United States, it is commonly believed that everyone who is willing and able has an opportunity to succeed. Thus the individual's effort to improve his or her conditions is most important determinant of socioeconomic position. When considering poverty, an agency-based premise would suggest that the poor are largely to blame for their impoverished state because they often exhibit aberrant attitudes and behavior. For example, a poor work ethic, failure to seek employment or to take jobs that are available, or lacking the skills and education to compete in society all represent personal choices that explain poverty. This positions suggests that certain groups of poor people, such as widows and orphans, would be more worthy of assistance than others but that most of the poor would be considered undeserving of governmental assistance or help through other organized channels. The culture of poverty thesis is usually associated with agency-based explanations for poverty.

Other Studies Related to the Culture of Poverty Thesis

Oscar Lewis' culture of poverty has been applied beyond its original scope, focus, and context. Although Lewis' research focused on poor barrios in Latin American cities, the thesis has been largely applied to explain the experiences of residents in poor U.S. urban settings. The original research examined the experiences of persons of Hispanic descent; but the thesis is commonly associated with commentaries about poor African Americans and, to a somewhat lesser degree, Native Americans, Chicanos, and Puerto Ricans. Lewis's original work also recognized the effects of structural forces, but such factors are secondary in many current applications.

Empirical studies testing the culture of poverty thesis have yielded conflicting findings regarding the culture of poverty on the part of members of disadvantaged minority groups. Edward Banfield suggested that, among inner-city residents, continued experience of and exposure to poverty resulted in a culture that undermined expectations of achievement and personal initiative. Like Lewis, Banfield argued that the poor tended to exhibit a present-time orientation rather than attitudes and behavior associated with delayed gratification, planning for the future, working hard, and frugality. More recently, in *The New Politics of Poverty*, Lawrence M. Mead (1992) focused on the experience of the nonworking poor and argued that poverty is not a result of limited employment opportunities, but rather, a result of failure to work. Mead contended that the majority of poverty-stricken people are female heads of families and single adults. Reminiscent of Lewis' terminology, Mead associated their behavior with "a culture of poverty that discourages work" (24).

However, other empirical studies have demonstrated the invalidity of the culture of poverty thesis. Chandler Davidson and Charles M. Gaitz (1974) examined work ethic among poor African American, white, and Hispanic people. Their findings showed that members of these urban poor are just as willing to work as nonpoor persons. Moreover, the poor racial/ethnic minorities in the sample were found to be more work-oriented than their white counterparts. According to William Ryan (1974), unequal access and distribution of resources and wealth and a disparate opportunity structure explain continued poverty among the urban poor in the United States as compared to countries that emphasize economic equity. Macrolevel societal factors that foster economic instability, rather than individuals, are to blame for poverty. Furthermore, Ryan contended that low aspirations among the poor are a *consequence*, rather than a cause, of poverty. Rather than blame the victims,

Ryan recommended policies to empower the poor economically and socially. Other studies, such as *Ain't No Makin' It* by Jay MacLeod (1995) and *No Shame in My Game: The Working Poor in the Inner City* by Katherine Newman (1999) also found the achievement-oriented attitude and strong work ethics among the poor and situated their experiences within a larger economic context.

Critique and Implications of the Culture of Poverty Thesis

Although Lewis's thesis was initially met with wide interest and support, it has been subjected to various criticisms, which can be summarized into the following three major categories. First, detractors have contended that the thesis is theoretically and methodologically limited because it emphasizes the individual initiative to escape poverty and other forms of disadvantage and minimizes possible negative effects of structural dynamics such as international and national economic changes that have reduced the number of high-paying manufacturing jobs. They suggest that failure to use a more comprehensive research approach has resulted in conservative policy implications.

Second, the culture of poverty thesis is believed to be overly simplistic in its presentation of who experiences poverty. Critics argue that it minimizes the existence of non-poor African Americans and Hispanics and their hard work, ignores poor whites and Asians, and may reinforce racial stereotypes. For example, despite the model-minority thesis's positive depictions of Asian Americans, many Asian American scholars are critical of it because it oversimplifies the Asian American experience in the United States, based on inappropriate interracial and intraracial contrasts, and tends to ignore social problems faced by Asian Americans.

Third, because the thesis tends to question other factors that result in economic disadvantage, it may make it difficult to objectively study the problem of poverty and result in placing blame on the poor for their condition. Although Lewis did not totally blame the poor for their state, his work has been heavily cited by persons who hold the poor largely accountable for their circumstances. Moynihan's pathology model, the model-minority thesis, and related studies represent applications of the cultural explanation that were widely accepted as ways to describe minority experiences in the United States. Some of these frameworks continue to be used today.

See also Black Family Instability Thesis; Blaming-the-Victim Argument; "Model Minority Thesis"; *The Negro Family: The Case for National Action*; Racial Difference in Poverty Rate.

Further Reading

Banfield, Edward. *The Unheavenly City Revisited.* Boston: Little, Brown, 1974.

Davidson, Chandler, and Charles M. Gaitz. " 'Are the Poor Different?' A Comparison of Work Behavior and Attitudes Among the Urban Poor and Nonpoor." *Social Problems* 22 (1974): 229–245.

Lewis, Oscar. *The Children of Sanchez.* New York: Random House, 1961.

———. "The Culture of Poverty." *Scientific American* 115 (1966): 19–25.

Mead, Lawrence. *The New Politics of Poverty: The Nonworking Poor in America*. New York: Basic Books, 1992.

Moynihan, Daniel Patrick. *The Negro Family: The Case for National Action*. Washington, DC: Office of Policy Planning and Research, United States Department of Labor, 1965.

Ryan, William. *Blaming the Victim*. New York: Vintage Books, 1976.

Sandra L. Barnes

D

Davenport, Charles Benedict

See Eugenics Movement.

Dawes Act

See Indian Allotment Act of 1887.

Declining Significance of Race, The

Published in 1978, William J. Wilson's *The Declining Significance of Race* generated an important polemic about race in America among diverse scholars. It was reviewed by a large number of academic and nonacademic publications and won prestigious academic prizes. Key parts of the polemic, namely the relative importance of race versus class, and the best policies to deal with the black underclass, are not completely settled today, and to this extent, the arguments set forth in *The Declining Significance of Race* are still relevant. The argument in the book, the debate it generated, and its legacy are considered here.

The Argument

Wilson's central argument is clearly stated in the book's first sentence: "Race relations in America have undergone fundamental changes in recent years, so much that now the life chances of individual blacks have more to do with their economic class position than with their day-to-day encounters with whites." While, in his view, the history of race relations is characterized by slavery, segregation, exploitation of black labor by white economic elites, and actions of the white masses to eliminate competition, particularly economic competition, in the last half of the twentieth century, "many of the traditional barriers have crumbled under the weight of the political, social, and economic changes of the civil rights era." To support his argument, Wilson made a historical analysis of the different race-relations systems in the United States. Each system was a combination of economic characteristics that included dominant production forms, economic groups generated by these forms, and their influence on or dominance of the political system. He distinguished three major periods.

The first period of racial-caste oppression began with slavery and lasted until the end of the Civil War. This system was based on a plantation economy, with a hegemonic, small slave-holding elite that controlled economic power and had great influence in the political life of the South. Economic relations in the plantation economy implied a simple division of labor in which slave owners and slaves were the major actors and there were few gradations in between. Because slaves performed tasks at lower costs than free whites, white free labor had few economic opportunities and resources and therefore lacked political and economic power. The polarity between slave owners and slaves, and the absence of a middle class and an influential working class was not universal in the South, but it was the most representative pattern of the racial-caste oppression system (41). Social relations, in turn, followed paternalistic racial patterns that "reveal[ed] close symbiotic relationships marked by dominance and subservience, great social distance and little physical distance. . . ." (13). The slaveholders' domination of Southern politics provided the basis for their influence on national politics.

The second period of class conflict and racial oppression started with the end of slavery and ended with the New Deal in the late 1930s. It was marked by the growth of industrialization based on manufactures and by the presence of a more complex class structure that, significantly, included a white working class that competed with black labor. In the different economic and political contexts of the North and the South, the competition between white and black labor was critical in producing two outcomes: a split labor market in the North, in which the demise of slavery was followed by laws designed to curtail black economic competition, and Jim Crow segregation in the South, in which the demise of slavery threatened white labor to a greater extent than in the North (50–67). In both contexts, however, there was a combination of class competition between blacks and whites in the labor market, accompanied by racial oppression in the form of physical exclusion and segregation of blacks from public spaces in the South, and exclusion from entering occupations controlled by organized labor in the North. Wilson emphasized that these systems of race relations were erected with the interests of the white working class being taken into account. Free labor had to compete with slave labor, creating labor-market conflicts along racial lines.

The third period, this one of predominant class oppression and declining racial oppression, was characterized by modern industrialization and by two critical processes: mass migration of blacks from the South to Northern cities and an increasing geographic dispersion of business that had begun to move away from central cities. The timing of black migration, accompanied by an extensive concentration of blacks in the cities, had important consequences for the slow growth of their urban political power. Wilson argued that since migration took place only after 1940, blacks were already several decades behind the European whites who had migrated in the 1920s and earlier, and this belated entry left them without the sociopolitical influence that the cities had provided to other immigrant groups (79). Further, after the 1950s, economic shifts meant that business decentralized and moved out of the cities, while the industrial structure shifted from manufacturing to service jobs. This economic shift generated white-collar positions for skilled, educated workers, and low-paying, dead-end jobs that did not offer wages high enough to support a family. Thus, demographic and structural economic factors conjured the development of an economic chasm among blacks: a middle social class, and an underclass of largely unemployed or underemployed blacks.

A critical aspect of Wilson's argument was that educated (middle-class) blacks were beneficiaries of the increasing demand for skilled workers and of government civil rights laws that basically eliminated overt discrimination. He documented the growth of the middle class with statistics showing that an increasing number of blacks were employed in middle-class occupations. Conversely, he argued that uneducated blacks had higher rates of unemployment than educated blacks, and that the highest gap in unemployment between whites and nonwhites during the 1970s was with nonwhites who had less than twelve years of education. Marginality and redundancy created by modern industrial society affected all the poor, regardless of race, including whites, Native Americans, and Hispanic Americans. And, according to Wilson, the fact that one-third of the total black population was in the "underclass" in the 1970s reflected more than the legacy of past racial oppression. Drawing a logical implication from this argument, he argued that "the challenge of economic dislocation in modern industrial society calls for . . . programs . . . to attack inequality on a broad class front, policies that go beyond the limits of ethnic and racial discrimination. . . ." (154).

The Debate

The book caused a widespread controversy, and critics' responses were varied. Some critics claimed that the thesis of the book was true but that it did not really advance any new arguments and was poorly documented (Sowell 1979), whereas others focused on the lack of direct evidence to support the decline of the importance of race, claiming that the author's belief that an increase in the predictive power of one variable (class) necessitated a decrease in another (race) was a fallacy (Pettigrew 1980). However, the core of the controversy centered on three related points, the issue of race versus class in explaining the socioeconomic status of blacks, the particular role of race in explaining the black underclass, and the policy recommendations drawn from the book.

Race versus Class. For Wilson, the very existence of a black middle class was proof that race as a sole criterion to allocate blacks in the economic structure was declining. This conclusion was logical from the standpoint of the author's conceptual apparatus: a racial system is one that, with the help of institutional sanctions, systematically uses race as the only or as the fundamental criterion to allocate blacks in the economic and social structure, and therefore, it is a system that precludes substantial economic differentiation of blacks. A class system, on the other hand, allocates people according to market resources (156). Wilson did not argue that racial discrimination had disappeared; he rather argued that it was less enveloping than before. While class factors were now operating in the economic sphere, race was displaced to the social and political spheres.

The role of the black middle class in the book's overall argument made it the subject of critics' comments. For example, Joe Feagin (1991), based on in-depth interviews with middle-class blacks, argued that they still encountered discrimination in different places, including workplace and educational sites, and particularly in public places, such as restaurants, stores, and motels. Feagin added that this discrimination in public places that existed in spite of the assumed protection of the civil rights laws contradicted Wilson's argument. And Stephen Steinberg pointed out that Wilson minimized the current importance of race, because although "class disabilities are real enough, . . . they are the byproduct of past racism, they are reinforced by present racism, and they constitute the basis for perpetuating racial divisions and . . . inequalities" (1988, 291). Steinberg also noted the extraordinary dependence of middle-class blacks on government jobs, arguing that "without this public sector employment . . . much of the black middle class would not exist" (291). This dependence of the middle class on government jobs contradicted the argument that market mechanisms were responsible for its creation and were symptoms of the increasing importance of class. Other critics also pointed out that the black middle class was precarious and weak, very much subject to economic cycles, and that by calling attention to class differences, he was inviting the dismissal of the racial inequities prevalent in America (Bagley Marrett 1980).

Race and the Black Underclass. Particularly controversial was the idea that the black underclass was the creation of market forces and not of racial discrimination. Wilson stressed that the lingering effects of past racism, mass migration, the existence of many young people among blacks, the movement of the middle class out of cities, and especially a mismatch between uneducated blacks and the skills that many service jobs required, contributed to the creation of a black underclass. Critics argued that contrary to Wilson's claims of a skills mismatch and implicitly of a lack of education among the poor, blacks were generally excluded from whole sectors of jobs, and from entry-level jobs with career ladders, such as waiters and cooks in full-service restaurants, and relegated to menial, low-paying and dead-end jobs (Steinberg 1982, 290). Others pointed out that blacks were excluded from construction jobs and that only black protest in the 1960s and government programs partially eliminated entry barriers (Waldinger 1996, 183).

Policy Recommendations. Also disputed were the policy recommendations that followed from the book. Wilson recognized the multiple problems that afflicted underprivileged blacks and was not optimistic about the future: "Economic recovery is not likely to reverse the pattern of unemployment, underemployment, poverty, welfare, and female headed households," and "there are clear indications that the economic gap between the black underclass . . . and the higher-income blacks will very likely widen and solidify" (134). However, for him, the solution for the problems of the underclass resided in policies that should affect all poor Americans, not in programs specifically designed for blacks. These policy recommendations provoked an intense controversy, especially since affirmative action programs were, in the eyes of many critics, precarious, poorly implemented, and always under political attack. Critics argued that the elimination of the most urgent problems of the underclass required race-specific policies and a national commitment to eliminate ghettos. Diluting the solutions for the black underclass under a general economic program for all poor people would help blacks last and least (Steinberg 1982, 292).

The Legacy

Recent reappraisals of the book, as well as research on race, indicate that *The Declining Significance of Race* made durable contributions to black studies in particular and to ethnic studies more broadly. It acknowledged class divisions among blacks, criticizing the talk about blacks as a monolithic block in academic and political writings, and forced students of race to examine more carefully the interactions between race and class. One long-term result has been a growing methodological and conceptual sophistication in academic studies specifying and isolating the current role of race, especially for the underclass. Today, it is commonly accepted that the two dimensions do not exclude each other and that market and racial factors are both frequently present in, for example, employers' decisions about hiring.

Furthermore, Wilson's argument that affirmative action programs were helping mainly educated middle-class blacks, those who needed help least, induced a broader discussion about the limitations and advantages of government policies toward blacks. Yet, the debate about the benefits of and the need for such programs is far from settled.

Above all, Wilson's analysis of the underclass and the complex interconnected factors that perpetuate it has been a lasting contribution to the national debate about blacks and low-income communities. In *The Declining Significance of Race*, Wilson attributed the rise of the underclass to economic transformations, the rise of low-paid service jobs that drastically reduced the number of jobs paying wages sufficient to support a family, the geographic concentration of poor blacks, and the cumulative effects of these problems on black neighborhoods. Many subsequent studies have built on the dynamics of the underclass that Wilson set forth in *The Declining Significance of Race* and expanded on in his later books *The Truly Disadvantaged* and *When Work Disappears* (see, for example, Massey and Denton 1993).

Wilson's book was not the first to call attention to the impact of class on the socioeconomic status of blacks. And the debates it generated are certainly not settled, or at least not in a manner that makes the arguments of the book right or wrong. Yet, by making compelling arguments about largely underanalyzed issues, and by articulating central political and analytical concerns of both scholars and politicians at the time it was published, *The Declining Significance of Race* set forth the coordinates that guided scholarly research and political debate on race in America for many years.

See also Deindustrialization and Racial Inequality; Jim Crow Laws.

Further Reading

Bagley Masset, Cora. "The Precariousness of Social Class in Black America." *Contemporary Sociology* 9, no.1 (1980): 16–19.

D'Amico, Ronald, and Nan L. Maxwell. "The Continuing Significance of Race in Minority Joblessness." *Social Forces* 73, no. 3 (1995): 969–991.

Feagin, Joe R. "The Continuing Significance of Race: Anti-Black Discrimination in Public Places." *American Sociological Review* 56 (February 1991): 101–116.

Jaret, Charles. *Contemporary Ethnic and Race Relations*. New York: HarperCollins, 1995.

Massey, Douglas S., and Nancy A. Denton. *American Apartheid: Segregation and the Making of the Underclass*. Cambridge, MA: Harvard University Press, 1993.

Pettigrew, Thomas F. "The Changing—Not Declining—Significance of Race." *Symposia on the Declining Significance of Race in Contemporary Sociology* 9, no. 1 (1980).

Sowell, Thomas. "On Race and Class in America." *The Heritage Foundation Policy Review* 7 (1979).

Steinberg, Stephen. *The Ethnic Myth: Race, Ethnicity and Class in America*. Boston: Beacon Press, 1988.

Waldinger, Roger. *Still the Promised City? African Americans and New Immigrants in Postindustrial New York*. Cambridge, MA: Harvard University Press, 1996.

Wilson, William Julius. *The Declining Significance of Race: Blacks and Changing American Institutions*. Chicago: University of Chicago Press, 1978.

———. *The Truly Disadvantaged*. Chicago: University of Chicago Press, 1987.

———. *When Work Disappears*. New York: Random House, 1996.

Carmenza Gallo

De Facto Segregation

See De Jure and De Facto Segregation.

Deindustrialization and Racial Inequality

Deindustrialization refers to the decline in employment and economic capacity of the manufacturing sector. This process, which has occurred in the United States and Europe since roughly 1980 and is occurring in other nations as well, has led to a fundamental shift in the employment opportunities available to workers in these nations. Of particular importance is the fact that manufacturing facilities offered jobs that did not require a college education but had relatively high pay, job security, and union representation. Many of these jobs were located in proximity to inner-city neighborhoods and thus allowed the African American and Latino/a residents of these neighborhoods to secure employment that would enable them to support their families.

As deindustrialization has proceeded, the factories have closed and the manufacturing jobs have dried up. They have been replaced with information and service-sector jobs. Few of these jobs have union representation or job security, and those that pay well tend to require a college degree or graduate education. Residents of the inner city have found that their options are, to a large degree, limited to work in low-paid jobs with poor working conditions and no benefits, often on a part-time basis. Representative of this type of work is employment at fast-food restaurants. If residents cannot find a job of this type or do not wish to take this type of employment, their other options are usually outside of the legal labor force, either in unreported domestic service or similar jobs or else in illegal occupations like drug sales or prostitution. Those residents who do have the education necessary to secure an office job face the additional barriers of the long distance between their homes and the locations of these jobs, often locations not serviced by public transportation, and their lack of the cultural capital that employers desire. In both types of work, employers may use consciously or subconsciously racist criteria in evaluating applicants, such as examining where the applicants live, whether they speak with an unsuitable accent, whether they wear the same types of clothing as other employees, and non-job-related interview questions. Also, as much hiring is done through social networks, inner-city residents may not even have access to information about desired job openings.

Even those facilities that could provide low-skill jobs in the inner city (such as movie theaters, malls, and customer-service call centers) often choose not to locate there and offer their jobs to the black and Latino/a residents. Instead they locate in the suburbs and offer employment to teenagers, retirees, and stay-at-home mothers on a part-time basis. These strategic choices enable employers to offer lower wages and fewer benefits on the principle that suburban part-time workers do not "really" need the money. Those who do not have another major income source are forced to string together multiple part-time jobs to try and make ends meet. In addition to human resources–related justifications for locating outside of the inner city, corporations want to avoid the perceived environment of these neighborhoods (including crime rates, disorder, and undesirable patrons), regardless of whether these problems are real or imagined.

The result of these economic shifts has been a widening of economic inequality as work is bifurcated into low-paid service work and well-paid work requiring advanced education. This inequality is closely linked to race, as a high proportion of those employed in low-paying jobs in the service sector (like the proportion of those living in inner-city neighborhoods) are black, Latino/a, or Third World immigrants. But the impacts are not limited to the individuals and families who cannot find work and do not have enough money to get by. As mentioned, the lack of well-paying lawful employment forces individuals to turn to illegal methods of acquiring income, which increases crime rates and incarceration rates such that in the United States on any given day, almost one in four black men between the ages of twenty and twenty-nine is either incarcerated or on probation or parole. These contacts with the criminal justice system can make it even harder for individuals to find good jobs.

See also The Declining Significance of Race; Mismatch Hypothesis; "Second Generation Decline."

Further Reading

Bluestone, Barry. *The Deindustrialization of America: Plant Closings, Community Abandonment, and the Dismantling of Basic Industries*. New York: Basic Books, 1982.

Wilson, William Julius. *The Truly Disadvantaged: The Inner City, the Underclass, and Public Policy*. Chicago: University of Chicago Press, 1987.

Mikaila Mariel Lemonik Arthur

De Jure and De Facto Segregation

Most books, discussions, and court decisions dealing with racial segregation draw a distinction between the two forms of segregation known as de jure and de facto. The distinction made between them, in most definitions, hinges on whether or not segregation is a state's or a local government's official and legal policy. De jure segregation occurs when a community or state makes and abides by laws that require separation of two or more races (in schools, public accommodations, seating arrangements, and so forth). People who practice racial integration in a society where de jure segregation principles are in force are liable to be arrested, fined, or jailed by the criminal justice system (or worse if caught and punished by vigilante groups that try to uphold the "color line"). In this situation, attempts to make legislative bodies rewrite the segregation laws, or to have the courts overturn them, are a central part of the antiracism movement. Much of the history of the U.S. civil rights movement's battle with "Jim Crow" laws involved that sort of struggle against de jure segregation.

In contrast, de facto segregation occurs when members of two or more races live and pursue their life activities apart from each other because of social customs, norms, preferences, choices, and power relations that are not dictated or required by law. This covers several situations. Members of different races may avoid one another out of mutual indifference, unfamiliarity, dislike, or fear. Or one racial group, typically one in a dominant position, may reject another's desire to be treated as equals and neither invite nor allow them into certain social circles or areas. The stronger or more assertive group may claim a particular beach or park as its turf and informally enforce a norm that excludes other races from using it. School board members might draw the attendance zone boundaries of a city's best high school in such a way that it excludes the streets or neighborhoods where members of a stigmatized racial group live. In each case of de facto segregation, the racial separation arises from traditions, choices, preferences and/or power relations rather than the requirements of law. Those who favor racial integration and oppose de facto segregation may not be arrested for breaking a law, but in the eyes of those who support segregation, they are deviants and often are subjected to verbal and physical abuse. Civil rights history includes many such instances.

The two most well known court decisions dealing with racial segregation focused on the de jure form. The U.S. Supreme Court's 1896 *Plessy v. Ferguson* decision upheld a Louisiana law that required train companies to have separate cars for whites and nonwhites and to enforce separate-race seating policies. The Court stated that separate cars for each race had to be of equal quality to be legal, but it had no way of enforcing that requirement, and the whites who wanted to impose segregation had no interest in providing equal facilities for blacks. So the precedent of "separate and unequal" rather than "separate but equal" was rapidly extended to schools, stores, buses, parks, and other public areas throughout the South.

In the other case, *Brown v. Board of Education of Topeka* (1954), the Supreme Court ruled against de jure school segregation. It asserted that state laws requiring or permitting racial segregation are unconstitutional violations of the Fourteenth Amendment because the racially separate schools they create are inherently unequal. At that time, seventeen Southern states had laws requiring racial segregation, and four others made it a local option. They were ordered to dismantle their segregated systems and establish integrated systems, but most of them stalled and resisted for many years. School systems that were racially segregated by de facto arrangements were not affected directly by the *Brown v. Board of Education* decision until other law suits challenged de facto segregation in the 1970s (e.g., *Keyes v. Denver School District no. 1*, 1973). These resulted in rulings to require busing or other efforts to desegregate schools if there is evidence that school officials intentionally try to maintain a segregated, unequal school system, for example, by gerrymandering attendance zones to keep racial minorities out of certain schools, by unequal school funding or teacher-assignment patterns, or through decisions to close certain schools closings and on the locations of new school construction. More recently, advances in school desegregation have slowed or even been reversed, largely by de facto causes that are difficult to alter (e.g., residential segregation, whites shifting from public to private schools).

See also Brown v. Board of Education of Topeka; Fourteenth Amendment; Jim Crow Laws; Residential Segregation; Segregation, Voluntary versus Involuntary; Separate but Equal Doctrine.

Further Reading

Goodman, Frank. "Some Reflections on the Supreme Court and School Desegregation." In *Race and Schooling in the City*, edited by Adam Yarmolinsky, Lance Liebman, and Corinne S. Schelling. Cambridge, MA: Harvard University Press, 1981, 45–83.

Stephan, Walter G., and Joe R. Feagin, eds. *School Desegregation: Past, Present, and Future*. New York: Plenum, 1980.

Charles Jaret

Democracy in America

In his 1835 book *Democracy in America*, Alexis de Tocqueville analyzed the nature of American democracy in the early part of the nineteenth century. Of two essential features of democracy—equality and freedom—the author identified, he focused almost exclusively on the equality aspect of democracy. To the author, true equality means an equality of conditions or equality of opportunity. The author began with the assumption that early-nineteenth-century America provided equal opportunity, and he probed the basic questions, How do people respond to equal opportunity? and How do individual activities affect the whole society.

According to de Tocqueville, persons living in a democratic society are enlightened in the sense that they eagerly discover means to improve their present fortunes. That is, people are motivated to seek more education, become more productive, and keep what they have earned and achieved. He concluded that the self-interest of individuals and the resulting activity benefit and vitalize the whole society under the structure of equality. In today's America, however, the author's assumption of equality is rather difficult to uphold.

Further Reading

Tocqueville, Alexis de. *Democracy in America*. New York: Library of America, 2004.

Shin Kim and Kwang Chung Kim

Derogatory Terms

Anyone on the receiving end of racial or ethnic slurs such as gook, spic, coolie, and nigger can testify to the tremendous psychological and social impact of such words. Race-based derogatory terms are not a new phenomenon: they have complex historical and political origins.

Defining Derogatory Terms

Derogatory terms are words that label or mark an individual in a negative, often harmful way. In the context of race relations in the United States, derogatory terms slander the entire minority community. Because other categories of derogatory terms are usually based on singular, alterable aspects of a person (such as their ability or behavior), their negative effects can be somewhat tempered. However, race-based derogatory terms, because they label a person on the basis of unalterable physical characteristics (such as skin color), more completely mark, classify, and reduce the identity of the receiver. Furthermore, racial and ethnic labeling carries the threat of "other-ing," which can increase the alienation felt: those who use racial epithets reaffirm their position at the center of mainstream culture and power and cast the objects of these slurs as a deviant "other."

It is at this point useful to distinguish between stereotyping and using derogatory term. A stereotype is a mental image one assigns to others. Ethnic or racial stereotypes are created when distinctive behavioral or physical characteristics of a group are chosen by members outside a particular group to signify them. Stereotypes operate to reinforce the preconceived beliefs of those using them and help sow the seeds of prejudice. A derogatory term is the verbal expression of a stereotype, rather than the stereotype itself. A derogatory term is given life through language, and as such, must be spoken or written to exist.

Because of this inherent connection to language, both the evolution and interpretation of derogatory terms are complicated. As the following history of racial derogatory terms suggests, determining which labels constitute a derogatory term is often highly subjective and affected by relations of power.

A given term may not be spoken with the same injurious intent with which it is received. Words can gain or lose their potency based on changing historical circumstance. As minority groups gain political voice and access to mainstream media and culture, they may choose to reappropriate words previously used against them. A derogatory term can thus metamorphose from a slur to a symbol of solidarity and power.

History of Derogatory Terms

Derogatory terms have a complex history rooted in both social and political circumstances and shaped by those who use them and by those who are their objects. Some key dynamics emerge from the African American and Asian American historical experience.

Derogatory terms are not formed in a historical vacuum. They arise out of a particular set of social and economic conditions. For Asian Americans, the term coolie (see Coolie for a fuller explanation) grew out of the context of Chinese immigration to the United States in the latter half of the nineteenth century. Whites perceived the Chinese as a "threat" to working-class solidarity, which was predicated on racial solidarity. Thus, the Chinese were marked as coolies, and their labor denigrated as coolie labor. This labeling reflected the larger exclusion of Chinese from the working class, especially from skilled labor.

As the historical context changed, so did the terms chosen to mark and degrade Asian Americans. The term gook gained popularity in the 1960s and 1970s. Its origins may be traced to the Korean War (1950-1953). *Megook* is the Korean word for "American," and GIs who heard the phrase mistakenly believed Koreans were referring to themselves "me (I am a) gook." *Gook* embodied the "invisible enemy" of the East and was used extensively by U.S. soldiers in the next major conflict in Asia: the Vietnam War. Back on home soil, the term helped single out Asian Americans of any ethnic origin—Korean, Vietnamese, Chinese—for opprobrium, and to equate Asian Americans to the same faceless enemies that fought, and in Vietnam, conquered, U.S. forces. Thus, *gook* can be seen as a term that found purchase in a destabilized, post–Vietnam world.

Racial resentment was shaped and channeled in different ways. Changing social and political landscapes created new racial discourses, from which new derogatory terms could develop. However, some derogatory terms have remained embedded in the racial lexicon and in public consciousness for a long time. The epithet *nigger* is one such word, and tracing its evolution can provide more clues as to how racial slurs find new meaning with time.

The origin of the term *nigger* can be traced to the word *negro*, the Latin origins of which denote the color black. The term *nigger* first appeared in the late eighteenth century in England, used by such literary notables as the poets Robert Burns and Lord Byron. From the nineteenth century, the term had been used in combination to refer to a wide variety of flora and fauna, suggesting more their color than any racial connotation: thus a "nigger" daisy, a "nigger fish," "nigger pea," and so forth. It is unclear precisely when or how *nigger* became derogatory, but the term had become recognized as a significant insult by the beginning of the nineteenth century.

Anti–African American writing on a South Boston building during school busing integration, 1974.

Photo by Lee Lockwood/Time Life Pictures/Getty Images.

As racialized slavery became increasingly coercive and oppressive, so also did the potency of the term *nigger*. This association with the darkest period of African American history continued to give the epithet a transcendent and deeply layered meaning and a particular venom. In the South during the segregation period between 1890 and 1954, the persistent usage of the term by anxious whites conveniently and effectively recalled blacks' previous position at the bottom of the social and economic ladder. However, as blacks continued to make headway into mainstream U.S. society and politics, any use of the word in public became progressively more unacceptable. The virtual absence, at least in public, of *nigger* from whites' vocabulary in the twenty-first century can thus be traced to effective political mobilization and African Americans' own changing socioeconomic position.

That said, the term has found a new lease on life in recent years. African Americans have appropriated the term for use amongst themselves—a subversive, if ironic, act of self-definition. First popularized in the 1970s by prominent black comedians such as Richard Pryor and increasingly an integral part of present-day hip-hop, rap, and street cultures, the use of the word *nigger* by African Americans has evolved to express affection, closeness, or a subtly joking familiarity. However, it is widely agreed that this new usage is confined strictly within the bounds of the black community. Only then can the term retain its noninflammatory quality. Tracing the evolution of the various meanings associated with the word amply shows how dramatically a given derogatory term's meanings can shift. Once a signifier of the deepest of racial prejudices, *nigger* has been given a second life by those who were once the object of its poison.

Social and Political Implications

What is the significance of derogatory terms? At the heart of the debate is the issue of language. Language has become an increasingly important subject of study, particularly as postmodernist theories have encouraged scholars to view reality not as an objective occurrence, but constituted by subjective experience and relations of power. It is through language that humans conceive the world and express their place in it. Some argue that language is inherently political—that not only do words express our ideas, they have the ability to shape our ideas and experiences as well. In an unequal social order, therefore, language is able to serve the interests of the dominant class. Language can help entrench unequal social institutions and perpetuate an ideology of inferiority among the dominated class.

In this context, derogatory terms have important social and political implications. Derogatory terms express power differentials; however, through their utterance, racial epithets may also reinforce and perpetuate inequality. In this interpretation, the use of the word *nigger* up until the civil rights era did not just reflect underlying white prejudice, it actively helped to maintain a layered and coercive system of racial oppression.

Psychological impact is one mechanism through which derogatory terms may accomplish this end. Some argue that because race-related stigmatization is based on an unchanging aspect of one's being (their race), its harm is far more direct and personal than any other negative speech. Minority groups who repeatedly struggle with racial stigmatization develop low self-esteem and low expectations of success. Also, those who are frequently exposed to racial epithets may develop a hypersensitivity to issues of race and experience increased psychological and social stress levels, all of which further impede emotional, social, and economic well-being.

Some people believe that a derogatory term can never lose its harmful impact. Within the black community, debate continues as to the appropriateness of using the word *nigger*. Black intellectuals, musicians, and performers have weighed in on both sides (gunned-down rap star Tupac Shakur was said to have asserted that *nigga* stood for "Never Ignorant, Get Goals Accomplished," while comedian Bill Cosby stressed that the word could never lose its destructive potential).

What Should Be Done?

For those who believe that derogatory terms exact a long-lasting and harmful toll on their victims and that racist speech perpetuates a larger social inequality, inaction is unthinkable. However, the extent to which all racial epithets need to be stamped out, and the steps by which they should be removed from public discourse have been subjects of heated debate. At one end of the spectrum are the people who believe the eradication of words such as *nigger* from the public arena is the only solution. That would mean censoring literary classics such as *The Adventures of Huckleberry Finn*, which used the word repeatedly, and attempt to prevent its continued use under any circumstance.

Opponents of this view argue that eradicationists fail to see racial epithets in their historical context. For example, Mark Twain's use of the word *nigger* was not intentionally pejorative; he was attempting to accurately portray local use of the term. To erase it would deprive the novel of its historical relevance. Also, erasing the term *nigger* would deny legitimacy to the ways in which African Americans have reappropriated the word as a signifier of their own.

Critics of eradication further emphasize that an overzealous pursuit of elimination of all forms of hate speech may create a climate of intolerance and ignorance, precisely at odds with eradicationists' own goals. For example, in 1999, educator Ken Hardy was removed from his position at Jefferson Community College after using the word *nigger* in a class about taboo words. The same year, a white director of a Washington, DC, municipal agency was forced to resign when he used the word *niggardly*, although the term has no etymological connection to *nigger* and the director had used it in the appropriate context. A University of Wisconsin professor who similarly used *niggardly* in a literature class provoked a campus protest. Thus, critics argue that heightened vigilance against racial epithets may yield unintended consequences: racial scapegoating and the creation of an environment that discourages open communication and debate.

Those who believe hate speech should be regulated as opposed to eliminated support a legal response to its use. "Regulationists" argue that the only effective, long-term solution can be effected through the courts. Several different avenues of action are possible. Some private institutions have developed speech codes, which may in future become models for the public domain. For example, Stanford University in 1990 instituted a code that prohibits "harassment by personal vilification" and prevents verbal assault on the basis of race, color, handicap, religion, sexual orientation, or national and ethnic origin. Also, regulationists point out that some anti-discrimination statutes already exist that can be used to help monitor the use of derogatory terms and make provisions for appropriate action in cases of abuse. For example, the provisions of Title VII of the Civil Rights Act of 1964 were meant to prevent racial discrimination in employment. Black employees may cite repeated use of the term *nigger* by white colleagues as possible proof that the company has created a "racially hostile environment," grounds for action under Title VII.

A second means of redress is through tort law. Many jurisdictions already protect against what tort law terms as "the intentional infliction of emotional distress." Supporters of a tort law for racial slurs argue that the legal system does protect an individual's right to humane treatment, and therefore victims of hate speech should have recourse to legal action. Supporters contend that tort law would create an institutional arrangement in which discriminatory behaviors have no room to exist. Detractors argue that litigation would be expensive and time-consuming, it would be difficult to prove intent to cause emotional distress, and free speech may be threatened.

Finally, there are those who argue that both regulationists and eradicationists are missing the point. Focusing on derogatory terms detracts from the real mission at hand—to stamp out the racism that breeds them. W.E.B. Du Bois penned the following words in response to growing debate in the early twentieth century within the black community about the political ramifications of racial labeling: "Names are only the conventional signs for identifying things. Things are the reality that counts. If a thing is despised, either because of ignorance or because it is despicable, you will not alter matters by changing its name." His words have a striking relevance in contemporary debates concerning derogatory terms. Supporters of Du Bois's viewpoint contend that the continual use of derogatory terms is but one manifestation of the racism that flows through American society and that only by stemming the flow of racism itself will discriminatory behavior, including the use of derogatory terms, cease.

See also Civil Rights Act of 1964; Coolie; Fu Manchu; "Nigger"; Political Correctness (P.C.).

Further Reading

Delgado, Richard. "Words That Wound: A Tort Action for Racial Insults, Epithets, and Name-Calling." *Harvard Civil Rights-Civil Liberties Law Review* 17 (1982).

Gates, Henry Louis, Jr. "War of Words: Critical Race Theory and the First Amendment." In *Speaking of Race, Speaking of Sex: Hate Speech, Civil Rights and Civil Liberties*, edited by Henry Louis Gates, Jr. et al. New York: New York University Press, 1994.

Grant, Ruth W., and Marion Orr. "Language, Race and Politics: From 'Black' to 'African-American.'" In *Notable Selections in Race and Ethnicity*. 3rd ed., edited by David V. Baker. New York: McGraw-Hill, 2001.

Green, Jonathan. *Words Apart: The Language of Prejudice*. London: Kyle Cathie Publishing, 1996.

Kennedy, Randall. *Nigger: The Strange Career of a Troublesome Word*. New York: Vintage Books, 2003.

Kramarae, Chris, Muriel Schulz, and William O'Barr, eds. *Language and Power*. Beverly Hills, CA: Sage, 1984.

Rebekah Lee

Detroit Race Riot of 1943

On June 20, 1943, a series of small conflicts erupted between white and African American residents in Detroit. Around 11 p.m., a near riot occurred on the bridge that connected Belle Isle, a recreational oasis on the Detroit River, to the city. As the news of the fight on the bridge spread, the conflict between white and African American residents escalated and spread into the city. In the wee hours of June 21, many African American and white residents vented their rage on the street. The riot continued throughout the day. Responses by the Detroit Police Department were racially biased: 82 percent of 1,800 arrests made during the riot, and 25 out of 34 persons who were killed, were African American. Of the 25 African Americans, 17 were killed by the Detroit Police. In contrast, none of the 9 white casualties were the result of police action.

Like many race riots that had occurred before, the Detroit Riot of 1943 was caused by racial contacts and competition for scarce resources after the mass migration of African Americans to northern cities. African Americans had mi-

A white man assaults an African American man escorted by police during the Detroit race riot, June 21, 1943.

AP/Wide World Photos.

grated in large numbers to Detroit from the South in search of the war-related industrial jobs. By 1943, African Americans numbered 210,000 in a city of 1.6 million residents. They were allowed to live only in certain dilapidated yet overpriced areas. They were subjected to other forms of discrimination as well. The Detroit race riot of 1943 was the consequence of different forms of racial discrimination.

See also Detroit Race Riot of 1967; Race Riots.

Further Reading

Lee, Alfred McClung, and Norman D. Humphrey. *Race Riot, Detroit 1943*. New York: Octagon Books, 1968.

Shin Kim and Kwang Chung Kim

Detroit Race Riot of 1967

Almost exactly a quarter century since the 1943 riot, Detroit erupted again. This time Detroit was not alone: more than fifty American cities experienced race riots in 1967. The Detroit race riot was one of the most serious riots that occurred that year, though. The immediate triggering event was a police raid on Twelfth Street—the hub of the African American community in Detroit—late in the evening of Saturday, July 22. In the early hours of the next day, a crowd of three thousand flocked to Twelfth Street and looting began. At first, the looting was somewhat carefree, with the police benignly looking on. With the spreading rumor that a black man had been bayoneted by the police, though, the looting turned to violence, including stoning and arson. By Sunday evening, the riot became quite violent and the National Guard was brought in. With the deployment of the National Guard, the riot waned. In all, thirty-three African Americans and ten whites were killed during the riot. It was estimated that the riot cost $22 million in property damage.

As in other race riots at that time, the root cause of the Detroit riot of 1967 was a high concentration of African Americans in certain high-stress, high-crime areas of the city with substandard housing. By 1967, about 40 percent of Detroit's population was African American and 25 percent of Twelfth Street's housing had been declared substandard. Under such conditions, even a slight provocation would likely erupt in a violent disturbance.

See also Detroit Race Riot of 1943; Race Riots.

Further Reading

U.S. Riot Commission. "Profiles of Disorder, VIII Detroit." Chap. 1 in *Report of the National Advisory Commission on Civil Disorders*, 84–108. Washington, DC: U.S. Government Printing Office, 1968.

Shin Kim and Kwang Chung Kim

Diallo, Amadou (1975–1999)

Amadou Diallo was an innocent victim of police brutality, shot to death by four New York City police officers in 1999. An immigrant from Guinea, he was working as a street vendor in the Bronx. On February 1999, the twenty-three-year-old man was shot forty-four times in the doorway of his apartment by the four officers in the plainclothes Street Crime Unit. The police officers said later that Diallo resembled a rape suspect and that he had drawn a gun on them when they approached him.

In a hotly contested state trial and a federal investigation, the officers were acquitted of murder and even of misconduct. The brutal killing of Diallo by the police officers, and their subsequent acquittal, led to a series of demonstrations by civil rights organizations and African American leaders, who protested against racial profiling and police brutality toward minorities and immigrants. In the process, many politicians and protest leaders were arrested on civil-disobedience charges. But the tragedy of Diallo's death and the ensuing criticisms of police brutality led the New York City Police Department to abolish the Street Crime Unit and initiate an antiprofiling policy. In connection with a civil suit filed against New York City, Diallo's mother accepted a $3 million settlement in January 2004.

See also Bensonhurst Incident; Byrd, James Jr.; Hate Crimes; Howard Beach Incident.

Further Reading

Amadou Diallo Educational, Humanitarian and Charity Foundation. http://www.
amadoudiallofoundation.org.

Pyong Gap Min

Dillingham Report

The Dillingham Report was a voluminous report issued in 1911 by the U.S. Commission on Immigration, a congressional commission chaired by Senator William P. Dillingham. After extensive hearings held between 1907 and 1911, the Dillingham commission issued a report that contained four major conclusions: (1) new immigrants tended to congregate residentially and were slow to assimilate; (2) they were less skilled and educated than the native born; (3) they had a greater criminal tendency; and (4) they were willing to accept low wages and a low standard of living. As a solution to these negative characteristics of new immigrants, the Commission suggested that immigrants be given a mandatory literacy test and that the number of immigrants be restricted based on the racial and ethnic compositions of the population in the United States.

Prodded by this report, the U.S. Congress passed a literacy-test bill, which was vetoed by President William Howard Taft. This report provided an empirical justification for the racially biased immigration restriction laws passed in subsequent years, which culminated in the National Origins Act of 1924. Analyses of empirical findings in this report were flawed because it was based on simplistic categories, an unfair comparison of different waves of immigrant groups, little consideration of the differences in native countries of immigrant groups, the length of residence in the United States, the changing socioeconomic conditions of the United States, and other factors.

See also National Origins Act of 1924.

Further Reading

U.S. Immigration Commission. *Brief Statement of the Conclusions and Recommendation of the Immigration Commission with the View of the Minority*. Washington, DC: U.S. Government Printing Office, 1910.

Shin Kim and Kwang Chung Kim

Discrimination

See Adaptive Discrimination; *Affirmative Discrimination: Ethnic Inequality and Public Policy*; Anti-Semitism in the United States; Archie Bunker Bigotry; Asian Americans, Violence against; Black Anti-Semitism; Blacks, Wage Discrimination against; Caribbean Immigrants, Experience of Racial Discrimination; Chinese Immigrants and Anti-Chinese Sentiments; *Closed Doors, Opportunities Lost: The Continuing Costs of Housing Discrimination*; College Admission, Discrimination in; Covert versus Overt Discrimination; Criminal Justice System and Racial Discrimination; *Discrimination, American Style*; Economics of Discrimination; Education and Racial Discrimination; Financial Institutions and Racial Discrimination; Haitians, Discrimination against in Refugee Policy; Hispanics, Prejudice and Discrimination against; Housing Discrimination; Irish Immigrants, Prejudice and Discrimination against; Italian Americans, Prejudice and Discrimination against; Mexican Americans, Prejudice and Discrimination against; Muslims, Prejudice and Discrimination against; Native Americans, Prejudice and Discrimination against; Reverse Discrimination; September 11, 2001 Terrorism, Discriminatory Reactions to; Statistical Discrimination.

Discrimination, American Style

In his book *Discrimination, American Style* (1978), Joe Feagin emphasized that racial discrimination in American society is more than just a product of prejudice. Feagin argued that racial discrimination is embedded in institutions and policies whose main objective is to address the concerns of white European males. Although an individual ultimately carries out the act of discrimination, the institutional setting is important for that individual to act.

Feagin outlined four types of discriminatory practices that take place in American society to explain the extent to which racial discrimination permeates all aspects of life. The first type is isolated discrimination. It is an individual act toward minority members or women that is not linked to any institutional pattern or behavior. For example, an individual may refuse to sit next to a black person in a restaurant or decide not to rent his or her house or property to a person of color. Minorities may encounter isolated discriminatory acts in their daily interaction with whites on the job, in police precincts, or in social gatherings. The second type of discrimination usually takes place in small-group institutions where there is intent to discriminate even though society at large may not support it. The Ku Klux Klan is an example of such behavior. Although it is a small group, its aim is to discriminate against people of color with the intent to harm them. Since the 1964 passage of the Civil Rights Act, minority groups have had more leeway to challenge the action of the Klan because the legal system forbids discrimination.

The third category is direct institutionalized discrimination, where actions taken against minorities and women are embedded in the practices and policies of the institutions that exist to serve the community. Usually these actions are carried out on a routine basis, and individuals who implement them may not be aware of their discriminatory character. Examples of these practices are found mostly in housing, employment, and education. Requiring a large down payment to buy a house can be discriminatory, because blacks, who have been discriminated against for generations in this society, may not be in a position to save the large sum of money required.

Feagin calls the last type of discrimination indirect institutionalized discrimination. It has to do with practices that have a negative impact on minorities and women even though official rules and requirements of the institution may forbid it. This form of discrimination often takes place in public institutions such as fire, police and sanitation departments. These public institutions are forbidden to discriminate against minority members and women. But they discriminate anyway through the physical requirements that they demand to admit candidates. For many years, police and fire departments required candidates to have at least a certain weight and height to be admitted in their ranks. As Asians and women who are interested in applying for these positions usually do not meet these requirements, they are automatically barred from pursuing a career in these fields.

See also Civil Rights Act of 1964; Ku Klux Klan (KKK).

Further Reading

Feagin, Joe. *Discrimination, American Style*. Englewood Cliffs, NJ: Prentice Hall, 1978.

Francois Pierre-Louis

Diversities, Ethnic and Racial

Much of the racial and ethnic diversity found in the United States today can be attributed to the liberalization of U.S. immigration brought about by the U.S. Immigration Act of 1965, also known as the Hart-Cellar Immigration Act. The enforcement of the liberalized immigration law, along with the U.S. government's military involvement in many countries in the world, has resulted in the influx of immigrants and refugees from Latin America, Asia, and the Caribbean Islands. Between 1970 and 2000, more than 20 million immigrants were admitted to the United States. The vast majority of them originated from Third World countries; Europeans made up less than 15 percent of the total number of immigrants during the period.

In 1970, non-Hispanic white Americans made up 87 percent of the U.S. population. African Americans made up the majority of racial minority members in 1970, and three Latino groups (Mexicans, Puerto Ricans, and Cubans) and some Asians in the West Coast composed the other racial minority groups. Thirty years later (in 2000), the proportion of white Americans decreased to only 70 percent. As immigrants are heavily concentrated in large metropolitan areas, white Americans in many cities have become numerically minority groups. In fact, according to 2000 census data, in forty-eight of the one hundred largest cities in the United States, racial and ethnic "minorities" comprised the majority of the population. The black population currently includes not only African Americans, but also a large number of Caribbean blacks (Jamaicans, Dominicans, Haitians, and Guyanese), Africans, and their children. The Latino population includes Colombians, Ecuadorians, Salvadorans, Brazilians, and Peruvians, as well as Mexicans, Puerto Ricans, and Cubans. Asian Americans include Indians, Pakistanis, Koreans, Vietnamese, and Filipinos, as well as the Chinese and the Japanese.

In addition to the influx of non-European immigrants in the post–1965 era, two other factors have made American cities far more culturally diverse now. One is the change in government's policy toward minority and immigrant groups, from Anglo conformity to cultural pluralism. In the early twentieth century, the U.S. government enforced the assimilationist policy to make immigrants and their children give up their cultural traditions and acculturate to American society. By contrast, the government and public schools currently encourage immigrants and their children to preserve their cultural traditions. The government and schools gradually adopted this multicultural policy beginning in the late 1960s.

The other factor that has contributed to ethnic and cultural diversity in contemporary America is transnational ties facilitated by technological advances. Immigrants and their children can now watch television programs made in the home country in the form of videotapes or satellite broadcasting. Most immigrants in large American cities watch television programs in their native language more often than they watch American television programs. They can buy almost all grocery items in American cities that they can get in their home country, making it much easier for contemporary immigrants to eat ethnic food than earlier white immigrants at the end of the nineteenth century.

See also Immigration Act of 1965; Multiculturalism.

Further Reading

Farley, Reynolds. *The New American Reality: Who We Are, How We Got Here, Where We Are Going*. New York: Russell Sage Foundation, 1996.

Min, Pyong Gap, ed. *Mass Migration to the United States: Classical and Contemporary Periods*. Walnut Creek, CA: AltaMira, 2002.

Portes, Alejandro, and Ruben Rumbaut. *Immigrant America: A Portrait*. 2nd ed. Berkeley: University of California Press, 1996.

Khyati Joshi

Dominative Racism

See Racism, Aversive versus Dominative.

Dot Buster Attacks

In the summer of 1987, a gang in Jersey City, New Jersey, calling themselves the "Dot Busters," published a letter in a local newspaper stating that they would "go to any extreme to get Asian Indians to move out of Jersey City." Calling Indian Americans "a weak race physically and mentally," the Dot Busters threatened physical violence and vandalism. The name "Dot Busters" refers to the red *bindi*—the "dot"—that married South Asian women wear on their foreheads. The Dot Busters were predominantly Latino.

In the months that followed the letter, the already-existing tension between the city's immigrant communities exploded into incidents of egg throwing, verbal harassment, physical intimidation, and violence against Indian women in public places, and vandalism against Indian-owned businesses. In July 1987, the Dot Busters used bricks to bludgeon Navroze Mody, a South Asian man. The attack left Mody in a coma, and he later died. During the attack, his killers taunted him with the epithets "Hindu" and "baldy." (The slur *baldy*, directed at South Asian Americans, is a reference to Indian independence leader Mohandas Gandhi, who was bald.) Most of the attackers served short sentences in juvenile facilities, and three are now police officers in Jersey City.

For what was then a small but growing Indian community in New Jersey, the "Dot Buster" attacks led to a siege-like climate. According to the 1980 census, Jersey City's population was 28 percent black, 19 percent Hispanic, and 1 percent Asian Indian. In the 1980s, however, more and more Indians moved into the area; many purchased small businesses, making them very visible in day-to-day life. By the late 1980s, when the Dot Buster attacks occurred, there were about 15,000 Indian immigrants in Jersey City, and approximately one in three Jersey City businesses were owned by Indians.

See also Asian Americans, Violence against.

Khyati Joshi

Douglass, Frederick (1817–1895)

Possibly the most famous American abolitionist, Frederick Douglass was also a prolific writer, orator, and social activist. Frederick Augustus Washington Bailey was born near Easton, Maryland, to Harriet Bailey, a black slave, and an unknown white man. After a failed first attempt, Frederick escaped slavery in 1838 and took the name Douglass.

Douglass found work as a laborer and later learned to read with the help of a white woman in Baltimore. According to history, his extemporaneous speech during a meeting of the Massachusetts Anti-Slavery Society in 1841 was so eloquent that he was solicited to be one of its agents and took part in lecture tours to inform the masses about the evils of slavery. As a central figure in the abolition movement, Douglass made frequent speeches to rouse support for the cause, founded the abolitionist newspaper, *North Star*, and edited it for seventeen years. In 1845, Douglass wrote his autobiography, *Narrative of the Life of Frederick Douglass*. Douglass supported political redress as the primary mechanism to both abolish slavery and deal with its aftermath. Douglass was the first black citizen to hold high political rank. His numerous posts included secretary of the Santo Domingo Commission (1871), marshall of the District of Columbia (1877–1881), and U.S. minister and consul general to Haiti (1889–1991). Douglass also served as advisor to President Abraham Lincoln during the Civil War and championed

Portrait of Frederick Douglass, perhaps the most famous American abolitionist.

constitutional amendments to guarantee civil and voting rights for blacks. He died in Washington, DC, in 1895.

See also Abolitionist Movement.

Sandra L. Barnes

Draft Riot of 1863

During the midst of the United States Civil War (1861–1865) it became necessary for President Abraham Lincoln to enact a draft to attain more Union soldiers, as fewer and fewer men were willing to volunteer. The draft was enacted on March 3, 1863, and called for 300,000 men. Able-bodied males aged twenty to forty-five were eligible to be conscripted into the Union Army, with some curious exemptions. One could find a suitable substitute or pay a fee of $300. Generally, the wealthy were able to avoid service by paying the fee. This left poor immigrants—particularly Irish immigrants—to bear the brunt of the draft. The draft was also instituted at a time when the population was tired of the war, which was already two years old. Additionally, by the time the names of draftees were being issued—July 11, 1863—an enormous battle at Gettysburg (July 1–3, in which the Union won the strategic battle but federal losses numbered approximately 23,000) would have been fresh in the minds of those to be drafted.

For these reasons, there were disturbances in many cities of the North

An angry mob watches the body of a lynched black man burn during the New York Draft Riot of 1863.

Courtesy Library of Congress.

against the draft, but the riot in New York City from July 13 to 16 was exceedingly violent. Mostly poor, Irish immigrants took part in the riot. The situation was especially volatile because the Irish were, at the time, on the receiving end of enormous prejudice and discrimination. In fact, they competed with blacks—who were also widely discriminated against—for the lowest-paying jobs. The Irish felt they were being forced to fight for the emancipation of their competitors. A mob of about 50,000 people rampaged through the city, causing mayhem, including the lynching and beatings of blacks. By the end of the rioting, there were about 1,000 casualties, although no exact figures exist. To restore order, President Lincoln had to send federal troops into the city. However, it should be noted that a good portion of soldiers in both the Northern and Southern armies were Irish.

See also Emancipation Proclamation; Irish Immigrants, Prejudice and Discrimination against; Race Riots.

John Eterno

Dred Scott Decision

The tensions between the North and the South over slavery had built up over several decades, especially since the Missouri Compromise of 1820. Under the terms of the Missouri Compromise of 1820, Congress decided that Missouri should be admitted as a free state but that slavery should be forever prohibited. The U.S. Supreme Court's denial of slave Dred Scott's suit for freedom in 1857 exacerbated the tensions, which in turn contributed to the South's desire to cede from the Confederacy. Scott was born as a slave of army surgeon John Emerson in Missouri, a slave state. Emerson took Scott to Northern free states (Illinois and what became Minnesota), living there for four years, and then returned to Missouri. At his white friends' advice, Scott sued for freedom on the grounds that he had resided for a prolonged period in free states. The Missouri Supreme Court and the Federal Circuit Court of Missouri denied his request for freedom. Scott's lawyers appealed the case to the U.S. Supreme Court.

In February 1857, the Supreme Court, which had a Southern majority, ruled that Scott's residence in free states did not make him free once he returned to Missouri, a slave state. Furthermore, it also declared that Congress never had the right to prohibit slavery in any state, thus arguing the unconstitutionality of the Missouri Compromise. The Dred Scott decision threatened not only abolitionists but also those politicians, such as Abraham Lincoln, who believed slavery should be contained in the Southern states.

See also Free Persons of Color in the Antebellum North; Lincoln, Abraham, and the Emancipation of Slaves; Missouri Compromise.

Further Reading

McPherson, James. *Battle Cry of Freedom: The Civil War Era*. New York: Oxford University Press, 1988.

Pyong Gap Min

Driving while Black, Stopping People for

One area in which some police agencies and officers have admitted to abusing their authority is stopping cars solely because the driver and/or its occupants are black. That is, some police officers and, in fact, entire agencies conduct illegal stops, because they have no evidence of wrongdoing on the part of the driver or the occupants. In the United States, law enforcement does not have the power to stop a car or, for that matter, a person, merely because of the race or ethnicity of the driver and or the occupants. Law enforcement must have, at a minimum, a level of proof called reasonable suspicion.

Various legal powers have been conferred upon police officers to allow them to enforce laws. These powers are written in what is called the law of criminal procedure. Officers, for example, have the power to arrest, write summonses, and forcibly stop people or cars. The law of criminal procedure, however, does not merely give officers power; it also places important limitations on that power. Officers may not, for example, forcibly stop just anyone they please; rather, police in the United States have the power to forcibly stop a person only if they *reasonably suspect* that individual has committed, is committing, or is about to commit a crime. Reasonable suspicion is defined as "the quantum of knowledge sufficient to induce an ordinarily prudent and cautious man under the circumstances to believe criminal activity is at hand" (Eterno 2003, 28). The U.S. Supreme Court, in the case *Terry v. Ohio* (392 U.S. 1 [1968]), and most state legislatures (e.g., New York State Criminal Procedure Law, §140.50) recognize that police have the power to conduct forcible stops. However, officers may stop the person only if he or she has reasonable suspicion to do so.

Law enforcement has tried to justify forcible stops of minorities by claiming that certain minority groups are more likely to engage in crime. That is, they try to use racial stereotypes rather than specific evidence to justify their actions. For example, a New Jersey chief of police troopers was fired in 1999 after he stated that "mostly minorities" were drug dealers (Harris 1999, 3). For the New Jersey State Police, there were not only statements but empirical studies indicating law enforcement's illegal behavior. One study showed that "although blacks and Latinos were 78 percent of persons stopped and searched on the southern portion of the Jersey Turnpike, police were twice as likely to discover evidence of illegal activity in cars driven by whites, relative to blacks, and whites were five times more likely to be in possession of drugs, guns or other illegal items relative to Latinos (Wise 2003). Such studies show the fallacy of the officers' racial stereotyping. Because of these egregious illegal actions, the New Jersey State Police are under a consent decree and must stop conducting the illegal stops.

These actions by police are sometimes termed *racial profiling*. The U.S. Department of Justice defines racial profiling as "any police-initiated action that relies on the race, ethnicity, or national origin rather than the behavior of an individual or information that leads the police to a particular individual who has been identified as being, or having been, engaged in criminal activity" (Ramirez, McDevitt, and Farrell, 2000). In its essence, this means that law enforcement may use race in the case of specific descriptions but may not use racial stereotypes as a basis for an action.

With respect to car stops, a 1996 U.S. Supreme Court case, *Whren et al. v.*

United States (517 U.S. 806) complicates the situation. In *Whren*, the Supreme Court ruled that a car could be stopped with probable cause for a violation. The concern with this case has to do with police using the probable cause from a traffic violation as a pretext to investigate other activity. As one scholar noted, "The average driver cannot go three blocks without violating some traffic regulation . . . [and] police will use the immense discretionary power *Whren* gives them mostly to stop African-Americans and Hispanics" (Harris 1997: 122–123). According to Justice Antonin Scalia, an unanimous Supreme Court decision directed that there was no alternative but to allow police the power to stop cars based on probable cause that a traffic infraction occurred. Even more liberal states such as New York are also adopting this rule. Interestingly, a recent study does indicate that police are conducting illegal car stops based on the driver's race, particularly black males (Lundman and Kaufman, 2003). However, more study is needed to confirm those findings.

More recently, President George W. Bush adopted a new policy that essentially prohibits racial profiling by federal law-enforcement authorities. However, this policy further complicates matters by including an exception that allows agents to use race and ethnicity if there is a terrorist threat or something similar (Lichtblau 2003). Indeed, balancing civil liberties with the threat of crime and terrorism will be a major issue for the foreseeable future (see, e.g., Eterno 2003).

Further Reading

Eterno, John A. *Policing within the Law: A Case Study of the New York City Police Department.* Westport, CT: Praeger, 2003.

Harris, David A. "Driving while Black: Racial Profiling on Our Nation's Highways." *American Civil Liberties Union: Special Report.* June 1999.

————. " 'Driving while Black' and All Other Traffic Offenses: The Supreme Court and Pretextual Traffic Stops." In *Taking Sides: Clashing Views on Controversial Legal Issues.* 9th ed. edited by Ethan M. Katch and William Rose, 119–125. New York: McGraw Hill, 2000.

Lichtblau, Eric. "Bush Issues Racial Profiling Ban but Exempts Security Inquiries." *New York Times,* June 18, 2003, A1.

Lundman, Richard J., and Robert L. Kaufman. "Driving while Black: Effects of Race, Ethnicity, and Gender on Citizen Self-Reports of Traffic Stops and Police Actions." 41, no. 1 (2003): 195–220.

Ramirez, Deborah, Jack McDevitt, and Amy Farrell. *A Resource Guide on Racial Profiling Data Collection Systems.* Washington, DC: U.S. Department of Justice, 2000. See esp. p. 3.

Wise, Tim. "Racial Profiling and its Apologists." In *Annual Editions Criminal Justice 03/04.* 27th ed., edited by Joseph L. Victor and Joanne Naughton, 91–94. New York: McGraw Hill, 2003.

John Eterno

Dual Housing Markets

Dual housing markets refer to racially segmented housing markets that provide different resources and opportunities (one for whites and one for blacks in particular). The persistent racial segregation in U.S. metropolitan areas has turned many scholars' attention to the existence of a dual housing market, in which racial minorities are served by a different set of housing and real estate practices than are whites. These scholars argue that dual housing markets have reinforced and perpetuated racial segregation through the use of racial steering, block-busting, home-mortgage programs of various public and private lending institutions, and the redlining activities of mortgage lending agencies and real estate firms. Moreover, it has been found that housing prices and rents are generally higher for blacks than for whites and that conventional loans for home purchases and remodeling tend to be more available to whites, whereas blacks are often forced to buy with cash, on contract, or through federal loan programs. There is also evidence that dual housing markets have channeled blacks and whites into different types of dwellings. Blacks at every income level tend to live in lower-quality dwellings than their white counterparts. As a result, a white majority occupies the outlying areas of new construction and existing zones of superior residential amenity in metropolitan areas, while blacks and other minority groups are restricted to multifamily projects, public housing units, and deteriorating housing in inner cities.

See also Housing Discrimination.

Sookhee Oh

Du Bois, W.E.B. (1868–1963)

William Edward Burghardt Du Bois (1868–1963) was the most prominent African American social critic of racism in the United States and a leader of the early civil rights movement. Born in Great Barrington, Massachusetts, Du Bois received a bachelor's degree from Fisk University and became the first African American to earn a PhD from Harvard University.

As a prominent scholar of race relations, Du Bois devoted his life to studying racism and the black community. In *The Souls of Black Folk* (1903) Du Bois explained the meaning of the emancipation and its effect and prophetically stated, "The problem of the twentieth century is the problem of the color-line." This phrase became the cornerstone of scholarly thought about racism in the United States in later generations. With this statement, he suggested that, instead of looking at blacks merely as the oppressed "folk," they should be studied within the context of systemic racism and colonialism.

As a social scientist, Du Bois also innovated a new scientific approach to studies of racial issues. In *The Philadelphia Negro* (1899), he employed a historical investigation of racism, statistical and anthropological measurements of local community dynamics, and sociological interpretations of racial disparity between whites and blacks. Du Bois's analysis based on these methods revealed that blacks were "a striving, palpitating group, and not an inert, sick body of crime," and racial disparity was "a long historic development and not a transient occurrence." Thus, he suggested that the "Negro Problem" was "a symptom, not a cause."

In addition to these pioneering treatises, Du Bois wrote about various themes pertaining to the black community, such as morality, religion, crime,

W.E.B. Du Bois, a leader of the early civil rights movement, cofounded the NAACP and coined the phrase, "the color-line."

Courtesy Library of Congress.

education, urbanization, and the economy. Later, his study also extended to the history of Africa. He demonstrated the complexity and mutuality of African culture and renounced the widely held view of Africa as a vast cultural cipher. These scholarly works were broadly presented by his numerous books, such as *The Suppression of the Slave Trade* (1896), *John Brown* (1909), *Quest of the Silver Fleece* (1911), *The Negro* (1915), *The Gift of Black Folk* (1924), *Color and Democracy* (1945), *The World and Africa* (1947), and a trilogy entitled *Black Flame* (1957).

Du Bois also involved in the early civil rights movement. Booker T. Washington, another black leader of the era, proposed that blacks should accept racial segregation and try to gain technical and industrial skills to be useful to white business owners. Rejecting Washington's accommodating position, Du Bois argued that blacks should develop professional and intellectual classes, in additional to technical and industrial classes, and that achieving social and political equality is as important as improving economic conditions. In 1905, Du Bois and other activist leaders organized the Niagara Movement, through which he called for full civil liberties for blacks and an end to the racial caste system. In 1909, in place of the Niagara Movement, Du Bois and his fellow activists cofounded the National Association for the Advancement of Colored People (NAACP). He served as the director and editor of many journals published by this organization, including *The Crisis*, until 1934. *The Crisis* became a major vehicle of communications between Du Bois and his followers.

While directing the domestic black movement, Du Bois broadcast the international implications of racism to the world audience. In 1919, he initiated the Pan-African Conferences in Paris and suggested "economic democracy" and a united black humanity. In 1945, through the speech he gave to the United Nations as a representative of the NAACP, Du Bois pressed the United States for a firm anticolonial commitment. In 1947, he presented a protest against the Jim Crow laws to international political leaders.

However, on the issue of racial segregation, Du Bois increasingly disagreed with black civil rights leaders such as James Weldon Johnson, Kelly Miller and Joel Springarn. While civil rights leaders emphasized the harmful effects of all forms of racial segregation, Du Bois claimed that voluntary segregation could be beneficial to blacks by enhancing their self-respect and economic and social power through cooperative economic enterprises and schools. As the civil rights movement focused on racial integration as its main goal from the 1950s on, Du Bois completely broke away from the NAACP and was disillusioned with the United States. In 1961, accepting an invitation from Kwame Nkrumah (who later became the president of Ghana), he emigrated to Ghana and became the director of *The Encyclopedia Africana*. He later died in Accra, Ghana, on August 27, 1963—ironically, on the eve of the March on Washington. By emphasizing the importance of voluntary segregation, Du Bois bridged civil rights and Black Nationalist leaders, who provided different goals and strategies for black racial empowerment.

Du Bois's work for peace and the rights of oppressed minorities was greatly appreciated by many international leaders during his lifetime, and he received the World Peace Council Prize in 1952 and the Soviet Lenin Peace Prize in 1959. But his contributions had been neglected in his home country because of his racial affiliation and long-standing "radicalist" label. In 1992, nearly thirty years after his death, the U.S. government finally recognized Du Bois's contribution to civil liberty for racial minorities and honored him by issuing his portrait on a national postage stamp.

See also National Association for the Advancement of Colored People (NAACP); Black Nationalist Movement; Civil Rights Movement; Color Line; Washington, Booker T.

Further Reading

Du Bois, W.E.B. *Autobiography of W.E.B. Du Bois: A Soliloquy on Viewing My Life from the Last Decade of Its First Century*. New York: International Publishers, 1968.

———. *The Philadelphia Negro*. New York: Lippincott, 1899.

———. *The Souls of Black Folk*. Chicago: A. G. McClurg & Co., 1903.

Jaret, Charles. *Contemporary Racial and Ethnic Relations*. Upper Saddle River, NJ: Prentice Hall, 1995.

Etsuko Maruoka-Ng

Duke, David (1950–   )

For more than thirty years, David Duke has been a local and national advocate of neo-Nazi, anti-Semitic, and white-supremacist politics. He was perhaps the most widely known white supremacist in the United States in the 1990s.

As a student at Louisiana State University, Duke founded the neo-Nazi group White Youth Alliance. Duke attained national prominence as National Director (or "Grand Wizard") of the Knights of the Klu Klux Klan in the 1970s. During this time, he advocated the mainstreaming of the Klan, a tactic that boosted its national membership. After his association with the Klan, he founded the National Association for the Advancement of White People. He was elected in 1988 to the U.S. House of Representatives for Louisiana, where he authored anti-affirmative-action legislation. His election was widely under-

David Duke as a twenty-seven-year-old Ku Klux Klan leader in London, 1978.

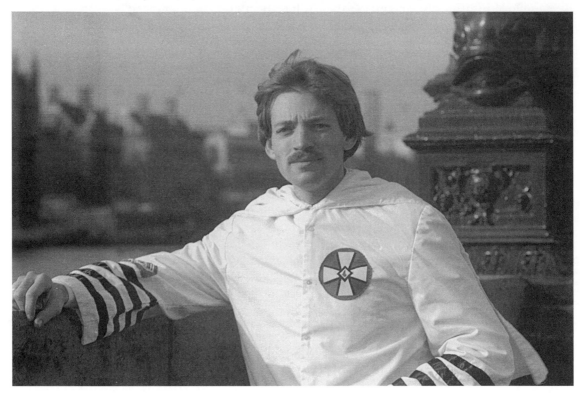

AP/Wide World Photos.

stood as a testament to the tolerance for, and popularity of, overt racism in Louisiana politics. He ran unsuccessfully for the U.S. Senate in 1990, although he received over 43 percent of the Louisiana vote. He also ran for Louisiana's governorship in 1991 and the White House in 1992, winning neither.

Throughout the 1990s, he continued to promote himself as an advocate of "white civil rights" through his radio program and his autobiography and other publications. In December 2002, he pled guilty to tax and mail fraud, a case that involved the sale of his list of supporters to Louisiana governor Mike Foster, and he was sentenced to fifteen months in prison. Currently, he is president of the European-American Unity and Rights Organization, which uses the Internet for the global advocacy of white supremacism and "white awareness" and for protesting affirmative action, U.S. immigration, hate-speech policies, and the Anti-Defamation League and other civil rights groups. He also sells products that appeal to racists and anti-Semites, including Confederate flags, videos like D. W. Griffith's *Birth of a Nation*, anti-Semitic books, and his own book, *Jewish Supremacism*.

See also Ku Klux Klan (KKK); Neo Nazism; White Supremacist Movement in the United States; White-Supremacist Underground.

Victoria Pitts

E

Ebonics

See "Black English" (Ebonics).

Economics and Politics of Race

In his book *Economics and Politics of Race* (1983), Thomas Sowell, a conservative social scientist, argues that culture makes a difference in the success of an ethnic group and that racial strife has affected all kinds of human relationships for thousands of years everywhere in the world. Despite the optimistic hope that education and time would erode racial and ethnic differences, evidence so far has shown that they have not been eroded. According to Sowell, it may be difficult for different ethnic and racial groups to cooperate politically, but, since all human beings excel at something, it is in their best interest to cooperate for economic purposes. Based on his analysis of the economic adjustment of various ethnic and racial minority groups in different countries, Sowell argues that their economic success or failure does not depend on matters of race or ethnicity but rather on the cultural messages that they carry with them from country to country. Therefore, one finds that the Chinese minority may succeed as well in the Philippines as in the United States because of the messages that they carry with them.

The author further argues that racial and ethnic differences have serious costs. These costs may range from difficulties of comprehension, misunderstanding of verbal communications, to outright hostility and violence. For Sowell, group separation is not something arbitrarily imposed from above by society but a way to minimize inherent costs.

Moreover, Sowell argues that the politicization of race tends to result in a process where redistributive and compensatory schemes are often bestowed on individuals who are inept or irresponsible, which then leads to a process where the human capital needed for prosperity is not created. Sowell is clearly against affirmative action or any other forms of social justice that would benefit a specific group of people.

See also Economics of Discrimination.

Further Reading

Sowell, Thomas. *Economics and Politics of Race*. New York: William Morrow, 1983.

Francois Pierre-Louis

Economics of Discrimination

Discrimination in the labor market can take many forms and be measured by differential market outcomes, such as wages and earnings, occupational attainment, and employment levels. After holding such factors as education, work experience, and productivity constant, any wage and/or occupational differentials are evidence of racial discrimination. The economics of racial discrimination differentiate between premarket factors that may be an outcome of past discrimination, such as disparities in educational quality, aspirations, and child rearing, and discrimination in the labor market, although premarket factors may have consequences in the labor market. Labor-market discrimination occurs as a result of the valuation of ascriptive characteristics such as race, gender, physical handicap, religion, sexual preference, and ethnicity, which are unrelated to worker productivity.

There are two general explanations for labor-market discrimination, and each proposes different rationales. One explanation is based on personal prejudice. In his 1971 book *The Economics of Discrimination*, Gary S. Becker, the University of Chicago economist and 1992 Nobel Prize recipient, explained that employers, fellow employees, and customers may have a "taste" or personal preference to associate with workers of a given race or sex. Becker contends that employers, employees, and customers who discriminate are utility maximizers, because they are willing to forego profits and/or pay higher prices and wages to satisfy their discriminatory preferences, that is, prejudices. According to Becker, discrimination is economically irrational because it is not profit-maximizing behavior.

The second explanation, statistical discrimination, proposes that labor market discrimination may not necessarily be an outcome of personal prejudice but rather a lack of information about an individual's potential productivity. Because of imperfect information, employers resort to attributing information or statistics about the average performance of a group to individual members in making hiring decisions. Employers may use race and gender as predictors of worker productivity. If an employer perceives that, on average, blacks or women are unproductive workers, they will then use this information in individual hiring decisions.

See also Economics and Politics of Race; Statistical Discrimination.

Further Reading

Beckeer, Gary S. *The Economics of Discrimination*. 2nd ed. Chicago: University of Chicago Press, 1971.

Tarry Hum

Education and Racial Discrimination

In modern, post industrial economies, education is a key to getting a good job and earning enough money to support oneself at a comfortable standard of living. If access to and success within the educational realm is distributed unequally according to race, then life chances in general will be uneven. Throughout the history of the United States, race has been an important factor in dictating educational opportunity, from the times of slavery when people of African descent were forbidden from receiving an education to today's systems of funding inequity that prevents schools in inner-city neighborhoods from obtaining the resources they need.

During slavery, many states had laws that forbade anyone from teaching African Americans to read or write. Not only did many whites believe that African Americans in general had subpar intelligence, they also believed that if African Americans were literate, they would become more dangerous. When African Americans were finally allowed to go to school after the Civil War, they attended segregated and underfunded schools. These schools often did not provide education beyond the first few grades, and they certainly did not educate their students enough for them to work in professions such as medicine or teaching. The education system was governed by the doctrine of "separate but equal" facilities and educations, though while the separateness was always maintained, the equality was seldom enforced. School segregation and exclusion is not only a black-white issue. In many areas, students of Asian and Latino/a descent were also sent to segregated schools—sometimes to the same schools as the African American students, sometimes to their own. While the grade levels taught in the schools slowly increased, schools in many states (particularly in the South) remained segregated by law until the landmark Supreme Court case *Brown v. Board of Education* in 1954, which forced the desegregation of public schools.

What this case meant, however, was not that every school would be integrated. It meant that public schools were no longer able to exclude students solely on the basis of their race. Although some districts and states instituted busing to integrate schools in all-white neighborhoods, these busing programs have been largely abandoned. Schools in segregated neighborhoods remain segregated schools: according to a Harvard University study, 70 percent of black students attend schools that enroll at least half students of color, whereas more than a third of both black and Latino/a students attend schools that enroll ninety to one-hundred percent students of color. In addition, some private schools have been largely able to keep students of color out through restrictive, but not openly race-based, admissions policies (particularly through class-based requirements and preferences for relatives of alumni).

The segregation of students of color, particularly those of low socioeconomic status, in underfunded school districts means that these students attend schools in substandard buildings, do not have sufficient textbooks, and often are taught by underqualified teachers or permanent substitutes. Underfunded schools lack many programs common in middle-class schools, such as special classes for gifted students, Advanced Placement exams, art and music, competitive sports teams, and SAT preparation courses. Students often have a hard time making it to graduation, and if they do graduate, their high school records are not competitive enough to gain them admission to selective colleges. These schools lack sufficient funding because school funding relies mainly on the local tax base, which is small in poor neighborhoods. States rarely step in to level the playing field by redistributing available funds from rich districts to poor ones.

Even when poor students of color attend adequately funded schools, they do not necessarily receive the same education as white students at the same school. There is some evidence that poor students of color are disproportionately tracked into vocational and technical courses that do not prepare them for college, as well as into special education. Tracking is a particular problem in schools where movement between tracks is one way; that is, where students can move to less academically rigorous tracks but not back in the other direction. Students are tracked on the basis of their scores on standardized tests, and these tests often exhibit pervasive racial biases. Additionally, students' behavior and parental pressures often come into play. Tracking continues to occur in higher education as well, when Asian American students, for instance, are encouraged to pursue scientific majors or African American students are encouraged to focus on athletics because of racial stereotyping.

Even when African American and Latino/a students are in the same courses as white students, their performance as measured by grades and retention falls behind. Though socioeconomic status and access to such resources as a parent with an advanced education are part of the explanation for this achievement gap, other explanations have been advanced. Anthropologist John Ogbu has argued that African American students exhibit an oppositional culture. This means that these students are aware of the fact that their economic and educational opportunities are constrained by their race, and so they develop an opposition to the values of hard work in school, which could help them get ahead. Oppositional culture is intensified by peer pressure that punishes students who work hard and do well in school and by the lack of African American role models in many schools. Ogbu believes that the oppositional culture is specifically developed by African Americans because of their history as a racial group that was brought to the United States against their will. Although many people have found Ogbu's explanation persuasive, other charge that it leaves out essential information, such as the fact that some Asian Americans' ancestors were brought to the United States essentially as slave labor and yet their children continue to do well in school.

Another explanation for the achievement gap is the stereotype threat. This explanation is advanced by Claude Steele, who believes that students are aware of the stereotypes that others hold regarding their academic abilities and that their consciousness of these stereotypes in academic situations leads them to focus more on the stereotype than on performance in school. Steele administered a standardized test to a number of college students and found that African American students performed at a lower level on the test when they were aware that there was a correlation between the race and test results—and in fact, they even performed lower when they were asked to indicate their race than when they were not. Stereotypes in general are pervasive in education, ranging from the idea that African Americans are good at sports and music to the conception of Asian Americans as "model minorities" who work hard and do well in school.

Others have suggested that an important reason for African American and Latino/a students' lesser academic achievement is that their experiences are not reflected in the curriculum. This has led to increasing pressures to develop multicultural education, which is often achieved by adding special units into the curriculum, such as a section on important African American writers during Black History Month. These "add-on" approaches do little to address the fact that the histories and achievements of people of color are excluded from the history and literature taught in many public schools in the United States, as well as in colleges and universities. In addition, many politicians, scholars, and activists have pointed to the cultural biases in IQ and other standardized tests. For instance, IQ tests may include questions asking the test taker to complete culturally specific proverbs. It is clear that an individual's ability to complete a specific proverb does not demonstrate his or her intelligence, but these tests use such items anyway, resulting in test scores that are lower for students of color and poor students in general.

In higher education, students have been somewhat successful in pushing for the development of departments of ethnic studies that focus on teaching pertaining to the experiences of people of color in the United States. At some colleges and universities, all students are required to take one or more courses with a focus on peoples and cultures other than those originating in Western Europe. These programs and requirements have brought more awareness of African American, Asian American, Latino/a, and Native American experiences into the college curriculum, but these issues are still academically ghettoized in many colleges and universities rather than being an essential part of the curriculum as a whole.

Multiculturalism in education is still a raging debate, with some scholars and pundits talking about how it is essential to include multicultural content to educate the next generation of world leaders and others arguing on how multiculturalism dilutes the canon of important history and literature about and by dead white males. The debate has thus shifted away from the needs of students of color themselves and toward what multicultural education can do for the student body as a whole. The multiculturalism debate in higher education has also involved controversies around the provision of cultural spaces and racially themed dorms as "comfort zones" for students of color. There are other important controversies currently raging around issues of race in education as well, including affirmative action, race-based decision making in admissions to college, and the distribution of special scholarships based on race.

In public schools, one of the most important controversies affecting students of color is the debate over bilingual education. With increasing numbers of Latino/a and Asian immigrant students in many school districts, particularly those in large urban areas such as New York City and Los Angeles, schools are faced with the task of educating students who do not speak English. Some educators favor rapid immersion in English, others favor a limited period of intensive English-as-a-second-language course work, and still others favor long-term bilingual education, both to ensure that students are fully competent in their other courses and to help them maintain fluency in their original language. Research has not yet confirmed which approach is best for students' educational success, but some states (most notably California) have banned all but the most cursory bilingual education programs.

Educators have proposed many plans to mitigate the effects of racial discrimination and disparities in the educational system and to help close the achievement gap. Two of those currently on the political scene that have stirred up significant controversy are school choice/school vouchers and standards-based education. School choice and school vouchers refer to policies that would allow students to control which school they attend. In the least radical sense, school choice can describe an educational system in a large metropolitan area that allows students to choose whichever public school in the system they wish to attend. The most radical voucher programs would replace standard state funding of schools by giving parents a set amount of money to spend on school tuition, which they could choose to spend at any school of their choosing, public, private, and even religious. Supporters argue that these systems would liberate poor students of color from failing inner-city schools, while opponents argue that they will just shortchange the public school systems and those students who are left behind in them.

Standards-based education, on the other hand, keeps students in their traditional schools. The most significant change that it makes is increasing achievement testing of students, teachers, and entire schools. Students who fail the tests would be forced to repeat a grade or would be unable to graduate. Teachers who fail would be fired, and schools that fail would face funding cuts, takeovers, or even closure. The supporters of these plans talk about how they would hold inner-city schools to the same standards as those in more wealthy areas and force them to value academic achievement. Opponents, on the other hand, emphasize the fact that achievement tests are almost inevitably racially biased and that it does not make much sense to give a failing school less money to work with.

Related to these two proposals for change is the increasing use of standardized curriculums and the rise in privatized magnet schools that are exempt from normal state regulations. Some people contend that these innovations can force a public school system to realize that it is shortchanging inner-city students and shape up or risk losing their students to other schools. However, many of the inner-city students that these programs are ostensibly designed to help do not have access to information about their choices.

A final plan for helping students of color gain academic achievement is the proliferation of junior and community colleges. These colleges, which grant two-year associate's degrees instead of four-year bachelor's degrees, are supposed to be low-cost options to help students on their way to attaining a bachelor's degree. For some students, they do just that, providing two very inexpensive years of general coursework that can then be transferred to a university, as well as a chance to improve their GPA and maybe fill in some gaps in their high school education. For many other students, however, the associate's degree becomes a terminal degree, even if they were originally planning to go on. Transferring can be very difficult—students often lose many credits, especially if they enrolled in a vocational major at the associate's level.

Educational opportunities continue to be distributed unevenly by race, despite the civil rights movement of the 1950s and 1960s and the supposed legal guarantees of equal access and equal opportunity. African American, Latino/a, and Native American students graduate from high school, enroll in college, earn college degrees, and earn advanced degrees all at lower rates than whites. These educational credentials are increasingly important in finding a rewarding and well-paying job in the postindustrial economy.

See also Brown v. Board of Education of Topeka; Deindustrialization and Racial Inequality; Hidden Curriculum; Intelligence and Standardized Tests, Cultural Biases in; Intelligence Tests and Racism; Tracking.

Further Reading

Fischer, Claude S., et al. *Inequality by Design: Cracking the Bell Curve Myth*. Princeton, NJ: Princeton University Press, 1996.

Gibson, Margaret A., and John U. Ogbu. *Minority Status and Schooling: A Comparative Study of Immigrant and Involuntary Minorities*. New York: Garland, 1991.

Hacker, Andrew. *Two Nations: Black and White, Separate, Hostile, Unequal*. New York: Scribner, 1992.

Henig, Jeffrey R., et al. *The Color of School Reform: Race, Politics, and the Challenge of Urban Education*. Princeton, NJ: Princeton University Press, 1999.

Jencks, Christopher, and Meredith Phillips, eds. *The Black-White Test Score Gap*. Washington, DC: Brookings Institution Press, 1998.

Lucas, Samuel Roundfield. *Tracking Inequality: Stratification and Mobility in American High Schools*. New York: Teachers College Press, 1999.

Margo, Robert. *Race and Schooling in the South, 1880–1950: An Economic History*. Chicago: University of Chicago Press, 1990.

Orfield, Gary, and Susan E. Eaton. *Dismantling Desegregation*. New York: New Press, 1996.

Mikaila Mariel Lemonik Arthur

El Teatro Campensino

El Teatro Campensino, the Farmworkers Theater, is a popular theatrical troupe founded in 1965 by Luis Valdez as part of Cesar Chavez's United Farm Workers union. In its early years, it fought for the rights of Mexican American farmworkers, particularly grape pickers in Delano, California. Touring rural areas, the theater group performed a series of agitprop-style *actos* (short skits) on a flatbed truck and in union halls to raise farmworkers' consciousness about their socioeconomic reality and the struggle for social change. The conflict revolving around four social actors—striking farmworker, scab, grower, and farm-labor contractor—was captured in a comical but poignant dramaturgic representation.

Spontaneous improvisations, using the everyday language of Mexican farmworkers, helped address their daily experience. In 1968, El Campensino became independent of the United Farm Workers union and worked to reflect a larger Chicano experience. It developed a unique agitprop theatrical style, combining the styles of Italian Renaissance comedy and Mexican folklore and popular culture. In 1971, the group settled permanently in San Juan Bautista, California, a small, rural town between San Jose and Salinas. Among its important works are *Los Vendidos* (The Sellouts), *Vietnam Campensino*, and *Munnified Deer*. The influence of El Teatro Campensino was felt beyond its own productions: it also ignited the entire Chicano theater movement, and in the late 1960s and 1970s, more than seventy Chicano theater groups were created.

See also Chavez, Cesar; United Farm Workers (UFW).

Dong-Ho Cho

Emancipation Proclamation (1862)

The Emancipation Proclamation issued by President Abraham Lincoln in September 1862 freed slaves in Confederate-controlled areas effective January 1, 1863. Contrary to popular belief, the scope of the Emancipation Proclamation was limited to slaves residing in Confederate states, including Arkansas, Texas, Mississippi, Alabama, Florida, Georgia, South Carolina, North Carolina, and parts of Louisiana and Virginia. President Lincoln's Emancipation Proclamation declared that "all persons held as slaves within said designated States and parts of States are, and henceforward shall be, free." It was not until the passage of the Thirteenth Amendment in December 1865, after the end of the American Civil War, that slavery would eventually be abolished throughout the nation.

Few slaves were actually freed immediately after the 1862 Emancipation Proclamation, because Confederate states and controlled areas did not heed President Lincoln's orders. Moreover, the proclamation did not apply to slaves in border states or Southern areas that were under Union control. Despite its limited jurisdiction, the proclamation made the abolition of slavery a central issue in the Civil War. Recognizing the untapped resources of African American men, the proclamation also called upon freed slaves to enlist in the Union effort, emphasizing that they would be welcomed "into the armed service of the United States to garrison forts, positions, stations, and other places, and to man vessels of all sorts in said service." As a result, in the two and a half years following the 1862 Emancipation Proclamation, nearly 200,000 African Americans joined the Union army.

See also Civil War and the Abolition of Slavery; Fourteenth Amendment; Lincoln, Abraham, and the Emancipation of Slaves; Slavery in the Antebellum South.

Tarry Hum

A Union soldier reads an announcement of the Emancipation Proclamation.

Courtesy Library of Congress.

Emergency Labor Program

See Bracero Program.

Employment

See Immigrant Preference in Employment.

English Language Education for Children in Public Schools Initiative

See California Ballot Proposition 227.

English-Only Movement

Although English is the language of the U.S. Constitution, government, and laws, the United States, like Great Britain, does not have an official language. English is the principal, or common, language rather than the official language. The framers of the Constitution were silent on this issue, and the question of the national language probably never came up at the Federal Convention.

Despite the existence of controversies over language issues at the local and state levels in early periods, English-Only as a national movement did not surface until the early 1980s (Crawford 1991). In 1981, the late U.S. Senator S.I. Hayakawa introduced a bill calling for an amendment to the U.S. Constitution to declare English the official language of the nation. The bill was defeated. In 1983, Hayakawa and John Tanton, a Michigan ophthalmologist, environmentalist, and population-control activist, cofounded an organization called U.S. English, the principal force of the English-Only movement, as an offshoot of the Federation for American Immigration Reform (FAIR), a Washington-based lobbying group. U.S English later outgrew its parent organization, and it now claims 1.7 million members. The goals of the group are to pass legislation at the national, state, and local levels to declare English the official language, to eliminate or reduce bilingual education, to abolish multilingual ballots, and to prevent translation of road signs and government documents into other languages. The growing use of the Spanish language by newcomers is of particular concern to U.S. English.

Largely as a result of the pushes of the group U.S. English and its allies, twenty-seven states have designated English the official language of their states either constitutionally or by law, including Louisiana (1811), Nebraska (1920), Illinois (1969), Massachusetts (1975), Hawaii (1978), Virginia (1981 and 1996), Indiana (1984), Kentucky (1984), Tennessee (1984), California (1986), Georgia (1986), Arkansas (1987), Mississippi (1987), North Carolina (1987), North Dakota (1987), South Carolina (1987), Colorado (1988), Florida (1988), Alabama (1990), Montana (1995), New Hampshire (1995), South Dakota (1995), Wyoming (1996), Alaska (1998), Missouri (1998), Utah (2000), and Iowa (2002). Hawaii recognizes both English and native Hawaiian as the official languages. The effects of these laws are more symbolic than substantive. Bilingual education programs have remained intact in many states where official English-language legislation has been enacted.

Attempts were also made at the national level to pass English-only legislation. On August 1, 1996, the House of Representatives passed the English Language Empowerment Act, by a vote of 259–169. This bill declared English the official language of the United States. According to this bill, all government documents (including income-tax forms and instruction booklets) must be printed in English; government officials cannot conduct business in foreign languages; states cannot use bilingual ballots in elections in areas with significant immigrant population; and the Immigration and Naturalization Service cannot conduct citizenship ceremonies in foreign languages. However, the bill made some exceptions. For instance, the bill permitted the use of foreign languages in the census surveys, international trade and diplomatic relations, national security, public health and safety, criminal proceedings, language education (including bilingual education), and oral communications with the public by federal employees, officials, and congressmen. The Senate introduced a similar measure sidestepping the repeal of bilingual education and bilingual ballots, but it failed to act on the bill before the session was over. U.S. English is currently trying to push through the 108th Congress H.R. 997, The English Unity Act of 2003, introduced by Rep. Steve King (R-Iowa). The outcome remains to be seen.

Advocates of English-only legislation argue that such legislation is essential to preserve English as the common language and bond; it will encourage people to speak English, to succeed economically, and to fully participate in a democratic society; and more importantly, it will help maintain national unity.

There are several counterarguments to English-only legislation. First, English-only legislation is seen to be unnecessary. Currently, 97 percent of all Americans already speak English, and more than 99 percent of all government

Applauding Proposition 227.

AP/Wide World Photos.

documents are printed in English. Most new immigrants acknowledge the necessity for them to learn English as quickly as possible. The preeminence of English is not in danger. Second, such legislation has negative effects, including depriving Americans with limited English ability of their essential rights to vote and of free speech, encouraging cutbacks in services for non-English–speaking newcomers, reducing resources for programs such as bilingual education, and destroying cultural heritage. Finally, English-only legislation is divisive and may stimulate xenophobia and anti-immigrant sentiment and create a racially divided nation. It should be noted that English-Plus, which champions the acquisition of strong English language proficiency plus the mastery of other languages, is the countermovement to English-Only.

See also Bilingual Education; Multiculturalism.

Further Reading

Crawford, James. *Bilingual Education: History, Politics, Theory, and Practice*. 2nd ed. Los Angeles: Bilingual Education Services, 1991.

U.S. English. "Making English the Official Language." http://www.us-english.org.

Philip Yang

Environmentalists

See Hereditarians versus Environmentalists.

Environmental Racism

Environmental racism refers to the deliberate placement of toxic and hazardous waste sites, incinerators, landfills, and polluting industries in communities populated mainly by minorities, including Latinos, African Americans, Asians, migrant farm workers, and the working poor. It also includes "any government, institutional, or industry action, or failure to act, that has a negative environmental impact which disproportionately harms—whether intentionally or unintentionally—individuals, groups, or communities based on race or color." As a consequence of these actions, the inhabitants in minority neighborhoods suffer from many health problems, including shorter life spans, higher rates of infant and adult mortality, cancer, and asthma. Communities populated predominantly by minority residents tend to have more commercial waste sites than do predominantly white communities. Fifty percent of the country's African American population and sixty percent of Latinos live in a community where levels of two or more toxins exceed government standards. Half of Asian/Pacific Islander Americans and American Indians live in areas with uncontrolled toxic waste sites. Areas with working incinerators hold 89 percent more minorities than the national average.

In 1987, the United Church of Christ Commission for Racial Justice (CRJ) conducted a study (Toxic Wastes and Race in the United States) on environmental racism and how it affects those in its polluted environments. The study found that (1) race was the most outstanding factor in the location of hazardous waste sites; (2) communities with a majority of minority residents housed the highest number of commercial hazardous facilities; (3) communities with one commercial hazardous waste facility had twice the national average minority population than those communities without said facilities; and (4) even though socioeconomic status played an important role in the location of these sites, the most outstanding factor was race, even after accounting for urban and regional differences.

Severe environmental racism is found in Emelle, Alabama, a poor, predominantly African American community. The community houses the largest hazardous-waste landfill in the United States, receiving toxic materials from more than forty states and many foreign countries. Another community victimized by environmental racism is the south side of Tucson, Arizona, where Hispanics are the majority of the population. An industrial toxic waste site there has caused high levels of cancers, birth defects, and genetic mutations among the residents. Also, Native Americans have often been approached by waste disposal companies in the hopes that they would allow dumping on their reservations in return for promises of improved economic conditions.

Why is environmental racism happening? There are several reasons. One reason is simply institutional racism; minorities pay a great price in terms of their health and overall quality of life in exchange for economic development, resources extraction, and industrialism. A second reason is for business purposes and profit. The industries that are polluting areas are attracted to poor neighborhoods because of the low land values and overall business costs associated with development in minority areas. Minority communities return the highest profits because of the low costs of development. Also, these areas are developed because of the low rate of opposition. Communities with higher incomes are more successful in controlling and staving off pollutant industries. A third and very important reason is the lack of power the residents of these neighborhoods have. These people lack information that should be given to them for informed consent, and they lack the political power necessary for fighting back against these polluting industries and companies.

How have minority communities fought environmental racism? Community activists have used strategies of the civil rights and antiwar movements of the 1960s and 1970s. The movement's goal is to fix the negative actions of the past and promote fairness in environmental decision on a local, national, and international level. Many people have taken to protesting, marching, civil disobedience, and legal action. Community activists have tried to inform their residents on the issue with pamphlets, newsletters, classes, and other means in hopes of educating them so that they can help to fight environmental racism. They have begun using voter blocs as a way of forming the necessary clout to promote change. There is strength in numbers, and using these means will achieve the movement's specific goals.

Further Reading

Haltfield, Heather. Toxic Communities: Environmental Racism, 2003. http://cbcfhealth. org/content/contentID/1107.

Robinson, Deborah M. Environmental Racism: Old Wine in a New Bottle, 2000. http://www.wcc-coe.org/wcc/what/jpc/echoes/echoes-17-02.html.

Weintraub, Irwin. Fighting Environmental Racism: A Selected Annotated Bibliography. http://egj.lib.uidaho.edu/egj01/weint01.html.

Wigley, Daniel C., and Kristin S. Shrader-Frechette. Environmental Racism and Biased Methods of Risk Assessment. http://www.piercelaw.edu/risk/vol7/winter/wigley. htm.

Tiffany Vélez

Equal Employment Opportunity Act of 1972

The Equal Employment Opportunity Act of 1972 amended the provisions of Title VII of the 1964 Civil Rights Act in several important ways to extend its jurisdiction and coverage, and to improve its effectiveness in ensuring equal job opportunities. Title VII prohibited employment discrimination based on race, color, sex, religion, or national origin. All areas of the employment process, including job advertisement, recruitment, testing, hiring and firing, compensation, assignment, and classification of employees, were covered by Title VII provisions. Title VII was enforced by the U.S. Equal Employment Opportunity Commission (EEOC), whose primary mission was to deal with complaints and obtain remedies for individuals and classes of individuals who had suffered discrimination.

The Equal Employment Opportunity Act of 1972 has extended the coverage of Title VII to educational institutions and all levels of governmental employees. In addition, the act has reduced the number of employees necessary for an employer to be covered by the provisions of the act, from 25 to 15, thereby increasing the number of employers that are subject to adhering to the act. The 1972 Equal Employment Opportunity Act has also extended the period of time that a party has to file a discrimination charge. Most importantly, the 1972 amendment has empowered the EEOC with litigation authority. If an acceptable conciliation agreement cannot be achieved, the EEOC now has the option to sue nongovernmental respondents such as employers, unions, and employment agencies. Finally, the act has amended the sex-discrimination provisions to prohibit employers from imposing mandatory leaves of absence or terminating pregnant women employees.

See also Civil Rights Act of 1964.

Tarry Hum

Ethnic Myth: Race, Ethnicity, and Class in America

Ethnic Myth: Race, Ethnicity, and Class in America is Stephen Steinberg's classic 1989 sociological work that challenged various prevailing ideas or "myths" about race and ethnicity in the United States. He critiqued the idea of the United States as an "open society" where individuals are unrestrained by limitations of birth, family, or class. Instead, he depicted a racist society riven by social and economic inequalities. Deconstructing specific historical examples, he argued against the reification of ethnicity as an explanatory factor for differences among racial and ethnic groups and instead analyzed race and ethnicity within their unique historical, social, and economic structures and manifestations, as well as within a larger context of a society that had practiced systematic racial oppression. The book was organized into three parts. In the first part, Steinberg debunked the idea of ethnic pluralism as an idealistic nationalistic impulse and instead situated it in the context of the United States's economically exploitative relationships with minority groups, such as Native Americans, blacks, and Mexicans, as well as a brutal, racist history rooted in the conquest, enslavement, and importation of foreign workers. In the second part, Steinberg deconstructed various cultural arguments for the success or failure of particular minority groups, calling them "ethnic myths"; in contrast, he focused on the influence of social class and racism as the reasons for the varying economic and educational group outcomes. In Part III, Steinberg focused on the class nature of racial and ethnic conflict. He rejected the idea of a historically transmitted "culture of poverty" as the reason for economically struggling urban blacks, Puerto Ricans and Chicanos and attacked such ideas as unfair instances of "blaming racial victims for their own plight"; on the contrary, he traced these groups' poor economic standing to a system of institutionalized racism and social inequality that, he contended, was in conflict and at odds with the ethical, democratic ideology of this country. This critical analysis challenged dominant mainstream narratives that assumed a progressively improving racial climate.

See also American Dream Ideology; Black Family Instability Thesis; Culture of Poverty Thesis.

Further Reading

Steinberg, Stephen. *Ethnic Myth: Race, Ethnicity, and Class in America*. Boston: Beacon Press, 1989.

Rose Kim

Ethnic Options

In her book *Ethnic Options: Choosing Identities in America* (1990), Mary C. Waters first coined the term ethnic option to emphasize the tendency of many white Americans to choose their ethnic identity in the form of symbols. Ethnic options refer to people's voluntary choice of identification with one or more ethnic groups. The core element of ethnic options is this noncompulsory nature of white Americans' choice. A great majority of Americans are descendants of European immigrants. From this perspective, such a voluntary identification is generally possible from the third generation (grandchildren) of immigrants. But members of racial minorities do not have the choice, because ethnic and racial identities are imposed on them by U.S. society.

Immigrants tend to maintain their social ties with those who belong to the same ethnic group. They also practice the kind of lifestyle associated with their country of origin. Thus, the ethnic identity of immigrants and their spouses is generally determined by the country of their birth (national identity), hardly a voluntary choice of ethnic affiliation. The ethnic identification of the second generation is also heavily influenced, from the time of their birth throughout their childhood, by their parents' ethnic group. Although the children of immigrants have more freedom in selecting an ethnic group (to identify with) than their parents, they still identify with the ethnic group of their parents. They usually hold a hyphenated American identity (Irish American, Italian American, etc.). For example, because of their intensive association with their parents and people of the same ethnic group, most children of German immigrants retained identification with German Americans, even when they were rapidly assimilated into American society as adults.

As demonstrated by the children of European immigrants, the second generation exhibits a high rate of interethnic marriage. By virtue of their parents' interethnic marriage, third-generation white Americans (the children of the second generation) are naturally exposed to multiple ethnic groups. As it is practically too cumbersome to identify with all of their parents' ethnic groups, they feel the need to choose one or two ethnic groups as their own. This is the idea of ethnic option, a voluntary choice of or identification with one or more ethnic groups. In reality, their voluntary choice of ethnic groups is somewhat diversified. While many third-generation white Americans simply think themselves as Americans, a high proportion of them identify themselves with one or two ethnic groups, based on their parents' or grandparents' origins or heritage.

By the time they make a choice, however, the intensity of their identification with their chosen ethnic group tends to be considerably weakened. In fact, their ethnic identification resembles Herbert Gans's idea of symbolic ethnicity, meaning that they identify with symbols such as ethnic food and holidays, but little else. From the fourth generation on, their ethnic identification would be a result of ethnic options and selective identification with certain ethnic groups rather than acceptance of all the ascriptive ethnic groups. This option is available to whites only, so far. The basic condition for an ethnic option is the fact that members of white ethnic groups are not subject to discrimination. Thus, to a great majority of nonwhites in America, ethnic-group identification is not necessarily voluntary.

In a study published in 1990, Waters empirically examined the issue of ethnic options when she analyzed ethnic identification of multigeneration white Catholics using 1980 census data. She observed that many white Americans identify with several white ethnic groups, although they do not identify with all of the ethnic groups associated with their parents. She thus asked her informants about the meaning of their identification with multiple white ethnic groups. She further inquired about why and how many white Americans made their voluntary choice. These questions led Waters to interview white, middle-class Catholics in two communities, San Jose, California, and Philadelphia, Pennsylvania. She discovered that the respondents did not identify with all of their ancestors' ethnicity. They tended to simplify their ethnic identification. Second, their ethnic options varied with the respondents' age, social status, family structure, generation, and so on. Third, their ethnic identification was mostly that of symbolic ethnicity. Their choice of ethnic ties did not interfere with their daily activities. Still, most respondents identified with certain cultural traits of their chosen ethnic group(s) and felt they belonged to the chosen ethnic group(s).

Ethnic option is not always available to members of racial minority groups. Many white Americans assume members of racial minorities have the same option as whites. For example, blacks trace their origin to various ethnic groups in Africa and Caribbean countries. Nevertheless, U.S. society does not differentiate their various countries of origin. With their exposure to severe discrimination, moreover, blacks generally marry with each other. Consequently, their children are not exposed to multiple ethnic groups within the structure of the family. Even African Americans with multiple ethnic heritages do not have the option of making a voluntary choice.

Today, the children of Asian immigrants show a high rate of interethnic marriage among Asian Americans. Mia Tuan has shown that the children of such marriages have more experience of ethnic choice than do African Americans. However, what most of them experience is not an ethnic option but a shifting of their ethnic identity from a single Asian ethnic group (e.g., Chinese or Japanese Americans) or to a broader Asian American ethnic group (e.g., Chinese-Japanese Americans) or to a pan-Asian identity. In these cases, as members of a racial group different from the whites, even the native-born Asian Americans are compelled to retain an Asian American identity and are more likely to be treated as foreigners in the United States. But interracial marriages (marriage of Asian children with non-Asians, especially whites) among Asian Americans are quite common as well, and studies on the ethnic identity among children of such interracial marriages exhibit a complicated picture. Often their ethnic identity ranges from an Asian ethnic group to white, but as long as some Asian features are visible they are also forced to retain their Asian American identity irrespective of their wishes.

Descendants of Latino immigrants are likely to face a situation similar to that of descendants of Asian Americans. Racial diversification among Hispanics is much more extensive than Asians. Thus, their experience of ethnic options is more complicated than white Americans' experience.

Further Reading

Alba, Richard D. *Ethnic Identity: The Transformation of White America*. New Haven, CT: Yale University Press, 1990.

Tuan, Mia. *Forever Foreigners or Honorary Whites? The Asian Ethnic Experience Today*. New Brunswick, NJ: Rutgers University Press, 1998.

Waters, Mary C. *Ethnic Options: Choosing Identities in America*. Berkeley: University of California Press, 1990.

Shin Kim and Kwang Chung Kim

Ethnic Retention and School Performance

Ethnic retention refers to immigrants or people of color embracing the characteristics of their culture, such as language, values and priorities, daily routines, social networks, and ethnic identity. Traditionally, educators and scholars believed that ethnic retention impedes the academic performances of students. This belief was based on the zero-sum assumption that, if a person is embracing "the other" culture, she/he could not be fluent in the skills that were valued in the United States. The assumption was also frequently made that children of color and immigrant children came from families and communities where the "American values" concerning academic and occupational success were not shared. In addition, they assumed that speaking languages other than English would slow the development of the English-language skills, in turn hindering students' overall academic achievement.

Interestingly, however, recent studies of children of immigrants have provided empirical evidence that disputes these assumptions. They have shown that retention of ethnic values, bilingualism, and ethnic identity is positively related to school performance. For example, Vietnamese high school students who were more closely tied to the Vietnamese communities and more fluent in the Vietnamese language were more successful in school performance and more college oriented than those who were less integrated into the ethnic community and less fluent in their mother tongue. Similarly, bilingual Latino and Asian American children tend to perform better in school than their counterparts who are English monolingual. These phenomena are counterintuitive, since higher degrees of ethnic retention are usually thought to hinder children's school performance.

Researchers have identified several factors that have contributed to this somewhat surprising trend. First, most Latino and Asian immigrants have come to the United States seeking better living conditions and expanded career opportunities. As such, adult immigrants tend to be heavily work oriented and emphasize the value of a good education as the major channel for their children's social mobility. They have brought with them their work ethnic, frugality, punctuality, respect for adults, and value for education. Although these adults may not be able to directly assist children with schoolwork, they often attempt to enhance children's learning through other means. For example, they arrange for neighbors or relatives to supervise their children's homework study and/or enroll their children in after-school programs. In addition, immigrant parents instill in their children early on the importance of education and professional careers. It is further documented that Latinos and Asians who are new to the country are generally optimistic that success is the direct result of hard work. By contrast, African American children are often disillusioned by the realities of racism and think that their diligence frequently goes unrewarded.

Second, the children of immigrants who have retained their ethnic traditions are currently more successful in school than those who have not, partly because multicultural education in American schools makes their ethnic traditions valuable to their education. At the turn of the twentieth century, when many Europeans were immigrating to the United States, the main goal of public education was to Americanize students. Thus, the children of immigrant at that time had to lose their cultural traditions and assimilate to American culture as soon as possible to succeed in school. However, the children of contemporary immigrants benefit from multicultural education in the form of bilingual education programs, bilingual counselors, and multiethnic curricula. Accordingly, the children of immigrants who are fluent in their mother tongue and familiar with the history and culture of their parents' homeland have opportunities to connect their ethnic backgrounds to schoolwork.

Research on African American students, however, has shown a different trend. Scholars have suggested that strong ethnic retention among African Americans may, in many cases, be predictive of poor school performance. It is argued that, as a reaction to the long history of racism and cultural devaluation, African American youths often express their ethnic retention by resisting the characteristics that are valued by their oppressors (e.g., excelling in school). This phenomenon is often called cultural inversion, and it is reflected in the concept of "acting White," which is a criticism frequently used in African American communities to discredit the authenticity of their peers who perform well in school. It should, however, be noted that ethnic retention among African Americans may take another form, one in which the retention is based primarily on their bond with African American culture and communities, rather than on rejection of the mainstream culture. When strong African American ethnic retention takes this particular form, there is no compelling reason to speculate that it would lead to poor school performance. The type of ethnic retention, rather than the degree of retention per se, thus appears to predict African American students' school performance. Therefore, while ethnic retention clearly has great implications for school performance, the relationship between the two is both complex and population specific.

See also Oppositional Identity; School Segregation.

Further Reading

Akiba, Daisuke. "Effective Interventions with Children of Color: An Ecological Developmental Approach." In *Practicing Multiculturalism: Affirming Diversity in Counseling and Psychology*, edited by Timothy Smith. Boston: Allyn & Bacon, 2004.

Cross, William, Jr. *Shades of Black: Diversity in African American Identity*. Philadelphia: Temple University Press, 1991.

Rumbaut, Ruben. "The New Californians: Comparative Research Findings on the Educational Progress of Immigrant Children." In *California's Immigrant Children: Theory, Research, and Implications for Educational Policy*, edited by Ruben Rumbaut and Wayne Cornelius. San Diego: Center for U.S.-Mexican Studies, 1995.

Zhou, Min, and Carl Bankston. *Growing Up in America: How Vietnamese Children Adapt to Life in the United States*. New York: Russell Sage, 1998.

Daisuke Akiba

Ethnic Studies

Although scholars embarked on the study of racial and ethnic groups and their interrelations a long time ago, in the United States, ethnic studies as a discipline did not emerge until the late 1960s. The civil rights movement, the women's movement, anti–Vietnam War demonstrations, and the uprising of Third World peoples inspired student movements on university campuses. In 1968, students at San Francisco State College (now San Francisco State University) and the University of California at Berkeley occupied the administrative offices at both campuses and demanded fundamental changes in higher education. The movement soon spread to many other campuses throughout the country. Students of color, as well as their white supporters, demanded better access to higher education, changes in curricula to reflect their ethnic cultures and perspectives, recruitment of minority faculty, and establishment of ethnic-studies programs. As a result, ethnic-studies programs were created in the late 1960s and the early 1970s as "fire insurance" to assuage militant students. Among the pioneers programs were the School of Ethnic Studies at San Francisco State University and the Ethnic Studies Department at UC Berkeley. Following their lead, black, Asian American, Chicano/Chicana, and Native American studies programs mushroomed across the nation. Ethnic studies as a discipline grew out of this historical context.

As a discipline, ethnic studies is an interdisciplinary, multidisciplinary, and comparative study of racial and ethnic groups and their interrelations, with an emphasis on groups that have historically been neglected (Yang 2000). The domain of ethnic studies includes all social aspects of racial and ethnic groups (e.g., their histories, cultures, institutions and organizations, identities, experiences, and contributions) and intergroup relations along social, economic, spatial, and political dimensions. Ethnic studies seeks to capture the social, economic, cultural, and historical forces that shape the development of diverse racial and ethnic groups and their interrelations. Ethnic studies adopts interdisciplinary, multidisciplinary, and comparative methodologies by combining and integrating approaches of various disciplines (e.g., anthropology, economics, history, political science, psychology, sociology, philosophy, literature, linguistics, and visual arts) and by comparing the histories, cultures, experiences, and social institutions of racial and ethnic groups. Currently, the emphasis of ethnic studies is on the so-called minority groups such as African Americans, Asian Americans, Latinos, and Native Americans. A primary reason is that traditional disciplines have largely omitted the history, culture, and experiences of minority groups and their contributions to the shaping of U.S. culture and society. This partly explains why ethnic studies departments or programs are normally staffed with specialists in specific minority groups or in comparative studies of racial and ethnic groups. The discipline of ethnic studies seeks to recover and reconstruct the history of minority groups, to identify and credit their contribution to American culture and institutions, to chronicle their protests and resistance efforts, and to establish alternative values and visions, cultures and institutions (Hu-Dehart 1993, 52).

In the United States, ethnic studies currently consists of several subfields: African American studies or black studies, Asian American studies, Chicano/a studies, Puerto Rican studies, and Native American studies. All of these subfields share some common concerns, assumptions, and principles, but each subfield has its special interest in a particular minority group, is relatively autonomous, has its own constituency, and is represented by at least one national professional association, such as the American Indian Studies Association, the National Association of African American Studies, the National Council for Black Studies, the Association for Asian American Studies, the National Association of Chicano Studies, and the Puerto Rican Studies Association. Each organization convenes an annual meeting. All organizations have their own publications. There are further divisions within some of these subfields. Chinese American studies, Japanese American studies, Filipino American studies, and Korean American studies are some examples of such divisions within Asian American studies.

Today, there are more than eight hundred ethnic studies programs and departments in the nation (Bataille, Carranza, and Lisa 1996, xiii). The Comparative Ethnic Studies Department at UC Berkeley and the Department of Ethnic Studies at UC San Diego offer PhD degrees in ethnic studies. Scores of other universities offer master's degree and/or a bachelor's degree programs in ethnic studies or in one of its subfields. In recent years, an increasing number of elite research universities outside the West have been making genuine efforts in establishing ethnic-studies programs, partly as a response to student demonstrations or demands. The institutionalization of ethnic-studies programs has been accompanied by a growing number of faculty engaged in ethnic-studies teaching and research. The establishment of ethnic-studies departments or programs and the recruitment of full-time faculty in ethnic studies have resulted in a prodigious amount of scholarship. Increasingly, ethnic-studies courses have gained importance, becoming requirements for degree programs or a more prominent portion of curricula. This trend is likely to continue in the near future as American society becomes increasingly multiethnic and the ethnic composition of the college-student population continues to diversify.

See also Diversities, Ethnic and Racial; Multiculturalism.

Further Reading

Bataille, Gretchen, Miguel Carranza, and Laurie Lisa. *Ethnic Studies in the United States: A Guide to Research*. New York: Garland Publishing, 1996.

Hu-DeHart, Evelyn. "The History, Development, and Future of Ethnic Studies." *Phi Delta Kappan* (September 1993).

Yang, Philip. *Ethnic Studies: Issues and Approaches*. Albany: State University of New York Press, 2000.

Philip Yang

Ethnocentrism

Ethnocentrism is the tendency to evaluate other groups by the standards and values of one's own. It means that one's own group is the center of everything. Other groups, including their cultural practices, beliefs, lifestyles and even languages, are understood in reference to one's own. Such evaluation is usually negative. This produces a view of one's own group as being superior to others. Unlike racism, which is historically constructed, ethnocentrism is a universal belief and practice among people. Ethnocentric views have often been encouraged to help enhance group solidarity and cohesiveness. At the same time, this way of thinking has been the basis of separation, misunderstanding, misconception, hatred, and conflict between groups. Ethnocentrism encourages the creation of negative stereotypes, which lead to prejudice and discrimination and can escalate into xenophobia.

Throughout U.S. history, Americans have often demonstrated an ethnocentric view of the world. In the initial contact between European settlers and Native Americans, ethnocentrism was the dominant attitude of the settlers toward the "Indians" they encountered. The effort of Christianizing them was based on an ethnocentric assumption. White Americans' ethnocentric view of Chinese immigrants created the negative stereotype of the "yellow peril" that developed into the xenophobia of the 1870s and 1880s and culminated in the Chinese Exclusion Act of 1882. Nativism and anti-immigrant movements throughout U.S. history have been based on the ethnocentric view of white Anglo Protestantism as a superior culture into which all other groups should be assimilated. Movements against the Jewish immigrants and Catholics were also supported by white Protestants' ethnocentrism.

See also Afrocentrism.

Heon Cheol Lee

Ethnogenesis

The term *ethnogenesis* was coined by David Greenstone and made popular by Andrew Greeley in his 1974 book *Ethnicity in the United States: A Preliminary Reconnaissance*. Literally, ethnogenesis means "the creation of an ethnic group" or "ethnicization." In contrast to assimilationism, the aim of which is ethnic homogenization, Greeley proposed ethnogenesis as an alternative perspective for looking at ethnic differentiation in American society. The main argument of this perspective is that, over time, immigrant groups will share more common characteristics with the host group, but they still, to varying degrees, retain and modify some components of their ethnic culture, and they also create new cultural elements in response to the host social environment by incorporating their own culture and the host culture. This perspective emphasizes the importance of studying the genesis and history of ethnic groups.

Greeley developed the ethnogenesis perspective to explain the adaptation experience of European immigrants. According to Greeley, at the beginning the host group and the immigrant group may have some things in common. For instance, the Irish could speak English, and some groups were Protestants. As a result of adaptation over generations, the common culture enlarges. The immigrant group becomes similar to the host group, and the host group also becomes somewhat similar to the immigrant group. However, the immigrant group still keeps some elements of its culture and institutions, modifies some of its cultural and social structural characteristics, and creates some new cultural elements in response to the challenge of the host society. The result is a new ethnic group with a cultural system that is a combination of the common culture and its unique heritage mixed in the American crucible. The ethnogenesis perspective integrates assimilation theory and cultural pluralism theory by incorporating the ideas of partial assimilation, partial retention of ethnic culture, and the modification and creation of ethnic cultural elements in the same framework.

Philip Yang

Eugenics Movement

The ideas of the Eugenics movement come out of Social Darwinism. Social Darwinists took Charles Darwin's idea of the survival of the fittest in nature and applied it to human beings. They believed that desirable social traits such as intelligence and morality were inherited and that some groups—particularly racial groups—were superior to others. Sir Francis Galton, an English scientist and a cousin of Darwin, founded eugenics in 1883, and he referred to it as the science of manipulating the processes of evolutionary selection to improve a particular genetic stock or population. Galton's emphasis was on the role of social control to either improve or impair the qualities of future generations. *Negative eugenics* refers to efforts to decrease reproduction by those who are believed to have undesirable qualities. Positive eugenics refers to attempts to increase reproduction by desirable stock.

The eugenics movement in the United States began in 1906, forwarded by Charles Benedict Davenport, a biologist with a PhD from Harvard University. To create a strong American "race," the Eugenics movement in the United States attempted to promote childbearing among the "fittest" people and to discourage it among the "unfit." The eugenicists argued that the United States was in immediate danger of committing "racial suicide" as a result of the rapid reproduction of nonwhite, feebleminded, immigrant, and criminal classes, as well as the decline in the birthrate of the better classes. They advocated a program of positive eugenics, including eugenic education, tax preferences, and other financial support, to encourage reproduction among people of high class, character, and intelligence. They also advocated negative eugenic measures such as compulsory sterilization for the mentally ill, restrictive marriage laws, (including antimiscegenation laws), and strong restrictions on immigration. During this time, thirty of the forty-eight American states passed eugenic sterilization laws authorizing the voluntary or involuntary sterilization of certain citizens, such as the supposedly feebleminded. A 1927 U.S. Supreme Court decision (*Buck v. Bell*) upheld a state's right to do so. By 1936, when medical experts formally condemned compulsory eugenical sterilization, more than twenty thousand forced sterilizations had been performed and more than five hundred patients had died during surgery. Most of the sterilizations had been performed on poor patients—a disproportionate number of whom were black—in state-run mental hospitals and residential facilities for the mentally retarded.

Madison Grant was one of the leading proponents of eugenics. His 1916 book, *The Passing of the Great Race*, argued against the idea that all people are created equal and instead suggested that the "Negroid" and "Mongoloid" races (Blacks and Asians) were inferior to whites. Eugenicists feared that if the allegedly unfit were permitted to reproduce, they would create an inferior "race" of people and that this would threaten American democracy by making the American people unfit to govern themselves. Eugenicists also attempted to preserve the American "race" by limiting immigration of groups that they considered to be inferior, such as Jews, Greeks, and Italians. They also promoted antimiscegenation laws to prevent "race-mixing." The eugenics movement was popular and respectable in the United States until the rise of Nazism in Europe. The Nazi movement took the principles of eugenics to its logical and brutal extreme by murdering Jews, homosexuals, and other so-called undesirable groups in the name of racial purity.

See also Biological Racism; *The Passing of the Great Race*.

Robin Roger-Dillon and Tracy Chu

Executive Order 9066

On February 19, 1942, shortly after the American declaration of war on Japan, President Franklin D. Roosevelt signed Executive Order 9066, allowing military commanders, as a matter of national security, to prescribe military zones over the West Coast. Lieutenant General John L. DeWitt, the commander of the Western Defense Command, ordered that all individuals of Japanese ancestry, aliens and citizens alike, be removed *en masse* from the western half of the three Pacific states—California, Oregon, and Washington—and the southern third of Arizona and be relocated in internment camps inland, arguing these areas were most vulnerable to attack, invasion, espionage, and sabotage. Despite Attorney General Bibble's denial of the possibility of wholesale internment and Lt. Gen. DeWitt's initial unwillingness, a mass evacuation was soon underway in March 1942. People of Japanese ancestry in those states were forced to leave behind anything that they could not carry. They were first sent to fifteen "assembly centers," and then to ten "relocation centers," which were surrounded by barbed wires and watchtowers. More than 110,000 of the 126,000 individuals of Japanese ancestry in those regions, over 70,000 of whom were U.S. citizens, were forcefully relocated from their homes with no warrants or indictments.

This tragic policy, which inflicted indescribable economic and emotional scars, and undermined the belief in American democracy among Japanese Americans, can hardly be justified as a legitimate security measure in wartime, particularly because Japanese Americans in Hawaii and German and Italian Americans did not suffer the same fate. The political powerlessness of Japanese Americans in the West Coast in the face of popular racial prejudice would account for the war hysteria. In 1988, the federal government compensated Japanese internees for the damages.

See also Executive Order 9981; Japanese American Internment; Japanese Americans, Redress Movement for.

Dong-Ho Cho

Executive Order 9981

In 1948, President Harry S. Truman issued Executive Order 9981, calling for the racial integration of the military. The order stipulated that there should be equality of opportunity for all persons in the armed forces, without regard to race, color, or national origin. After World War II Jim Crow practices within the military became increasingly embarrassing to the U.S. leaders, because it bluntly highlighted the disparity between the American ideal and its reality. In 1948, Truman and Congress considered institutionalizing a peacetime military draft. A. Philip Randolph, an architect of the March on Washington, threatened a national boycott, unless the military was desegregated. He said, "I personally will advise Negroes to refuse to fight as slaves for a democracy that they cannot possess and cannot enjoy." Moreover, civil rights became one of the main issues in the 1948 presidential election. In spite of opposition from some of the top generals, Truman took decisive steps to end all segregation in the U.S. armed forces. By 1952, the army, navy, and air force were largely integrated. But the executive order was not as vigorously enforced in the National Guard.

Truman also issued Executive Order 9980, establishing the Fair Employment Board to ensure equal treatment of minorities in federal hiring. Although the actual achievements of these orders were limited, they nevertheless unleashed expectations and desires that the subsequent governments could hardly restrain.

See also Executive Order 9066.

Dong-Ho Cho

Expatriation

After World War I, Europe, especially France, became a popular destination for African American writers, artists, musicians, and intellectuals who wanted to live abroad. During World War I, the French population welcomed African

American soldiers, who were subject to widespread racial discrimination and mistreatment both in the military and at home. After the war, veterans and other African Americans continued to move to Europe, attracted by stories of a culturally accepting environment and by professional appreciation and acclaim that was not available to them in the United States. Expatriates included such notables as writer Langston Hughes, performer Josephine Baker, and jazz greats Miles Davis, Charlie Parker, and Bill Coleman.

After World War II, African American expatriates with Communist sympathies, including novelist Richard Wright, went to Europe to escape Senator Eugene McCarthy's investigations. Other expatriates of this era included writers James Baldwin and Chester Himes and jazz musician Lester Young.

Tracy Chu

Exposure Index

Researchers studying racial/ethnic segregation of residential areas or school systems sometimes use an "exposure index" as a measure, either in conjunction with or as an alternative to the index of dissimilarity. For ex-

Josephine Baker as an expatriate in Paris, 1949.

Library of Congress, Prints & Photographs Division, Carl Van Vechten Collection; LC-USZ62-93000.

ample, an exposure index can be computed to rank a city's schools in terms of how much interracial contact they provide in their classrooms. In doing this, exposure-index computations indicate, for students who are black (or for any race/ethnicity being studied), the average percentage of their classmates who are black and the average percentage that are of some other race/ethnicity. In other words, this index measures how much or little exposure the average member of one racial/ethnic group has in his or her classroom (or in a neighborhood, if one is studying residential segregation) to fellow members of the group and to members of other groups. Zero is the lowest value an exposure index can have, if a school's index measuring exposure of blacks to whites is 0, then black students in that school do not have any whites in their classes. If the black-to-white exposure index is 40 (or 0.40 if proportions are used), then the average black student is in a class in which 40 percent of his or her classmates are white; 100 (or 1.00) is the maximum value.

An interesting feature of exposure indexes is that they are "asymmetrical," unlike the index of dissimilarity and other measures of segregation. This means that exposure indexes reflect the principle that the level of contact experienced by a pair of groups can vary depending on from which group's perspective one views the situation. For example, in a school in which most classes comprise many whites and few Latinos (e.g., twenty-eight white students and two Latino students), the white-to-Latino exposure index is low, but the Latino-to-white exposure index is high. This distinction is important in comprehending the results of research on school re-segregation reported by organizations such as the Harvard University Civil Rights Project.

See also Index of Dissimilarity.

Charles Jaret

F

Fair Housing Act of 1968

The Fair Housing Act of 1968 (technically Title VIII of the broader Civil Rights Act of 1968) declared illegal most forms of discrimination based on race, color, religion, and national origin in the sale or rental of housing units. Later, Congress amended and expanded this act several times, notably in 1974, when housing discrimination based on sex was made illegal, and in 1988, when housing discrimination based on family status (e.g., having children under eighteen years of age) or on handicap or disability were outlawed. Because of the original and amended Fair Housing Act, sellers of housing units and their agents are not allowed to indicate in their advertising a preference for or bias against people of a particular race, color, religion, nationality, sex, familial status, or disability category. Neither can they use a person's membership in one of those categories as the reason for refusing to sell or rent a housing unit or for establishing different terms, conditions, or privileges regarding the unit being bought or rented. The act also prohibits racial "block-busting" and protects these categories against discrimination by financial institutions when seeking home mortgages or money for other home-related transactions. Block-busting refers to the tactic of real estate agents to create the impression among whites that the arrival of blacks in their neighborhoods will increase crime and decrease the value of their homes.

Fair-housing legislation faced much opposition in the 1960s. A similar bill failed in 1967. Many experts believe that the only reason it became law (on April 10, 1968) was to calm racial tensions and rioting that erupted right after the assassination of Rev. Martin Luther King Jr. the previous week. Initially, civil rights activists complained that the 1968 law had weak enforcement provisions, was underfunded by Congress, and had several loopholes, all of which enabled racial discrimination in housing to persist. Later amendments strengthened the law and gave the U.S. Department of Housing and Urban Development and the Department of Justice authority to investigate and bring lawsuits against people charged with housing discrimination.

See also Block-busting; Civil Rights Act of 1968; Fair Housing Amendments Act of 1988; Fair-Housing Audit; Federal Housing Administration (FHA); Housing Discrimination; King, Martin Luther Jr.; U.S. Department of Housing and Urban Development (HUD); White Flight.

Charles Jaret

Fair Housing Amendments Act of 1988

The Fair Housing Amendments Act of 1988 strengthened the provisions of the Fair Housing Act of 1968 by giving the U.S. Department of Housing and Urban Development (HUD) greater power to enforce the 1968 legislation.

What is known as the Fair Housing Act was actually Title VIII of the landmark Civil Rights Act of 1968. Title VIII made illegal public and private discrimination based on race, color, religion, and national origin in the sale, rental, and financing of housing. In 1974, discrimination based on gender was also prohibited. In the twenty years after passage of the original act, it became apparent that the compromises made on enforcement provisions left the act itself without clout. HUD could accept complaints, but its power ended with investigating them and seeking reconciliation. If settlement was not possible, private lawsuits with punitive damage awards of no more $1,000 were the alternative, although the Department of Justice did have authority to bring lawsuits in cases of actual discrimination and patterns of discrimination.

The 1988 amendments put teeth in enforcement by mandating HUD to enforce the law. They revised the fair-housing enforcement provisions by allowing HUD attorneys, in places where HUD has jurisdiction, to bring cases before HUD's administrative law judges for victims of discrimination and by expanding the jurisdiction of the Department of Justice to bring suit on behalf of victims in federal district courts. Complainants can also go directly to federal court. If a complaint comes from a state or region that HUD has certified as having similar fair-housing laws, the complaint goes to the local human-rights agency. Remedies were also increased and enhanced.

The 1988 amendments also extended the act to cover discrimination based on disability and discrimination based on family status, including pregnancy and the presence of children under eighteen. With these amendments, landlords and rental agents were required to make reasonable accommodations to allow a disabled person equal opportunity to enjoy housing. Multifamily housing to be first occupied on or after March 13, 1991, had to meet new federal design guidelines.

See also Block-busting; Civil Rights Act of 1968; Fair Housing Act of 1968; "Fair Housing Audit"; Federal Housing Administration (FHA); Housing Discrimination; King, Martin Luther Jr.; U.S. Department of Housing and Urban Development (HUD); White Flight.

Benjamin F. Shearer

Fair-Housing Audit

The best way to test for and detect the presence or absence of systematic discrimination in a housing market is to perform a series of fair-housing audits on real estate agencies and/or apartment-leasing managers. As the name implies, fair-housing audits check to see how often the official "gatekeepers" of housing (e.g., real estate agents and apartment managers) treat people equally when they seek homes or apartments, acting without regard to their race, ethnicity, sex, age, and so forth, and how often they provide unequal service to people who differ on those criteria.

In a typical fair-housing audit, many pairs of testers visit real estate agencies and apartment complexes in a metropolitan area. Each member of a pair of testers visits at a different time of day, but they request housing that is similar in terms of price, size, style, and age. Members of the testing pair pretend to have similar incomes and occupational standing, as well as a like marital status and lifestyle. To test for racial/ethnic discrimination, the only difference between each member of the testing pair is their race/ethnicity (e.g., one tester white and the other, black; one is Hispanic, the other, non-Hispanic, etc.). During their respective visits, each tester takes note of the real estate agent's responsiveness to him or her, especially on matters like the number and locations of homes described and inspected, offers of assistance in finding or applying for mortgage loans, and the professionalism and sincerity of effort evinced by the real estate agent. Each tester then independently prepares a detailed report describing the real estate agent's behavior. The last step in the audit involves the research staff, which analyzes the testers' reports to see whether there is a statistical pattern in which more favorable treatment is given to one group or another (e.g., racial steering to different quality areas). If so, this may be used to initiate or substantiate a claim of housing discrimination, and the audit data may be taken into account should there be mediation or a lawsuit on this matter.

See also Block-busting; Civil Rights Act of 1968; *Closed Doors, Opportunities Lost: The Continuing Costs of Housing Discrimination*; Fair Housing Amendments Act of 1988; Federal Housing Administration (FHA); Housing Discrimination; King, Martin Luther, Jr.; U.S. Department of Housing and Urban Development (HUD); White Flight.

Charles Jaret

Fair-Weather Liberals

"Fair-weather liberals," according to sociologist Robert K. Merton, are those who are not prejudiced but still discriminate against members of minority groups. They are inconsistent in their racial attitudes and discriminatory behaviors. What make them inconsistent are situational conditions such as normative expectations from one's reference group or any rewards for the discrimination. In other words, Merton argues that racial prejudice and discrimination do not necessarily go together. It is highly probable that people are prejudiced but do not discriminate because of the situational factors. It is also probable that people are not prejudiced and yet discriminate because of social expectations. He suggested four ideal types of people by combining the presence or absence of racial prejudice and discrimination: prejudiced discriminators as "active bigots," prejudiced nondiscriminators as "timid bigots," unprejudiced discriminators as "fair-weather liberals," and unprejudiced nondiscriminators as "all-weather liberals."

If a white college student joins a racist fraternity without knowing its racist practices, and yet wants to stay in the group as a member, he may have to discriminate against minority students to belong to the group. He is a fair-weather liberal. In the Old South it is probable that some white people had to discriminate against blacks to be accepted in their community. They were fair-weather liberals. The great contribution of Merton's theory of racial discrimination is his stress on the importance of social conditions in explaining discrimination. To reduce racial discrimination, people's behaviors, instead of their attitudes, should be changed through enacting and enforcing applicable laws. Then, eventually, their attitudes will change to meet the legally regulated behaviors.

See also Archie Bunker Bigotry; Bigots, Types of.

Further Reading

Merton, R. K. "Discrimination and American Creed." In *Discrimination and National Welfare*, edited by R. M. MacIver, 99–126. New York: Institute for Religious and Social Studies, 1949.

Heon Cheol Lee

Farrakhan, Louis (1933–   )

Louis (Abdul Haleem) Farrakhan is a controversial minister and the current leader of the Nation of Islam, a national religious organization in the United States that embraces elements of Islam, Black Nationalism, and separatism. Although he has detractors, Farrakhan has developed a reputation as a critic of racism and discrimination and is considered by some to be an influential leader in the black community. Farrakhan was born Louis Eugene Walcott, May 11, 1933, in New York City and grew up in Boston, Massachusetts. After attending Winston-Salem Teachers' College in North Carolina, Farrakhan worked as a musician and singer. In 1955, while in Chicago to perform, he attended an American Muslim Mission convention, subsequently joined the movement, and changed his name to Minister Louis X and later to Minister Louis Farrakhan. He served as Minister of the Muhammad Temple No. 11 in Boston. Although initially he was recruited and mentored by Malcolm X, Farrakhan would later renounce Malcolm X and, after Malcolm's death, replace him as the Minister of Temple No. 7 in New York City in May 1965. After the death of Elijah Muhammad in 1975, and due to ideological differences with Wallace Muhammad, his successor, Farrakhan formed his own sect, the Nation of Islam. Known for his charismatic and sometimes controversial speeches, Farrakhan emphasizes black economic development, self-help, black solidarity, and personal respon-

Nation of Islam Minister Louis Farrakhan gives a speech at a Baptist church in Brooklyn, 1996.

AP/Wide World Photos.

sibility for black men. In 1979, he developed the internationally circulated newspaper The *Final Call*. Farrakhan most recently gained recognition for his involvement in organizing the Million Man March in Washington, D.C., in 1995. Farrakhan is married to Betsy Farrakhan and is the father of nine children.

See also Malcolm X; Million Man March on Washington; Muhammad, Elijah; Nation of Islam.

Sandra L. Barnes

Federal Housing Administration (FHA)

The Federal Housing Administration (FHA) was created in 1934 as one of the many "alphabet" agencies of Franklin Roosevelt's administration. Its purpose was to stimulate home ownership in the depths of the Depression at a time when millions of construction workers were unemployed, maximum mortgage loans were 50 percent of the property's value, and only 40 percent of Americans owned a home. By 2001, 68 percent of Americans owned their own homes thanks in large part to FHA programs.

The FHA has increased home ownership by insuring mortgages made by approved lenders, to lessen their risk on unconventional loans. Unlike conforming conventional loans, FHA-insured loans require a smaller down payment and allow for more latitude in determining household income and payout ratios. But the FHA also discriminated against African Americans by using racially restrictive covenants as a means of ensuring the security of neighborhoods. In evaluating the stability of a neighborhood, the agency focused on whether properties there will continue to be "occupied by the same social and racial classes." As a result of this policy, the vast majority of FHA mortgages went to white, middle-class suburbs; few were awarded to black neighborhoods in central cities. The FHA's bias for granting mortgages for suburban white middle-class neighborhoods and pattern of disinvestment in black neighborhoods were most evident in the 1940s, but its racist practices continued in the 1950s. They contributed not only to the huge racial gap in home ownership, but also to racial segregation.

See also Housing Discrimination; Restrictive Covenants; U.S. Department of Housing and Urban Development (HUD).

Benjamin F. Shearer

FHA

See Federal Housing Administration (FHA).

Films and Racial Stereotypes

Does art imitate life or does life imitate art? This is an often-posed question, but the answer is all the more important when considering the racial stereotypes that are transmitted by films. Films are primarily sources of entertainment, but for many, they also serve as educational tools. They expose many people to worlds they have not had the opportunity to encounter.

In a media-obsessed world, films are tools that people frequently use to help them assess situations. Trying to categorize people is natural and serves as an efficient way to determine how to interact with others, but it is dangerous to rely on these categories when they are stereotypes, or exaggerated generalizations that are applied without consideration of natural variations. When such stereotypes were prevalent in society without any censure, it was inevitable that they would also be prevalent in films. Stereotypes have come to be denounced and treated as politically incorrect, and they have slowly faded from films. But the images have not completely faded and film is immortal, so the stereotypical images of the past live forever.

Early films, such as *Birth of a Nation* (1915), depicted minorities as savages whose predilection for violence was a constant threat to civilized white people. By the 1930s, minorities were no longer primarily depicted as savages. Instead, they were most often cast as servants for white families, e.g., *Gone With the Wind* (1939). Despite society's penchant for political correctness, examples of stereotypical images still abound. African Americans are frequently depicted as being sexually promiscuous, loud, uneducated, poor, and criminal. Few mainstream films depict African American males in intimate relationships. Most images of the African American family in film continue to promote the notion that all African American families are dysfunctional.

Images of Hispanic Americans in films have been every bit as stereotypical as images of African Americans. Silent films such as *Tony the Greaser* (1911), *Bronco Billy and the Greaser* (1914), and *The Greaser's Revenge* (1914) depicted Mexican Americans as violent, dishonest, and criminal. By the 1950s, Hispanic actors continued to receive few leading roles. Instead, white actors were frequently asked to portray Hispanic characters, as in films such as *Touch of Evil* (1958) and *Viva Zapata!* (1952). In the 1960s, the greaser image dominated films about Hispanics once again and led to the emergence of the image of the urban greaser in films such as *The Warriors* (1979), *Boulevard Nights* (1979), and *Walk Proud* (1979). By the end of the twentieth century, independent filmmakers began to provide more diverse images of Hispanic Americans. Still, many mainstream

Early films, such as D. W. Griffith's *The Birth of a Nation*, portrayed minorities as violent savages.

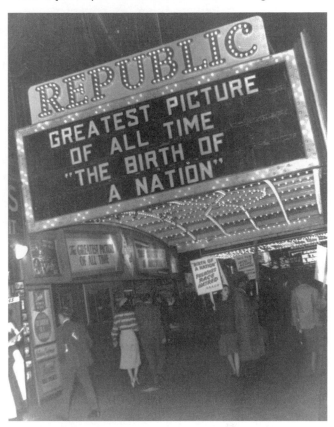

Courtesy Library of Congress.

films continue to present Latinos as uneducated, unable to speak English, poor, and primarily employed in menial occupations. Latino men in particular are treated as hypermasculine, cartoonlike characters.

Four dominant images of Asian Americans have emerged in mainstream films. The stock image treats Asian characters as expendable or interchangeable. The mysterious villain image plays into anti-immigrant attitudes. The Banzai war crime image became popular during World War II when the loyalty of Japanese Americans was called into question. The image that has been most difficult to shake is the China Doll or Geisha character. Asian American women were portrayed as submissive, exotic, sex objects in films such as *The Thief of Bagdad* (1924), *Old San Francisco* (1927), and *The World of Susie Wong* (1959). In modern films, Asian Americans are portrayed as docile, industrious, conservative, and cliquish. They are identified as America's "model minority." This term seems positive, but it also trivializes challenges that are faced by members of the Asian American community by suggesting that they have no problems that need to be addressed by the larger society. Although Asian Americans continue to be treated as foreigners in films, their role as the instantly recognizable villain has been passed onto Arab Americans in films such as *The Siege* (1998).

Perhaps the most influential stereotype is the most subtle one. Minority actors are frequently relegated to second-class status in films. Even at the start of the twenty-first century, minority actors are not equal to white actors in their roles. In most instances, African American actors are used to support or prop up the lead actors, who typically are white. Even in films in which equal billing is given to the lead white and nonwhite actors (e.g., *Lethal Weapon* movies), the white character usually takes on the high-profile, take-charge, heroic role. These limited images are transmitted time and time again, with very few alternative images to balance them. Certainly, white Americans are stereotyped in films as well. The difference, however, is that many alternative images of whiteness are offered.

See also Fu Manchu; *The Godfather*; Hollywood and Minority Actors; Music Industry, Racism in; Television and Racial Stereotypes; *West Side Story*.

Further Reading

Bernardi, Daniel, ed. *Classic Hollywood, Classic Whiteness*. Minneapolis: University of Minnesota Press, 2001.

Miller, Randall, ed. *Ethnic Images in American Film and Television*. Philadelphia: Balch Institute, 1978.

Toplin, Robert B., ed. *Hollywood as Mirror: Changing Views of "Outsiders" and "Enemies" in American Movies*. Westport, CT: Greenwood Press, 1993.

Romney S. Norwood

Financial Institutions and Racial Discrimination

In spite of federal laws that prohibit discrimination in lending, studies continue to demonstrate that racial discrimination persists in the lending of funds for homes, cars, businesses, and farms. A landmark study by the Federal Reserve Bank of Boston in 1990 documented disparities in mortgage-lending patterns between nonwhites and whites in the Boston area. It also found that African Americans were three times more likely than whites to have a loan application rejected. A supplemental report that controlled for important economic factors, like credit histories, still left whites with higher approval rates than blacks. The Geographic Information System Action for Economic and Social Justice project conducted a larger study of sixteen metropolitan areas in 1993 and found absolute evidence of redlining—lenders drawing theoretical red lines around minority neighborhoods—and not making mortgages available within those lines. This practice can account for higher loan costs to the borrowers and thus lower home-ownership ratios for those affected. If African Americans were no longer to bear the brunt of illegal lending policies, the federal government had to begin enforcing its laws. The government had indeed begun enforcing the law when the Justice Department brought suit against the Decatur Federal Savings & Loan Association of Atlanta in 1992. In a consent decree, Decatur paid damages of $1 million to loan applicants and agreed to adopt a marketing plan that did not exclude black neighborhoods or discriminate against potential loan applicants.

Still, discrimination continued. A 1998 study by the California branch of the Association of Community Organizations for Reform Now (ACORN) looked at nine thousand lenders in thirty-five cities around the country. It found that nationwide, of all those applying for conventional mortgages, African Americans were 2.1 times more likely, and Latinos, 1.76 times more likely, to be rejected than whites. Furthermore, as the number of conventional loans made to whites increased 24 percent between 1995 and 1997, loans to African Americans increased only 5 percent, and loans to Latinos, 1 percent. The Urban Institute reported in 1999 that mortgage-lending discrimination existed from the beginning of the process to its end. Another ACORN report found that, in 2001, the likelihood of loan rejections for African Americans and Latinos had not changed much. Even as the Department of Justice continued to prosecute discriminatory lending cases, like the 2002 redlining case against Mid America Bank in Chicago, many studies showed that the pattern of discrimination goes on in mortgage lending. A National Community Reinvestment Coalitions report issued in 2003 found that African Americans were more likely than whites to have high-cost subprime loans rather than conventional loans, even when their credit risk was factored out. That 74 percent of whites and only 47 percent of blacks nationwide are homeowners reveals the reality of mortgage-lending discrimination.

Lending discrimination in car loans is also a problem. It is legal for car dealers to increase the interest rates fixed by lenders, which are determined by credit history and income. When dealers mark up the rate charged to the customer, they split the profit with the lenders. However, if black car buyers' loans are marked up more than white car buyers' loan, there is discrimination. Studies showed that nationally, blacks were charged over $600 more than whites through these markups. General Motors settled a class-action suit against it alleging discriminatory markups by its General Motors Acceptance Corporation early in 2004. Class-action suits are pending against WFS Financial, Inc. (a lender that works with thousands of dealers), American Honda Finance Company, and Toyota Motor Credit Corporation.

It is estimated that minorities own nearly 15 percent of small businesses nationwide—Hispanics about 6 percent, and blacks and Asians each around 4 percent. However, numerous studies have consistently found that minorities do not have equal access to capital, or put another way, are discriminated against when applying for business loans. One study even found a loan denial rate for whites of 27 percent and for blacks, 66 percent. The National Community Reinvestment Coalition found disparities in small-business loans by income and percentage of minorities in Washington, DC, neighborhoods. Most controlled studies confirm a loan denial rate for black-owned small businesses twice that of white-owned businesses. Financial institutions make less than 1 percent of their small-business loans to black-, Latino-, and Asian American-owned businesses.

Black farmers have also experienced lending discrimination, most notably by the federal government itself. It came to light in 1997 that employees in the U.S. Department of Agriculture had for decades been systematically denying black farmers crop loans and other federal support to which they were entitled. In several southeastern states, the county committees that granted the loans processed loans of whites three times faster than those of blacks. Most of these local committees had no minority representation. As a result, many lost their land. Only 18,000 black farmers of the 925,000 who were counted in 1920 remained by 1992. In the class-action suit that followed this revelation, black farmers and former farmers who documented loan denials were compensated with over $630 million.

See also Capitalism and Racial Inequality; *Economics and Politics of Race*; Economics of Discrimination; Housing Discrimination; Laissez-Faire Racism.

Further Reading

Myers, Samuel, and Tsze Chan. "Racial Discrimination in Housing Markets: Accounting for Credit Risk." *Social Science Quarterly* 76 (1995): 543–561.

Shlay, Anne B. "Not in That Neighborhood: The Effects of Population and Housing on the Distribution of Mortgage Finance within the Chicago SMSA." *Social Science Research* 17 (1988): 152–163.

Benjamin F. Shearer

Henry Ford, best known for founding Ford Motor Company, was a notorious racist and anti-Semite.

Courtesy Library of Congress.

Forced Relocation

See Native Americans, Forced Relocation of.

Ford, Henry (1863–1947)

Best known for his role in starting Ford Motor Company and developing an assembly-line system for producing automobiles that made them affordable to the masses, Henry Ford was also a notorious racist and anti-Semite. He published many essays in the local newspaper he financed, the *Dearborn Independent*, alleging that Jews had an international conspiracy to cheat non-Jews out of money and power. These essays were later collected into a book called *The International Jew*, which was distributed free of charge at Ford dealerships. In addition, he contributed money to the Nazi party in Germany during its early years and was well respected by Adolph Hitler, who saw him fit to receive the Grand Cross, then Nazi Germany's highest honor. Ford also segregated the African American workers whom he employed in his early factories but did pay them as well as his white employees, which was a major cause for African American migration to Detroit from the rural southern states. Although a libel suit eventually forced Ford to issue an apology for his writing, he continued to express his anti-Semitic views for the rest of his life. The Ford Motor Company continues to this day to work to overcome its founder's reputation, through such actions as sponsoring a newtork broadcast of *Schindler's List*, Steven Spielberg's film about the Holocaust.

See also Anti-Semitism in the United States.

Mikaila Mariel Lemonik Arthur

Foreign Miners License Tax

In 1850, at the height of the gold rush, the California state legislature enacted the Foreign Miners License Tax to protect white miners from Mexican, Chilean, Hawaiian, and Chinese competition. The $20 monthly tax was levied on every foreign miner who was ineligible for citizenship. As the 1790 U.S. federal law precluded nonwhites from citizenship, Chinese and others inevitably fell under the tax. In 1852, the Foreign Miners License Tax was reenacted and directed at the growing Chinese population. Arguing for the tax, a committee of the California State Assembly reported that Chinese miners differed in customs and language, were "servile contract laborers," and by their presence discouraged whites from coming to California. By the time the tax was repealed by the federal Civil Rights Act of 1870, tax receipts in California totaled $5 million, representing up to 50 percent of all state revenues during the lifetime of the tax, almost all paid by Chinese workers. The Foreign Miners License Tax proved to be only the first among many laws aimed at excluding Chinese from full and equal participation in American society, a trend culminating in the Chinese Exclusion Act of 1882.

See also Asian Americans, Discrimination against; Chinese Exclusion Act of 1882.

Kenneth J. Guest

Fourteenth Amendment

Ratified July 9, 1868, the Fourteenth Amendment was central to the reconstruction agenda after the Civil War. Following the Thirteenth Amendment, which abolished slavery, in 1865, the Fourteenth Amendment was designed to protect the rights of Southern blacks, but it has had wide-ranging implications for all Americans. The amendment's most-noted clauses conferred U.S. citizenship on the basis of birth or naturalization, required equal protection under the law for all citizens, and barred states from depriving "any person of life, liberty or property without due process of the law." In addition, the amendment encouraged states to allow blacks to vote, though did not require it, barred from public office officials who had rebelled against the Union, and rejected claims of Confederate war debt.

Interpretation of the Fourteenth Amendment became a central battleground in landmark civil rights cases in the ensuing years. In *Plessy v. Fergusson*, an 1896 case involving the legality of segregating railroad passengers by race, the U.S. Supreme Court held that separate but equal facilities did not violate the Fourteenth Amendment. In 1954, however, a unanimous Supreme Court reversed course and ruled in *Brown v. Board of Education* that separate but equal school facilities did violate the equal-protection clause of the Fourteenth Amendment. The court's subsequent, 1955 decision, often referred to as *Brown II*, instructed the states to begin school desegregation plans as quickly as possible.

See also Brown v. Board of Education of Topeka; Reconstruction Era; Separate but Equal Doctrine.

Kenneth J. Guest

Frank, Leo (d. 1915)

The April 26, 1913, murder of Mary Phagan, a twelve-year-old girl employed in an Atlanta factory, initiated a sensational chain of events culminating in the lynching of Leo Frank, the man convicted of this crime but who was probably innocent. This bloody incident has been the subject of books, articles, films, exhibits, and a musical. It is of historical significance because bound up in these two murders and the reactions to them are the central tensions, changes, and conflicts that the American South experienced in the early twentieth century: industrialization and class conflict, anti-Semitism, new racial stereotypes and etiquette, discomfort with newcomers from the North, and changing gender roles and work roles for females.

The murder of a young girl who had to work in a factory outraged the public. Leo Frank, a Jew from New York, was superintendent of the factory in which Mary Phagan worked and was killed. He and six Georgians were arrested, and with little evidence the prosecutor put Frank on trial. During and after the trial, anti-Semitic rhetoric flowed, led by Tom Watson, who was well known for his hatred of blacks and Jews. Frank was convicted and sentenced to death. While appealing the verdict, threats on his life made it necessary to transfer him from Atlanta to a prison in Milledgeville, Georgia. After hearing evidence that cast doubt on the verdict, Governor John Slaton commuted Frank's sentence to life in prison. This enraged those who believed Frank guilty and wanted him to die. On August 17, 1915, a group calling them-

The lynching of Leo Frank, Marietta, Georgia, 1915.

Courtesy Library of Congress.

selves the Knights of Mary Phagan abducted Frank from prison, brought him to Marietta, and lynched him. This case soon led to organizing along very different directions: the Anti-Defamation League of B'nai B'rith gained support in its fight against anti-Semitism, while the Ku Klux Klan was revived to defend white Protestant Americans against perceived threats. Much later, in 1986, Georgia posthumously pardoned Frank.

See also Anti-Defamation League of B'nai Brith (ADL); Anti-Semitism in the United States; Ku Klux Klan (KKK).

Charles Jaret

Freedmen's Bureau

After nearly two years of debate, on March 3, 1865, Congress finally established the Bureau of Refugees, Freedmen and Abandoned Lands, known as the Freedmen's Bureau, in the War Department. It was to last only for one year after the war and had a broad mandate to supervise and manage all abandoned lands and control everything having to do with refugees and freedmen from rebellious states and army-occupied lands. With presidential approval, the appointed commissioner was to make rules and regulations as needed to carry out the bureau's tasks, which also included setting apart tracts of abandoned or confiscated land in Confederate states for freedmen and refugees in forty-acre parcels. These parcels were to be rented by the re-

The Misses Cooke's school room, one of the schools established for former slaves by the Freedmen's Bureau, Richmond, Virginia.

Courtesy Library of Congress.

cipients for three years, after which time they could be purchased with a clear title.

The bureau continued until 1872, over two vetoes in 1866 by President Andrew Johnson, who undercut the bureau when he returned land, sold to fund itself, to its former owners. Commissioner Oliver O. Howard nevertheless set out with nine assistants to close relief establishments gradually and make the freedmen self-sufficient through wage labor. The assistants helped the former black slaves with employment contracts, established schools, held court where and when needed, and began to establish the institution of marriage among them. By 1868, more than nine hundred Bureau officials were spread throughout the old Confederacy, trying to help four million former slaves find a place in emancipated America, their work often thwarted by the antipathy of Confederate sympathizers.

At the beginning of its existence, the bureau was successful in feeding and clothing black refugees and it established a legacy of justice in law, land ownership, compensated labor, and free education, none of which had existed before for blacks in the South.

See also Fourteenth Amendment; Ku Klux Klan (KKK); Reconstruction Era; Sharecropping.

Further Reading

Oubre, Claude F. *Forty Acres and a Mule: The Freedmen's Bureau and Black Land Ownership*. Baton Rouge: Louisiana State University Press, 1978.

Benjamin F. Shearer

Freedom Riders

Freedom Riders were individuals who took part in the Freedom Rides, integrated bus rides in which African American and white volunteers sat next to each other on chartered buses that traversed the southern United States in 1961. More than one thousand people participated in these rides, which were organized and sponsored by the National Association for the Advancement of Colored People, the Congress of Racial Equality, and the Student Nonviolent Coordinating Committee. Riders also participated in sit-ins at restaurants, lunch counters, and hotels. The riders experienced significant repression and violence, including the burning of one bus, often at the hands of the Ku Klux Klan. Eventually, President John F. Kennedy sent five hundred federal marshals to accompany the riders and ensure their safety. On November 1, 1961, the Interstate Commerce Commission desegregated bus terminals, largely as a result of the Freedom Rides. Later on, partly because of the success of the Freedom Rides, the same civil rights organizations organized Freedom Summer, a voter-registration and community-service project in Mississippi that drew on the multiracial group of volunteers and nonviolent philosophy of the Freedom Rides.

See also Civil Rights Movement; Congress of Racial Equality (CORE).

Mikaila Mariel Lemonik Arthur

Volunteers on a Freedom Rider's Bus, while police cars and soldiers line the streets, 1961.

Courtesy Library of Congress.

Free Persons of Color in the Antebellum North

After the American Revolution, the states in the North systematically began to liberate the slaves in their jurisdictions, preceding the emancipation of the slaves in the South by about a century. The New England states took the initiative, and Pennsylvania, New York, and New Jersey followed. However, free persons of color in the North before the Civil War had frequently been characterized by historians as being slaves without a master, because of the oppressive living conditions faced by African Americans. In the North, free persons of color faced economic, social, and political injustices on institutional levels. For instance, they quite clearly lived in poverty and were usually not allowed to vote or to testify against European Americans in court. In fact, there were open policies encouraging housing and vocational discrimination.

They also endured the harsh realities of racism in their everyday lives; mobs of European Americans routinely attacked free African Americans and places where African Americans gathered. To cope with such oppressive living conditions, African Americans developed support networks, typically based at church. Despite these hardships, free persons of color in the North participated actively in the Civil War, playing a crucial role in ending the slavery in the South.

See also Slavery in the Antebellum South.

Daisuke Akiba

Fu Manchu

In 1913, Arthur Henry Sarsfield Ward, an Irishman living in London and writing under the name Sax Rohmer, penned *The Insidious Dr. Fu Manchu*, the first in a series of novels introducing an evil, Western-educated Chinaman intent upon world domination and destruction of the West. The novels were popular into the 1950s and inspired a series of Hollywood movies, including *The Mysterious Fu Manchu*, *The Mask of Fu Manchu*, and *The Face of Fu Manchu*, and a 1950s television series, *The Adventures of Dr. Fu Manchu*. Rohmer's depictions played on stereotypes of the inscrutable, mysterious, dangerous Chinese and on the Western vision of Asian men as objects of fear and Asian women as objects of desire. Describing his main character, Rohmer wrote, "Imagine a person, tall, lean and feline . . . a close-shaven skull, and long, magnetic eyes of the true cat-green. Invest him with all the cruel cunning of an entire Eastern race, accumulated in one giant intellect, with all the resources of science past and present, with all the resources, if you will, of a wealthy government. . . . Imagine that awful being, and you have a mental picture of Dr. Fu-Manchu, the yellow peril incarnate in one man" (*The Insidious Dr. Fu Manchu*, 25–26).

The Fu Manchu movies, in which the title role was played by white actors in "yellowface," including Warner Oland, Boris Karloff, and Christopher Lee, continued to market these Asian stereotypes. The evil and dangerous Fu Manchu was eventually replaced in the entertainment media by the more benign and lovable Charlie Chan, a second-generation Chinese detective who displayed his insights in short Confucian-style proverbs. The success of the Fu Manchu series built upon anti-Asian sentiment of the time, and critics have suggested that Rohmer's writings revealed Western xenophobia and orientalist ideas of Asian race, class, and sexuality, more than they portrayed truths about Asia and Asians.

See also Asian Americans, Discrimination against; Derogatory Terms; Films and Racial Stereotypes; Orientalism.

Kenneth J. Guest

Furman v. Georgia

Furman v. Georgia (408 U.S. 238 [1972]) is a U.S. Supreme Court case in which the high court held by a close 5–4 vote that the death penalty is unconstitutional because decisions regarding its application are "capricious and arbitrary"; that is, eligibility for execution is too reliant on the discretion and judgement of prosecutors and judges and not clearly defined by established, statutory criteria. Each of the five concurring justices wrote a separate opinion, and the four dissenting justices wrote a united opinion, foreshadowing the Court's acceptance of the death penalty only four years later (*Gregg v. Georgia* 428 U.S. 153 [1976]). Only two of the justices in *Furman*—Thurgood Marshall, the only black justice on this Court, and William Brennan Jr.—thought that the death penalty, outright, was cruel and unusual, violating the Eighth Amendment. The other three concurring justices argued that the death penalty as applied in this case was unconstitutional.

The defendant, Furman, was black and killed a homeowner. He shot the deceased through a front door. Furman only completed the sixth grade and, as Justice William O. Douglas noted in his concurring opinion, Furman had a mild-to-moderate mental deficiency. Based on the recent case *Atkins v. Virginia* (122 S. Ct. 2242 [2002]), this mental deficiency makes it questionable as to whether Furman could get the death penalty even under today's revised statutes.

Several of the justices believed that the death penalty was being administered disproportionately against blacks and Anthony Amsterdam, who argued the case for Furman before the Supreme Court, continues today to argue that there are at least four reasons to revoke the death penalty: it is overwhelmingly used against the poor and minorities; it is imposed arbitrarily; it is so rare that it cannot be a deterrent to crime; and standards of decency have evolved past the need for legal killing.

See also Capital Punishment and Racial Inequality.

__John Eterno__

G

Galton, Sir Francis

See Eugenics Movement.

Garvey, Marcus (1887–1940)

Marcus Garvey was the first major leader of the Black Nationalist Movement and the proponent of the back-to-Africa movement. Born in Jamaica in 1887, he organized the Universal Negro Improvement Association (UNIA) there in 1914. He established its branches in New York (Harlem) and other cities for his political activities. Even though he never acquired U.S. citizenship, Marcus Garvey was one of the most influential Black leaders in the United States in the 1910s and 1920s.

In the early part of the twentieth century, African Americans debated intensely how to address their demeaning social status and their related experience of oppression and discrimination. Both Garvey and W.E.B. Du Bois rejected Booker T. Washington's approach of accommodation, but they advocated different approaches than each other as well. While W.E.B. Du Bois took the political-action approach to press for equal opportunity, Garvey did not foresee much to be gained by African Americans, remaining as a part of American society. He argued that, instead, African Americans would be best served by creating their own society in Africa. He was proud of being black and taught Black Pride. His popularity reached its peak in 1920 with two million followers; nevertheless, he was not accepted by the established African American leaders of the period. In 1922, he was indicted for mail fraud and served two years in prison. After being pardoned by President Calvin Coolidge, he was deported in 1927 to Jamaica. He died in London in 1940.

**Marcus Garvey, leader of the Black
Nationalist Movement.**

Courtesy Library of Congress.

See also the Back-to-Africa Movement; Black
Nationalist Movement; Du Bois, W.E.B.; Washington, Booker T.

Further Reading

Franklin, John Hope, and August Meier. *Black Leaders of the 20th Century*. Urbana: University of Illinois Press, 1982.

Shin Kim and Kwang Chung Kim

Genotype versus Phenotype

A genotype is the internally coded, inheritable
genetic information that is stored by all living or-
ganisms. A phenotype is any outward, observ-
able structure, function, or behavior of an
organism. Phenotype—how a person appears,
acts, or functions—is the consequence of both
a person's genotype and his or her environment.
People with the same genotypes may have the
same phenotype, or they may have different phe-
notypes. For instance, siblings may have different eye and hair color. Likewise, people with
different genotypes may have the same phenotype. Thus, inferring genetic characteristics or
qualities (i.e., what genes a person has inherited
from his or her parents) from phenotype can be
very difficult. This is strikingly true in the classification of race because race has no genetic com-
ponent and is based solely on the subjective classification of phenotypical
features, that is, the outward appearance of skin color, hair texture, eye color,
and so on.

See also Biological Racism; Eugenics Movement; Intelligence Tests and
Racism; Social Construction of Whiteness; Terman, Lewis.

Tracy Chu

Gentlemen's Agreement of 1908

With the formal exclusion of Chinese immigration through the Chinese Exclusion Act of 1882, the anti-Asian sentiment in America turned to the Japanese as the twentieth century began. For example, the San Francisco school
board attempted to exclude Japanese children from public schools. President
Theodore Roosevelt pressured San Francisco officials to back down from the
resolution and negotiated with the Japanese government to prohibit Japanese
immigration to the United States instead. In the 1907–1908 negotiations, Roosevelt persuaded the Japanese government to accept the infamous Gentle-

men's Agreement, whereby no immigration passport would be issued by the Japanese government to anyone except immediate families of Japanese workers already living in the United States.

Unlike Chinese immigrants, Japanese workers in the United States were allowed to bring their brides. Through this and other exceptions, the number of Japanese immigrants continued to grow, albeit at a slower pace than before: between 1908 and 1924, more than 120,000 arrived at Pacific Coast ports and another 48,000 entered the Hawaiian Island. In spite of this increase, both the 1882 Chinese Exclusion Act and the Gentlemen's Agreement were effective in curbing immigration from East Asia. Plantation owners in Hawaii turned instead to the Philippines to fill their labor demand. The National Origins Act of 1924 closed off immigration from Japan.

See also Chinese Exclusion Act of 1882; Asian Americans, Discrimination against; National Origins Act of 1924.

Further Reading

Kitano, Harry H. L., and Roger Daniels. *Asian Americans: Emerging Minorities*. Englewood Cilffs, NJ: Prentice Hall, 1988.

Shin Kim and Kwang Chung Kim

Gerrymandering, Racial

Racial gerrymandering is the process of drawing electoral districts with the intent to minimize racial-minority representation. Although African Americans were granted the right to vote in 1870, multiple barriers effectively disenfranchised them for many decades. Racial gerrymandering was one such barrier, and this means of diluting the black vote was accomplished by two different means. Racial gerrymandering includes packing and stacking. Packing occurs when large numbers of African American voters are concentrated in a small number of districts, whereas stacking disperses African Americans into majority-white districts.

Partly because of racial gerrymandering, historically, racial and ethnic minority candidates rarely won elections in majority-white districts. To remedy this problem and facilitate the representation of historically disenfranchised and underrepresented communities, minority-opportunity voting districts could be drawn. This is referred to as redistricting. Every ten years, after the decennial census, electoral district lines must be redrawn to contain approximately equal numbers of people to adhere to the constitutional mandate of "one person, one vote." In addition to equality in population size and opportunity for representation, the geographic criteria for redistricting are compactness, contiguity, and preserving the integrity of political boundaries. Electoral districts must also encompass "communities of interest," represented by groups of people who share similar values and interests or common characteristics.

See also Redistricting.

Tarry Hum

Ghetto

See Racial Ghettoes.

Ghost Dance Religion

The Ghost Dance was a religious movement that spread through Native American tribes in the 1880s. It offered its adherents hope, peace, and prosperity at a time when they were out-gunned, out-manned, and experiencing what seemed to be the death throes of their ancient cultural traditions.

The founder was Wovoka, born around 1858, the son of a Paiute medicine man. He was only fourteen years old when his father died and he went to live with the Wilson family near Yerington, Nevada. He even took the name Jack Wilson. Through the Wilsons he became familiar with Christian religion, which he sought to transform in combination with the shamanism he learned from his father, for the good of his people. Wovoka's message was simple: harm no one, hurt no one, do not fight, do not tell lies, always do right. The Ghost Dance came to him, he claimed, in a dream. By dancing for four straight nights and a fifth night until morning, then bathing in a river, heaven at some point would come to earth. The dancing should take place every six weeks.

As many as thirty different western tribes eventually took up the Ghost Dance religion, and thus, the promised rewards of dancing varied from tribe to tribe. There were, however, common elements. The day would come when the dead would join the living on an abundant earth without hunger, death, or disease. The old would be young and the blind would see. The whites would disappear, leaving Native Americans to live in peace and harmony as they had,

Arapaho Ghost Dance, 1900.

Courtesy National Archives.

at least ideally, before the whites appeared and disrupted their way of life. In a world without whites, war and fighting would no longer be necessary. It was ironic then that Ghost Dancing, misunderstood by fearful whites as war-like behavior, led to the atrocity at Wounded Knee in 1890.

See also Native Americans, Conquest of; Sioux Outbreak of 1890.

Further Reading

Hittman, Michael. *Wovoka and the Ghost Dance*. Expanded ed. Edited by Don Lynch. Lincoln: University of Nebraska Press, 1998.

Mooney, James. *The Ghost-Dance Religion and Wounded Knee*. New York: Dover Publications, 1991.

Benjamin F. Shearer

Goddard, Henry H. (1866–1957)

Henry Herbert Goddard was a major proponent of the idea that southern and eastern European immigrants entering the country in the first decade of the twentieth century were intellectually inferior. In 1912, Goddard was asked by U.S. government officials to use the newly developed intelligence test on immigrants entering the United States at Ellis Island in New York. The newly arriving immigrants were given a test in English that covered information about American life that was unfamiliar to most of them. Naturally, Goddard found that Italian, Jewish, Hungarian, and Russian immigrants did poorly on the IQ test compared with native-born Protestants. He labeled those immigrants with low IQ scores as "feebleminded." The results of his intelligence test were used by policymakers and other white supremacists to legislate restrictive immigration laws in the early 1920s, including the National Origins Act of 1924.

See also Biological Racism; Intelligence and Standardized Tests, Cultural Biases in; Jensen, Arthur; Terman, Lewis.

Further Reading

Kamin, L. J. *The Science and Politics of I.Q.* Hillside, NJ: Earlbaum Associates, 1974.

Pyong Gap Min

Godfather, The

In recent years, Italian American organizations have drawn attention the creation of negative stereotypes of Italian groups in American media. In February 2000, in response to the smash hit television series *The Sopranos*, the National Italian American Foundation wrote a press release announcing their campaign to end the nearly exclusive portrayal of Italians as mobsters. According to the coalition, beginning with the success of Francis Ford Coppola's *The Godfather* trilogy of films in the 1970s, Italians have been persistently overrepresented as Mafioso figures. The recent popularity of the HBO series *The Sopranos*, underscores this problem. The press release reads, "The HBO network and its series 'The Sopranos' are guilty of defaming and assassinating the cultural character of Italian Americans by using their religion, customs and values in violent and immoral contexts that damage the image and reputations of an estimated 20 million Americans of Italian descent." According to the Italian American Heritage Foundation, movies like *The Godfather* and television shows like *The Sopranos* are responsible for false perceptions of Italian Americans. In a survey conducted by the Commission for Social Justice/Sons of Italy in America, nearly three out of four Americans believe that Italian Americans are associated with organized crime. Since *The Godfather* trilogy, 57 percent of movies produced in the United States that portray Italian characters have been movies about the mafia. According to the U.S. census and the FBI, there are 14.7 million Italian Americans living in the United States, and 1,150 of them, or just 0.0078 percent of the total population of Italian Americans, are convicted criminals.

See also Films and Racial Stereotypes; Italian Americans, Prejudice and Discrimination against; Italian Americans, Violence against; Television and Racial Stereotypes.

Michael Roberts

Gonzales, Rodolfo "Corky" (1928–   )

In the 1950s, Rodolfo Gonzales became the first Mexican American district captain for the Democratic Party in Denver, in 1960, the Colorado coordinator of the "Viva Kennedy" presidential campaign, and, later that decade, a leader of the War on Poverty program during the Johnson administration. Growing disillusioned with establishment party politics, Gonzales left the Democratic Party and helped found the movement for Chicano self-determination and nationalism.

He founded the organization Crusade for Justice, which included a school teaching "liberation classes," a nursery, gym, Mayan ballroom, art gallery, shops, library, dining room, community center, legal aid service, skill bank, Barrio Police Board, health and housing social workers, athletic leagues, newspaper (*El Gailo*), bail bond service, and revolutionary theater. The organization issued a "Plan for the Barrio" calling for housing, education, economic opportunities, agricultural reforms including land reform, and the redistribution of wealth.

In March 1969, the Crusade convened the first Chicano Youth Liberation Front, a national convention of barrio youth in Denver, where the "Spiritual Plan of Aztlan" called for separate Chicano communities and self-determination on their own political, social, economic, and educational issues. The Crusade, led by Gonzales, also helped to organize La Raza Unida (The United People) party in Colorado, and participated in the Poor People's March of 1968 and the school walkouts at West Denver High School to end discrimination against Chicano children. Gonzales is also well known as the author of the poem "Yo Soy Joaquin" (I Am Joaquin) and the play of the same title, which presents the Mexican American experience from conquistador Hernán Cortés to the present-day farmworkers' struggle.

See also La Raza Unida; War on Poverty and the Great Society.

Dong-Ho Cho

Government Initiatives after the September 11, 2001, Attack on the United States

Immediately after the September 11 attack on the United States, the U.S. government initiated a series of directives aimed at combating terrorists who might have infiltrated the country. These initiatives will be discussed in chronological order to get a sense of the pace, sequence, and scope of the directives as they happened. It should be noted, however, that the long-term repercussions of these initiatives—how they have affected the lives of the immigrant men who were "caught" in the fray, the effects on their families, and the impact on targeted communities, namely, Arab and/or Muslim Americans—remains to be seen. A list of the major initiatives, announcements, and actions is provided.

- On September 17, 2001, the Immigration and Naturalization Service (INS) changed the regulation regarding detentions. A nonresident alien could be detained without charge for forty-eight hours or more if there were attenuating circumstances.

- On September 21, 2001, chief immigration judge Michael Creppy issues a memorandum regarding "secure" hearings, meaning that in certain cases, proceedings are closed to the public.

- On October 25, 2001, the attorney general, John Ashcroft, announced that the government had arrested or detained nearly 1,000 individuals as part of its antiterrorism offensive.

- On October 26, 2001, President George W. Bush signed the USA PATRIOT Act into law.

- On November 7, 2001, President Bush announced the creation of the Foreign Terrorist Tracking Task Force during the first formal meeting of the Homeland Security Council. The goal of the task force was to deny entry to, locate, detain, prosecute, and/or deport anyone suspected of terrorist activity.

- On November 9, 2001, the Attorney General sent a memo to the FBI to conduct voluntary interviews with some 5,000 men, ages eighteen to thirty-three, who entered the United States after January 2000 and who came from countries where Al Qaeda is suspected of having operations. If found in violation of immigration laws, these men were to be arrested and kept without bail.

- On November 19, 2001, President Bush signed into law the Aviation and Transportation Security Act, which established the Transportation Security Administration (TSA). The law empowered the new agency to use information from government agencies to identify individuals on passenger lists who may be a threat to civil or national security, and to prevent them from flying.

- On January 8, 2002, the Department of Justice added to the FBI's National Crime Information Center database the names of approximately 6,000 men who had ignored deportation or removal orders. This is known as the "absconder" initiative. The list profiles men of working age from a number of countries believed to be harboring Al Qaeda cells.

- On February 26, 2002, the *Final Report on Interview Project* stated that out of 5,000 Arab and/or Muslim men on the list, 2,261 were interviewed and fewer than twenty were taken into custody, three on criminal violations and the rest on immigration charges.

- In March 2002, the State Department updated its list of terrorists and terrorist organizations whose property interests were frozen in September 2001 by presidential order.

- On April 12, 2002, the INS established a new limitation on visitors to the United States of thirty days, depending on the reason. Visitors could not change their status to student or attend a school if their status was pending.

- On May 9, 2002, the attorney general ordered noncitizens who are subject to deportation to surrender to INS within thirty days of the final order or be barred forever from any discretionary relief from deportation.

- On May 14, 2002, President Bush signed into law the Enhanced Border Security and Visa Entry Reform Act. Like most of the government initiatives, this law was most consequential to individuals of Middle Eastern and South Asian birth, even if they were naturalized Canadian citizens.

- On May 16, 2002, the attorney general introduced the Student and Exchange Visitor System (SEVIS), which became law on January 30, 2003. SEVIS tracks student enrollment, start date of each semester, failure to enroll, dropping below nine credits per term (i.e., full-time status), disciplinary action by the institution, and early graduation, among other information.

- On June 5, 2002, the attorney general announced a new entry-exit system. Aliens from twenty-five predominantly Muslim countries (Afghanistan, Algeria, Bahrain, Djibouti, Egypt, Eritrea, Indonesia, Iran, Iraq, Jordan, Kuwait, Lebanon, Libya, Malaysia, Morocco, Oman, Pakistan, Qatar, Saudi Arabia, Somalia, Sudan, Syria, Tunisia, United Arab Emirates, Yemen) were required to register, submit to fingerprints and photographs upon their arrival in the United States, report to INS field offices within thirty days, re-report annually, and notify the INS agent of their departure, with possible criminal prosecution for those who fail to comply. The National Security Entry-Exit Registration System (NSEERS) was implemented on September 11, 2002, for men from Iran, Iraq, Syria, and Sudan.

- On June 26, 2002, the Department of Justice deported 131 Pakistani nationals who were detained for months at various INS facilities. Most were arrested for ignoring previous deportation orders. Another 100 men were deported on August 21, 2002.

- On July 11, 2002, the Department of Justice declared that most of the September 11 detainees were released and many of them deported.

- On July 24, 2002, the Department of Justice announced that the attorney general can deputize any state or local law-enforcement officer to exercise and enforce immigration laws, under certain provisions.

- On July 24, 2002, the U.S. Commission on Civil Rights reaffirmed its commitment to protect the rights of Arab and Muslim Americans.

- On November 6, 2002, the INS required males older than age sixteen who are citizens of Iran, Iraq, Libya, Sudan, or Syria, and who had entered the United States before September 10, 2002, and who were remaining at least until December 16, 2002, to register with the INS before that date. Failure to comply was cause for deportation. On December 16, 2002, other countries were added to this list, which then totaled twenty, mostly from the Middle East. Armenia was initially part of that list, but it was removed immediately. Some argue that the government put Armenia on the list to suggest it was not targeting only Muslim countries.

- On November 25, 2002, President Bush signed into law the Department of Homeland Security. This new cabinet-level department merges twenty-two federal agencies and thus employs about 170,000 individuals. President Bush also signs the Justice Department's Operation Terrorism Information and Prevention System (TIPS), which would enlist thousands of truck drivers, mail carriers, bus drivers as "citizen observers," but was defeated through media exposure and the resulting outrage by the American public.

- On January 16, 2003, the INS extended the date of deadlines for registration. Statistics are released stating that almost 1,200 were detained during the NSEERS "special registration." Five countries—Bangladesh, Egypt, Indonesia, Jordan, and Kuwait—were added to the existing list of twenty that requested males older than sixteen years of age to register with the INS and be fingerprinted.

- On March 24, 2003, the FBI declared that more than 5,000 Iraqis who live in the United States were "voluntarily" interviewed and, of these, thirty were detained on immigration violations.

- On April 29, 2003, Tom Ridge, Secretary of Homeland Security, launched U.S. Visitor and Immigrant Status Indication Technology (U.S. VISIT). The new system replaces NSEERS and integrates SEVIS. A minimum of two biometric identifiers (e.g., photographs, fingerprints, iris scans) will be used in the future to track all visitors to the country.

- On May 9, 2003, the General Accounting Office (GAO) issued its report on the "voluntary interviews." The report noted that 3,216 Muslim and Arab immigrants were interviewed by the Justice Department out of a possible 7,602 identified individuals. GAO doubted that the interviews were voluntary.

- On June 2, 2003, the Inspector General (OIG) of the U.S. Department of Justice issued its highly critical report on the detention initiative that followed the September 11 attacks.

- In November 2003, two facets of what had been NSEERS were suspended: the annual re-registration requirement and the 30- and 40-day follow-up interviews.

Though the government initiatives do not appear to have ended, a preliminary analysis of their impact thus far is warranted. Civil rights organizations, legal experts, immigrants' rights groups, and critical observers of the government's policies claim that these policies in the process of defending the security of the nation, are chiseling away at immigrants' rights and potentially even citizens' civil liberties. They also victimize innocent people. Even the U.S. Department of Justice's own Inspector General's Office issued a scathing report accusing the attorney general of breaking many laws he was meant to protect.

Arab and Muslim immigrant men suffered the most from these policies, and their ethnic/religious communities were left feeling extremely vulnerable. It is not yet known how many of those detained, interviewed, and registered have been deported, because the government has not published these statistics. However, from available information, one can gather that about 6,000 Arab/Muslim absconders were sought; 42 percent of those invited for supposedly voluntary interviews were questioned and about 20 arrested on immigration and criminal charges; at least 231 individuals were deported, more than half of them Pakistanis; and less than 1 percent of the 5,000 Iraqis were detained after being interviewed. Estimates of the detainees vary between the Inspector General's number of 762 illegal immigrants from the Middle East and South Asia to more than 1,200 from other sources. Almost 1,200 men were detained as a result of NSEERS, or "special registration," whereas by May 2003, it was estimated that more than 80,000 had obeyed orders to register. Although these numbers are not staggering, the dragnet nature of the government initiatives has created a perception that the backlash was far more encompassing.

As men usually contribute the primary income for the household, especially those originating from patriarchal societies, wives, children, and other family members were obviously drawn into the backlash unwittingly. The repercussions on the Arab and Muslim immigrant communities have yet to be assessed. The Pakistani immigrant community in Coney Island, New York, for example, has witnessed the closure of several businesses and rapid sales of vehicles and real estate. More seriously, constitutional scholars and observers of the nation's civil liberties have sounded the alarm. For example, law professor David Cole argues that the United States has adopted a double standard of "their liberty, our security," accepting abuse of foreigners that citizens would not tolerate. He warns that these civil-liberty abuses, if unchecked, may come to haunt citizens in the future.

See also Al Qaeda; Arab/Muslim American Advocacy Organizations, Responding to the Backlash; Middle Easterners, Historical Precedents of Backlash against; Muslim Philanthropic Organizations, Closure of after September 11, 2001; Muslims, Terrorist Image of; September 11, 2001, Terrorism, Discriminatory Reactions to.

Further Reading

Cole, David. *Enemy Aliens: Double Standards and Constitutional Freedoms in the War on Terrorism*. New York: The New Press, 2003.

Mehdi Bozorgmehr and Anny Bakalian

Great Society

See War on Poverty and the Great Society.

"Green Menace"

During the four decades of the Cold War, the Soviet Union—the "Red Menace"—was depicted as a sinister military and ideological threat to the American way of life. With the collapse of the Soviet Union and the rise of the United States as the dominant player in international politics, in recent years a "Green Menace" has emerged in the American popular and political imagination. The "Green Menace" represents the assumed danger posed by Islamic fundamentalism (Islam is represented by the color green). First given life in the 1970s through the Iranian Revolution and the Tehran embassy hostage crisis, the image of the Green Menace depicts Islamic revivalism as a virulent threat to American political dominance and the West's social and cultural order. Since the mid-1990s, terrorist activities against U.S. interests worldwide—culminating in the 2001 World Trade Center and Pentagon attacks—have cemented the picture of the United States under hostile attack from an ominous "green" power.

Like the "Red Menace" of previous years, the "Green Menace" is the product of political ideology, mass media, and popular culture. It is also the product of oversimplification. The creation of an identifiable menace may prove useful for political mobilization, because a clear enemy is presented against whom the United States can marshal military and financial resources. It may, however, have negative consequences as well, particularly for the rapidly growing Middle Eastern population of the United States. Television and media images that promote negative stereotyping of Arabs reinforce political messages of a sinister Islamic enemy. Islam is unfairly equated with fundamentalism, and fundamentalism with terrorist activity—this denies the immense diversity of Islam within both religious and political spheres. Also, propagation of the Green Menace imagery may encourage a monolithic, and wholly negative, view of Middle Easterners in America, who in fact have varied ethnic, national, and religious allegiances.

See also Middle Easterners, Historical Precedents of Backlash against; Muslims, Terrorist Image of.

Rebekah Lee

Gratz v. Bollinger

See Affirmative Action, University of Michigan Ruling on.

Guadalupe Hidalgo, Treaty of

Named for the city in which it was signed on February 2, 1848, the Treaty of Guadalupe Hidalgo concluded the Mexican-American War. The treaty called for Mexico to cede 55 percent of its territory, including the land area that later became the states of Arizona, California, and New Mexico, and parts of what are now Colorado, Nevada, and Utah. In exchange, the United States agreed to pay $15 million in compensation for war-related damage to Mexican property. In addition, the treaty established the border between Texas and Mexico at the Rio Grande River, 150 miles south of the traditional border on the Nueces River (Article V). Articles VIII and IX called for the United States to protect the property and civil rights of Mexican nationals living within the new U.S. border. The treaty also stipulated that the United States would police its side of the border (Article XI) and provided for compulsory arbitration of future disputes between the two countries (Article XXI). Article X originally guaranteed the protection of Mexican land grants, but the U.S. Senate deleted this clause when it ratified the treaty in March 1848. The treaty made Mexican Americans the only minority group in the United States, besides Native Americans, who were annexed by conquest and whose property rights were legally usurped.

The legitimacy of the war and the U.S. territorial ambition have been disputed from the beginning. In 1846, with the war barely begun, pacifist and naturalist Henry David Thoreau refused to pay taxes, denouncing the Mexican-American War. Newspaperman Horace Greeley doubted that the predictable military victories and annexation of half of Mexican territory would enhance liberty, morality, and industry. General Ulysses S. Grant declared the Mexican-American War to be "the most unjust war ever undertaken by a stronger nation against a weaker one." But in a widely circulated article written in 1911, David Saville Muzzey, a historian at Barnard College, Columbia University, justified the war, arguing that the United States had a right to annex Texas, which had been independent for nine years, and that the admitted military weakness of a country should not give immunity to continued and open insolence. With the Treaty of Guadalupe Hidalgo, he concluded, "The work of westward extension was done. Expansion, the watchword of the decade 1840–1850, was dropped from our vocabulary for fifty years."

Notwithstanding the promises of the Treaty to protect property rights and civil rights of the former Mexican nationals (now Mexican Americans), the U.S. government and judiciary have denied their claims to the ancestral land formerly granted under Spanish and Mexican rule. Recently, an increasing number of Mexican American families have begun to fight for the return of the land taken from them for decades by the injustice of predominantly Anglo-Saxon courts. Now those bringing land-related claims, disillusioned by the Treaty's unenforceability under the current judiciary procedure, have started focusing their attention on the federal legislature. Consequently, a small number of bills were introduced in Congress: House Resolution 2538 sought to create a presidential commission to determine the validity of the land-related claims; a Senate bill proposed to acknowledge the property claims outright and to develop a method of compensation; and in 2000, Senate Bill 2022 recognized that the loss of property subsequent to the war with Mexico has had serious repercussions in the Mexican American community in the southwest-ern Unites States, and specifically questioned whether the United States ful-filled its obligations under the treaty. These bills are significant in that Congress admits the accountability of the federal government and the Territory of New Mexico in the mid-to-late nineteenth century for the massive dispossession of Mexican American landholders. But the proposed legislation does not directly address the key issue, the Unites States' blatant failure to adhere the provisions of the treaty, but merely mentions the issue of fairness and equity in admin-istrative process, thus blurring the necessity of an official apology on the part of the federal government to those illegally dispossessed.

See also Mexican-American War.

Further Reading

Muzzey, David Saville. *An American History*. Boston: Ginn Company, 1911.

St. Mary's Law Review on Minority Issues (Spring 2001): 231–267, 232–236. http://www.loc.gov/exhibits/ghtreaty.

Zinn, Howard. *A People's History of the United States*. New York: Perennial Classics, 2003.

Dong-Ho Cho

Gulf War

The Persian Gulf War was an armed conflict between Iraq and a U.S.-led coali-tion of thirty-two nations during the administration of President George H. W. Bush. On August 2, 1990, Iraq invaded its neighbor, Kuwait, to take control of its oil reserves. Saddam Hussein, the president of Iraq at the time, accused Kuwait of breaking agreements by overproducing oil and reducing oil prices severely. Moreover, he claimed that Kuwait illegally pumped oil from the oil field of Rumaila in Iraq. Outnumbered by the Iraqi forces, Kuwait turned to the United Nations for help. In response, the UN Security Council called for Iraq to withdraw from Kuwait by January 15, 1991, and subsequently forbade trade with Iraq.

Hussein's refusal to comply by January 15 resulted in launching the five-week operation of intensive air attack, called Operation Desert Storm, under the leadership of General Norman Schwarzkopf and chairman of the joint chiefs of staff, Colin Powell. Iraq responded by calling for terrorist attacks against the coalition and dispatching Scud missiles at Israel and Saudi Arabia, allies of the United States. The U.S. troops retaliated with Patriot antimissile missiles and finally defeated the Iraqi forces. On February 28, President Bush declared a cease-fire.

Although the war was a military victory for the coalition, Kuwait and Iraq suffered enormous damage, and Hussein remained still in power. Iraq agreed to coalition peace terms, but every effort was made to frustrate implementa-tion of the terms, particularly UN weapons inspections.

See also Powell, Colin.

Sookhee Oh

Gutierrez, Jose Angel (1945–   )

Jose Angel Gutierrez, a political science professor at the University of Texas at Arlington, has been considered a leader of the political and civil rights movements among the Chicano communities since the 1960s. In 1970, Gutierrez cofounded a political organization, El Partido Nacional La Raza Unida, which was originally designed to increase political and civil rights awareness among Chicanos. Among Gutierrez's recent concerns have been the anti-Mexican-immigration movements in the United States. During a 2000 interview with the Dallas-Fort Worth Texas newspaper, the *Star-Telegram*, Gutierrez argued that "undocumented" Mexican immigrants belong in Texas anyway, because they are simply reclaiming parts of the United States traditionally known as Aztlan, which was taken by the United States from Mexicans.

See also Chicano Movement; La Raza Unida.

Daisuke Akiba

H

Haitians, Discrimination against in Refugee Policy

The Haitian government has a well-documented history of political oppression and violence against its people, including an aborted election in 1987 and a 1991 military coup d'etat overthrowing the democratically elected President Bertrand Aristide. Nevertheless, Haitians who have sought asylum in the United States have historically been denied asylum at rates far exceeding those of political-asylum seekers from other countries, including China, Cuba, and the former Soviet Union.

Haitians who have attempted to flee Haiti for the United States in boats have been intercepted at sea and automatically repatriated to Haiti, where they have faced violent retribution and imprisonment by the government. Haitians who have applied for asylum in person have been denied at a higher rate than any other asylum-seeking group. They have also been held in detention for longer periods of time and subject to harsher conditions than comparable asylum seekers from other countries. Beginning in 1981, the Immigration and Naturalization Service (INS) began a policy of systematically detaining Haitian asylum seekers, as opposed to detaining only those persons deemed likely to abscond or pose a threat to national security. Often the INS held Haitians in detention centers, including maximum-security prisons, for extended periods of time in overcrowded and harsh conditions and with limited access to legal representation. Detainees were also subject to forced transfers to other INS facilities in remote parts of the country, where legal resources, as well as Creole interpreters, were even scarcer.

In contrast, Cuban asylum seekers have had much higher rates of acceptance and have been offered better treatment by INS. In 1993, fifty-two Cubans who had hijacked a commuter flight and diverted it to Miami were released from detention within forty-eight hours. This incident sparked one of many serious

Haitian refugees seeking asylum are detained at a U.S. naval base camp.

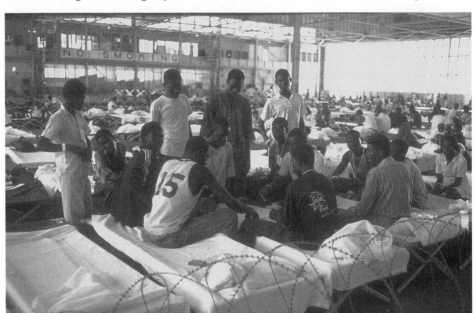

Photo by William F. Campbell/Time Life Pictures/Getty Images.

hunger strikes by Haitian detainees who protested their extended detention. Critics of Haitian refugee policies argue that it is because of blatant racism and classism that Cuban refugees have consistently received better treatment—Cuban refugees tend to be lighter skinned and of a higher social class than Haitian refugees. Moreover, Cubans have received preferential treatment by the U.S. government because of the United States' long-standing anti-Communist political policies in general, and its opposition to the Fidel Castro regime in particular.

See also Black Identities: West Indian Immigrant Dreams and American Realities; Caribbean Immigrants, Attitudes toward African Americans; Caribbean Immigrants, Class Differences in the Second Generation; Caribbean Immigrants, Experience of Racial Discrimination.

Tracy Chu

Harlem Renaissance

The Harlem Renaissance usually refers to the remarkable intellectual and artistic activity of African Americans in the 1920s and the 1930s around but not confined to the Harlem neighborhood of New York City. Its significance, however, lies not simply in the proliferation of literary, artistic, and musical works but in the radical transformation in the racial consciousness of African Americans that these works embody and evoke. Writers such as Alain Locke, W.E.B. Du Bois, Langston Hughes, Zora Neale Hurston, Countee Cullen, Claude McKay, Jean Toomer, and Nella Larsen, to name a few, expressed a new self-understanding and the mood of the "New Negro," deeply rooted in black folk-lore and Africa as the source of racial pride and new political militancy, through the newly founded journals including *Opportunity*, *The Crisis*, *Negro World*, and *The Messenger*. Large urban centers in the North, particularly in New York City, where African Americans migrated to escape the Jim Crow system in the South and to find a new life, provided fertile grounds for the New Negro movement. Also, the crisis of the world system based on Euro-centric values after World War I led African descendents to see the common historical roots of colonial domination and racial oppression. Pan-Africanism, which the Harlem Renaissance articulates, is part of the global self-assertion of colonized peoples.

See also Du Bois, W.E.B.; Harlem Riot of 1964; Jim Crow Laws.

Dong-Ho Cho

Harlem Riot of 1964

In the midst of the civil rights movement, African Americans' aspirations were raised. But the social reality of their lives remained the same. This gap be-

Civilians run from police during a riot in Harlem, July 18, 1964.

tween aspirations and reality created a great deal of discontent in the early part of the 1960s, and it was expressed in the form of riots in large U.S. cities. The Harlem Riot was one of those riots. In July 1964, a white policeman shot and killed an African American boy in Yorkville, New York. In response to the shooting, a riot began in Harlem and spread quickly to Brooklyn's Bedford-Stuyvesant neighborhood. Throughout the six days of rioting, 8,000 persons were involved and 118 people were injured. Police made 465 arrests. As in other racial riots, participants were heavily male teenagers perceived as hoodlums or criminals by some local residents.

Although the immediate cause of the riot was the police shooting of an African American boy, African American residents perceived the real causes of the riot to be social and economic discrimination and deprivation in the face of heightened aspirations. In other words, the riot was an expression of African Americans' frustration of their social reality. In this respect, a study of the riot by Joe Feagin and Paul Sheatsley (1968) is interesting: they showed that one in three whites believed that Communists were responsible for stirring up riots and one-fifth of whites thought that there were outside agitators. Whites also believed that the social conditions of African Americans were improving significantly.

See also Harlem Renaissance; Race Riots.

Further Reading

Feagin, Joe R., and Paul B. Sheatsley. "Ghetto Residents' Appraisals of A Riot." *Public Opinion Quarterly* 32 (1968): 352–362.

Shin Kim and Kwang Chung Kim

Hate Crimes

Hate crimes are violent acts committed against people, property, or organizations and that are motivated by the offenders' prejudice or bias against the groups. Most hate crimes are committed against people in the form of assault, rape, or murder. Lynching, which was frequently committed against blacks in the pre–civil rights era, is the most severe form of hate crime. But about 30 percent of hate crimes are committed against property owned or used by members of minority groups, taking the form of vandalizing, destroying, stealing, or setting fire to vehicles, homes, stores, or places of worship. Hate crimes are "message crimes" in that through their violent actions the offenders are sending the message that members of a certain group are unwelcome in a particular neighborhood, community, school, or workplace.

The target of hate crimes can be minority groups with cultural differences from the dominant population, such as minority religious groups (Muslims, Sikhs, and Jews), ethnic minority groups (Italians and Irish immigrants in the early twentieth century), and homosexuals. They can be groups with physical differences from the dominant population, such as racial minority groups, women, and disabled people. But the most significant determinant of hate crimes in the United States is racial bias, with African Americans at the highest risk of victimization. In 1996, about two-thirds of hate crimes reported to the FBI (about eight thousand cases) were committed against members of racial minority groups, with two-thirds of them targeting African Americans. Hate crimes against Latinos and Asians in the West and Southwest at the end of the nineteenth/beginning of the twentieth century were closely related to anti-immigrant sentiments.

Some white Americans think that minority groups are a threat to their position in society. They believe that minorities are unfairly getting ahead in the workplace and that whites are in danger of losing their jobs, neighborhoods, and schools to these groups. It is believed that the white Americans who are the most threatened by minority groups are at the bottom of the socioeconomic ladder. There is evidence that these working-class and lower-class whites are committing most hate crimes. These whites also make up the primary memberships of extremist groups, such as the Ku Klux Klan. The Ku Klux Klan is one example of a white group that harasses, intimidates, and acts physically violent toward blacks.

A major hate crime against African Americans has been the burning of black churches. Churches have always been a vital part of the black community, and the burning of these institutions sends a message that intimidates the entire group in the community. The burning of black churches can be

A crowd watches as FBI bomb experts comb the street for clues to the bombing of a Baptist church.

© Bettman/CORBIS.

dated to the beginning of the nineteenth century. After the Civil War, the Ku Klux Klan made the black church a target for arson. Many instances of arson took place in the South, specifically along two "arson zones": one in the mid-South, stretching from western Tennessee to parts of Alabama and Mississippi, and the other zone stretching across the Carolinas. For example, the St. John Baptist Church in Dixiana, South Carolina, which was founded in 1765, was subject to attacks from the times of slavery, through the Civil War, Reconstruction, segregation, and the civil rights periods, until it eventually was burned to the ground in 1995.

There are other examples of attacks against African Americans, such as burning crosses on the front lawns of black residents in predominantly white neighborhoods, random acts of violence against blacks who were attacked solely on the basis of their race, and threatening letters of attack or death threats sent to the homes of black residents in white neighborhoods. Even though there has been a decrease in the number of racially motivated hate crimes between 1995 and 2000, these types of crimes still constitute the majority of hate crimes, according to statistics.

See also Hate Crimes Statistics Act of 1990; Ku Klux Klan (KKK).

Further Reading

American Psychological Association. "Hate Crimes Today: An Age-Old Foe in Modern Dress." http://www.apa.org/pubinfo/hate/.

The Civil Rights Coalition for the 21st Century. "The Human Faces of Hate Crimes." http://www.civilrights.org/publications/reports/cause_for_concern/p8.html.

Healey, Joseph F. *Race, Ethnicity, Gender, and Class*. Thousand Oaks, CA: Pine Forge Press, 1998.

Tiffany Vélez

Hate Crimes Statistics Act of 1990

Sponsored by Representative John Conyers Jr. of Michigan, and having over one hundred co-sponsors, the Hate Crimes Statistics Act was passed in 1990. Hate crimes are defined in the legislation as "manifest prejudice based on race, religion, sexual orientation, or ethnicity." The act requires the U.S. Department of Justice to compile national data annually on the incidence of hate crimes and to publish an annual summary of findings. The act was intended to help create a hate-crime index and to allow for the tracking of the incidence of hate crimes. The act arose out of a growing concern in the late twentieth century over an increase in hate crime.

The FBI collects this information through the Uniform Crime Reporting System, which compiles aggregate data based on crime statistics reported by state and local policing agencies. The Higher Education and Reauthorization Act of 1998 mandated that hate crimes on college campuses be included in these data. Since the passage of the act, the federal definition of hate crimes has been expanded. In 1994, the Violent Crime Control and Law Enforcement Act amended the Hate Crimes Statistics Act to include manifest prejudice based on disability. The Hate Crimes Statistics Improvement Act of 2003, introduced in the House by Representative Carolyn Maloney of New York, would also add manifest prejudice based on gender.

See also Hate Crimes.

Victoria Pitts

Hawaii, Annexation of

Hawaii, previously a sovereign nation governed by a monarchy, was annexed by the United States in 1898. The century before this annexation was marked by multiple trade treaties between the United States and Hawaii, many aimed

The Hawaiian flag is lowered from a staff atop Iolani Palace in Honolulu, marking the annexation of the Hawaiian islands by the United States.

Courtesy Library of Congress.

at preventing European powers from gaining a foothold in the nation. The events directly preceding annexation involved a move by Hawaii's last monarch, Queen Liliuokalani, to strengthen the monarchy; the deposing of the queen by American planters was related to their economic interests in avoiding U.S. tariffs on the sugar they grew, as well as nationalism spurred by the Spanish-American War. Hawaii was made a territory in 1900, two years after its annexation, but it did not become a state until 1959, owing in large part to the United States' unwillingness to accept the unique racial conditions in the Hawaiian Islands, including a high percentage of people of color and those with mixed racial backgrounds.

Not only were the decisions about how to incorporate Hawaii into the nation politically based on racial factors, the administration of the islands themselves was racially motivated. The new U.S. government of the islands worked to Americanize the Hawaiian and Asian people living there by trying to force them to abandon their language and religion while simultaneously segregating them residentially and educationally and keeping them out of political power. While social scientists on the mainland pointed to Hawaii as a laboratory of racial coexistence, native people, Asian immigrants, and those of mixed racial backgrounds found themselves in a subordinate position both politically and socially. Efforts to gain sovereignty for the Hawaiian Islands and the native people are also ongoing.

See also Manifest Destiny; Texas, Annexation of.

Mikaila Mariel Lemonik Arthur

Hayes-Tilden Compromise of 1877

The controversial results of the 1876 presidential election between Samuel J. Tilden, a Democrat from New York, and Rutherford B. Hayes, a Republican from Ohio, led to a political deal that dramatically affected Southern history and race relations throughout the United States. This election was so tainted by allegations of voting fraud and other irregularities that it was unclear who won the popular vote in four states. Supporters of each candidate claimed the electoral votes of the states in question, and the decision as to who would be declared the winner was given over to the House of Representatives. In February 1877, after intense political negotiation, a deal was struck whereby Democrats conceded the election to Hayes (the Republican), and in return Hayes promised to remove all remaining federal troops from the South and to recognize the white-dominated state governments that remained committed undermining political and social gains that blacks had made during the Reconstruction Era.

Although some saw this arrangement as a gesture toward regional reconciliation and a first step toward ending Northern dominance over the South, many others saw it as sign that Northern whites had lost interest in protecting African Americans' civil and social rights, as established by the Thirteenth, Fourteenth, and Fifteenth Amendments to the Constitution. In more partisan terms, it was seen as evidence that the Republicans—the party of Abraham Lincoln, "The Great Emancipator," and congressional leaders such as Thaddeus Stevens and Charles Sumner, who supported equal rights for freed slaves,—had "sold out" the cause of black equality in exchange for taking over the office of the presidency. Indeed, in the decades after this compromise, black oppression deepened in cruel and brutal ways as whites disenfranchised African Americans, exploited their labor, institutionalized "Jim Crow" segregation laws in many facets of life, and without fear of punishment lynched thousands of blacks.

Given the ineffectiveness and corruption of the previous Republican administration, led by President Ulysses S. Grant, the Democrats had appeared likely to win the 1876 election, and Tilden actually won the total popular vote. But disputes over ballots cast in South Carolina, Louisiana, Florida, and Oregon prevented either candidate from obtaining the needed number of electoral votes to become president. The House of Representatives then created a bipartisan commission to investigate the election and resolve the matter. Its deliberations were contentious, and a bargain was worked out to give each side something. In return for Republican candidate Hayes receiving all the electoral votes of the states in question (which would allow him to become president), Hayes promised several things that southern Democrats wanted. The most important of these was to withdraw federal troops that were still stationed in the South and have the federal government refrain from interfering in white southerners' efforts to subordinate blacks. Other elements of the compromise involved Hayes promising to include at least one Southern white in his cabinet, to appoint some Democrats to patronage offices in the South, and to support federal legislation that would assist in industrializing the South. Soon after he was inaugurated in March 1877, Hayes ordered federal troops out of the South. This set the stage for many years of social and political control by supporters of white supremacy. Among other things, they established white-only primary elections, created racially segregated schools, and tolerated Ku Klux Klan violence. Until Franklin D. Roosevelt was elected president in 1932, the federal government remained mute as blacks were ensnared in racist systems that denied them their rights and excluded them from a host of educational, economic, political, and social opportunities.

See also Fourteenth Amendment; Jim Crow Laws; Ku Klux Klan (KKK); Reconstruction Era.

Charles Jaret

HCSA

See Hate Crimes Statistics Act of 1990.

Hereditarians versus Environmentalists

The age-old debate over which shapes human behavior, nature or nurture, is at the root of the debate between hereditarians and environmentalists. Hereditarians tend to emphasize the importance of inherited traits. Hereditarians have often argued that some racial groups are inherently superior to others and that inherent racial differences explain why some racial groups are generally more advantaged than others. Environmentalists tend to stress the importance of the environment and opportunity structures in which a person is embedded. Today, this debate might be seen as being between genetics and environment, but the differences between hereditarians and environmentalists have historically been more complex. For example, Social Darwinists of the Progressive Era were strongly hereditarian, but they tended to see inherited traits as being shaped by the behavior of the parents. In other words, in their view, a child born to parents who had been criminals could inherit a criminal tendency that they would not have inherited if those same parents had not engaged in criminal behavior.

This is a much more flexible view of inherited traits than we have today. It is as if DNA, which had not yet been discovered in the Progressive Era, could be changed by the actions of individuals. Although this might seem to be a less restrictive view of human potential than the contemporary genetics-based view, it had within it frightening implications: for instance, that the downward spiral of a family could continue with each generation, becoming progressively more criminal, stupid, or otherwise undesirable. Hereditarians of this era viewed this process as being similar to the process of breeding animals for particular traits: with generations of breeding, it would be difficult to reverse the traits.

Today, hereditarians tend to focus more on genetic predisposition. There is relatively little talk of people being genetically programmed to be criminals. Instead, hereditarians tend to focus on inherited traits as setting the parameters for behavior. In other words, they may view aggression as an inherited trait, but whether that aggression is expressed as criminal violence or corporate advancement depends on personal choices and social opportunities. Similarly, few contemporary environmentalists deny any role to biology or genetics in shaping behavior. The idea that children are blank slates and can be turned into anything at all has fallen out of fashion. Today, the main difference between hereditarians and environmentalists is in which is seen as the dominant factor in people's lives: inherited traits or social and environmental factors. Hereditarians and environmentalist also tend to differ in their assessment of social inequality.

Hereditarians as a group view social inequality as reflecting innate differences between groups. For example, in the early 1990s, prominent hereditarians such as Arthur Jensen have argued that there are real and measurable differences in the intelligence levels of different racial groups. These real—in other words, biological—differences, they argue, account in part for social inequality. In contrast, environmentalists tend to view social inequality as primarily the result of social structures that perpetuate the power of some groups over others.

Hereditarians are often accused of being racists. In response, they argue that scientists must study the world as it is and not as they wish it to be. Critics of hereditarianism, such as Stephen Jay Gould, argue that hereditarians misuse science to justify social inequality. Debates between hereditarians and environmentalists often focus on both concrete issues of research methodology and more abstract philosophical questions, such as how much science can be detached from its social context.

See also Biological Racism; Genotype versus Phenotype; Social Darwinism.

Further Reading

Gould, Stephen Jay. *Mismeasure of Man*. New York: Norton, 1981.

Herrnstein, Richard J., and Charles Murray. *The Bell Curve: Intelligence and Class Structure in American Life*. New York: Free Press, 1994.

Robin Roger-Dillon

Hidden Curriculum

The hidden curriculum refers to everything the formal curriculum does not explicitly cover but that students learn through the organizational arrangement, unwritten rules, routines, rituals, and cultural milieu of their schools. Through the hidden curriculum, students are taught dominant values and attitudes, such as obedience to authority and conformity to cultural norms, hard work, punctuality, "proper English," and acceptable manners, that employers would require of their workers. The hidden curriculum embodies and reproduces at the same time the structural inequality of a society by class, gender, race, national origin, religion, and sexual orientation. The hidden curriculum works against the optimistic hope of educator John Dewey that universal education will eventually lead to democracy and equality.

Even well-intended educators, when they are not fully aware of the hidden curriculum, may contribute unwittingly to the perpetuation of racial stratification. The hidden curriculum is present in the formal curriculum, the teaching process, and the culture of the school. In the formal curriculum, what counts as knowledge reflects the cultural biases of the white middle class. Even the IQ test, which appears neutral and objective, is culturally tilted in a way that disadvantages ethnic minorities as well as lower class and female students. Assessment procedures in general that are culturally and racially biased can lead to misevaluation and reinforce racial stereotypes. Teaching materials often contain linguistic expressions and graphic illustrations that reproduce racial and ethnic stereotypes.

In the teaching process, teachers' preconceptions and expectations of their students based on their race play a significant role in students' development. Generally, black students get less attention and encouragement from teachers and thus tend to have lower self-esteem. Even though African American girls start out with positive behaviors, teachers give them less academic feedback. Even worse off are African American males, who are more likely to be negatively labeled as "a problem" and referred to special-education programs. In contrast, Asian American students tend to be viewed as the best. Often, teachers encourage ethnic minority children to participate fully only in stereotypical areas. For example, African American boys are often thought to be naturally good at sports.

The culture milieu of the school is also an important part of the hidden curriculum. The rules of conducts, ceremonies, and rituals in the U.S. school system represent the dominant white Anglo-Saxon Protestant culture. They are not updated yet to represent the cultural diversity of ethnic groups that make up U.S. society. The specific religious reference in the Pledge of Allegiance and the insistence on school prayer can alienate students who are from non-Western religious backgrounds. The historic symbols that are inherited from the bygone years of ethnic extirpation, slavery, Jim Crow, and colonialism still survive in ceremonies and rituals to damage the self-esteem of the non-white students. For example, the use of the Confederate flag or war whoops, tomahawks, and "savage" mascots at sports events creates a hostile environment for African American and Native American students.

Although the hidden curriculum has a significant influence on students, students are by no means passive containers. The process of socialization always involves struggle and conflict. For example, as Paul Willis's 1970s ethnographic study shows, working-class kids may develop a rebellious counterculture, a possibly embryonic form of working-class culture, against the dominant culture the school system embodies. In this sense, the hidden curriculum may be said to be a cultural battlefield, in which the dynamics of social, political, and economic conflicts unfold around the assumptions, stereotypes, and social structure taken for granted in everyday routines.

See also Education and Racial Discrimination; Intelligence and Standardized Tests, Cultural Biases in; Intelligence Tests and Racism; Political Correctness (P.C.).

Further Reading

Gillborn, David. "Citizenship, 'Race,' and the Hidden Curriculum." *International Studies in the Sociology of Education* 2, no. 1 (1992): 57–73.

Irvine, Jacqueline Jordan. "Teacher-Student Interactions: Effects of Students' Race, Sex, and Grade Level." *Journal of Educational Psychology* 78, no. 1 (1986): 14–21.

Willis, Paul. *Learning to Labor*. New York: Columbia University Press, 1977.

Wren, David J. "School Culture: Exploring the Hidden Curriculum." *Adolescence* 43 (1999): 593–594.

Dong-Ho Cho

High Yellows

See Yellows.

Hispanics, Prejudice and Discrimination against

In the United States, the term *Hispanics* includes a wide variety of people from diverse countries with different cultures, ethnicities, races, languages, social and economic backgrounds, and histories of settlements in the United States. Even though the term seeks to denote Spanish-speaking people, in its most inclusive meaning, *Hispanics* embraces Brazilians, as well as some Guatemalans or Mexicans whose first language is not Spanish. Major components of discriminatory practices, including race or phenotypic characteristics, command of the English language, legal status, and legacy of a history of low socioeconomic status, do not equally fit all Hispanic groups, much less all individuals within the groups. Thus, significant inter- and intragroup differences, along with those factors, have led to a wide variety of experiences and of perceived reasons for discrimination.

The Hispanic groups with the longest history of settlement in the United States include Mexicans, Puerto Ricans, and Cubans. Discrimination and prejudice against Mexican Americans date to the nineteenth century, when Mexicans in the South and Southwest were incorporated into American society as a defeated group, against whom economic dispossession and discrimination were easily justified. Geographic concentration in these regions was accompanied by concentration in agricultural jobs that not only paid lower wages than most other jobs but also were seasonal. With poorly paid jobs, marginal neighborhoods, and poor schools for their children, Mexican Americans were excluded from channels of social and economic mobility. For many decades, prejudice and discrimination against Mexicans involved the common negative stereotypes applied to many subordinated and undervalued groups, including, those of being lazy, unclean, deceitful, and prone to criminality. Later, as Mexican Americans migrated to the cities, they struggled against direct and indirect institutional discrimination by the police, the political system (in the form of violations of voting rights), and poorly funded schools. After the 1930s, large numbers of Mexicans migrated to the United States under special programs (like the Bracero Program instituted in 1942) to fill jobs in the agribusiness of the South and Southwest, and other Mexicans crossed the border illegally to work in agricultural jobs or in the cities. Today, "Mexicans" include Mexican Americans whose families have been part of the United States for many generations, as well as many second- and first-generation Mexicans. Discriminatory practices are currently based both on history and on the variety of social and economic characteristics that put more recent Mexican immigrants at a disadvantage.

Puerto Ricans migrated to the United States in significant numbers after Puerto Rico became a Free Associate State by a referendum vote in 1952. Since then, Puerto Ricans have been U.S. citizens, have settled mainly in cities in the Northeast, particularly in New York City, and were incorporated into service and manufacturing jobs in the 1960s. Unlike Mexican and other Hispanic immigrants, discrimination against Puerto Ricans is not based on legal status. Yet, Puerto Ricans have a range of skin colors, from white to mestizo to black, and a significant number have experienced high levels of unemployment and poverty. Discriminatory practices have been seen to reinforce the permanence of many Puerto Ricans in a low socioeconomic status and in identifying them stereotypically with poverty and welfare dependency (Marger 1991, 305).

Cubans migrated to the United States after the Cuban revolution in 1952, settled mainly in Miami, and acquired the status of political refugees. This first wave of immigrants were mostly of European descent and largely from a middle-class background and highly skilled, and they quickly gained considerable economic power in Miami. Consequently, early Cuban immigrants did not face discrimination based on their skin color or socioeconomic status. But their most important confrontations have been based on the use of Spanish in Miami and on the nature of their interaction with African Americans in that city. The widespread use of the Spanish language in Miami by Cubans and other Latin American immigrants has met with Anglo resistance. A sign of this resistance was the narrowly passed referendum in Dade County in 1980 geared to bar the use of Spanish in the conduct of official business, thereby promoting American culture. The referendum polarized the community along ethnic lines (Marger 1991, 308). Regardless of the merits of the referendum's results, a 1996 study on second-generation Cubans found that children of immigrants "not only possess widespread competence in English but also demonstrate an unambiguous preference for it in everyday communication" (Portes and Schauffler 1996, 28). In addition, Cubans and African Americas in Miami clashed in 1980 and 1989 when African Americans rioted against perceived injustices in the legal system and in police treatment, and Cubans were a visible target of the rioters (Parrillo 1994, 429).

Other Hispanics from Central and South America started to arrive in large numbers in the 1960s. They are of mixed races with diverse cultures, socioeconomic backgrounds and skills, legal status, and levels of command of the English language. Although numbers, culture, and language make Hispanics a visible minority and a target of resentment and hostility, some Hispanics have achieved social mobility and are integrating to some degree into the larger society. On the whole, scholars agree that Hispanics are subject to less discrimination and have integrated to a greater degree than African Americans, as measured by the level of intermarriages and neighborhoods shared with whites.

See also Barrios; Bilingual Education; English-Only Movement; Mexican Americans, Prejudice and Discrimination against; Mexican Americans, Violence against; Operation Wetback.

Further Reading

Marger, Martin. *Race and Ethnic Relations: American and Global Perspectives.* Belmont, CA: Wadsworth, 1991.

Parrillo, Vincent N. *Strangers to These Shores: Race and Ethnic Relations in the United States.* Boston: Allyn & Bacon, 1994.

Portes, Alejandro, and Richard Schauffler. "Language and the Second Generation: Bilingualism, Yesterday and Today." In *The New Second Generation*, edited by Alejandro Portes. New York: Russell Sage Foundation, 1996.

Carmenza Gallo

Hollywood and Minority Actors

Hollywood is where people go to pursue their dream of becoming a movie star. But for many members of the acting community, Hollywood is not a place where dreams come true. The Hollywood community has been accused of limiting the talent and the stories that emerge from the minority acting community.

For the last few television seasons, watchdog organizations, such as the National Association for the Advancement of Colored People (NAACP), have called attention to the dearth of roles for minority actors and the lack of programming that introduces elements of minority culture. The NAACP threatened to sue the broadcast networks for violating the Communications Act of 1934, which mandates that broadcasters must act in the public's interest. This resulted in the addition of many supporting roles for minority actors at the end of 1999. Still, in 2004, few shows feature minority characters in leading roles, and those that do are frequently ghettoized. Programs with predominantly minority casts are typically shown in blocks on marginal networks, such as UPN and the WB.

The 2002 Academy Awards made banner headlines when African Americans won Oscars for Male Actor in a Leading Role and Female Actor in a Leading Role. This was the first time the Lead Actor Oscar was awarded to an African American woman and the first time in more than forty years that an African American men had received this award. In 2003, only two minorities were nominated for acting awards, and neither was considered a front-runner. In 2004 however, five of the twenty acting U.S. nominees were African Americans.

When the racial composition of the population is considered, the proportion of minority nominees in the acting categories is not representative. At most, nonwhites have earned only three out of twenty acting nominations in the history of the Academy Awards in any given year. This represents only 15 percent of the nominations, while the nonwhite population in the United States is 30 percent and growing. In 2002, the percentage of roles for minority actors declined by almost 1 percent, from 22.9 percent to 22.1 percent. Clearly, 22 percent is not representative of the proportion of ethnic minorities in the population.

Not only are there few roles for minority actors, many of the roles written for minority actors offer stereotypical and in some instances degrading images of minorities. African American actors receive an inordinate number of scripts featuring gang members and poor, single mothers. Hispanics receive a great number of scripts about drug dealers and menial workers, and Asian Americans are regularly depicted as foreigners and small-business owners who have poor social skills. Many minority actors think they must take these limited roles to maintain their visibility and to make a living.

Some insiders believe the entertainment industry is not capable of producing films and shows that address the experiences of minorities, because

Actress Hattie McDaniel (right) as the most famous of her maid-mammy characters, "Mammy" in *Gone with the Wind*. Although the role won her an Oscar for Best Supporting Actress, McDaniel, like many African American actors/actresses, was relegated to supporting roles that portrayed stereotypical images.

© Bettman/CORBIS.

most of the writers, producers, and directors are white. Moreover, minority actors are being penalized by a system that devalues them. Not only are stories that examine the minority experience less often explored, but minority actors are also marginalized and excluded from films that explore mainstream culture as if they have no relationship to it.

This less-than-diverse view in Hollywood does not reflect the diversity of the viewing audience. African American households watch 50 percent more television than other Americans and account for a quarter of movie ticket sales, although they make up only 12 percent of the U.S. population. Since the target audience for film and television tends to skew young, one might expect to see more roles for minority actors, given the fact that the white population is older than the minority population. Some believe the solution to this problem is to increase the percentage of minority-owned media outlets. Some minority actors have developed their own production companies, talent agencies, and film festivals to showcase their work, in an effort to increase the presence of racial minorities in Hollywood.

See also Films and Racial Stereotypes; Television and Racial Stereotypes.

Further Reading

Lester, Paul M., ed. *Images That Injure: Pictorial Stereotypes in the Media.* Westport, CT: Praeger Publishers, 1996.

Ryan, Joel. "Fall TV an 'Outrage,' NAACP Charges." July 12, 1999. E!Online. http://www.eonline.com/News/Items/Pf/0,1527,5033,00.html.

Xing, Jun, and Lane Ryo Hirabayashi. *Reversing the Lens: Ethnicity, Race, Gender, and Sexuality through Film.* Boulder: University Press of Colorado, 2003.

Romney S. Norwood

Homelessness and Minority Groups

There is remarkably little solid research on who is homeless in the United States. Part of the problem is that it is difficult to define who is homeless. Most people would agree, for example, that individuals who live exclusively on the street are homeless. Similarly, people who live in homeless shelters are also widely considered to be homeless. But there are other groups for whom it is not so clear. For example, consider a family who lose their home or are evicted from their apartment. If they stay in the living room of friends and family, are they homeless? Many researchers and advocates say yes, because this family has no stable housing. Others say no, because the family, however unstably, is currently housed by friends and family. In addition, this definition of homelessness can include people whom most of us would not consider homeless, such as college students who are temporarily without a place to stay. However, if this group is omitted, there is a risk of missing a large number of people who do not have steady or reliable shelter.

The face of homelessness changes depending on who is counted as being homeless. The homeless who live on the streets are overwhelmingly men.

Women and children make up a greater proportion of the homeless who temporarily stay in other people's homes. There are also considerable regional differences in who is homeless. The homeless are a diverse group. Even if one agrees on a definition of homelessness, it is hard to create a reliable demographic portrait of this group, because they are often a hidden population. Simply counting the number of people who appear to be living on the street can be misleading. Some of the so-called street homeless may be in areas that are not easily accessible or visible. In addition, some of the people who may appear homeless to the researcher may, in fact, have a home. Trying to learn who is homeless solely by looking at information from homeless shelters creates similar problems. Not everyone who is homeless will be willing to go to a shelter. More importantly from a demographics perspective, those who go to a shelter may be different from those who do not. It is even more difficult to get an accurate count of the homeless who are temporarily staying with friends or family.

In the early 1990s, Anne Shlay and Peter Rossi conducted an extensive review of the literature on the homeless. This comprehensive review is arguably one of the most reliable sources on homelessness. They found that more than 40 percent of homeless persons were blacks, although the black population accounted for only about 12 percent of the U.S. population in 1990 (1992, 135). Therefore African Americans are disproportionately represented among the homeless. Latinos composed 9 percent of the U.S. population in 1990 but represented 12 percent of the homeless population. There has been considerable growth in the Latino population in the United States since 1990. Therefore, the percentage of Latinos in the homeless population is likely to have grown. The proportion of Asian homeless was too small to note in the early 1990s.

Why are some people homeless? There are two types of explanations, individual and structural. Individual explanations focus on the characteristic of the homeless themselves, such as their prevalence of mental illness and substance abuse. Structural explanations focus on external factors, such as expensive housing and high unemployment. In fact, it is hard to completely separate individual and structural factors. For example, external factors, such as a weak economy, can create unemployment and homelessness. Housing instability and homelessness can exacerbate substance use and abuse problems, which can make locating stable employment and housing even more difficult. Similarly, more and more people are being incarcerated, and there may be an increase in homelessness as people leave prison and have no stable housing. This would be a result of both individual factors, the decision to commit a criminal act, and structural factors that contribute to criminality and the social response, such as increased criminalization of drug offences in the United States and limited assistance available to former inmates in reentering society.

Although research on the homeless is limited, there are a few clear patterns. First, men and women have different patterns of homelessness. Men are more likely to be single and on the street than are women, and women are more likely to be doubled up and to have children with them. Minorities, particularly blacks and Latinos, are also far more likely to be homeless than are whites.

These differences suggest that there are strong structural influences on who is homeless, although these external influences may be mitigated by individual factors such as addiction and mental illness.

See also Housing Discrimination.

Further Reading

Ringheim, Karin. "Investigating the Structural Determinants of Homelessness." *Urban Affairs Quarterly* 28, no. 4 (June 1993): 617–640.

Shlay, Anne B. "Social Science Research and Contemporary Studies of Homelessness." *Annual Review of Sociology* 18, 129–160.

Robin Roger-Dillon

Housing Discrimination

This discussion of housing discrimination is divided into three sections. The first discusses what racial/ethnic discrimination is, and the second explains why it occurs. The third section describes the many ways housing discrimination has been practiced in the United States at different times and covers opposition to and prevention of housing discrimination. Racial and ethnic discrimination are discussed, although some discussion may apply to housing discrimination against people based on other attributes (e.g., age, sexual preference, family type, or disability status).

Definition and Examples

Racial/ethnic housing discrimination refers to direct actions or institutional arrangements that result in adverse or inferior treatment of a person or category of people based solely on their membership in a particular racial or ethnic group, which has a negative impact on their ability to find, purchase, rent, or live in residential property (Yinger 1995). Listed here are the most significant forms of racial/ethnic housing discrimination, all of which are now illegal. A discussion of them is provided in a later section.

- local residents of an area using real or threatened violence to intimidate minority group members from looking for housing in their area or to frighten them into moving out of the area (e.g., vandalizing property, threatening phone calls, or physical assaults).

- local residents of an area (or their representatives or agents) attempting to exclude minority groups from the neighborhood or local area (e.g., through racial zoning or racial steering).

- homeowners or landlords refusing to rent or sell particular housing units to members of specified minority groups (e.g., racially restrictive covenants).

- sellers of housing setting more onerous terms or conditions on minorities who rent or purchase the housing unit than on similar non-minorities (e.g., requiring a higher security deposit or a higher down-payment).

- real estate agents or apartment managers providing false, misleading, or less information or giving poorer-quality assistance to minority-group home-seekers than to majority-group home-seekers (e.g., telling a black person that no apartments are vacant when in fact some are; showing a white customer more houses for sale than a black customer).

- banks or mortgage companies requiring higher credit ratings for minority than for majority applicants, higher rejection rates for minority applicants than for financially similar majority applicants, or designating minority neighborhoods as areas in which home loans are not to be made or only made on very expensive terms (e.g., "red-lining" black neighborhoods).

- marketers of housing avoiding potential minority-group customers by selectively advertising only in majority-group geographic areas or in media that few minority group members listen to, read, or watch (e.g., targeting marketing of new suburban homes only to whites).

Since the 1970s, the federal Department of Housing and Urban Development (HUD) has sponsored national surveys, called fair-housing audits, to gauge the extent of some of these forms of housing discrimination. One, done in 1989, found that real estate agents and rental agents showed blacks and Hispanics about 25 percent fewer housing units than they did to equally qualified whites, and that in 5 percent to 10 percent of the cases, blacks and Hispanics were told that no house or apartment was available, when in fact the agents did have housing units available (Yinger 1995). In 2000, HUD completed another housing-discrimination survey in twenty-three metropolitan areas across the United States. In 2000, there was a slightly lower amount of housing discrimination against blacks compared to 1989 but a small increase in housing discrimination against Hispanics, and Hispanics were somewhat more likely to encounter housing discrimination than were blacks. Another problem is housing discrimination by banks and other lending institutions that favor white residential areas over others or disproportionately reject black applicants' mortgage applications. Federal legislation in the 1970s and private negotiation in the 1990s have tried to reduce this problem, but it remains an issue in some places.

Why Does Housing Discrimination Occur?

Housing discrimination brings real or perceived benefits to those who practice it and disadvantages to those who are discriminated against. Because norms and laws against housing discrimination are not well enforced, many individuals or groups who want those benefits ignore the law or seek loopholes in it and discriminate in the housing market. Examining the various benefits people seek via housing discrimination illuminates the motivation behind it. One important reward that arises from housing discrimination is the social-psychological sense of elevated status and gratification that comes from rejecting others as "not good enough" to be one's residential peer. Some people derive feelings of security, superiority, and prestige from residential exclusiveness that establishes social and physical distance between them and those whom they look down on.

Associated with the social-psychological benefits accruing from housing discrimination are important financial and material rewards. Sellers of housing often find that many buyers are willing to pay more to rent or buy in racially/ethnically exclusive areas, and purchasers in those areas may find their property appreciating in value more than houses in other areas. Another benefit for members of a dominant or privileged group is that housing discrimination and the racial residential segregation it produces enable them to take as their own many geographically based advantages: better access to areas of the community with the finest schools, the best shopping areas, the least pollution, the best drainage, and the most scenic spots.

Real estate agents typically engage in housing discrimination for financial reasons. They steer racial minorities because neighborhood associations tell them that if they arrange for the "wrong" kind of person to purchase in a locality, no one else in that area will use them or their firm again. Or real estate agents find that by block-busting—a practice in which a black family is brought in to look at a house in order to scare whites into selling—and provoking racial fears they can generate a large number of easy sales and commissions, thereby increasing their earnings. Bankers, too, have financial motivations for their discrimination. They used to defend their lack of mortgage loans to blacks desiring to move to predominantly white suburbs by saying such moves would reduce the property values of the homes in the nearby areas in which they had already invested. Banks' redlining of poor minority areas was rationalized by saying that the profits made in transactions on such low-cost housing were too small to bother with compared with the large profits made on more expensive homes in other areas. These are but a few of the various social-psychological and economic motivations behind housing discrimination.

Historical Overview

Ignoring the 1866 Civil Rights Act, which stated that blacks have the same property and contract rights as whites have, white private citizens, organizations in the housing industry, and state and local governments devised a variety of ways to deny African Americans (and other racial minorities) freedom of choice in selecting a place to live. However, in the past century fair-housing advocates have challenged each form of housing discrimination in court and public forums. The first such struggle was over racial zoning. In the 1910s, soon after many U.S. cities started to use zoning to regulate and separate urban land use for residential, industrial, and commercial purposes, some municipality also passed zoning ordinances specifying that certain streets or districts can only be occupied by whites, and others only occupied by "colored" people. Typically, the areas reserved for blacks had lower-quality housing and received inferior services (e.g., schools, sanitation, roads, public health) from the city. By 1917, courts in fifteen states had upheld laws establishing such residential segregation, but in that year the U.S. Supreme Court struck down those laws (*Buchanan v. Warley*), asserting that government did not have the authority to dictate where people of different races could live.

Although some local governments sought loopholes in the ruling against racial zoning, the primary mechanism of housing discrimination, from the 1920s through the 1940s, was the racially restrictive covenant. Usually these were private agreements made by white homeowners associations stipulating that white residents would only sell their homes to a purchaser who was also white (in other cases, it took the form of landlords agreeing that only whites could be tenants in their apartment buildings). In some areas, restrictive covenants were also used to prevent Asians, Mexicans, Jews, or other ethnic minorities from entering exclusive residential areas. Racially restrictive covenants covered a significant percentage of the U.S. housing stock in the first half of the twentieth century but were actively opposed by the NAACP and other civil rights groups. In 1948, the U.S. Supreme Court ruled, in *Shelley v. Kraemer*, that no government court or official could enforce a racially restrictive covenant, though private individuals remained free to abide by them as long as no government agency was involved. This meant, in theory, that government was "neutral" with regard to housing discrimination—it would not penalize anyone who broke or disregarded a racially restrictive covenant and it would not assist or punish anyone who abided by a racially restrictive covenant. As a result, many racially restrictive covenants continued as "mutual understandings" among whites about whom to sell or rent housing to, and usually the consensus was to exclude people of color (e.g., in the post–World War II era, real estate agents and residents in many suburbs had agreements to exclude blacks).

Before and after the 1948 *Shelley v. Kraemer* decision, federal and local governments often engaged in racial discrimination when they chose locations for public-housing projects and selected which residents would live in which public-housing units. The federal government provided most of the money for constructing public housing, but it did not require that this housing be racially integrated in cities or states where local authorities insisted that blacks and whites should reside separately. As a result, Southern and many Northern public housing authorities decided which housing project to assign a resident to based on the applicant's race. Moreover, when and where public housing became a predominantly black mode of residence, local government officials and public-housing authorities usually abided by politically well-organized white residents' demands that public-housing projects, especially large ones, not be built in or next to their neighborhoods. This meant that most federally funded public-housing projects built in the 1950s and 1960s (and their residents) were put in predominantly black neighborhoods or in less-desirable, peripheral areas of cities.

In the post–World War II years, black resentment over housing discrimination was strong, especially in the North. Major civil rights organizations and a coalition of civic and religious organizations (the National Committee Against Discrimination in Housing) lobbied local, state, and federal government to outlaw housing discrimination. By 1962, they had made some gains. In that year President John F. Kennedy signed Executive Order 11063 (prohibiting discrimination in federally funded housing) and by then, more than a dozen states and fifty-six cities had passed laws or resolutions against racial discrimination in housing. But black-white residential segregation still was increasing, and these actions were having little effect in preventing it, because they did not cover much of the nation's housing stock, had many loopholes, and were not well enforced. The difficulties blacks had in finding housing outside the less desirable ghetto areas was an important underlying factor in many of the large urban race riots and rebellions of the 1960s. Indeed, it was the violent turbulence following the assassination of Martin Luther King Jr. that pushed the federal government into taking a more proactive stance against housing discrimination by passing the Fair Housing Act (Title VIII of the 1968 Civil Rights Act), which outlawed many forms of housing discrimination against people based on their race, color, religion, or national origin. This law has been amended several times to increase the enforcement powers of HUD and the Department of Justice and to extend protection against housing discrimination to several other categories of people. Also in 1968, the Supreme Court made a strong ruling against racial/ethnic discrimination in housing (*Jones v. Alfred H. Mayer Co.*).

Housing discrimination by private individuals rather than by government authorities can take many forms. Although it is illegal and against real estate ethics, some agents may practice racial steering, defined as behavior that directs a customer toward neighborhoods in which people of the customer's racial or ethnic group are concentrated (Yinger 1995, 51-52). Real estate agents, often acting at the behest of neighborhood associations, show homes in white areas only to white clients, whereas they show black or Hispanic clients homes in "transitional" areas or in areas where blacks or Hispanics already live in significant numbers. Fair-housing audits show that in some areas it is still commonly practiced. These audits and other research have found real estate agents engaging in other forms of racial discrimination: minimal advertising of homes in black or mixed neighborhoods to whites; showing Hispanic clients fewer homes than white clients; slower or less service provided for black than white clients. Apartment managers and rental agents also have been found to discriminate by telling blacks and Hispanics there are no vacancies when in fact there are, by charging higher deposits to racial minorities, and by assigning minority residents to different buildings or parts of the apartment complex.

Other housing "gatekeepers" besides real estate and rental agents are involved in housing discrimination. In some higher-status residential settings (e.g., condominiums, cooperatives, and country club communities), a residents committee reviews applicants' financial and personal characteristics and can screen out unwanted racial/ethnic minorities by finding some "defect" on their application. In less affluent, tight-knit areas, housing vacancies sometimes are made known only through "word-of-mouth" social networks that are racially or ethnically homogeneous. That way, unwanted racial/ethnic minorities are excluded because they do not see or know about available houses or apartments in these neighborhoods (DeSena 1994).

In the 1970s, fair-housing activists and researchers became concerned about discrimination by banks and businesses that provide mortgage or other home-related loans. Research in Atlanta, Milwaukee, and Boston found that banks did not offer mortgage loans in many black neighborhoods and/or had much higher rejection rates for blacks (and in some studies, Hispanics) than whites, even when applicants were of similar economic status (Ladd 1998; Ross & Yinger 2002; Squires & O'Connor 2001). Racial/ethnic housing discrimination by lending institutions has several negative consequences: (a) it contributes to lower rates of home ownership among minorities than whites; (b) it prevents or hinders residential and commercial upgrading or revitalization in minority neighborhoods; and (c) it makes minority borrowers more likely to rely on companies that make home loans on adverse terms (e.g., higher interest rates and fees). As the extent and seriousness of home-loan discrimination became clearer, civil rights groups pressured and sued banks and sought legislative remedies.

Three important federal laws address home-mortgage discrimination. The 1974 Equal Credit Opportunity Act made it illegal for banks or other lenders to discriminate against minority groups and made it illegal for them to "redline" local areas, that is, use the racial composition of a neighborhood as a basis for not making loans in that area. The 1975 Home Mortgage Disclosure Act (amended and strengthened in 1989) requires each lender to provide data on its mortgage loans by census tract and give additional information about its loan applications, which makes it more difficult to conceal housing discrimination. The Community Reinvestment Act (CRA) (Title VIII of the Housing and Community Development Act of 1977) reinforced the principle that banks have a responsibility to serve the credit needs of the entire community in its service area, regardless of race or income level, rather than to just focus on more affluent customers. It also required federal financial regulatory agencies to monitor banks' CRA performance and take this into consideration when making decisions on banks' requests for mergers, relocations, and expansions. Some banks have found it expedient to increase mortgage loans to minorities to avoid jeopardizing their merger and acquisition plans. These laws have reduced housing discrimination by lending institutions, but by how much is a controversial matter. The banking industry seeks to weaken the CRA, while fair-housing advocates try to strengthen it, so this area will remain one of the hottest fronts in the battle against housing discrimination.

See also Block-busting; *Closed Doors, Opportunities Lost: The Continuing Costs of Housing Discrimination*; Dual Housing Markets; Fair-Housing Audit; Fair Housing Act of 1968; Fair Housing Amendments Act of 1988; Federal Housing Administration; *Shelley v. Kraemer*; U.S. Department of Housing and Urban Development (HUD).

Further Reading

DeScna, Judith N. "Local Gatekeeping Practices and Residential Segregation." *Sociological Inquiry* 64 (1994): 307–321.

Ladd, Helen F. "Evidence on Discrimination in Mortgage Lending." *The Journal of Economic Perspectives* 12 (1998): 41–62.

Ross, Stephen, and John Yinger. *The Color of Credit: Mortgage Discrimination, Research Methodology, and Fair-Lending Enforcement.* Cambridge, MA: MIT Press, 2002.

Squires, Gregory D., and Sally O'Connor. *Color and Money.* Albany: State University of New York Press, 2001.

Yinger, John. *Closed Doors, Opportunities Lost.* New York: Russell Sage Foundation, 1995.

Charles Jaret

Howard Beach Incident

On December 20, 1986, Michael Griffith, a 23-year-old, black Trinidadian immigrant was killed after he and two men, Cedric Sandiford, 36, and Timothy Grimes, 18, were attacked by a gang of white teenagers. The three men had landed in the working-class white neighborhood of Howard Beach in Queens, New York, after their car had broken down. Seeking a telephone or other means of help, the three left the car under the care of a fourth passenger, Curtis Sylvester, 19. The men eventually entered a pizzeria; after learning there was no public phone, they ate some pizza. As they left the eatery, they were taunted, attacked, and then chased by more than a dozen white teenagers who were armed with baseball bats and tree limbs. Jon Lester, 18, originally a South African who had emigrated from England with his family four years earlier, was said to be the ringleader. While Grimes escaped major physical injuries, Griffith was killed when he was hit by a car after running onto a busy expressway to flee his attackers, and Sandiford was brutally beaten. More than a dozen teenagers were arrested and variously charged with murder, manslaughter, assault, and riot.

The savage assault and tragic death inflamed racial tensions in the city and mobilized radical black activists, who decried the assault as emblematic of black-white relations nationwide. The activists led marches through Howard Beach, where they were met by hostile residents. The residents claimed that the three men were burglars and that the teenagers were acting only in self-defense. A year later, Lester, Jason Ladone, 17, and Scott Kern, 18, were convicted of manslaughter and assault, receiving charges ranging from fifteen to thirty years; three others received community service; and three others were acquitted. The case highlighted the physical dangers blacks faced in contemporary white society, even in cosmopolitan urban centers such as New York City. Social scientists also observed how the event served to awaken awareness of white racism in the Caribbean American community. Although many recent Caribbean and African immigrants had prospered in America, this event—and later the brutal attack on Haitian immigrant Abner Louima and the killings of Haitian American Patrick Dorismond and West African immigrant Amadou Diallo—underscored a racial hierarchy that privileged whites and subordinated blacks.

See also Bensonhurst Incident; Caribbean Immigrants, Experience of Racial Discrimination; Diallo, Amadou.

Rose Kim

Human Trafficking

See Indentured Servants.